A VICTORIAN GENTLEWOMAN

IN THE FAR WEST

A Victorian Gentlewoman in the Far West

THE REMINISCENCES OF MARY HALLOCK FOOTE

EDITED WITH AN INTRODUCTION BY

RODMAN W. PAUL

HUNTINGTON LIBRARY

SAN MARINO, CALIFORNIA

Copyright © 1972 by The Henry E. Huntington Library and Art Gallery
All rights reserved
Published 1972. Fifth printing 2000
Printed in the United States of America

Published by the Huntington Library Press
1151 Oxford Road, San Marino, CA 91108
http://www.huntington.org

Library of Congress Cataloging-in-Publication Data

Foote, Mary Hallock, 1847–1938.
A Victorian gentlewoman in the far West: the reminiscences of Mary Hallock Foote / edited
with an introduction by Rodman W. Paul.
        p. cm.
Includes bibliographical references and index.
1. Foote, Mary Hallock, 1847–1938—Homes and haunts—West (U.S.)
2. Novelists, American—19th century—Biography.
3. Novelists, American—20th century—Biography.
4. Illustrators—United States—Biography.
5. Frontier and pioneer life—West (U.S.)
6. West (U.S.)—Biography.
I. Paul, Rodman W. (Rodman Wilson), 1912–1987.
II. Henry E. Huntington Library and Art Gallery.
III. Title.
PS1688.A4   1992
813'.4—dc20   92-3480
[B]   CIP
ISBN: 0-87328-057-1

Front cover: Huntington Library

Rodman W. Paul (1912–1987) was Edward S. Harkness Professor of
History at the California Institute of Technology. He was particularly interested in the history of mining in the west, and among his many publications
are *Mining Frontiers of the Far West, 1848–1880*, and *California Gold: The
Beginning of Mining in the Far West*.

Preface

WHEN Mary Hallock Foote was writing these reminiscences, she was aware that she was telling two stories at once. The first story was her own: a narrative of the mixed rewards and anxieties experienced by a sensitive eastern lady of the Victorian era who was simultaneously wife and mother, novelist and artist in the Far West. One learns the inner thoughts of a singularly honest lady who took west with her the value system of the genteel tradition and the social standards of the eastern upper class. But Mary Hallock Foote's adjustment to the West involved much more than her personal attitude. In an age in which few women had professional careers, she became a highly successful writer and illustrator of "local color" stories about the West. Even if she had mixed feelings about life out there, nevertheless she learned to write about it and to draw it, and thereby to reach an audience of thousands of easterners.

The second story told by Mary Hallock Foote was an intensely personal explanation and defense of the role played in the West by the little group of engineers to which her husband, brother-in-law, and their close friends belonged. The engineers were a tiny and anomalous minority. Quite aside from their tendency to think in terms of quantitative relationships, graphic representation, strengths of materials, and natural phenomena, the engineers were an oddity in this new region of self-made men because they had had an extensive formal education and came often from sophisticated social backgrounds — "professional exiles," Mary Hallock Foote

v

termed them. They had long been a favorite subject for her short stories and novels; now she was able to write about them in terms of episodes in her own life.

All of this makes it very appropriate for the Huntington Library to be publishing this book. The Huntington Library has today a great collection of manuscript and printed materials that deal with the mining West and more particularly with the work of mining engineers and geologists. This collection was started twenty-five years ago when James D. Hague, in association with his aunts, the Misses Marian and Eleanor Hague, gave to the library a large body of business and personal papers relating to the man for whom the present James Hague was named, his grandfather. The elder James D. Hague, a mining engineer trained at Harvard and in Germany, was one of the most successful mining consultants of his generation, and was at the same time a notably sophisticated individual whose friendships and intellectual interests kept him in touch with leading figures throughout the Anglo-American world of the Victorian era. His own papers and the papers he collected as a tribute to his close friend, Clarence King, provided a rich base around which to assemble materials that illustrated the role of a kind of person whose significance was overlooked in the older histories of the West.

During the years since his original gift, the present James Hague has found many more of his grandfather's letters, diaries, and account books, and has given them to the library together with comparable materials relating to his father, William Hague, a young mining engineer whose very promising career was cut off all too soon by his death during the First World War. Possession of the Hague and King papers has encouraged the Huntington Library to seek similar collections from the families of other mining engineers and geologists.

Mary Hallock Foote was the wife of an engineer who specialized in mining and water supply, and the sister-in-law of the elder James Hague. Her husband, Arthur D. Foote, and the elder James Hague were for a dozen years the superintendent and president, respectively, of the famous North Star gold mine at Grass Valley, California. Upon the death of James Hague, William Hague took over primary responsibility for the North Star, at first in association with Arthur D. Foote and later with Arthur B. Foote, son of the elder Foote. A copy of Mary Hallock Foote's reminiscences came to the Huntington Library as a document of obvious importance for the Huntington's growing collection.

In preparing the reminiscences for publication, I have received much assistance from Mary Hallock Foote's grandchildren. At Grass Valley two of the granddaughters, Mrs. Raymond Conway and Mrs. Tyler Micoleau, were my hostesses during long and rewarding talks about their grandparents. Mrs. Conway and Mrs. Micoleau made available to me all of the photographs, drawings, and other memorabilia in their possession. Another granddaughter, Mrs. Evelyn Gardiner, gave her endorsement to the project and helped me by summarizing her impressions of the Foote family. Still another granddaughter, Agnes Swift, whom I have not had the privilege of meeting, sent me versions "A" and "B," which were the originals of this autobiography and have proved to be essential to the restoration of it. Sarah Swift loaned me the charming girlhood diary kept by her mother, Mrs. Rodman Swift, during the Footes' first summer at Grass Valley.

Helen Bontecou recaptured her personal impressions of Mary Hallock Foote and recalled her conversations with Mary Hallock Foote on precisely the questions that were most troubling me after I had finished research. Donald M. Harris loaned his copy of the Foote family genealogical book, without which many of Mary Hallock Foote's family anecdotes would have been at least confusing, perhaps inexplicable.

Mrs. Helena Sherman Sims and Mrs. Mary Sherman Harper supplied reminiscent accounts by their grandmother, Bessie Sherman, and their father, Gerald Sherman.

Merle Wells, director of the Idaho Historical Society, and the librarian, Judy Austin, gave invaluable help in the attempt to discover the truth about the Footes' somewhat controversial experiences at Boise. The Idaho phase of Mary Hallock Foote's life was the most elusive and yet in some respects the most crucial topic covered by research for this book. Dr. Wells and the Idaho Historical Society set a high standard of service.

Patricia Palmer of the Stanford University Library handled the difficult business of obtaining reproductions of the 500 Mary Hallock Foote letters in that library. These letters proved to be of essential importance. Dr. Josephine L. Harper of the State Historical Society of Wisconsin supplied facsimiles of Mary Hallock Foote's correspondence concerning a biographical sketch, and Professor Gene M. Gressley of the University of Wyoming provided facsimiles of a biographical article.

The Library of Congress and the National Portrait Gallery made available everything in their possession that was pertinent to this topic. The California State Library, in Sacramento, the Bancroft Library, in Berkeley, and the library of the University of California at Los Angeles supplied information or facsimiles of contemporary publications.

Here in Pasadena the bulk of the research and editing was done at the Huntington Library, which proved to be superbly equipped and staffed for that purpose. The "Bibliographical Note" suggests the rich manuscript and printed materials available there, but that essay does not indicate how much help I have received from members of the two notable scholarly communities in Pasadena and San Marino: the Huntington Library and the California Institute of Technology.

James Thorpe, director of the Huntington Library, saw to it that the whole operation was viable. He and his colleague Ray A. Billington made very helpful comments on the preliminary draft of the introduction. When the introduction was in its late stages, two other friends, Daniel J. Kevles of Caltech and Claude Simpson of Stanford, then on leave to work at the Huntington, gave that document a most perceptive reading. Kent Clark of Caltech spent hours advising the copy editors concerning Mary Hallock Foote's punctuation, a distressingly complex subject. Robert A. Huttenback of Caltech supplied answers to my questions about India, and Paul C. Eaton of that same institution advised on matters relating to Penobscot Bay and oceanic navigation, while Lance Davis, again of Caltech, explained why Arthur Foote's business venture was so ill-timed from the point of view of investment capital. Hallett Smith, of Caltech and the Huntington, has somehow remained good humored through twenty years of my exploiting his wisdom and his remarkable breadth of knowledge.

Mary Isabel Fry, warm friend to all who work at the Huntington, was especially interested in this project because she grew up next door to the family of Mary Hallock Foote's nephew, Gerald Sherman, in the copper mining town of Bisbee, Arizona. Virginia Rust of the manuscript department of the Huntington did a splendid job of processing recent additions of Hague papers so that they were available for study within a very short time of receipt. Constance Lodge of the accessions department solved some of the editor's needs for materials from other institutions. Betty Leigh Merrell of the publications department made all arrangements for publication, while Jane Evans has shown great patience as chief copy editor.

At Caltech Edith Taylor typed the Introduction and Daphne Plane of the Division of Geological Sciences once more made the books and maps of that excellent library available to me.

A very special tribute should go to Carol Pearson, who took on the job of research assistant. This would have been a much less complete and less interesting book if Mrs. Pearson had not, on so many occasions, refused to accept defeat when a quotation or a name seemed to have eluded all attempts at identification, or when a piece of evidence seemed unobtainable. Her resourcefulness and her enthusiasm for the project kept her searching long after a lesser person would have quit. She is the source also of the genealogical tables and of many other features that add to the book's usefulness and understandability. To Mrs. Pearson, warmest thanks for a stellar performance.

Finally, I owe a great deal to James Hague's interest in this project. For years he has urged that his great-aunt's memoirs be published. When work finally started, he replied patiently and precisely to all appeals for information and for leads to promising material. He gave many hours to talking with me about complex questions that were not clear from the written record, and when some subjects still remained obscure, he did first-hand research himself in his grandfather's diaries. James and Hanneke were the best of hosts during rewarding "Mary Hallock Foote visits" to Pebble Beach.

RODMAN W. PAUL

Pasadena, May 16, 1972

It is a pleasure to hear that Mary Hallock Foote's reminiscences have been received so favorably that now a third printing is justified. My friend of school and college days, James D. Hague, would be delighted. It was James who persuaded me to edit his great-aunt's reminiscences in which James's grandfather and namesake appears so prominently. Thereafter James not only supplied clues out of his prodigious memory for family details, but he also enlisted his cousins in a successful search for the document that I needed most, Mary Hallock Foote's original typescript, with her penciled changes and tentative revisions. As the project neared completion, James's health was failing rapidly. I had page proofs sent to him as quickly as they came from the printer and he read them with enthusiasm. He did not live to see the final product. Death came on November 15, 1972, at Pebble Beach. This new printing is dedicated to his memory.

R.W.P.

Pasadena, January 11, 1984

Concerning the Text and Illustrations

WHEN the present editor began work on Mary Hallock Foote's reminiscences, there seemed to be only one known version of the text. This was a clean typescript that had been prepared by Mary Hallock Foote's daughter, Mrs. Rodman W. Swift (the "Betty" of these reminiscences), and Mrs. Swift's daughter, Agnes. Since the Swifts did their work with care and discrimination, it has been possible to use their typescript as the basic working copy for the present book. But, as the Swifts' marginal comments frankly stated, the text still contained too many abrupt breaks and too many places where Mary Hallock Foote's meaning was not clear. An appeal to Agnes Swift to search for the original produced not one but two earlier versions. They were found at Southwest Harbor, Maine.

These two were typescripts that originally were identical: the one called by the Swifts "Version B" was merely a carbon of the top copy, "Version A." Many small identical revisions had been penciled into both versions by Mary Hallock Foote. But at some point thereafter the "A" and "B" versions parted company. The split probably came when Mary Hallock Foote's family and intimate friends persuaded her to submit her reminiscences to her publisher, instead of leaving them as merely a family document preserved in typed form, as she had at first intended. Seizing upon "Version A" as her working copy, the author slashed out chunks that ranged in size from a phrase to a chapter. Some of the deletions were merely scratched out in pencil, others were cut out with scissors or crumpled up and thrown away. Fortunately, most of the passages physically removed from "A" were left intact in "Version B," and the latter received also the benefit of some changes in punctuation and wording that made for greater clarity and smoothness and yet, for some unknown reason, were not inserted in "A." The drastic cuts from "Version A" not only lessened the text's color and warmth, but also left awkward transitions and puzzling references to people and places that had now been cut off from their antecedents.

Family legend has it that the deletions from "A" were a reason for the publishers declining to accept the book at the time the reminiscences were written, which was during the early 1920s. Mary Hallock Foote's motive in treating her text so harshly seems to have been a desire to protect the privacy of people then living or of recent memory. Today, nearly half a century later, this restraint no longer is a substantial one. When the Swifts prepared a smooth copy for retyping, they very wisely restored the passages in "Version A" that Mary Hallock Foote had marked for deletion but had not physically destroyed. The present editor has extended the Swifts' practice still further by salvaging from "Version B" passages that no longer exist, even in scratched-out form, in "Version A."

The intent has been to recapture the autobiography in its fullest form, as Mary Hallock Foote originally wrote it, including her revisions of it but not accepting her drastic excisions from "Version A." Save for the few instances that are indicated by brackets, the editor has inserted nothing that is not Mary Hallock Foote's own wording, as found in either "A" or "B" or in her handwritten or typed revisions. The revisions, in themselves, have constituted an editorial problem, since they were not always identical as between the two versions and in some cases were left still as tentative possibilities when Mary Hallock Foote ceased work on the manuscript. Where there were discrepancies between the two versions or between their varying or incomplete revisions, the editor has used his own judgment. In extreme cases this has meant choosing between as many as three or even four alternatives. But such instances were the exception and usually concerned only small matters of wording and punctuation.

As one might expect of a literary person, Mary Hallock Foote was fond of quoting poetry and prose. Since many of her quotations were from memory, and others were the result of hasty or careless copying, few are exact. Therefore quotations have been checked whenever the source could be identified and have been corrected where necessary. Similarly, misspellings and typographical errors have been corrected, even though this has meant eliminating some rather attractive phonetic spellings, such as consistently putting an extra "r" in the participle of "murmur."

For a veteran writer, Mary Hallock Foote was surprisingly erratic in deciding which words to capitalize or to hyphenate, and how to use parentheses, dashes, and commas. The editor has sought to reduce this confusion to a single usage that would be consistent throughout the text. *Webster's International Dictionary*, 3rd edition, has been used as the standard in determining spellings and the *Chicago Manual of Style* in determining style, even though this has meant adjustment to present-day practice rather than to that of the Victorian era. In the special case of Spanish words, the decision has been to define or explain words unless they have been sufficiently accepted into modern American usage to appear in *Webster's Dictionary*. The demands of hardworking copy editors have compelled the addition of many commas that were not in the original and the deletion of many commas, dashes, and hyphens that were. Because Mary Hallock Foote sometimes continued a single paragraph for a fatiguingly long distance — more than a page — it has seemed wise to spare the modern reader by breaking up such passages into two or three paragraphs.

Mary Hallock Foote made a rather frequent use of several

dots to indicate ellipsis. This habit of hers has been left undisturbed, and in the few cases where the editor has needed to use the same symbol to indicate that there is a break in the text, he has conveyed that fact by verbal explanation, thus hopefully avoiding confusion.

Since Mary Hallock Foote was also an illustrator, it has seemed logical to supplement her text with a large selection of her very attractive drawings. Some of these are copied from contemporary periodicals, especially the *Century Illustrated Monthly Magazine*. Others are from unpublished collections, chiefly in the Library of Congress or in the possession of Mary Hallock Foote's grandchildren. In addition to reproducing these examples of Mary Hallock Foote's work, it has been possible to include some surprisingly good photographs. This was the beginning of the age of amateur photography, and the Foote and Hague families were pioneers in that art. Some additional excellent photographs of the Idaho years have been supplied by the Idaho Historical Society, apparently from pictures taken by the Cobb family.

Contents

THE LAST TRIP IN.

DRAWN BY MARY HALLOCK FOOTE.

ENGRAVED BY J. H. E. WHITNEY.

ILLUSTRATIONS

All drawings reproduced here are the work of Mary Hallock Foote.

A VICTORIAN GENTLEWOMAN

IN THE FAR WEST

Arthur De Wint Foote

Mary Hallock Foote

Introduction

I

THESE fluently written memoirs give an unusual insight into the private life of a cultivated Victorian lady whose circumstances happened to bring her into the Far West at the close of the frontier era. With grace and tact, but also with honesty, Mary Hallock Foote looks back upon the years of mixed happiness and anxiety, of partial accomplishment and disheartening failure, that characterized her own and her family's experience as they followed her husband's varying fortunes as an engineer. But the memoirs offer more than personal history. Because Mary Hallock Foote was such an unusual person to settle in the West, the story of her career as wife, mother, artist, and writer challenges many of the stereotypes of western history and raises provocative if sometimes unanswerable questions.

What, for example, were the distinctive qualities that caused a Victorian American to be considered a "westerner," particularly a feminine "westerner"? Was it mere residence beyond the Great Plains, more specifically, residence in the kinds of communities that were regarded as characteristic of the raw new West, such as mining towns, engineers' camps, and embryonic irrigation settlements? Or, to go a bit deeper and into the realm of attitudes, to be a true westerner did one have to adopt the West's ever-hopeful "boomer" psychology and accept its aggressive materialism? If one were a woman, was it necessary, like the pioneer wife of popular legend, to live in drab hardship and frontier privation, and display stoic courage, in order to be considered a real westerner?

Far from being mere rhetorical questions, these are very

real reflections that would occur to anyone who has given thoughtful consideration to Mary Hallock Foote's account of herself. In her own day, which was from the late 1870s to the First World War, Mary Hallock Foote was one of the best-known writers and illustrators who made the Far West their genre. She was a part of that enthusiasm for "local color" that produced such notable figures as Bret Harte, George Washington Cable, Sarah Orne Jewett, and Frederic Remington. Her short stories, serialized novels, and illustrations appeared regularly in the best periodicals, especially *Century Magazine* and the *Atlantic Monthly*, and were reprinted in book form by one of the most prestigious of eastern publishing houses, the Boston firm of Houghton, Mifflin.

Critics and book reviewers hailed her as "an authentic voice of the West," and praised her for writing so charmingly and vividly about dramatic scenes that were as intriguingly different from the life of the eastern reader as were Stanley's reports on Africa. The very facts of the lady's life seemed to justify these favorable verdicts. By following her engineer husband to his successive jobs, Mrs. Foote had actually lived and kept house in the tumultuous and bizarre new mining town of Leadville, located at 10,000 feet altitude in the magnificent Colorado Rockies. Under quieter circumstances she had gone as a bride to live at the famous quicksilver mine of New Almaden, California, where she had both sketched and described the picturesque Spanish-speaking and Cornish miners. In the barren cañon of the Boise River of Idaho, she and her children had endured the loneliness, uncertainty, and ultimate failure that attended her visionary husband's efforts to promote an irrigation system that would indeed make the desert to blossom as the rose. After the total miscarriage of all their Idaho plans and the loss therein of all their money, the Foote family had struggled through years of mounting anxiety as the husband searched the Far West for new employment. Finally the family had found safe haven at the mining town of Grass

Valley, California, famed alike for its deep gold mines and its Cornish miners. What could be more "western"? How could any writer have had personal experiences that better qualified her to speak with authority about this dramatic new region?

And yet, was Mary Hallock Foote really a westerner? She was not born one, of course, but did she become one? In a few respects, yes; in greater part, no. The reminiscences contained in this volume offer revealing evidence of the pervasive influence throughout her life of attitudes and desires that tied her psychologically to the East in which she had spent her childhood and young womanhood — that is, her formative years. Among those attitudes and desires were nostalgia for her Quaker family and its quiet farm on the Hudson River; hunger for the bright literary and artistic world of New York City, which she had come to know during art-student days; and instinctive sharing of the eastern upper-class social biases that her husband had before he went west and never shed during his long years of strenuous work in that region.

The psychological pull was not all in one direction. There was a continuing tension in Mary Hallock Foote's personality between loyalty to her husband, whose work kept him in the West, and affection for close friends and relatives, who were mostly in the East; between enthusiasm for the West's natural beauty and expansive way of life, and yearning for the intellectual and social stimulation of the eastern seaboard. Negatively there was comparable tension between the characteristics of western society that repelled her and the implications of eastern social and literary life that intimidated her. That is, although she complained that western women were dowdy and dull, and western society correspondingly uninteresting, it is equally true that she felt insecure whenever she thought of returning to New York City to compete for attention in that glittering world of fashion and intellect.

These relentless tensions were a central fact of Mary Hallock Foote's mature life. The surprising thing is that she coped with them as well as she did, and somehow managed to handle her own uncertainties simultaneously with well-justified apprehensions about her husband. Nothing about Mary Hallock Foote suggested the quiet courage and stoic endurance popularly attributed to the western wife of pioneer days. Delicate both physically and psychologically, she was a constant sufferer from insomnia and anxiety, and an overprotective mother to her several children. She expected and usually obtained an amount of attention and a degree of physical comfort utterly at odds with the realities of their successive western situations, including their always precarious finances. Yet she stood by her man in all these (to her) difficult places, raised their children, and learned how to convert the scenes of her daily western life into stories and pictures for which publishers would pay desperately needed cash.

These are the reminiscences of old age, written in the early 1920s and from the relative security of the home in Grass Valley. Save for the affectionate and nostalgic introductory chapters on her childhood and youth, they deal primarily with what Mary Hallock Foote termed the "restless years," that is, the twenty years between her first trip west after marriage, and her ultimate haven at Grass Valley. Of the mixed tension, happiness, and disappointment of that era, sometimes she speaks frankly and fully, sometimes she merely hints, leaving the reader to look between the lines. At still other times family loyalties cause her to be entirely silent, and thus make it necessary to supply missing insights from other sources, such as her extensive private correspondence.

II

In curious ways, Mary Hallock Foote's childhood prepared her psychologically for the experiences she was to undergo in the West. Born in 1847 on a peaceful but worn-out farm outside the Hudson River town of Milton, near Poughkeepsie, she was always in the presence of financial "unsuccess," as she once termed it. Her father, she remarked in the present reminiscences, "belonged to the last of his breed of thinking and reading American farmers working their own land which they inherited from their fathers." Unable to recognize that he had entered a new age in which the value of his property was eroding away under the simultaneous forces of decreasing yields, increasing costs, and inefficient hired hands, Hallock left the farm so reduced and indebted by the time of his death that the family lost possession. Other members of their immediate family and their cousins experienced comparable misfortunes, amounting in some cases to thorough disaster.

Theirs was a close-knit, affectionate family that gave warm and unselfish support to its children and sent them out into the world only reluctantly and, whenever possible, in the custody of relatives. The Hallocks were Quakers, which would normally have meant participation in a considerable local fellowship, but as described in the first chapter, an inherited dispute, as relentless as a Kentucky feud, cut off their little family group from all larger Quaker bodies, while at the same time their Quakerism tended to set them apart from their neighbors of other faiths. As Mary Hallock Foote confessed in her reminiscences, her family "ignored" the village in which they lived. Being thus relatively isolated from general society, the Hallocks gathered their kith and kin around them and turned inward. Just so, although for different reasons, Mary Hallock Foote and her husband were to create at each new home in the West a little enclave that maintained only limited relations with most neighbors and potential friends. Confining their little circle to their immediate family, a cousin or two, several retainers, and one or two very congenial friends, the Footes impressed their western neighbors as being aloof and snobbish, just as the Hallocks seemed to Milton villagers to be "superior."

One would expect the graduate of such a distinctive up-bringing to display in later life either a pronounced continuing attachment for her family and their home, or else an attitude of total rebellion. In the Victorian era the latter alternative would have been difficult for a woman; probably it never occurred to one as basically conventional as Mary Hallock Foote. In fact the migratory nature of her husband's engineering assignments prior to the middle 1880s made her dependent on her childhood home for a recurrent refuge whenever it was impracticable for her to accompany her husband to some strange new place.

Even when the decision to settle in Idaho, the land of her husband's irrigation hopes, finally brought unavoidable separation in the 1880s, Mary Hallock Foote ("Molly," for short) carried with her her beloved older sister, Bessie Sherman, and the latter's husband and children. A lady who was notably self-sacrificing, hardworking, and dedicated to family responsibilities, Bessie was also a person of greater practical resourcefulness than Molly. For a dozen years in Idaho, throughout the most severe tests that the Footes were ever to endure, Bessie was there to help, strengthen, and comfort her younger sister when crises struck, just as her children were there to be playmates for the Foote son and daughters. Thus a transplanted Milton and Hallock influence persisted even in the dry desert air of southern Idaho.

III

If the circumstances of her Milton childhood were the first major continuing influence on Mary Hallock Foote's life, the second was the result of her formal education. After a high school preparation at the Poughkeepsie Female Collegiate Seminary, Mary Hallock persuaded her family to let her try to develop her youthful talent for drawing. As one of her friends later explained, "the School of Design for women at the Cooper Institute [Cooper Union, New York City] was the only place, at that time, where anything approaching an art education could be had for a girl."[1] Here Mary Hallock began her studies in the fall of 1864, when she was not yet seventeen. Her friends of that period remembered her as a delicate yet energetic little figure with some surprising skills. She could sew "exquisitely"; she could make bread in her family's huge old-fashioned oven and butter in their dairy; she could ride with enviable proficiency. But above all, they remembered, "She skated on her little feet like a swallow flying, and danced with the same grace and lightness. She could outskate and out-dance us all."[2]

Formal instruction over a period of several years sufficiently matured the young lady's artistic skills so that by the early 1870s she was doing her first professional work as an illus-trator — something quite unusual for a woman in that era. New friendships did even more for her than art studies. The move from Milton to New York City had been a momentous one. In New York, Brooklyn, and on Staten Island and Long Island, Mary Hallock met relatives and friends who were part of a much bigger, more sophisticated world than anything known to Milton. This was a world in which bright people and dogmatic people talked of art, literature, and the political con-troversies of the post–Civil War era. If many of the relatives were Quakers, they were worldly and wealthy urban Quakers.

Among people of her own age, the young art student met one who was to be her closest friend, her most intimate confi-dante for the rest of their lives. Helena de Kay, descendant of New York aristocrats, had had the kind of rich cultural up-bringing in Europe and America that Mary Hallock would have loved. It spoke well for both young ladies that from their

[1] Helena de Kay Gilder, "Mary Hallock Foote," *The Book Buyer*, 11 (August 1894), 338.
[2] *Ibid.*, p. 339.

first meetings at Cooper Union the society girl and the rural Quaker accepted each other wholeheartedly, and presently came to love one another with a warmth that found embarrassingly naive expression in their private correspondence. As the two moved on into their respective marriages, the numerous letters between them mixed terms of endearment with news of pregnancies and miscarriages—the latter always clouded with Victorian euphemisms — and anguished reports of their children's and husbands' distressingly frequent illnesses and their own periods of exultation and black discouragement. This lifelong intimacy flourished despite — or perhaps because of — Molly's unashamed conviction that her friend was a being superior to herself.

The friendship so well launched in student days survived Helena's marriage in 1874 to one of the most brilliant literary figures of the oncoming generation, Richard Watson Gilder, poet, critic, reformer, public personality, and, most important of all, editor of *Century Magazine* from its founding in 1881, and before that de facto editor of *Century*'s predecessor, *Scribner's Monthly*. During the brief recurring periods of Molly's eastern residence and through all the long years of her western adventures, Helena and Richard Gilder served as her never-failing link with, her means of participation in the brilliant eastern and European world of intellect and social purpose. The Gilders sent her books and magazines and supplied rich details concerning each of Richard's literary and political enthusiasms. Helena wrote long descriptions of the Gilders' receptions for literary lions and political leaders.

Richard and Helena encouraged Molly to try writing about her bizarre new environment when she first found herself in the West, at the New Almaden quicksilver mine. Thereafter Richard read and revised Molly's manuscripts as they were submitted, and always won her grateful, almost humble acceptance of his revisions. Richard saw to it that Molly was offered contracts for illustrations.

Through this remarkable dual friendship with the two Gilders, nourished by more than five hundred exchanges of letters over the course of several decades, a Mary Hallock Foote who was living in a cañon in Idaho or on a mountainside in Colorado or California was able to share vicariously in a life that was utterly unknown to most of her western neighbors. To Molly this vicarious experience was of deep importance; she was shameless in confessing how eagerly she awaited each letter from the Gilders, how much those letters did to compensate for the deficiencies that she felt in the intellectual and social setting of the West. But, for this dependence on the Gilders she paid a price. Already a part of the genteel tradition when she first went west, her continued reliance on the Gilders, who were the embodiment of eastern culture, kept her subject to what would today be called the viewpoint of the Eastern Establishment, at a time when she was becoming known as a leading writer and illustrator of scenes that were regarded as being "authentically western."

IV

Molly was still an eager participant in the cultural world of New York City when she met her future husband, Arthur De Wint Foote, whose ambitions to practice his profession in the West were to be the reason why this eastern-raised, eastern-thinking young artist reluctantly abandoned both the quiet family life on the Hudson River and the new intellectual and social circles to which the Gilders had introduced her. Foote was eighteen months younger than his prospective wife. He came of a prominent rural Connecticut family in which the head of the household had a status more nearly equivalent to that of an English country squire than to that of an American farmer. Arthur's father, in addition to managing his farm properties, was senior warden of his Episcopal parish, colonel of the militia, and member of the state legislature.[3] Young Foote was as instinctively upper-class in his social outlook as he was eastern in his origins. His personality and the demands of his career became the third major continuing influence on his prospective wife.

Arthur had less than two full years at Yale's Sheffield Scientific School from 1866 to 1868, before eye trouble interrupted his formal training in engineering. After a first trial elsewhere, presently he went west, where the best opportunities in engineering were to be found. Foote had many of the qualities that ordinarily made for success in a new country. He had imagination, fierce physical drive (despite neuralgia and headaches when frustrated), and skill with machines, human subordinates, and work animals. Sharply conscious of the incomplete nature of his academic training, he made each new project the occasion for intense study and self-education.

After trying his luck on several quite different engineering jobs in the Far West, Arthur finally found employment at New Almaden, where the initial discoveries of cinnabar ore had been made as far back as 1845. By the middle 1870s the New Almaden deposits had been developed so extensively that the mine was one of the greatest producers of quicksilver in the world, and the settlement at New Almaden had become a company town, peaceful, paternalistic, socially stratified, and an entirely safe place to which to bring a bride. Being only sixty miles south of San Francisco, it was not even especially isolated.

In coming west as a bride in 1876, Mary Hallock Foote was, however unconsciously, accepting a life in which many of her future friendships would be drawn from among the engineers with whom Arthur was to be associated professionally. It is, of course, a universal experience for a wife to find her list of friends and acquaintances somewhat determined by her hus-

---

[3] Abram W. Foote, *Foote Family, Comprising the Genealogy and History of Nathaniel Foote of Wethersfield, Conn. and his Descendants* (Rutland, Vermont, 1907), p. 203.

band's choice of careers, but in this case the tendency was accentuated. Engineers and geologists came much more often to the Footes' western homes than any other type of visitor — not just any engineer or geologist, but rather a special type. Usually eastern born and eastern or European trained, possessed thus of an extensive formal education and coming often from established families, engineers and geologists of this background fitted comfortably into Arthur's and Molly's preconceptions as to desirable friends. And the Footes had a rich field from which to choose. The late nineteenth century was the age of opportunity for the engineer; his was the glamorous new profession, and the West was the scene of many of his exciting achievements. No wonder that so many able, bright, and attractive young men, fresh from good professional schools, could be found in the mining towns and construction camps.[4]

The Footes' tendency to stay within the ranks of those who shared Arthur's professional interests was reinforced by the opportunities opened to them by James D. Hague, Arthur's brother-in-law. Boston born, Hague attended Harvard and Göttingen before going to the famous Royal Mining Academy in Freiberg, Saxony, where so many of the notable American mining engineers and geologists received their training. Experience in the South Seas, at the Lake Superior copper mines, and as a geologist and mining expert on Clarence King's famous scientific survey of the Fortieth Parallel preceded his beginning a successful consulting practice in California in the 1870s. Later he transferred his office to New York, where his services were sought by the great mining concerns and individual investors of the day.[5]

A worldly, distinguished-looking man of cultivated tastes

---

4 For a discussion of the mining engineer, see Clark C. Spence, *Mining Engineers & the American West: The Lace-Boot Brigade, 1849-1933* (New Haven, 1970). T. A. Rickard, *Interviews with Mining Engineers* (San Francisco, 1922), pp. 171-189, gives Arthur Foote's own account of his professional career.

5 Rossiter W. Raymond, *Biographical Notice of James Duncan Hague* ("Author's Edition," n.p., 1909). Read before the American Institute of Mining Engineers, October 1908.

Richard Watson Gilder   *Helena de Kay Gilder*

James D. Hague

and catholic interests, Hague moved easily in what contemporaries called "the best circles" of eastern America and Europe, yet was equally effective in the rough atmosphere of western mining camps, partly because he had so much poise, tact, and self-confidence. As Mrs. Foote once remarked, "Mr. Hague has an important manner." His wife, Arthur's sister Mary, possessed a beauty, charm, and generous kindness that complemented her husband's qualities.

When James and Mary Hague became the sponsors who introduced Mary Hallock Foote to western "society" in 1876, that lady found herself encountering not the "raw new West" of eastern fancy but rather the Hagues' professional friends and a few other Hague acquaintances of similar social and geographical origins. San Francisco was the headquarters for a considerable group. There the husbands left their wives and children while they themselves went off to inspect mining properties located in places deemed too rough for Victorian ladies of breeding. In her reminiscences Mrs. Foote referred to such people as "professional exiles." Whether the members of this elite class always regarded themselves as "exiles" may be questioned, but in any event, they were precisely the kind of individuals that the Footes instinctively liked to meet in their successive western homes. As with this first meeting in San Francisco, James Hague, who knew everybody, was apt to be the one who directed interesting new personalities to the Footes' door.

Often associated with the engineers were other young easterners or young Englishmen of comparable educational and social background, but not trained in engineering, who came west as managers of investments, especially in mines, or simply as restless young men out for adventure and advancement before settling down. These two types of educated "exiles"— the engineers and the other young men — were to be found much more frequently in the mining west than in the less exciting, less speculatively appealing agrarian regions. In

Mary Hallock Foote's own mind the principal additional group of acceptable young men in the West was offered by the United States Army. In one of her novels she spoke of her interest as being confined to "the mining and engineering and military, not the rural West."[6]

Given this highly selective circle of friendships in the West, when Mary Hallock Foote began to write, her subject matter was bound to be restricted. But in practice her husband's personality narrowed still further that lady's opportunities for observation and experience. Foote had difficulty with many types of men. Children, servants, employees, and animals were apt to be devoted in their trust of him, and a few associates and subordinates who came to know him intimately remained sympathetic friends for life, but he developed hostility toward many who would normally have been his allies or superiors in business.

A man of unbending integrity himself, he recoiled from anyone whose conduct suggested something less than complete honesty — and the West was full of such types. Or again, any attempt to patronize Arthur Foote cut off further relations. So did coarseness or crudity in manners — and the West had much of that, too. There were, as Mary Hallock Foote remarked regretfully, too many people that her husband "couldn't work for."

V

Taken together, her own preconceptions and those of her husband severely limited the types of personalities and types of living scenes that Mary Hallock Foote would encounter during the half century that she ultimately spent in the Far West. There her career as a professional writer started modestly enough. Having gone west as a successful illustrator whose

[6] *The Last Assembly Ball; and The Fate of a Voice* (Boston, 1889), p. 39.

artistic talents were in demand for poems and stories by authors as famous as Longfellow and Whittier, Mary Hallock Foote was encouraged by the Gilders to try writing about the picturesque scenes that she had described to them in her letters from the mercury mines at New Almaden. Indeed, her first published writing was a scissors-and-paste job reconstructed by the Gilders out of "Molly's" letters to them. This was done after Arthur had resigned his job at New Almaden and had moved his family to the seaside resort of Santa Cruz, California, to await an upward turn in Arthur's professional career.

With the Gilders' aid, an article about New Almaden, written and illustrated by Mary Hallock Foote, appeared in *Scribner's Monthly* for February, 1878, and a comparable article on Santa Cruz, again both written and illustrated by Mrs. Foote, followed in the August issue of that same periodical. At children's level the New Almaden material was used again for a story and illustration in *St. Nicholas Magazine* for December, 1878.

Success with these initial offerings encouraged further experimentation during the next two to three years. From descriptive essays that stressed the "color" of particular localities and their inhabitants, she made the transition to short stories that utilized essentially the same elements for fictional purposes — always within the limits of places and people very similar to those that had been a part of Mary Hallock Foote's personal experience. Short stories with settings borrowed from New Almaden and Santa Cruz were sold to the *Atlantic Monthly* and *Scribner's Monthly*, while a long Quaker story for the latter magazine was based on the history of the Hallock family and their farm at Milton.

By the time these varied efforts appeared in print, however, the newly established authoress had long since joined her husband at Leadville, where she spent much of 1879 and 1880. There she found the richest material for purposes of fiction and art that she had yet encountered, and out of the Leadville days came short stories, illustrations, and her first novels, which last were published in serialized form before being reprinted as books.

Leadville was as lively and picturesque a town as the West could offer at that late date in the history of the mining frontier. Haphazardly built near the site of a "played out" placer gold camp, and located at high altitude near the head of the Arkansas River, Leadville scarcely existed before 1877, when a metallurgist's experiments proved that the district was rich in carbonate ores that would yield silver and lead when smelted. From a population of less than 200 in the autumn of 1877, Leadville boomed up to a total of 14,820 by the time the census was taken in 1880. Of necessity, everything was extemporized, nearly everything was in short supply. The constantly changing crowd walked the streets and the plank sidewalks twenty-four hours a day; the saloons never closed. Large contingents of Irishmen, Cornishmen, Canadians, and Germans mingled with the American-born majority, who came from all parts of the United States.[7]

It was the Leadville books and stories, far more than the articles about New Almaden and Santa Cruz, that gave Mary Hallock Foote her reputation as a western writer, and, significantly, most of her early book-length fiction dealt not only with mining scenes but even more so with a colorful little minority among the mining population, a minority that did in fact exist and that remarkably resembled the Footes' Leadville friends, as one finds them described in these memoirs. The central figure in the novels she published in the 1880s and 1890s was usually an attractive, educated, young eastern mining engineer or manager, who had among his intimates one or two others of similar background. Often the hero was hiding a secret sorrow that had caused him to escape westward to the land of fresh beginnings. Some at least of the eastern "exiles"

7 Rodman W. Paul, *Mining Frontiers of the Far West, 1848-1880* (New York, 1963), pp. 127-31.

had the further interest of having fallen somewhat from grace
through yielding to the temptations to dissipation so readily
available in that bizarre setting. The villains were apt to be
either coarse western men or depraved eastern outcasts. The
heroines were invariably young ladies of remarkable prettiness and cultivation that was visibly of an eastern type, including an ability to quote poetry. In *John Bodewin's Testimony* (1886) the handsome young mining engineer from
Connecticut expressed surprise that a girl from Kansas City
could be so charming.

The process by which Mary Hallock Foote's novels were
created, and the effect of her decidedly specialized personal
observation, was shown by Mrs. Foote's own comments on *The
Led-Horse Claim: A Romance of a Mining Camp* (1883),
which was based on her experience at Leadville. As she explained forty years later:

The Led-Horse Claim was my "first novel" — written on demand.
The Scribner's Monthly people said I had the material and I could
do it if I'd try. As a fact, you see, I hadn't the material except from
the woman's point of view, the *protected* point of view — My poor
Cecil! What a silly sort of heroine she would seem today. Yet girls
were like that, "lots of them!" in my time. I ended the story at Leadville — as I believe it would have ended; the young pair would, in
the order of things as they were, never have seen each other again.
But my publisher wouldn't hear of that! I had to make a happy ending. I think a literary artist would have refused to do it.[8]

Mrs. Foote was aware that there were plenty of crude realities walking the streets of Leadville, "but the men of Leadville
whom I *saw* were the 'sifted pickings' and they were very able
men, most of them, and very charming." The examples she
then cited were three distinguished geologists, including Clarence King, plus a well-known mining engineer-journalist,

[8] Levette Jay Davidson, ed., "Letters from Authors," *The Colorado Magazine*,
19 (July 1942), 123.

Rossiter W. Raymond, who had been at Freiberg "a couple of years" behind James Hague.[9] Hardly a representative sample.

Something more complex than snobbery was involved here. Precisely because upper-class Victorians such as Arthur Foote and James Hague had seen the mixed and often rough elements in the society of the mining West, they were exceedingly careful as to whom they allowed into the presence of their womenfolk, or even what local happenings they permitted to be recounted in their ladies' hearing. Writing in 1922, Mrs. Foote pointed out that if realism was missing from her novels, "I could not get that sort of realism into my stories for I was one of the 'protected' women of that time — who are rather despised nowadays. As much of Leadville life as my husband thought I could 'get away with' he told me." But when Leadville had a lynching that his wife could have seen from her front porch through the use of a telescope or field glasses, Arthur carefully neglected to explain why there was unusual excitement and noise in the town that evening. [10]

Neither then nor subsequently did Mrs. Foote make false claims as to breadth of her experience in the West. When asked to draw a full-page picture of a sheriff's posse for the *Century Magazine* in 1889, she prefaced her introductory remarks with the confession:

This picture is not so sincere as it might be. The artist, in the course of many rides over these mountain pastures, by daylight or twilight or moonrise, has never yet encountered anything so sensational as a troop of armed men on the track of a criminal.[11]

If she was thus restricted in her opportunities to study human conduct at Leadville, no comparable limitation applied to the spectacular mountain scenery. A person who loved horseback rides and picnics, Mrs. Foote had an artist's eye for

9 *Ibid.*
10 *Ibid.*
11 "The Sheriff's Posse," *Century Magazine*, 37 (January 1889), 448.

telling details along the mountain trails, and an artist's imagination for reconstructing the details into a pleasing composition. The physical settings that Mrs. Foote created for her western stories were often more striking and persuasive than the personalities and actions of the principal characters. She indicated why this was so in a letter to James Hague in 1882, written just after she had completed *The Led-Horse Claim:* "The story, with the exception of one incident, which is very much changed, is *entirely* a *story* — but I cannot write a story without seeing the *places.*"[12]

A lively and surprisingly detailed description of Mary Hallock Foote, as seen in her picturesque setting at Leadville, happens to have survived in the reminiscences of Thomas Donaldson, a highly intelligent and useful political officeholder whose governmental assignments and connections with the Smithsonian Institution had won him the friendship of many a scientist. At Leadville on a late summer day in 1879, Clarence King persuaded Donaldson to join him in making "a call upon James D. Hague's relative, Arthur D. Foote."

King and I forged along through a forest, crossed a mining ditch, and in a little clearing espied a cozy log cabin. As we approached, we discerned a rustic porch made comfortable by armchairs built of barrels sawed in half and stuffed with straw and covered by gunnysacks. To the right a hammock swung lazily, suggesting that an eastern woman, and a cultivated one, lived at the house . . . .

King had known her, but it was the first time I had met Mary Hallock Foote, afterwards well-known through her literary works. She was dressed in white and she rounded out a pleasing picture in contrast to rugged nature all about her home. Mrs. Foote put us at ease with her sweet manners, and King fell into a conversation interesting and bright. We went inside the house and saw every evidence of artistic taste and culture . . . .

12 MHF (Mary Hallock Foote) to James D. Hague, Milton, N.Y., May 27, 1882. MHF's letters to members of the Hague family are in the Huntington Library in manuscript form, while her letters to the Gilders are in that library as photographic facsimiles of the originals in the Stanford University Library.

Mrs. Foote settled herself for a chat until her husband returned, and my, my, how she did talk! She was well read on everything and ripped out an intellectual go-as-you-please backed up by good looks and brightness. She told us of their hopes, hers and Arthur's, in Mr. Foote's engineering schemes. What was more interesting, she showed us some of her black-and-white illustrations for the work of other authors.[13]

After Leadville came Arthur's assignment in 1881 to inspect silver mines in the interior of Mexico, the trip that Mary Hallock Foote always described as sheer romance. As her first adventure in a foreign and exotic land, the Mexican visit remained vividly in her memory for the rest of her life, and for that reason occupies an amount of space in these reminiscences that is out of proportion to the time span involved but is not excessive in terms of the importance of the journey to the author herself. Besides, in retelling that episode Mrs. Foote was able to follow closely her own admirably written and well-illustrated travel articles that she prepared for Gilder, who thought so highly of them that he used the first in the series as the lead piece with which to open the initial number of the *Century Illustrated Monthly Magazine*, when that periodical succeeded the old *Scribner's Monthly* in November, 1881.

The real test of the Footes' individual characters, of their attitudes toward each other, and of their acceptance or rejection of western life came when dreams of settling permanently in Mexico gave way to the more prosaic reality of Arthur's scheme for an irrigation project in Idaho. At New Almaden and Leadville their stay had been brief compared with the dozen years in Idaho. The period at New Almaden was "poetic," Mrs. Foote once said to Helena, while that at Leadville was "gay and frantic." The year at New Almaden was suffused by the glow of being a bride and giving birth to their first baby. There, too, Mary Hallock Foote's adjustment was

13 Thomas Donaldson, *Idaho of Yesterday* (Caldwell, Idaho, 1941), pp. 359-60.

eased by the Hagues' kindnesses. Leadville had so many congenial people that it was continuously interesting, save for the
exhausting periods when the baby was sick or Mrs. Foote was
having a miscarriage. Of the lasting and basically satisfying
nature of the Leadville experience, no better evidence could be
cited than that it remained Mary Hallock Foote's favorite setting for short stories and novels. As for Mexico, that trip stood
out in Mrs. Foote's mind as partial compensation for never
having been able to finance the customary Grand Tour of
Europe.

But Idaho threatened to be different. That Territory's original gold placer boom of the 1860s had long since "played out,"
and agriculture and stock raising had started slowly, because
of aridity and remoteness from markets, so that only at the
end of the 1870s, after a decade of economic decline and
dwindling population, had Idaho finally begun to advance
under the twin stimuli of approaching railroad transportation
and a new mining boom based on silver discoveries. The
Footes' involvement with Idaho began nearly a year after
their return from Mexico, when Arthur was sent out to inspect
some of the new silver mines for prospective investors, while
his wife remained at Milton.

With an enthusiastic display of independence that was all
too typical of him, Arthur soon turned from silver mines to
plans for promoting an irrigation system in the cañon and
valley of the Boise River. Idaho had been the scene of intermit-
tent, small-scale irrigation efforts ever since 1855, when Mor-
mons, coming into southeastern Idaho from Utah, dug the first
ditches. Irrigation in the Boise valley dated back to 1863-64,
but major canals were not attempted there prior to Foote's
scheme. The incorporated company that he helped form needed to raise nearly one and a half million dollars to finance its
first stage of construction, and even the limited preliminary
work that the concern was able to pay for when it started up in
1883, such as surveying, filing claims, and preparing an

elaborate map and promotional pamphlet, came to $4,000 a month.[14]

A long-term project that was intended for a new and underdeveloped region, but was dependent upon eastern or British private funds that tended to dry up every time a tremor ran through the New York or London financial markets, was bound to be speculative. Nor was there much about Idaho to encourage distant investors. The census of 1880 listed only 1,885 farms in the whole Territory and a population of only 32,610, half of whom must have arrived recently, since the preceding census had recorded a mere 15,000. The "city" of Boise, the nearest place to Arthur's project and therefore the Footes' prospective home, was a small supply center that served miners, farmers, and ranchers, and was a resting place for "emigrants" who still moved west over the old Oregon Trail, but it was also the county seat and the capital of the Territory, and was adjacent to a small army post. The social life of the town thus drew upon a more varied constituency than would have been found at most western settlements. Boise's population was 995 in 1870 but had risen to 1,899 by 1880 and to 2,311 by 1890.

Mary Hallock Foote was not eager to go to Idaho. Her husband had to resort to his most confident assurances and most optimistic persuasion to convince her that the venture was worthwhile, and even when reluctantly converted, she still was agonizingly aware that because of the necessarily long-term nature of the project, this time they were going west for a long stay, perhaps permanently, and thus she must reconcile herself to diminution of so many eastern relationships, and of so much of the position that she had won for herself on the edge of the Gilders' cultural world. How sharp she conceived the break to be was indicated by an assertion she later made in one of her novels:

[14] Paul L. Murphy, "Early Irrigation in the Boise Valley," *Pacific Northwest Quarterly*, 44 (October 1953), 177-84; and typewritten essay by Merle W.

When an Eastern woman goes West, she parts at one wrench with family, clan, traditions, clique, cult, and all that has hitherto enabled her to merge her outlines — the support, the explanation, the excuse, should she need one, for her personality.[15]

For Mary Hallock Foote the impending break came at a time when she was well into mature life and might reasonably have expected a quieter, more predictable future. She was past her mid-thirties, mother of two children, and a hardworking, successful author and illustrator. Contemporaries reported that she was still youthful in appearance and manner and was apt to be shy among strangers. When a New Yorker who cultivated artists and writers met her with the Gilders, at a Sunday literary tea in March, 1884, he noted admiringly:

Mrs. Foote, for one whose name is so well known as writer and illustrator, retains her ladylike, bashful ways and prettiness wonderfully well.[16]

Under certain conditions, which is to say when she found herself in congenial and stimulating surroundings, Mary Hallock Foote was quite likely to burst into animated and prolonged conversation, as she did that day in Leadville when Clarence King and Thomas Donaldson called upon her. Usually the flow of words would cease only when she heard her husband's gentle admonition, made the more acceptable by his use of the Quaker mode of address, "Thee is talking too much." A psychologist would probably consider her shyness and compulsive talking to be merely opposite ways of expressing the same feeling of insecurity.

Wells, "The Beginning of the New York Canal," Idaho Historical Reference Series No. 190 (October 1971).

[15] *The Last Assembly Ball*, p. 39.

[16] James Herbert Morse, manuscript diary in New-York Historical Society (microfilm in National Portrait Gallery, Washington), entry for Sunday, March 16, 1884, at Robert Underwood Johnson's home.

This Sunday literary tea must have been a part of Mary Hallock Foote's farewell to New York City, for a few weeks later she departed with her family for Idaho and for the beginning of a major testing. While the reminiscences give an extensive account of the Idaho years, it is important to recognize that virtually every aspect of the Footes' experience there is decisively understated. By the time she came to write her autobiography, Mary Hallock Foote was anxious to bury painful memories, to avoid hurting her husband anew, and, in keeping with her Quaker beliefs, to live in peace with former neighbors and associates for whom in fact she had felt little liking.

VI

From the beginning Mary Hallock Foote's attitude toward Idaho was ambivalent. Her arrival there was made happy by the paradoxical sense of reuniting with part of Milton and the Hallocks out in this strange new land, for Bessie Sherman and her husband and children, together with Arthur Foote, had preceded Molly and the Foote children to Boise by many months. All her life Mary Hallock was dependent on the companionship and support of a few women: her mother, Bessie, Helena de Kay Gilder, Mary Hague.

The house that Arthur had rented for the joint use of his family and the Shermans was splendidly located, with unbroken views that stirred the newly arrived artist to rhapsodies. Close by was the comforting sight, so unexpectedly reminiscent of Milton, of apple trees, flower beds, kitchen gardens, and a row of well-groomed Lombardy poplars. "It seems strangely homelike to walk there at twilight," Mary Hallock Foote wrote to Mary Hague.[17] "I cannot tell you the thankfulness I feel for this place. This is an awkward little corner of the world to get to or away from, but once here, with good reasons

[17] MHF to Mary Hague, Boise, June 1, 1884.

for staying, it is uncommonly restful and pleasant. The children are well and happy."

Yet to Mary Hallock and Arthur Foote one reason for liking their rented house was that it was so far outside the settled part of Boise. "We are, indeed, I am happy to say," Molly's letter to Mary Hague continued, "so far 'out' that we are scarcely aware of the town at all." Their nearest neighbors were the rather pleasant officers and rough enlisted men of the unobjectionable army post on the far side of "a wild sort of picturesque common."

The town itself aroused the newcomer to only limited enthusiasm. When she first saw it in May, 1884, as Arthur was driving his family from the railroad toward their new home, Boise appeared to be "a very proper, decent little town quite unlike the wild [mining] camps where my married morals have been cultivated."[18] Three weeks later she reported to Helena that Boise was a "little oasis in the desert. . . . But this is its best season — when all its little ugly houses are smothered in apple blossoms and roses — and locust blossoms and the poplars, Lombardys — tall and splendid — give great distinction. It is a soil where everything grows apace" [when irrigated].[19]

She found no reason to live in the town or to cultivate its society or to educate her children in the new public school of which the local citizens were so proud. On the contrary, in a letter written three years later to James Hague, she reported that their continued residence outside the "city" had had many advantages, including "keeping our children, for instance, away from the commoness [sic] of the Boise atmosphere, to say nothing of its bad drainage."[20]

Despite the protective distance from Boise of the Footes' successive homes, Molly wrote Helena that well-meaning,

[18] MHF to Helena (de Kay Gilder), Boise, May 8, [1884].
[19] MHF to Helena, Boise, May 25, [1884].
[20] MHF to James D. Hague, The Cañon, December 31, 1887 (punctuation added).

kind, and yet dowdy and dull provincial ladies kept making courtesy calls, which doubtless would have to be returned, she added wearily.[21] The fortuitous presence of one stray acquaintance from Cooper Union days was scarcely sufficient compensation for the shortcomings of the other Boise ladies, whose conversation, social ambitions, and ill-conceived attempts to outshine the fashionable young army wives never ceased to arouse irritation in the lady who was at once a Quaker from Milton and a member of the literati from New York City. The irritation increased when her own growing fame as a writer and illustrator caused the local ladies to try to lionize her. Arthur was even less enthusiastic about local entertainment than was his wife — and much less prepared to suffer through the unavoidable minimum of it.

With relief the Footes escaped to still greater isolation when they went to live in a cañon ten miles from town, on the route of Arthur's projected irrigation system. The retreat to the cañon was an expedient to save rent, because of the irrigation company's troubled finances. After first living in the cañon in makeshift quarters, they built a stone house that was Arthur's design, done under his direction, and built of native materials of his discovery. There they assembled a domestic staff of surprising proportions for a family of precarious means: a Chinese cook, an English governess-tutor, a local girl for a nurse after baby Agnes arrived, plus all the assistance so cheerfully volunteered by the little irrigation company crew, who were delighted by the unexpected addition of a charming lady and her appealing small children. Ultimately, finding their stone house cramped and isolated even by their standards, the Footes moved to a new house that they built closer to town, but still far enough from Boise to assure privacy.

Throughout the Idaho years a critical attitude toward most of the people of this rural west, other than her husband's engi-

21 MHF to Helena, Boise, May 19 and July 27, 1884.

The Stone House in the Cañon

The Cañon of the Boise River

neering crew, marched side by side with Mary Hallock Foote's admiring appreciation of the beauty of mountain, cañon, and desert. During the happier phase of their stay in the cañon, as one of her letters to Helena shows, she expatiated upon the soft loveliness of moonlit nights in which she climbed to the top of the bluff to look down upon their firelit camp and upon the silvery gleam of the river as it wound its way toward the gate of the cañon.[22] On another occasion she wrote of the peacefulness of sunset over the bluffs, as the wind died and the cooing of wood pigeons rose above the sound of the river.[23] "Did I tell you," she asked Helena in still another letter, that "we had a glorious fishing trip up the river beyond Dowlings. Spent a week; with a tent and a cook, and pack animals — and rode over some wonderful trails high above the river — Coming home we forded the river twice and Moors' Creek once. I never forded on horseback before — The river's current was so swift, it made me feel rather giddy, but there was nothing to do but go ahead!"[24]

On quite a different occasion, writing to Helena from their house in the cañon, she described a day in which the relentless wind would have upset many people:[25]

This is one of those days when the wind blows up the cañon. . . . It is cross-grained weather. Baby cannot go out in her carriage. The sky is full of wind clouds. The sage bushes on the hills quiver in their stiff way, and the poplars lean and sway. This yellow fall color is beautiful against the sage green and brown of the hills. I have been riding again on horseback, which means good health & spirits.

Mary Hallock Foote was sufficiently objective to be aware of her ambivalence. She realized that quite aside from the imperatives of Arthur's career, the Foote family was able to enjoy

[22] MHF to Helena, The Cañon, June 26, [1885].
[23] MHF to Helena, The Cañon, June 6, 1885.
[24] MHF to Helena, undated, perhaps September 1885.
[25] MHF to Helena, Boise, November 1, 1886.

in the West many advantages that they could never have afforded in the East: ample space, a pleasing remoteness from undesired people, horses to ride, superb scenery. What was more, after years in the West Mrs. Foote's instinctive shyness and a tendency toward self-depreciation made her feel that she was too out of touch with Helena's cultivated East ever to live there again permanently. Her Quaker blood, she felt, was coming out more and more as she grew older, and would make her increasingly ill at ease in the rich world of celebrities in which the Gilders dwelt. After four years in Idaho she wrote resignedly to Helena:[26]

For us, a home here [in the West] for a few years is inevitable, so there is nothing for it but to make the best of it. The best is not at all bad: it is only that there are people in the East I love, who draw my thoughts and longings away from what I should be wrapped up in, here. The only way to come west happily is to embrace the country, people, life, everything as colonists do, jealously maintaining its superiority and refusing to see a blemish. I love my West when I am in the East.

She made a gallant effort to understand and write about the kinds of people whose lives would be influenced by her husband's irrigation system. Of several short stories that made use of Idaho rural scenes, one centered in the love affair of a young ditch tender whose official duties brought him into collision with an angrily uncoöperative farmer — who happened to have a pretty daughter. A full-length novel, *The Chosen Valley* (1892), took as its theme an irrigation project. Not surprisingly, the hero was an attractive young engineer of eastern and European training. Still another novel, despite its irrigation-sounding title, *The Desert and the Sown* (1902), took the nearby Boise army post for much of its setting. But more characteristically, she continued to write mining-town stories,

26 MHF to Helena, May 23, 1888.

merely transferring her stock types of personalities from Leadville to the new silver-lead mines of northern Idaho.

In a revealing letter to Helena, Mary Hallock Foote
showed how intrinsically difficult for her was any attempt to
move past her few tangential approaches to the rural West and
into use of it as a more central literary theme:[27]

I have a good subject — the sorrows and the wrongs of some of the
settlers here, not [that] I'd take it up in a partisan spirit but if possible in a spirit of human sympathy. I have the little story all
planned and I feel that it is worth doing, but I *cannot* write! The *talk*
of the men, particularly, is a stumbling block. I have *no* command
of dialect — and in fact there is no distinct form of dialect here,
rather a mingling of various kinds of slang and of local speech, and
it is very much more subtle and *surprising* than anything I can hope
to do. Perhaps after we are here longer it will soak into me
gradually.

There is great poetry to hear in the country life here. The valley
farmers with herds of cattle on the high pastures ("ranges") — the
life of the women — There is so much dignity in lives of people who
are building up their little fortunes slowly out of the ground, and
here there are entirely new risks. Nature is not subdued [but is]
awful and takes the place of Fate. There is a fascination about the
darkly tanned faces of the men and their clothing that shows the
effect of weather like old sails of barks that have just come into port
after long voyages. The long, long lines of mesa and plains are im-
pressive.

Her ability to reach a more satisfactory adjustment to western rural people, more nearly comparable to her enthusiasm
for mining and engineering, would have been greater if the
Idaho experience had not been overshadowed by disheartening
delays in financing Arthur's irrigation scheme, and by growing doubt as to whether the project had a future at all. Settlers
who had been attracted to the Boise valley by the company's

[27] MHF to Helena, March 8, [1885].

enthusiastic publicity became bitter when they discovered that after a few bursts of activity, the company was able to finance little more than the nominal amount of work required to keep water-right claims legally alive. As resident manager, it was Arthur rather than his absentee-owned corporation that became the target of an increasing local hostility. At the same time, bits of evidence gradually began to suggest what effect years of uncertainty and frustration were having on the whole family, but especially on Arthur himself.

Until 1887 Arthur would not permit his wife to tell even her most intimate friend Helena that in fact the great irrigation scheme had failed and the Footes were without adequate income.[28] Not until 1889 could Molly bring herself to confess to Helena that under the weight of prolonged strain and disappointment, and in an atmosphere of enforced inactivity that was demoralizing to a physically and nervously overcharged man, Arthur had given way to bursts of excessive drinking. In shifting moods that ranged from despair and alienation to affectionate sympathy and loyalty, Molly reported on Arthur's fight to regain his self-respect. She felt, she said, a "mother's" yearning that he might succeed — as in the end, courageously, he did.[29]

Arthur was a good, a generous and magnanimous husband, Molly argued to her skeptical confidante, a plain, physically strong man who had to work very hard in order to be happy and who had few resources outside his work. When he read, he read for a purpose, in annoyingly expensive books on engineering and water systems. Yet he had dreamed a great dream, a poetic dream, that saw a desert transformed by long lines of gleaming ditches into a fat land of farms and cattle. The happiness of everyone in the Footes' little group, each in his own way, was committed to the fulfillment of that dream.[30]

Absorbed in his own struggles, Arthur often left his wife to

[28] MHF to Helena, March 6, 1887.
[29] MHF to Helena, Boise, August 8, 1889.
[30] MHF to Helena, The Cañon, December 16, 1887.

find her own company, her own conversation, her own means
of exercise and fresh air. The person who helped her most,
save when Bessie could come out from Boise, was young Harry
Tompkins, an attractive, very young engineer who was a recent graduate of St. Paul's School (Concord, New Hampshire)
and "Boston Tech," as they called the Massachusetts Institute
of Technology. The son of the president of Arthur's irrigation
company, he was also Arthur's completely trusted assistant
and had become virtually a member of the family.

Like the artist she was, Mary Hallock Foote described Harry
Tompkins to Helena as being so superbly proportioned that he
resembled a very youthful figure by Michelangelo, with a
beautiful head and a rather "tragic" profile. Better educated
and more intellectually versatile than Arthur, Tompkins was
the one who could talk poetry and novels with Mary Hallock
Foote. He became, with Arthur, one of the two critics to whom
she read her manuscripts before deciding whether they were
ready for submission to the publisher. During Arthur's frequent absences, Harry Tompkins was in charge of both the
irigation project and the Foote household. He took Mary Hallock riding, served as her model when she wanted to sketch,
nursed the family when they were sick, and was a good host
when she had guests. He was the one whose influence decided
that the Footes' son, Arthur, should go to St. Paul's School and
thence to "Boston Tech."[31]

Certainly there was a time when the continuance of the
Footes' marriage, on any substantial basis, was in doubt. Mary
Hallock was under her own strains. She had miscarriages, as
she had earlier in Colorado and in the East before leaving for
Idaho, and one or the other of her children, husband, or retinue seemed always in the sickroom. In between sickroom
service she labored, sometimes almost mechanically, to crank
out the stories and illustrations that had become a major
source of greatly needed income. She made no pretense about

31 MHF to Helena, The Cañon, March 28, 1888.

it; many times she confessed to Helena that she was writing because she must earn money.

That she was able to continue her work at all under such circumstances is remarkable. A. J. Wiley, a quiet, competent young engineer who, like Harry Tompkins, was both an assistant to Arthur Foote and almost a member of the family during the years in the cañon, later commented:[32]

The vast amount of work she produced under conditions that would have absorbed all the energies of an ordinary woman, is accounted for by the fact that she seemed not to be dependent upon propitious moods or favorable surroundings, but had the faculty of absorbing herself in artistic or literary work whenever the more pressing claims of family life relaxed.

In his own unobtrusive way, Wiley was as deeply impressed by Mary Hallock Foote as was his colleague Harry Tompkins. Speaking of her in retrospect, Wiley stressed "the extraordinary and indescribable charm of her personality."[33] Throughout her life Mary Hallock Foote's other friends would have echoed Wiley's words of praise, and that makes it the more unfortunate that so few people in Boise ever had an opportunity to know her intimately. During much of their dozen years in Idaho the Footes were absorbed in their discouragements or isolated by their self-imposed distance.

By 1888 Arthur was telling Molly that she must try to see more people, to have a change from this unhealthily small circle of personalities. She herself acknowledged that she felt thin-skinned, tense, and more prone than ever to insomnia. Everyone in the household, her letters showed, was getting on everyone else's nerves.[34]

A long-planned trip east late in 1888, to see her mother and the Gilders, and to help with the mournful task of settling her

[32] Boise *Idaho Sunday Statesman*, December 3, 1916.
[33] *Ibid.*
[34] MHF to Helena, The Cañon, January 8, 1888.

parental family's tangled financial affairs, provided at least a change of scene. More successfully, she conceived what she called the unprecedented scheme of taking her family to the quiet British colonial seaport of Victoria, British Columbia, in 1889 for a summer vacation in an oceanic climate. She had persuaded Arthur to accept a low-paying but honorable and flattering offer to participate in a government survey of western water resources. While Arthur remained in Idaho to organize his survey, the wife and children tried the experiment of life without husband and father.

After weeks of interesting but often lonely vacationing in a totally unfamiliar setting, Mary Hallock Foote reached a major decision. In three terse sentences in a letter to Helena, she suddenly revealed the alternative that she had been considering, and her dismissal of it:[35]

This experiment has settled one thing in my mind. There is no use my thinking I could go anywhere with the children for their improvement and my own away from my old boy. I'm irrevocably committed to the part of an anxious wife.

So she went back to Boise. Back to a husband whose drinking had slipped out of control on at least one dramatic occasion during her absence. Back to a husband who had no certainty of employment, who had stubbornly refused to work for men whom he did not like, and had proved inaccurate in judgment of projects that he ran himself. Back to a husband who had so much talent, vision, and generosity, and yet was so little interested in the non-material things that mattered to his wife. If at times there seems ground for dismissing Mary Hallock Foote as an eastward-looking woman of letters who never fully accepted her role as a western wife, then thoughtful consideration should be given to the immensity of her decision in 1889. As a letter to Helena shows, in her own mind hers had by then become a family "without a future," "without hope." Yet she

35 MHF to Helena, Victoria, B.C., July 5, 1889.

made her decision. Greater resolution has rarely been shown by any western woman, not even in the hardy days of the frontier.

VII

That period was the nadir. For several years more Arthur struggled to find an engineering job in mining or water supply. The West was supposed to be the land of opportunity, and yet this man with a quarter century of engineering experience to his credit found nothing but brief and tentative employment. In silent, uncomplaining humiliation Arthur watched his wife's earnings supplant his own as the primary support for their large household. With equal forbearance he learned to endure an almost total uncertainty as to his own future. Ultimately he must have suppressed his pride about appeals to relatives for assistance. His wife had already sensed that one of the few avenues of escape from an intolerable situation lay through the intervention of James Hague, who by now was one of the most successful mining consultants of his generation. In a spirit of fierce defensiveness Mary Hallock Foote wrote to James' wife, Mary, in 1893:[36]

You must remember your brother Arthur has *not* made a failure here, in the sense that there is anything against him, either professionally or against his character. The failure is one of over-confidence in our financial backers. We shall lose all our land, probably, and that means all our little stake which has cost a good deal in time & money. But we have gained quite the worth of that time in sobering experience; and you must not for one moment think that your brother Arthur amounts to nothing because he is not making money. He is making character, and is a better comrade and a tenderer, deeper, stronger man for his trials. It is only fine natures that can rise through bitter disappointment and unsuccess; and I have seen

[36] MHF to Mary Hague, Boise, September 26, 1893.

my husband progress grimly, in patience and silence, through bitter trials; and speaking as an outsider might speak I can say I have never admired him more than I have this past year.

One year later Mary Hallock Foote wistfully reported to James himself:[37]

My work prospers as far as it ever does — that is; the magazines pay me good big prices but the books sell but mildly. . . . If my dear old man could get an income again, enough for modest family expenses, I could easily, with my work, keep my big lad his four years at the Tech.

By the end of that year Hague was ready to intervene. Since 1887 he had owned a controlling interest in a well-known gold lode mine at Grass Valley, California, the North Star. The North Star was showing signs of running out of profitable ore in the ground accessible to its existing shaft. After first consolidating a group of adjacent claims into North Star ownership, so as to be able to work additional properties, Hague launched upon several momentous steps that were intended to rejuvenate the North Star. He was backing his own professional judgment that he could restore the mine's profitability by driving the main shaft much deeper and conducting extensive exploration underground, while at the same time totally rebuilding and re-equipping the surface operations — the whole at immense initial cost before any major return could be expected.

A discreet and observant man, Hague seems to have calculated his brother-in-law's qualities carefully and understandingly. First he retained Arthur in 1895 to study installation of electrical power in the mine. Arthur recommended against electricity and in favor of compressed air; the air was to be compressed through power generated by a high-speed waterwheel of unprecedentedly large dimensions. Hague decided to accept Arthur's recommendations, and to give him the further

37 MHF to James D. Hague, Boise, September 9, 1894.

assignment of supervising construction and installation of the equipment. Still there was no assurance of permanent employment.[38]

The reminiscences tell the rest of the story. Mary Hallock Foote and the two daughters were invited by Hague to visit at Grass Valley and to be guests in the company's cottage there, while son Arthur, who had been with his family, went east to Massachusetts Institute of Technology. At this critical moment, while her husband's future was still uncertain, Cooper Union, prodded perhaps by the Gilders, suddenly proposed that Mary Hallock Foote take a position as principal in the school in which she had been trained. She wavered, first agreeing to go, then reconsidering and deciding to stand by her husband, in accordance with the verdict reached in 1889. Soon thereafter James Hague offered Arthur a permanent job as resident superintendent of the North Star, and with continued use of the cottage as a home for Arthur's family, although the cottage would also provide quarters for James himself on his repeated visits to Grass Valley.

Out of the resulting agreement developed a division of responsibility that worked. Like the fortunate incidents that made possible happy endings to Mary Hallock Foote's novels, this arrangement gave Arthur a chance to demonstrate his very real talents as designer and operator of equipment and manager of subordinates, while James made the basic decisions and continued to shoulder the heavy burden of financing the mine until it could begin to pay. Almost timidly, as if afraid to be too optimistic, Mary Hallock Foote reported to Mary Hague about "the way Arthur's old enthusiasm has been roused by the beautiful chance James gave him here. I have never seen him happier in any work — the first that fate has ever allowed him to finish."[39]

---

[38] On the North Star mine, see Errol Mac Boyle, *Mines and Mineral Resources of Nevada County* (California State Mining Bureau, December 1918, published Sacramento, 1919), especially pp. 15-17, and Arthur B. Foote with George Starr collaborating, *Men and Mines of Nevada County and Adjacent Territory for Forty Years* (mimeographed, n.p., n.d.).

[39] MHF to Mary Hague, North Star Cottage, Grass Valley, May 24, 1896.

Arthur's work on his new job showed not only enthusiasm, but also imagination and resourcefulness in overcoming technical problems. As his son, Arthur B. Foote, later said of him: "Mr. Foote was a true pioneer. He was never afraid of trying something new."[40] He was also a perfectionist who insisted that the new waterpower system and all other new structures be built on a solid, permanent — and very costly — basis. For his labors he received only a modest salary until the mine finally began to yield a handsome profit. Just before Christmas in 1902, the Footes learned that James had caused the company to make a very substantial gift to Arthur of shares of company stock. In an emotion-laden letter of thanks, Mary Hallock Foote wrote to James:[41]

I know Arthur will feel a certain sacredness about that gift of stock. He'll take no risks with that. If we could have lived by your advice all our lives, our foolish sanguine temperaments would not have got us into scrapes. You pulled us out of the worst one, and placed a roof over our heads.

It does Arthur so much good to feel he hasn't worked (and spent!) in vain.

The spending has been terrible! How it must have worn on your nerve: what patience, what withheld generosity you have shown — all the time this good thought "up your sleeve"! I wonder if your faith never really was shaken? It has been a piece of heroism, the waiting on results: and oh, the relief!

The reminiscences end soon after reaching this point of apparent stability and security in the Footes' lives. There is little more than passing reference to the more than thirty-five years that the Footes spent at Grass Valley. Arthur won high praise from his peers for the technological innovations that he introduced at the North Star, including several instances in which

[40] Arthur B. Foote, "Memoir of Arthur DeWint Foote," American Society of Civil Engineers, *Transactions*, 99 (1934), 1450.
[41] MHF to James D. Hague, December 19, 1902.

he actually invented new types of equipment to solve difficult problems at that mine. On the other hand, Arthur's family and the company would have been richer if he had been able to curb his ill-justified enthusiasm for opportunities that he kept discovering in connection with mines other than the North Star. Like many another westerner, Arthur's judgment was inferior to his imagination. That is why he was fated to die poor.

His son stated the problem delicately: "Mr. Foote could never accumulate money for himself. He was always supplying money to some prospector to develop a mine."[42] The big loss of the later years, however, was caused by a road-building scheme that was only indirectly part of a mining venture. Having invested in the Tightener mine, which was located high up in the Sierra Nevada and was accessible only by an execrable road that was closed by snow in winter, Arthur Foote persuaded the public authorities and some local mine owners to appropriate what appeared to be the amount of money needed to construct a modern all-weather road. Always a believer in his own projects, Foote took the contract for it himself, but soon found that the proposed route was leading him into construction costs far beyond anything anticipated in the estimates. Grimly he completed the contract, but according to his son, the venture stripped him of virtually "all he had"[43] — that is, of all that the prosperous years at the North Star had brought him. No wonder that the local people nicknamed the road "Foote's Folly"!

For Arthur and Mary Hallock Foote the significance of this episode and of several contemporaneous unsuccessful mining ventures was that they came so late in the lives of this hard-working couple, when both husband and wife were in their sixties, when Arthur was shifting from active management of the North Star to the lesser position of consulting engineer,

42 Foote, "Memoir," p. 1451.
43 Ibid., p. 1452.

and when Mary Hallock Foote was writing less and finding a diminished literary market. In short, unlike their recovery after the Idaho disaster, this time there was no chance to re-build their personal fortunes and thus provide money that would make possible travel, independence of their children, and assurance against the inevitable uncertainties and ex-penses of old age.

Fortunately the worst consequences of these latter-day fail-ures were not felt immediately. For many more years the Footes continued to have a comfortable place in which to live at the North Star's official residence, which remained available to them and their family even after Arthur had retired as superintendent. Mary Hallock Foote's letters from this later era show an affection and loyalty between husband and wife that is a tribute to both parties. Probably that is why "Foote's Folly" finds no mention in these reminiscences. During their early years at the North Star their son Arthur spent his sum-mers with them, and after finishing at M.I.T. in 1899, did his first practical work at Grass Valley, before going off to Korea for additional mining experience. Ultimately he was to suc-ceed his father at the North Star. Bessie Sherman's son Gerald likewise found employment at the North Star and at its neigh-bor, the Empire mine, before going on to bigger things else-where. Employment at the North Star came to be regarded as an unusually instructive internship for young mining engi-neers at the start of their careers. One "graduate" of service there said of Foote: "His fine kindly character and high ideals permeated the whole North Star organization."[44]

The two daughters grew up at Grass Valley until they were ready for boarding school. After the turn of the century the family's life was a comfortable, even luxurious one. Early in the present century the company built for them, in accordance with the Footes' ideas, the big stone mansion (North Star House) that still stands atop the hill on which the mine was

44 *Ibid.*

situated. Surrounding the house were handsomely planted grounds that reflected Arthur's skill and taste as a gardener. A considerable retinue of servants and hired hands maintained the property. To North Star House came other well-to-do mining people from the cluster of profitable mines in Nevada County. In the Footes' home they found a quiet atmosphere of cultivation and graceful living. Distinguished people from afar came to be guests at North Star House, and mingled there with the inevitable cousins, nephews, and nieces who were always a part of the Footes' lives. In the predominantly Cornish town of Grass Valley, Mary Hallock Foote was respected and looked up to, but was not known intimately.

One who would catch some impression of the later years, after Arthur's retirement from active management, can do so by reading Mary Hallock Foote's novel of the First World War, *The Ground Swell* (1919), which deals with relations between a retired couple and their daughters. The death of the fictional girl in that novel is based upon the actual tragedy of the loss of the Footes' real daughter Agnes, which is so movingly described in these reminiscences. Placing the fictitious girl's death in France, while nursing soldiers, was probably suggested by the actual death in France in 1918 of the Hagues' only son, William, who had assumed principal direction of the North Star after his father's death in 1908.

It was characteristic of Mary Hallock Foote to use an incident or happening in her own family's life as the inspiration for a story. Many of her short stories were almost autobiographical, just as many of her illustrations depicted members of her family retinue. From Milton and New Almaden in the 1870s to Grass Valley after 1900, she was constantly seeking themes for fiction and models for illustrations, and within the limits of her upper-class Victorian life, she found it none too easy to discover them, despite the unusual places in which she lived.

In an undated letter to the editors of *Century Magazine*,

written in this late period, she submitted a manuscript written "in a dramatic form" and dealing "with very contemporaneous subjects."

My tragedy shop is closed for awhile. I must get in a new stock. . . . Students, co-eds, women's rights girls, soldiers, prosperous middle-class citizens; you can't make tragedy out of them.
It is here, in the lives of the miners, the underground world, and the pine-woods, but I can't get at it yet.[45]

She did less with Grass Valley, its deep gold mines, and its Cornish workmen than one might expect. Two short stories, published in 1898 and 1899, made a very promising beginning. In both Mary Hallock Foote showed that she had learned enough about the technology of vein mines to write convincingly about the peculiarities and dangers of life underground, and that she knew her husband's employees well enough to make effective use of the dialect and distinctive attitudes of Cornishmen.[46] But she turned from this theme to experiment fairly widely, not only with the "contemporaneous subjects" that she mentioned in her letter to *Century Magazine*, but also with historical novels whose setting was based upon recollections of Milton and New York State. Always modest and honest about her writing, she ceased to submit manuscripts when she came to feel that "my vogue" has "passed away."
If today her fiction is much less remembered than the romantic mining-camp tales of Bret Harte, who preceded Mary Hallock Foote, or the equally romantic western novels of Owen Wister, who followed her, and if her western illustrations are clearly not in the same class with those of Frederic Remington,

45 MHF to Editors, *Century Magazine*, (n.p., n.d.), in "The Century Collection," Archives of American Art (microfilm in National Portrait Gallery, Washington, D.C.).
46 "How the Pump Stopped at the Morning Watch," *Century Magazine*, 58 (July 1899), 469-72, and "The Borrowed Shift," *Land of Sunshine*, 10 (December 1898), 13-24.

nevertheless her work was widely and appreciatively enjoyed in her own day, and, what is more, her readers included western people whose daily experience put them in a position to distinguish between convincing and false fictional situations. Particularly during the isolated Idaho days, her incoming mail brought a flow of unsolicited letters from unknown mining men and mining and irrigation engineers, who had liked her stories, were impressed by her apparent knowledge of their activities, and wanted to know how she ever learned all this. (Her invariable answer: from my husband.) The engineers, "the sons of Martha," she called them, were delighted to have someone at last recognize the dramatic possibilities of their supposedly prosaic profession.

If, again, her plots and personalities seem to the modern reader to be thin and artificial, nevertheless consider the verdict of two well-known contemporaries who had a good basis for knowing whereof they spoke. Charles F. Lummis, the enthusiastic southwestern editor and writer, and a leading spokesman for the literary and artistic values of his region, declared in 1898:[47]

If those who have carefully followed American literature for the last ten years were bidden to make choice of the most typical series of Western stories written by a woman, I fancy a majority would promptly elect Mary Hallock Foote. Western in very truth of scene and "color" and outlook, marked by all the instincts at once of woman, artist, poet and story-teller, *The Led-Horse Claim* and its fellows are of a quality that refuses to be forgotten. . . . [Her work has] that undefinable but unmistakable largeness of soul which belongs to our horizons.

W. A. Rogers, for many years an illustrator for *Harper's* and a veteran firsthand observer of western scenes in the later nineteenth century, tells in his autobiography of making a

47 Charles F. Lummis, "The New League for Literature and the West," *Land of Sunshine*, 8 (April 1898), 208.

pilgrimage to Mary Hallock Foote's cabin at Leadville in 1879. The recollection inspired him to remark:[48]

If Mrs. Foote were not so identified with her work as a novelist she would be better known as one of the most accomplished illustrators in America. There is a charm about her black-and-white drawing which cannot be described, but it may be accounted for by the fact that, more than any other American illustrator, she lived the pictures from day to day which she drew so sympathetically.

Somehow she and Owen Wister, two products of the most refined culture of the East, got closer to the rough frontier character than any writers I know, and Mrs. Foote supplemented this with pictures that one feels were made while looking from the rim of some deep cañon or by the light of a lantern in a lonesome cabin.

After spending nearly the first third of the twentieth century at the North Star mine, Arthur and Molly Foote decided to move to New England to spend their few remaining years with their daughter, Betty.[49] The editor of Grass Valley's little newspaper came up to North Star House for a long farewell interview.[50] His printed report spoke of Arthur, his achievements at the North Star, and "the Great Failure" in Idaho, but most of all the newspaper account stressed "this exquisite gentlewoman of an era now closed, but with surprising understanding and toleration of the foibles of the present era."

---

48 W. A. Rogers, *A World Worth While: A Record of "Auld Acquaintance"* (New York, 1922), p. 188.
49 Arthur died August 24, 1933, and Mary Hallock Foote, June 25, 1938.
50 *Grass Valley-Nevada City Union*, June 5, 1932.

BOOK I

Quaker Beginnings

1

THERE was a difference of fourteen years in the ages of our parents. My father, being questioned on the subject, said he fell in love with little Ann Burling in her cradle: she was eighteen and he thirty-two when he took her up the river and set her in his "lot and heritage."[1] He had worked hard and saved money but he could not have built his bride as good a house as the one his children were born in. It might have been called a Burling house on Hallock land for some of our Grandfather Burling's money, and more of his advice, went into it; also a legacy to our mother from her step-grandmother Burling who had no children of her own. She was an English-woman, Mary Shepherd, of a suitable age for a third wife.

Her name in our childhood was connected with certain pieces of London furniture that were "good" and a row of old Quaker tomes that we never read but were expected to dust at housecleaning when they were turned out of the back-parlor bookcase. One of them would be a collector's prize: Robert Barclay's *Apology for the People Called, in Scorn, Quakers. Written in Latine, for the Information of Strangers.* "From Ury, the place of my Pilgrimage." This was the English translation printed in London, 1678.[2] Not being acquainted with the word *Apology* in its "Latine" use, it struck me, as a child,

---

[1] See genealogical chart of the Hallock family, endpapers. Mary Hallock Foote's parents were Nathaniel Hallock (1802-87) and Ann Burling (1815-90). They were married in 1833. The maternal grandfather referred to here was Thomas Hull Burling, who died in 1861.

[2] The actual title of Robert Barclay's treatise was: *An Apology for the True Christian Divinity, as the same is held forth, and preached by the People, called, in Scorn, Quakers. . . . Written and Published in Latine, for the Infor-*

unpleasantly. In the village — our village of Milton half a mile away — they called us Quakers, "the Quaker Hallocks," but they did not scorn us. And the village did not matter. I don't remember when it was we first read Whittier's "Barclay of Ury" — but that cleared up part of the mystery of Barclay's *Apology*.[3]

I don't remember that we took any part in the village life, certainly not in its social or its churchgoing life, and we escaped its gossip and petty wranglings. A few of the neighbors who wanted private teaching for their children sent them to the Friends' school in the old Meetinghouse, joint property of the Hallocks and their kin. Half the room inside was ample for the shrunken gatherings there on Sundays (First Days). One of these little schoolmates came to play with me now and then but I was not allowed to go to "her house." The question was never discussed — we accepted these inhibitions as a matter of course, and we had company enough: cousins on the neighboring farms and cousins in New York who visited us for weeks in summer and we returned their visits; but these Brewster cousins were not Friends. Grandfather Burling's lively sister Polly ran away at sixteen and "married out of meeting." She came back as it were in these children who were a different brand of cousins. They taught us all we knew about dancing and sang songs we never else should have heard, and wore low-necked dresses every evening at supper, and were a distinct element in our education of a kind we should have missed; certainly we enjoyed them!

---

mation of Strangers, by Robert Barclay. And now put into our own Language, for the Benefit of his Country-Men (London [?], 1678). The additional phrase "From Ury, the place of my Pilgrimage" occurs at the end of the dedication.

[3] John Greenleaf Whittier's poem "Barclay of Ury," first published in 1847 and often reprinted, was prefaced by this explanatory note: "Among the earliest converts to the doctrine of Friends in Scotland was Barclay of Ury, an old and distinguished soldier, who had fought under Gustavus Adolphus, in Germany. As a Quaker, he became the object of persecution and abuse at the hands of the magistrates and the populace. None bore the indignities of the mob with greater patience and nobleness of soul than this once proud gentleman and soldier."

But to the Quaker society in New York we seemed no nearer than to the village that we ignored. It was not so in our father's time. Gradually we began to wonder why this should be — why our parents never attended the New York Yearly Meetings, which were held to be a great social as well as spiritual opportunity, why we never had visits from Friends at any time, unless they were relatives or connections by marriage. We learned, when we were older, that back of our remembrance there was a reason for this isolation: the glory of persecution for a principle belonged in a mild way to our little Milton Meeting.

Our Uncle Nicholas,[4] no longer living, was held in the family to have been a remarkably gifted preacher. That would have been a matter of opinion, but he had enough power in words to get himself thoroughly disapproved of by the New York General Conference, where country preachers went down and relieved their minds of their spiritual burdens. The "concern" on his mind was slavery. Shut in on their farms, with hours of silence in their fields or by their firesides for reading or brooding, coming in contact with the emotional politics of the day through newspapers remarkably well edited, they ate their hearts, these single-minded Quaker farmers, over matters which may have called for greater patience than even they possessed. Nature tried what patience they had in the course of each season's work; you can't fight Nature but you must fight Wrong when it is "on the throne."[5] He carried his message to the Yearly Meeting where he was listened to with uneasiness, not for the matter but the manner, I suppose, since all Northern Friends were antislavery. New York was not so far from Baltimore that Southern Friends might not have been present.

His language was too strong for those shrinking times and

4 Nicholas Hallock, one of Nathaniel's numerous brothers. Each generation of the Hallock family produced a number of preachers.
5 From James Russell Lowell's poem "The Present Crisis" (1844): "Truth forever on the scaffold, Wrong forever on the throne."

stirred emotions contrary to the spirit of unity among Friends. He was visited and admonished but refused to withhold or modify his testimony. A man of blameless life, nothing on personal grounds could be alleged against him, and in order to reach the preacher the meeting that bred and endorsed him was "laid down," awaiting a change of heart in individuals or the body. I can't explain this form of discipline in the proper words but it resulted (as nobody did change) in the stiff-necked Hallocks up the Hudson finding they had no one but one another to preach to. No authentic voice arose among them after Uncle Nicholas died. They were now on the open roads of thought and they did not lack company nor great allies. The character of the meetings changed: instead of silence or mild personal testimonies such as Uncle Townsend or one or two others might have supplied, there was reading aloud from the Bible and printed discourses by men of note who filled the Unitarian pulpits of the day. But I can remember the charm of the silences, before and after — with our elders seated on the benches above us. "How reverend is the view of these hushed heads, looking tranquillity."[6]

---

[6] So quoted in Charles Lamb's "A Quakers' Meeting," in *The Essays of Elia*, although in fact it is a very free adaptation from Congreve's *The Mourning Bride*.

2

THERE were dark winter mornings when we woke as it were in the night, in a room where an airtight stove blared away with the draft open, panting and reddening on its legless feet; and the youngest lay in bed and watched a person named Charlotte doing her hair by candlelight. She went through the same gestures every morning, sweeping the comb through its long black streamer after she had freed it from tangles, and the same shadows mimicked her, shooting up the wall and across the ceiling where it sloped down towards the eaves. (This must have been in the west wing before it was "raised.") I thought she was very good looking but I did not know why she always wore black dresses, or why she came to live with us and then went away. She was a young widow of the neighborhood who took over the housekeeping for a time to spare our mother when she needed a complete rest. She was seldom ill but never very strong....

Then, I remember a morning when my winter coat was put on before breakfast to go with father — a great privilege — to the upper barn along the icy lanes in March, to see him feed cut-turnips to the yearling lambs. The sun just risen at our backs made our shadows all legs streaking ahead of us; his seemed to end over in the next field, and he pointed to it and quoted from one of his old classics (Thomson's *Seasons* very likely), "Prepost'rous sight! the legs without the man."[1] I missed the context, but that word "prepost'rous" I never forgot

[1] The quotation is actually from Book V ("The Winter Morning Walk") of William Cowper's *The Task*, first published in 1785.

— nor the low light so different from sunset streaming across the glistening fields; nor the faces of the lambs crowding about my father's knees as he waded through their warm, bleating bodies to the barn.

And there were sounds: the millponds in spring, up in the hills overflowing their wasteweirs; the frogs on summer nights — we young ones gathered on the piazza steps — and the plash of the fountain unseen in the dusk and sometimes silent when the wind scattered it on the grass. The peculiar whining cadence of the cider mill rising and falling on still autumn mornings, fog hanging over the river; and another sound in cold weather, up in the neighborhood of the pigsty, which little girls did not like to think about, though they were greatly interested in some of its results . . . . And then, in that house of Quaker traditions, awoke a thrill, when our first musician came home from boarding school, and all hands on the place were summoned to unload a piano and set it up in the back parlor, and the men waited outside the open windows to hear Miss Bessie play.[2] They were the old-time Irish whom we read about in *Traits and Stories of the Irish Peasantry*;[3] they brought over their ineradicable habits and speech and adopted our father and mother and all of us as the Family, and they were as much a part of our childhood as the farm itself.

Children of my generation (I was born in 1847) came to their consciousness of public events at a very forcing period. It was our father's custom in the evening to read aloud to the family assembled the Congressional debates and the editorials in the *New York Tribune*.[4] A child of eight or nine would have been lacking in ordinary intelligence if she had not gathered some

[2] Mary Hallock Foote's older sister, Bessie, was born in 1841 and married her cousin, John Sherman, in 1861.

[3] By William Carleton, first published in Dublin in 1830.

[4] Horace Greeley's great newspaper, founded in 1841. It was widely read throughout the North, and was noted for its high intellectual and moral tone, its advocacy of advanced causes, and its uncompromising opposition to slavery.

notion of what they were talking about, the great speakers in Congress who were battling for or against the extension of slavery. I had brought the mail from the village one day, dreaming along the half mile of road I knew so well, and on the front page of the *New York Tribune* was the news of the assault on Charles Sumner, beaten senseless on the floor of the Senate chamber by a fellow member, Brooks of South Carolina. The color left my mother's face and Grandfather Burling said those words which, I thought then, were his own: "Whom the gods destroy they first make mad." The Fugitive Slave Bill had been passed and the Dred Scott decision made it obligatory to enforce it to the letter; and William Lloyd Garrison put forth his challenge to that law: "The Constitution of the United States is a covenant with death and an agreement with hell."[5]

The voters of our family were Free Soil Republicans; they believed slavery would die of itself if kept within its own borders, but as to the new territories in dispute since the Mexican War, they said, "No further."[6] The women were for the most part silent, but not Aunt Sarah! She was Uncle Edward Hallock's second wife, a comparatively young woman when he died. She had no children and her stepsons were married men. With half her life's energies unspent she gave herself to books and gardening and friendship and reform. At intervals, between 1856 and the Civil War, we were visited by missionary

[5] Mary Hallock Foote's crowded references here are to famous episodes in the slavery controversy: Congressman Preston S. Brooks' brutal beating of Senator Charles Sumner of Massachusetts in 1856, because of Sumner's philippic against Brooks' uncle, Senator Andrew Butler of South Carolina; the Fugitive Slave Act of 1850 that was intended to stop the loss of southern runaway slaves, but in fact roused the North to fury; the Dred Scott decision of 1857 that seemed to leave Congress powerless to exclude slavery from new territory; and the harsh and relentless abolitionist crusade of William Lloyd Garrison's *Liberator*, which began publication in 1831.

[6] The Free Soil party, organized in 1848 around the principle of "no more slave states and no more slave territory," merged into the Republican party after the latter came into being in 1854.

lecturers sent forth by the New York Anti-slavery Society.[7] Aunt Sarah, who belonged to the society, invited them, and the Republicans, those weary voters, got up meetings for them and met their trains, and they were the guests of the Hallocks at large.

I have always regarded this phantasmagoria of idealists and propagandists and militant cranks and dreamers as one of the great opportunities of our youth, shut up as we were and cut off and "laid down"! For they were brilliant talkers; all the villages in the valley of the Hudson and the Mohawk put together could not have furnished such conversation as we heard without stirring from our firesides.[8] Frederick Douglass was our guest upon a time and the second girl (Irish, of course) refused to come into the dining room and wait on a "naygur." But Douglass, son of a southern aristocrat and a black slave woman, had a breadth of experience and humor that turned the incident into comedy. . . . But none of it was comedy — it was the seed of bitter tragedy we were sowing North and South.[9]

Aunt Sarah was far ahead of all the men and most of the women of the family on the question of Woman's Rights,[10] which they thought might wait till slavery was settled. But

7 The New York Anti-slavery Society was organized at a convention held in Utica in 1835, with Mary Hallock Foote's uncle, Townsend Hallock, as one of its vice-presidents. The object was the "entire Abolition of Slavery in the United States."

8 Records of conventions held by antislavery and women's rights organizations in the 1850s and 1860s show that Sarah H. Hallock was a constant, militant, and articulate participant.

9 Frederick Douglass (1817?-95), the famous abolitionist, was the son of a white father and a slave mother. He began his own life in slavery and was a runaway slave until his freedom was purchased.

10 After the first women's rights convention was held at Seneca Falls, New York, in 1848, agitation was constant to improve the status of women, and especially to win for them the right to vote. Of the two leaders mentioned here, Susan B. Anthony (1820-1906), reared in a Quaker household, became interested first in temperance, then in abolition, and then in women's rights, and was for many years a leader of the woman suffrage movement. Ernestine L. Rose (1810-92), born in what was then Russian Poland, married William E. Rose in 1829, came

with her they were "spirits twain": if at her instigation you invited an antislavery lecturer to come and wake up the lazy-minded little village, you were in for the sister reform, and if argument did not start on one head it did on the other. It was a school of controversy, but without loss of temper, for those minds were bent on bigger game than petty personal differences. I have never known a more argumentative or a less quarrelsome family.

Aunt Sarah would have been no mean platform figure herhelf, a Deborah with a Greek profile somewhat heavily molded. She wore too many curls falling over her cheeks Mrs. Browning fashion, and she had too much hair altogether for the classic knot. It came below her knees when she let it down and was that part of her woman's glory she would have sacrificed last on the altar of her convictions. Some of those militant ladies of her time bobbed their hair in a ruthless and purposeful manner and wore short skirts and a pantalet or trouser business beneath, ending in the shoes of the period which might be congress gaiters[11] — what sights they were! — there was no danger of Aunt Sarah's making a guy of herself. But they were not all of them guys by any means: Susan B. Anthony was young and handsome when she laid her head on those Quaker guest-room pillows; Mrs. Ernestine L. Rose was a veritable rose of Sharon, and our guest for many summers, when she came not to preach but to charm. Introduced by Aunt Sarah in her public capacity, to us she was beauty and fashion and sparkling black eyes, and large boxes of candy from New York, and a fan in a hand covered with rings that tossed the curls about her brilliant face, and a strangely accented speech which made us hang on her every word. When she parted with the company at bed time she would assume

---

to New York in 1836 and thereafter gave many lectures on religion, free schools, abolition, and women's rights.

[11] Congress gaiters were a type of boot, apparently introduced in the late 1840s, that was worn by both sexes.

her platform manner playfully, make a little formal curtsy ending with "Ladies and gentlemen, I think I will say good night!"

She was the daughter of a Polish rabbi, betrothed in childhood to a man whom she refused to marry; hence, according to the law of her people, her dowry was forfeit. She carried her case into the courts (I can't be sure of the modus operandi here), denying the justice of an order which penalizes for breach of contract one who has had no hand in making that contract. She couldn't have won anything but publicity, and her father's house was home to her no longer. Young and handsome and eloquent and without fear, she fled to England and married a mild little Englishman of her own choosing. Her Rights were safe enough as the wife of William Rose. He had the means also to dress her according to the taste of Judah, and support her career of unpaid lecturer in behalf of the Rights of others.

I can see our front parlor of a summer afternoon, the shutters, that had been closed all day against the heat, open on the shaded lawn; our mother and her guest in their afternoon dresses, the little Quaker conservative and the Jewish rabbi's daughter with her stormy eyes. In dress they were equally contrasted. Our mother's skirts were full but plain; she wore "flowing sleeves" but her undersleeves were gathered in a band of embroidery at the wrist to match the round collar fastened with a cameo brooch. Her soft thin hair lay in puffs close to her temples crowned by a little Mary Stuart cap. When she did fine sewing she took off her spectacles, and if she looked up, her blue nearsighted eyes had that vague, wistful look of eyes accustomed to glasses.

There was nothing vague about her companion in the mahogany rocking chair. Her dress skirt flounced to the waist spread a yard on either side; her full lace undersleeves showed her plump bare arms clasped by bracelets; a long gold watch chain fell below her waist-belt; she was trimmed and decked wherever it was allowable to be so. She wore yellows and greens, and beside our mother in her lavenders and grays they must have looked like a cockatoo conversing with a wren. Mrs. Rose was one of our disenchanted foreign residents who love us to chasten us. She knew more about what we should do and think and demand in the name of democracy than our undemocratic founders ever dreamed of. But she was charming to a listener while scolding the multitude, from unfaithful servants and stupid dressmakers (one would gather she might be a rather hard person to serve) to the Supreme Court and Constitution of the United States. It was the age of showing others their duty; even the poets were on the platform with their lyres. Whittier rhymed his indignation against slavery; Lowell's best satires were the *Biglow Papers*, and now and then Emerson sent a peal from his belfry tower.[12]

The Prince of Wales came to America and the cities vied with one another in his honor. New York gave him a grand ball at the Academy of Music, and little girls in the country who had never seen a ball, and never expected to see a prince, hung over the pictures in *Harper's Weekly* and sighed to think they should probably never wear dresses like those nor waltz with elegant partners in side-whiskers. . . .[13] They were reading *A Tale of Two Cities*, and Aunt Sarah, the family purveyor of literature, had just lent them the *Idylls of the King*.[14] They were deep in the romance and poetry of old wars when that new and terrible war was gathering over their uncon-

---

[12] Whittier's collected works list 93 poems under the heading "Anti-Slavery Poems." The second series of *Biglow Papers* was published in the *Atlantic Monthly* during the Civil War. Emerson was deeply interested in the antislavery movement and, of course, in the northern cause during the Civil War.

[13] The American tour of the Prince of Wales (later Edward VII) took place in September and October 1860.

[14] Dickens' *A Tale of Two Cities* was published in 1859 in both England and America. The first four of Tennyson's *Idylls of the King* were published in London in 1859 and in America in 1860.

scious heads. Hoops were wider than ever — the Lyons looms
were weaving silks "to deck our girls for vain delights.". . .[15]
And three of the tall cousins who skated and played chess
with us and talked over the stories in the *Atlantic Monthly*
were to die — two on southern battlefields and one in a southern prison. Their white marble shafts in the old Friends' burial
ground stand tall above the low gray stones of their ancestors
— the familiar names look strange with military titles before
them. That was all that came of Quaker blood in 1861.[16]

[15] Mary Hallock Foote's free adaptation of Julia Ward Howe's war poem, "Our
Orders":

>Weave no more silks, ye Lyons looms,
>To deck our girls for gay delights!
>The crimson flower of battle blooms,
>And solemn marches fill the nights.

[16] These boys were the sons of Mary Hallock Foote's aunt, Martha (Hallock)
Ketcham. See below, p. 62.

A BIRD'S-EYE VIEW.

❴ 3 ❵

I AM the last one living who can remember our sister Bessie at eighteen. Hers was the face that launched my ships when about this time I began to be called the artist of the family. . . . In this house[1] there is a little fair-haired artist of the new generation who kneels at the bench where her paper is spread and the short locks fall forward over the flushed cheeks while the pencil rushes across the page, and there is "joy in its mighty heart"[2] — we need no models at that age! But from the time I began to "see" things to draw until I was sent away to learn the trade, Bessie was my inspiration; she was the embodiment of human loveliness in my eyes as she was in character to everyone who knew her. I must have been twelve that winter when she was finishing at Dr. McClellan's, the school I went to later under a different Head. Its brass doorplate looked down on shady Mill Street of the old river city and bore the name "Poughkeepsie Female Collegiate Seminary." That dates it —

[1] I.e., North Star House, Grass Valley, in which the reminiscences were written. The "little fair-haired artist" must have been one of the grandchildren, presumably one of Arthur B. Foote's children.

[2] One of Mary Hallock Foote's typical free adaptations from a well-known poem. This is from Rudyard Kipling's "The Conundrum of the Workshops," which in the collected editions is usually printed in the volume entitled *Verses 1889-1896:*

> Our father Adam sat under the Tree and scratched
>   with a stick in the mould;
> And the first rude sketch that the world had seen
>   was joy to his mighty heart,
> Till the Devil whispered behind the leaves, "It's
>   pretty, but is it Art?"

there was no Vassar then; "Collegiate" was as far as any Female Institution of learning dare go.[3]

Milton, on the west shore of the Hudson, is but four miles below Poughkeepsie, and Bessie came home on Friday afternoons for over Sunday. She would arrive in the early winter dusk with cold, pink cheeks after her drive down from the ferry, to be kissed all around and stand in front of the open fire in her dark wool dress and smile at us all quietly — the first daughter, the first sister to grow up, and such a beauty! — an artist's beauty. We hear a great deal of small heads and long throats but her head was in the Greek proportion and she carried it high on a long throat, not from pride but obedience to a mother's incessant reminder all the years she was growing fast: "Straight, Bessie — *straight*, Child!" She had a heart-shaped face, broad brows and a long pure sweep of eyebrow over her large brown eyes, and her long braids were crossed and recrossed making a chaplet for that stately little head. But her eyes were her great beauty, and her eyelids looking down as I loved to draw her in my favorite tragic roles. She was the Lady of Shalott, she was the Duchess May, she was Guinevere, the long braids hanging down as she knelt at the feet of the king; she was Ethel Newcome, she was Nora Nixon — she was the Queen of Fancy, whoever ruled the hour. . . .[4]

Vanity of vanities! My beautiful sister married when she was only twenty — a cousin,[5] of course — and not even the

3 The Poughkeepsie Female Collegiate Institute was founded in 1848 by Dr. Charles H. P. McClellan.

4 Tennyson's poems "The Lady of Shalott" and "Guinevere" were favorites in Mary Hallock Foote's family. Ethel Newcome is a character in Thackeray's novel *The Newcomes*.

5 John Sherman. Connections between the Sherman and Hallock families had been close for many years. James Sherman, father of John, came to Milton from Long Island as a boy and learned the wagonmaker's trade under Nicholas Hallock, one of Mary Hallock Foote's uncles. In 1818 he married Philadelphia Hallock, one of her aunts, by whom he had three sons that appear in this narrative: Isaac, Townsend, and John. The three sons were described as men who read a great deal, "stalwart Republicans," active Quakers, and industrious men who developed the Sherman farm into a valuable property.

youngest and handsomest cousin who was in love with her too (a family secret), but the one she had seen least of as she grew up. He came into her life a stranger, a man over thirty, very much at his ease, very welcome as the nephew who had been long away; full of jests and witty stories; the one who argued best in those endless discussions between Abolitionism and constitutional Republicanism.

My sentiments towards him after the startling news of the engagement were very mixed, though I had been proud of his notice before. I greatly approved, however, his gifts to the Well Beloved whom he was taking from us. The influence of two books that came into the house in this way I count as a valuable part of my casual and desultory education. One was Dana's *Household Book of Poetry*[6] — well named! you lived with it — you carried it about with you and sat on the floor with it in your lap and listened to voice after voice at the age when such words are the "sweetness of the world edged like a sword." The other was the Moxon edition of Tennyson, bound in tree-calf with hand-cut illustrations by the Rossetti group, Holman Hunt, and all the new lights in art.[7] But not only the Pre-Raphaelite brotherhood — Millais was there too, at his best. If any of my sister's descendants should be the fortunate possessors of this old book, let them cherish it, for nothing better in the way of illustration and woodcutting could be done at that time. See "The Lord of Burleigh," Millais' drawing — that exquisite faded little face sunk in the pillow, the dim, casement-lighted room, the sense of sorrow which the artist has conveyed — you almost hear the whispers of the women who bring the dress to put it on her "That she wore when she

---

[6] Charles A. Dana, comp., *The Household Book of Poetry* (New York, 1858, and subsequent editions).

[7] Of the several editions of Tennyson's poems published by Edward Moxon in London, that of 1857 contained illustrations by members of the Pre-Raphaelite "brotherhood" of artists and poets, formed in 1848 to protest against the low standards of British art. The Rossettis, W. Holman Hunt, and John E. Millais (afterwards Sir John) were leaders in the movement.

was wed." Millais' illustrations (of Orley Farm for instance) made you know England of that time; so looked an English lady, hoops and all, in her English home. So looked the home, even to the bedroom candlesticks and the housekeeper's black silk dress.

There was another cousin, the youngest of those three fine young men that Quaker family lost in the Civil War — his home was but a field away from our house, yet he did not come to Bessie's wedding. I couldn't understand why! I was only thirteen — and I never knew till twenty-five years later, and then it almost broke my heart. It brought back all those subtler tragedies of the war I had missed at the time. He hated war — he only went because it was *that* war, and for the other reason they never told me. He was his mother's last son, and the family embittered his farewells with useless protests against his going; and all his experience of the war was sheer heartbreak. He buried his brother on the battlefield after Gettysburg; he spent weeks wasting away in hospital with fever and rejoined his regiment only to be captured — trapped at the loop of a ford during a retreat. He had no support and to spare the lives of his men, picked off one by one, he surrendered. Those who were with him in Libby prison said he died because he did not wish to live.[8] Aunt Martha was a widow when she lost these sons and her part in life was over. I don't mean that she died too; she lived many years and it was whispered that "they" came and comforted her in her long sleepless nights, made their presence manifest to her senses in ways she could not doubt. She spoke seldom and to one or two persons only of these experiences, knowing the family scepticism

8 See Mary Hallock Foote's earlier mention of these cousins, above p. 58. Lt. Edward Ketcham is listed in the records as having been killed at Gettysburg on July 2 or 3, 1863, and Lt. John Ketcham as having died in the notorious Libby prison, Richmond, October 8, 1863. The third cousin's death does not appear in the official listing, but there is much confusion in the military records, including a dispute as to whether the name was spelled Ketchum.

(which she had shared) on the subject of spiritualism, as they called it then.

The overshadowing event of our grandparents' middle years — that which drove Grandfather Burling to give up his business and grandmother her housekeeping and join the younger family up the river — was the sudden, useless death of their only son at twenty-one — Thomas Hull Burling III, killed by a young horse he was training; just a toss, but he struck on his head — and that line was extinct without any pride of sacrifice to compensate. His death made an old maid of Anna Haviland, the girl he was engaged to. We called her Cousin Anna; she became an honorary member of the family, and I was given her name combined with her mother's, Mary Haviland. Part of each year she spent in a round of visits, singing the praises of one household she loved in the home of the next one. She loved the Walters of Brooklyn Heights — she raved about Sarah the eldest daughter; and whether she had any matchmaking designs or not, she never rested till this paragon had been persuaded to accept our mother's invitation and came with Cousin Anna to Milton on one of her yearly pilgrimages. I think she had a partiality for our brother on account of his name, Thomas Burling, not that he wasn't a nice boy — still, his own family, I believe, were surprised when out of that visit came his engagement to Sarah Walter.

She was a daring choice — it would have been an honor to love her even to be refused. She was two years older than he, a much more finished person socially who had had many more worldly advantages. But there was something that distinguished him in her eyes and made her trust him. However he did it, he won his wife, and it was his greatest achievement. Perhaps nothing matters as much in a man's life as the mother he chooses for his children.

There was much thinking and doubting on her side before

the marriage went through. Once she broke it off — after the death of the second Mrs. Walter, leaving three young children motherless. Such a loss is not always a personal sorrow to the daughter of the first mother, but it was in Sarah's case; and it doubled her responsibilities. Her life was differently oriented from that hour. She could not make plans for herself alone. There was no one to take her place at the head of her father's widowed household. He accepted the sacrifice but said that her marriage must go on; she should live her own life under his roof and bring her husband home. So, after the marriage, Ellwood Walter's house on Columbia Heights became our brother's address, and the winter following it was mine.

Ellwood Walter was a thoroughbred Quaker, though shaped by circumstances into a man of a different type from any of our kin whom I have tried to describe.[9] He was a city Friend, holding a position in the world of affairs, a man of distinguished presence and great personal dignity, with, for those times, considerable wealth. He had no reason to be pleased with Sarah's marriage, yet he seemed satisfied. He liked Tom's blood and breeding, and he respected his character, his good health and heart and disposition. Perhaps he had grown wise to the worth of these assets; he had seen a good deal of life. As for Sarah, she came to us clothed in prestige of all kinds, yet she put beneath her feet at once the family attitude of humility as to the marriage — that Tom had got more in winning her than he could ever give in return. She took a leading part also in the family councils; my attempts at illustration were brought out for her criticism and she said the place for me was in the School of Design for Women in New York,[10] and as I was

9 New York and Brooklyn city directories list Ellwood Walter (the spelling of the first name varies) as president of the Mercantile Mutual Insurance Company (marine insurance) and owner of a large block of land fronting on Columbia Street, Brooklyn.

10 The Cooper Union for the Advancement of Science and Art, also known as Cooper Institute, was founded by Peter Cooper, and was incorporated and built by him in 1857. See the Introduction to these reminiscences, p. 7.

nearly seventeen my serious training could not begin too soon. And she procured from her father an invitation to spend the following school terms in his house.

I went down prepared with many thrills for this wildly unexpected opportunity, only to find there was no room for me; the classes already were full. Then Sarah took my artless efforts over to Mrs. Cudahy, who was principal of the school that year, and showed her the desire of the moth for the star (I think one of them was my Lady of Shalott). Whatever they did show, Mrs. Cudahy made the most of. The school at that time needed an enthusiast and she was one. I was hailed as a budding genius and squeezed into the school. A third-story room in Uncle Ellwood's crowded house, light, cold, with a view of the bay, was assigned me as my bedroom, and I learned the way down Columbia Street hill and across Fulton Ferry; my apprenticeship had begun.

I︎ᴛ ᴛᴏᴏᴋ some effort to call my awe-inspiring host "Uncle Ellwood," but that was the form Friends' usage demanded. "Mr. Walter" would have jarred, from a young connection of Quaker antecedents. . . . The change from autumn temperatures in the country to city warmth and luxury indoors was softening to my hardy habits, but the daily walk of two miles morning and afternoon on the New York side kept me in exercise. I suppose there were days when walking could hardly have been called a pleasure; I remember only being absolutely well and gloriously happy all those months, and counting the days as they fled as a miser his store depleted by necessity.

Among other joys connected with living in that house was a library crammed with books where on Saturdays and Sundays I had free pasture alone. And at the end of each rear room on every floor was that great picture of the Upper Bay out to Governors Island and the New Jersey shore — all the maritime life and motion crossing it from morning to evening and far into the city's restless, lamp-starred night. Uncle Ellwood would often stand beside me at the end-parlor window and explain the signals and name the character of the vessels and their errands as they plied past or vanished on the verge. He was then secretary of the Board of Underwriters, and president of a bank of marine insurance, and his life in office hours brought him in touch with the sea and with seafaring men and their troubles.

The rich Quaker set of Brooklyn Heights, in 1864-65, would have been no mean taste of society for a girl of seventeen, even one less fresh from the pasture than I. They were styled "gay

Friends," and in a little clique of their own they enjoyed most of the gaiety of the time. They danced, they went to the theatre, they dressed as the World did, only better, with a chastened taste much needed in a misguided period when the fashions required the sternest editing. Sarah's younger sister, Annie, was going out that winter for the first since Mrs. Walter's death; I should think she must have been a belle by the carriages that rolled up to the door almost every evening to take her away.

On the next block lived the Havilands, the "china Havilands," cousins to the Havilands of Limoges. The war had made havoc of George Haviland's business, but I heard this incredulously: he was in the gayest form always and his young wife elegantly dressed, diamond solitaires sparkling in her ears as she turned her beautiful little head — which had turned his. She was not of Quaker blood; not of anything they recognized as blood. The marriage, I gathered from subdued gossip, was one that you could "understand," but it was looked upon as a problematical one. . . . Things went steadily downward with George Haviland in a worldly way, and the world counted with him undoubtedly. Sarah told us a few years later that he had taken his own life in a fit of despair or disgust. The only way left him of supporting his family had become insupportable to his pride. . . . There was, after that war, a period when inexplicable things were done, just such things as we hear of today. He was, in spite of his austere ancestry, a child of luxury and disillusionment — the most sophisticated person and the most fascinating man altogether that I had ever hitherto met.

Our mother often spoke of a school friend of hers, Mary Miller,[1] who married a Haviland and went to France and became the first Madame Haviland of Limoges — of purest Qua-

---

[1] Mary Conklin Miller married David Haviland, who was then conducting a crockery business in New York. Going to France in 1840, he decided to establish his own chinaware manufactory at the great French porcelain center of Limoges. To handle the imports of his product at New York, he founded a

ker and American stock. This would have been about the year our mother sailed up the Hudson, after her marriage, to live her life upon a farm. It sticks in my mind that they met, after twenty-five years, at Tom and Sarah's wedding — I know that Mrs. Haviland of Limoges was visiting the family in America that year. An incident I am quite sure of was very characteristic of that gathering of city and country Friends. One of the elders of the New York Meeting, who had been most active in disciplining the Milton Meeting, took occasion when he met our father to reopen the subject, shaking him warmly by the hand and owning that in his later view of the action taken, it had been "a great mistake." This generous-minded protagonist was John Merritt, another good old Quaker name.

Sarah would have had many things on her mind that winter, more than I conceived of in my inflated happiness. She managed however to steer a young sister-in-law's course with a touch now and then and introduce her to some of the ordinary conventions. She was tact itself with me: she saw everything without too much participation — and it was a large and complex household that green country girl was plunged into. Uncle Ellwood, unconsoled, a deeply wounded man, with cares connected with the living which he kept to himself, unless he shared them with Sarah; Annie, who had a love affair developing on her hands which she must have known would be sure to meet with opposition; the children of the second marriage — beautiful, unruly little Helen, three years old, and Emily with the face of a young saint, condemned to limp about the soft-carpeted floors on a thick-soled shoe (hip-joint disease) — Sarah never looked at her without anguish. Alfred, on whose head none of the blights but all the blessings of his inheritance rested, was at boarding school rampant with health and happiness.

---

business house that became known as Haviland Brothers in 1852. George Haviland must have been a part of this family, although not one of the three founding Haviland brothers.

Sarah's own brother, Ellwood Jr., was living at home, a young man of twenty-five dependent on his father. He had finished his law course, and if he had practiced he might have made a brilliant pleader at the bar. He had inherited his Grandmother Coggeshall's eloquence and personal magnetism and with these endowments the want of balance which often goes with them. Webster was his idol in statesmanship and Sydney Carton (it was the age of Dickens) in fiction,[2] and occasionally he copied the well-known weakness of both his heroes. He would have been capable of any sacrifice which did not last too long, yet since his earliest manhood he had walked on the hearts and the pride of his family. For years after that winter our preposterous friendship continued with lapses, breaking out now and then in letters as amusing and reckless as his talk. Then for more years Sarah ceased to speak of him; but like Launcelot he died a holy man. He joined a Catholic brotherhood whose rule of life is abstinence from everything carnal; and so he left the world — but I don't believe he ever abstained from talk. The brothers must have enjoyed him.

There was another house on Columbia Street with the same great view from its back windows — I must have passed it scores of times that winter without the faintest notion I should ever enter its doors. In that house, five or six years later, I met the man I was to marry, and but for the introduction any little sign of artistry gave a young woman at that time, I should hardly have been asked there — out of a clear sky — for there was no link, family or social, to begin the acquaintance which became a friendship with Emma Beach, the eldest daughter of that house. The Beach family were great appreciators, I might say appraisers — they distinctly knew a good thing when they saw it. But there was in Emma a generous inclusiveness and in-

---

[2] The dissipated young man who dies a hero's death in Dickens' *A Tale of Two Cities.*

terest in others all her own, and which her home life encouraged.

Moses S. Beach was an ardent communicant, a pillar of Plymouth Church, though hardly up to the part in physical stature.[3] The whole neighborhood was a hotbed of Beecherites and Hicksite Friends. It may sound disrespectful to call them Beecherites, though I don't know why, more than to say Hicksites; still, it was the name generally used by those who did not admire them. Henry Ward Beecher[4] admired the Early Friends and their writings, as I have heard him say: he and Elias Hicks[5] would have had some great ideas in common. Both were thorns — bombs were a better word — in the ironclad sides of doctrine; both were mocked in their day. But their followers on Brooklyn Heights were men and women with dissimilar tastes and prejudices living in sight of each other's houses. Great war sermons thundered from Henry Ward Beecher's pulpit; the Friends did not hold with preaching the Sword from any Christian pulpit. They did not approve of auctioning church pews to the highest bidder, nor of such conspicuous worship of any human man. That he was a great man

3 Moses S. Beach (1822-92) was at this time proprietor of the *New York Sun*, which he sold to Charles A. Dana in 1868. He was indeed an "ardent" admirer of Henry Ward Beecher and a major supporter of Beecher's Plymouth Church. His home was on Columbia Street, Brooklyn.

4 Henry Ward Beecher (1813-87), graduate of Amherst and a seminary in Cincinnati, was the immensely popular and influential pastor of Plymouth Church (Congregational) for forty years, beginning in 1847. His theatrical denunciations of slavery and his other moral crusades attracted huge crowds — and controversy. He was the defendant in a famous adultery suit, in which the jury failed to agree. Although this case did not become an open scandal until 1872-74, an accusation against Beecher by the aggrieved husband was made as early as December 1870, and rumors were about well before that.

5 Elias Hicks (1748-1830), one of the most famous Quaker preachers of his day, was the leader of the "liberal" or "Hicksite" branch of the Quakers, as distinct from the "Orthodox," in the great and enduring separation in the Society of Friends that began in 1827-28. Believing that the inner light is the center of life and religion, he argued that salvation is entirely within man and cannot be achieved by external acts, as current evangelical doctrines suggested.

they did not deny, but they saw him too frequently on the street; they were too familiar with his thickset figure and his powerful, unshrinking eye and orator's throat exposed by the backthrown folds of his cape-overcoat. He of course, born conspicuous, the most naturally self-conscious man in the world, took no note of them. All that winter at Uncle Ellwood's I lived in an atmosphere of intense and but half-suppressed repulsion towards everything connected with Henry Ward Beecher and his church — and I married one of his first cousins. . . .

And now comes the hitch in all that youthful reverence for Uncle Ellwood. It has been sufficiently shown what we thought of Democrats up the Hudson and how we felt about slavery and the war. Uncle Ellwood was a Democrat, as much as he could be anything political, and he was what is called a southern sympathizer, absolutely opposed to coercion of the South by means of war. Antislavery in principle he must have been; the Friends almost without exception were so in the North, but they hated war and hated the disruption of old ties of faith and kindred. "Unity" was their favorite word. The war, and the loss of his wife, and those constant hurts through his son which were the torment of his life of outward dignity and calm, kept him thinking by himself in his library evenings or pacing the empty parlors before dinner when the gas was lit and turned low and no one down yet but a young girl unseen behind the curtains, watching the stream of businessmen from the ferry hurrying to their homes.

All that winter of 1864-65 the silence in that house on the subject of the war was formidable. My brother did not talk — he was his father-in-law's guest. I supposed he still believed the same, but I dared not ask — sometimes I doubted. The daughters did not so far as I can remember once refer to the war in their father's presence. April 14 the news of Lincoln's assassination struck New York and you could almost hear the city groan. There were strained looks at table but not a word. Yes; there were one or two deep, harsh sentences from Uncle Ellwood that gave the key to his thoughts. It was plain his first feeling was for the wretched South and what the Nation's vengeance recoiling from that horror might do to her. He had loathed Abraham Lincoln "in the chair of Washington." That day of assassination I wished myself for the first time at home.

My progress in art that winter is not worth speaking of, but I had lived in the house of a "Copperhead," as the Peace Democrats were called, and revered him like a father; I had spent delighted and trustful hours in the company of a young man who "drank," and who would have died sooner than have said one word to hurt that trust; I had seen what wealth can give in the things of this world, without happiness or rest.

My brother's first venture in business ended that winter in the loss of all he had put into it, and a knowledge of his partner he did not possess in the beginning. It was a foretaste of years of defeat from various causes less easy to define. But there were reasons enough why a young man not trained to business, and ambitious to give his wife all she had been accustomed to, should make mistakes founded on that optimism our brother was blessed or cursed with. It made him a very pleasant person to live with.

Disgusted with the wiles of the city, his heart turned towards the great spaces of the West — a boy's heart and a boy's will. He would have gone, and Sarah with him (that was the stuff she was made of), in a covered wagon by the plains' route had not an outbreak of Indian troubles just then halted his enthusiasm. Eventually Sarah's father bought for them a beautiful tract of land in the mountain glades of Maryland, picked out by Tom himself while the pioneer fever still ran in his blood. It was pioneering among the poor whites of the South, a population we were just beginning to read about in Miss Mur-

free's stories.[6] There was no labor or servant class; your hired
men, if you could get any, would leave the crop on the ground
and ride forty miles to a funeral or a circus; there was no transportation and nothing to transport except scenery as beautiful
as any in the world. And still it was one of the after-war falla-
cies in the North that there were fortunes in southern lands.
This land's face was its fortune later on. . . .

Our lives build on to themselves; "mansions" or hovels —
we seldom cross the same threshold twice. I am unable even to
imagine what Brooklyn Heights may look like now! The house
on Columbia Street that I once knew room by room was sold to
John A. Roebling, who died there. His son, succeeding him in
the great bridgework, added interest to the neighborhood
where the house became known as the Roeblings' home.[7]

Uncle Ellwood retired to his country place in the New Jersey Highlands at Englewood. Once I spent a Sunday there and
walked with him and his great Cuban bloodhound, out to the
Palisades, when all the way led through woods. He called his
place "The Wilderness." His family was small by that time.
The fates that wait upon inheritance had worked out in the
children, one by one. Sarah had married for love, unselfishly,
and love was all she had and the chance to exercise unselfish-
ness to the end. Annie's social triumphs ended in a happy marriage, opposed however by her father to the extent that he refused to have it performed in his own house or to be present at
the ceremony. She married her double first cousin, one of the
dark and handsome Coggeshalls of Philadelphia who used to

[6] Mary Noailles Murfree (1850-1922), whose pen name was "Charles Egbert
Craddock," became noted for her stories about the southern mountain folk. She
was publishing in magazines as early as 1874, although her first book did not
appear until 1884.

[7] John A. Roebling (1806-69) and his son Washington A. Roebling (1837-1926)
were the engineers who built Brooklyn Bridge.

come on to visit her so often that winter of '64; there was the same blood on all sides. A witty friend of both families, soon after this much discussed marriage, enquired after the young couple who waded "through slaughter to a throne."[8] None of the headshakings and warnings were justified by the sequel, at least in my time. They had but one child, a daughter, but that has happened to other young couples who were not double first cousins. . . . Emily and Helen, children of the second Mrs. Walter, died in young womanhood, beautiful and cherished, joining that procession of tragic young figures doomed, as it used to be thought, from birth. There was no cousinship to account for that woe. Alfred, with the same inheritance, lived and made a signal success in his profession of civil engineer. Sarah, who had perhaps the hardest life of them all, lived to the greatest age.

[8] The quotation is adapted from Thomas Gray's "Elegy Written in a Country Churchyard":
> Forbad to wade through slaughter to a throne,
> And shut the gates of mercy on mankind.

I T WAS during Christmas week, a few years later, I was driven in Mrs. Beach's brougham up to that other door on the street I knew so well, which I had passed so many times and never dreamed I should enter. And that was a "summer clime" of welcome too! But it was strange, in that same city atmosphere of flower-scented warmth, to be walking down a vista of rooms again towards that same great view — with Moses Beach beside me as host instead of Uncle Ellwood. There was the same wide and wintry scene outside which we seemed about to step into, for at the Beaches' they had a plate-glass window all in one pane, nearly filling the end of the extension-parlor looking on the bay.

I was there on the invitation of Emma Beach, a little person with engaging manners and what Arnold Bennett calls "an agreeable snub nose." She had a kind, clever, bizarre countenance and a head of such hair as Nature often bestows in lieu of some other things we value in youth. She was entirely individual, yet at this time she seemed to get her greatest good in life out of other people's experiences. She did a little in the way of Art, yet seemed more interested in artists. The genius of the man she married,[1] and did so much to protect in his use of it,

[1] Abbott H. Thayer (1849-1921), the distinguished artist, was married twice. In 1875 he married Kate Bloede, daughter of a leader in the Revolution of 1848 who fled to America when the revolt failed in Germany. Kate and their two daughters and son frequently served as models for Thayer's paintings. When mental illness blighted Kate's life, Thayer began to retreat into isolation from the world. After Kate's death, he married "Emma" (Emeline B. Beach) in 1891, and a decade later withdrew to a still more secluded life in New Hampshire.

must have satisfied her very soul of an enthusiast. But this was years later. . . . Beautiful, dark-eyed Katie Bloede, Abbott Thayer's first wife, was one of that oddly assorted group of girls at Cooper, the second year I was there, who gathered around Helena de Kay, our link and mutual exponent. Katie was of German parentage — her father a Liberal in a most unliberal time in Germany. He had come to America for political reasons connected perhaps with being a journalist on the Liberal side. They were a highly educated family, extremely poor and out of sympathy with the American grade of poor, their neighbors. Abbott Thayer married her on an art student's prospects, and her face was his inspiration (or her type of face repeated in her daughter) in some of his most beautiful and noble work. The great spiritual eyes and pure forehead and small, pinched mouth of the early saint. It was strange to have known both these two girls, destined to link their so contrasted lives by marrying the same man.

From various circumstances I should have said that Emma and her father were just home from abroad. It couldn't have been the *Quaker City* trip, for the Innocents returned in 1876; but I know Emma wore a dress bought in Paris,[2] a sage green silk that I particularly admired her in with her red gold hair, and she sat on the floor in it and allowed her sister Violet's kitten to claw it, and she said the beauty of French clothes was that every hook fitted its eye and every loop was in place and the dress ready to "jump into even to the neck ruffles." Neck ruffles — in a French dress! So such things were, and very becoming we thought them, those boned, high-necked waists and bunched-up skirts with trains.

Mrs. Beach had a passionate love of flowers and a genius for arranging them. It was the day's pleasure to her to change

[2] Mary Hallock Foote's memory misled her. The famous voyage of the steamer *Quaker City*, which Mark Twain immortalized in *The Innocents Abroad* (1869), took place in 1867, not 1876. But in 1873 Beach went on an extended tour through Europe, and it was perhaps on this second trip that the Paris dress was purchased.

them in every vase when they were brought up from their night's sleep in a cold room in the basement, and in this way she expressed herself to the household. She seldom talked — she spoke to the point, a sentence at a time. She never fussed, yet nothing escaped her. Once I was "spoken to" by her and I have never forgotten it. It was my last day, my packing not begun and the expressman due to arrive at any moment. Mr. Beecher was there talking to the room at large; there might have been a dozen persons present. I rose to slip upstairs unobserved, my seat being near the door. Mrs. Beach had observed me: "Mary Hallock, sit still!" I murmured something about my packing. . . . "Lizzie will see to it." (Mrs. Beach's maid.) Of course! but I was not used to Lizzies. I sat me down and I think no one noticed this little byplay.

Mr. Beecher was in and out of the house every day; no one could have been more informal than he; and still he was sacrosanct: to leave the room where he was in full tide of speech was an incredible offense against that homage everyone was expected to pay him. Often he came in the evening, letting himself in with a latchkey, and went down the hall into the library unannounced and he might remain there thinking or reading by himself for hours. He came frequently to escape from guests in his own house; he was pursued by cranks and enthusiasts and men with axes to grind. No man was more open to imposture or more of a temptation to parasites. He might and occasionally did fall asleep over his reading and not wake till after midnight. It might occur when no one ever knew that he was there, but if it were known it was understood; it was deemed a compliment to the library and an honor to the house that he should use it as if it were his own. But if you were a Quaker lady from the country, sitting up perhaps with a sick person in one of the opposite (and opposition) houses on that block, and saw Mr. Beecher, that unmistakable figure, let himself out of Moses Beach's house hours after the house was dark, you thought it "strange" and if you were something of a gossip, as many Quaker ladies were, you mentioned it to a friend in awed whispers — and Quaker ladies were not the only gossips: Mr. Beecher laid himself open in a hundred ways; he was the center of legend in a world not made of angels.

Emma had asked me for these dates the winter before. It was one of her unconventional impulses; but invitations however tempting were not accepted impulsively in our family. It was the general decision that I had better decline. But when the invitation was repeated I was a year older and more sure of myself, and after a little talk with our mother I found her instinct in the matter coincided with mine, so I naturally thought she was right. Sarah would not have disapproved of the Beaches, of course — she did not know the young people but she was a great admirer of Mrs. Beach; but — in short, it was the old hitch between Friends Meeting folk and Plymouth Church folk that prejudiced her. *I* wanted a good time! That was my first break for open country, so to speak, and that visit had long consequences for me.

There were six girls, including Emma and her younger sister, receiving with Mrs. Beach on New Year's Day. The old custom was at its height. Who the others were I can't be sure, with one exception; no one could forget Nelly W. who had ever had the pleasure of being petted by her — though she smiled on everyone, a tolerant, rather disillusioned smile. She was a generously modeled blonde from Chicago, which is not supposed to be a city of illusions, and probably a great belle. She was the daughter of Success in the business world and she had the perfect approach that a very good businessman's daughter might be expected to have. I don't know why I may not say at once she was Nelly Wheeler and her father's wealth came from the Wheeler and Wilson sewing-machine warehouses, and there was a great deal of it.[3] She was dressed before any of us in the yards and yards of silk girls had about them in those days, but that merely gave her time to hook up other girls and cozily approve their looks in a way to comfort the most doubtful. She had too much humor to flatter; she mothered one in a competent way with an eye for little details to be set right; her soft hands were as clever as a lady's maid's. Her features were rather heavy and common, but she was not common. She remains to me typical of the great Midwest we knew so little about at that time, in her approachability, her humanness, her common sense, her humor, her competence, her atmosphere of luxury carried lightly, and her *rrr*'s in speaking. She must have added dozens of young men to the success of the day.

It was exciting, hour after hour, to hear the cabs and carriages rolling up and stopping at our block; they were rolling up to all the other houses and often they were not for us. Some of the young men were almost too boastful of the fractional time they had to stay, with so many hostesses awaiting them. Houses where the girls were favorites were left to the last, and whoever happened to arrive when dinner was served got asked to stay and all was informal and the evening the best time of all. After the ordeal of those refreshment tables in the back parlors which were not set out according to any Volsteadian rules,[4] not all the young men were very fit for dancing after eight o'clock. But there was nothing like that at Moses Beach's. Mrs. Beach had a nonchalant independence in social matters that made short work of any custom she did not approve of.

[3] Mary Hallock Foote's reference to Chicago is hard to explain. Nathaniel Wheeler (1820-93) was the proverbial Connecticut Yankee, ingenious with mechanical contrivances. He lived in Connecticut all his life and manufactured the Wheeler and Wilson sewing machine, first at Watertown, Connecticut, and then at Bridgeport. He did have a daughter named Ellen.

[4] After the Eighteenth Amendment was passed, Congressman Andrew J. Volstead of Minnesota achieved lasting fame by sponsoring the National Prohibition Act (1919) to outlaw sale of liquor.

My own callers did not take up a very large part of my day. In the afternoon I slipped into the library and in the quiet there, with the noise of carriages and company shut out, I grubbed away at a piece of work I had brought with me, a front-page drawing for *Hearth and Home* which had to be finished on time. The door behind me opened with a burst of sound and closed again. A young man stood there who apologized for his entrance and asked if he might stay.

As a matter of fact, I didn't believe that I could draw a stroke with him there; but I did! I had noted, the evening before, when he was introduced to me, a restfulness of manner which seems to go with certain occupations or with the temperaments that seek them — sailors and horsemen and farmers; he was of the breed I had known, yet he was different. He did not praise my work; he merely said how jolly it must be to have work that one liked and make it pay. I gathered that he had a job which paid but he hated it and was thinking hungrily of some other work that should have been his. His eyes had given out — permanently, he was told by an oculist who made a mistake that cost the stunned patient his last two years at Yale [Sheffield] Scientific School. No years are wasted necessarily, of course; he accepted the verdict and went south to raise oranges and laid up more chills and fever than money and came north and had his eyes looked at by a better man, who said there was nothing the matter with the optic nerve — his eyes were exceptionally strong; all he needed was the right pair of glasses. His class had been graduated that June — and there he was, done out of those two years which would have put him in line with the other fellows.

But why worry about Yale if he had his eyes? "Why not go ahead and be an engineer on one's own?" I think I said, but it's rather mixing in these memories to sort what one said one's self from what one merely thought or someone else said. But one speech of his I can't be mistaken about. Having heard of the relationship so honored by my hostess and everyone in the house, I ventured to allude to his "Beecher blood." He corrected me with emphasis: "I have no 'Beecher blood.'" And without another word I knew that as the one dissident in that house of unqualified worship and adulation, I did not sit alone.

The connection was on the Foote side: Roxanna Foote, his father's sister, was the mother of Henry Ward and Thomas and Catherine Beecher and Mrs. Stowe, and "Cousin Mary Perkins," who was heard to say once that she began life as the "daughter of Lyman Beecher" and grew up as the "sister of Harriet Beecher Stowe," and now she was finally settled and accounted for as "the mother-in-law of Edward Everett Hale." It was the general opinion that for an all-around endowment, including common sense, she was blessed beyond any of the geniuses of the family. She probably had an easier life.[5]

I have forgotten the name of the street that transacted its business of the waterfront below the back gardens of Columbia Heights. The future of this thoroughfare was even then regarded as a menace, but none of its buildings had yet obstructed to any extent the view from those commanding residence blocks. When you went down the parlors at the Beaches' just at sunset or while the splendor lived out there beyond the bay, you seemed to have stepped out of doors into that cold, supernal beauty, yet still to be in an atmosphere of warmth and indoor luxury. A few years later, in E. S. Nadal's "New York and London Winters," I came upon a description which might have been written of that very view.[6]

[5] To summarize this extraordinary family, Roxanna Foote was a shy, sensitive, artistic lady who bore her husband nine children before she died of consumption at a relatively early age. Her husband, Lyman Beecher (1775-1863), was one of the most famous and controversial Presbyterian clergymen of his day. Their children included Henry Ward Beecher, previously discussed; Catherine Beecher, who became noted for her educational reforms; Harriet Beecher Stowe of *Uncle Tom's Cabin* fame; and Mary Foote Beecher, who married Thomas C. Perkins, by whom she had a daughter Emily, who became the wife of Edward Everett Hale, the Unitarian clergyman and author of *The Man Without a Country*. But Thomas K. Beecher, whom Mary Hallock Foote also mentions, was the son of Lyman Beecher by his second marriage, not by Roxanna. He, too, was a minister.

[6] Ehrman S. Nadal (1843-1922), who attended Columbia and Yale, had a varied

On a late Sunday, looking over the bay at sundown, there arose a scene so wild, strong, and sublime, that the beholder could scarcely believe himself in the midst of a city of a million people. The desolate bay, jammed with ice from the wharves to the wood-fringed Jersey hills, lay as silent and stern as any untrodden unfamiliar place in the heart of the Andes or the Himalayas. There is a vital hour of the landscape, which, at summer sunsets, is very evanescent. The day concentrates into its parting glance a swift, intense meaning. Turn your back upon it a moment, or shut your eyes, and it is gone; but, on this evening, all around the city roofs, the hills, and the ice-fields, there lingered a deep, strong crimson almost frozen into the sky.

The parlors that New Year's evening were filled with a large company of persons moving about and changing places, and but few were in the room of the window. Dark had fallen outside. I was sitting close to the great pane and I saw in it, as in a mirror, all the persons assembled within the rooms; we were there reflected on that background of night starred with specks and clusters of lights, but these did not obtrude. Our images were softened and mysteriously beautified — it was charming. One face in the foreground showed distinct on the darkness of the world outside. There was a drawing block and pencil within reach and I made an attempt to draw it — it was the face in line with my view — and, as it happened, it was the only one of all those mirrored in the window that has stayed in my own life. All the others are gone out of it years ago; most of them are out of the world. It was the face of my future husband.

---

career as teacher, journalist, essayist, holder of minor Federal offices, and was twice secretary of legation in London. The quotation is from "New York and London Winters" in his *Impressions of London Social Life* (New York, 1875), pp. 174-75.

How long John and Bessie were in Wisconsin while John was closing up his affairs out there, after their marriage, I am not sure. They were needed at home; John to take our brother's place who had repudiated the family occupation, Bessie to be our mother's right hand, her eldest daughter, born for the part. Tom, when he went into business in New York, had asked for an advance on his share of the estate to invest in the new partnership; it has been told how it came out. The withdrawal of this amount of capital was something of a jar to the finances of the farm, and upon that came the hard times following the Civil War. I am not enough of an economist to say just what the farmers' troubles were — the usual troubles, I suppose, after all wars. John Sherman had done much the same thing — invested his family portion and lost it, in the West, but he never went back to his family for further assistance, not until he could do so on a strictly business basis.

The arrangement between him and our father must have included a share of the profit of the farm, as John had no salary for his services; but there were no profits, after the hard times set in, and appeals from Tom had been met from time to time, as a man like our father would be sure to meet them, and a man like John Sherman would have been too proud and too scrupulous to protest. My own memories of this time are based on the impressions of a young girl explained to a certain extent in later confidences from her elders. I recall visits from our brother without his wife, short visits which left our father more silent than usual and our mother looking worn and white. These consultations were always too late for anything but help; Tom never wanted and never took advice. But if father had been strictly just with his son and had disciplined him to face his own results, Sarah would have been the chief sufferer. Fate may educate a man through his wife and children, but human hearts are not always equal to the part of Fate.

Judging by the change in our circumstances, this must have gone on for years; the *entente cordiale* went on too — of that I was equally a witness. It was a situation that might have been used in a modern novel, but a realist would have been apt to treat it from the point of view which seems to be considered the only real one: sordid selfishness, meanness, and recrimination. Magnanimity may not be as common, but it is just as natural to some minds. I can speak as one who had no share herself in the sacrifices that were called for; as long as I lived at home my work was protected and my profits, after paying my board as a son would, if he could, were my own. With John and Bessie and with Phil, my next oldest sister, it was quite another matter. Seeing what was before her if she never married, Phil asked only the means to fit herself for teaching, and teaching became her life and all her life except its generosity and its courage and its love.

Our father might be blamed, and no doubt he was, for so partial a distribution of his goods, but one asks what are goods? When Aunt Martha (who lost her soldier sons) died without heirs of her body, she left Phil a little legacy which gave her the one adventure of her life, a summer abroad, and a small deposit was left for that rainy day we had so much reason to expect in our family. It came, but it was Tom's rainy day. . . . "Has he ever paid it back?" was asked when this fact was extracted from her — it was hard to ask and harder for her to answer — but suddenly her pained smile became beautiful and proud. "Not in money, but a thousand times in love and kindness!" They all loved Aunt Phil in Tom's family and that made everything right to her.

But it was not all right, though it is not for me to say so! Not the wisest among us could account for this idiosyncrasy in our brother so worthy to be loved; how it got into his blood of the old Quakers who were so proud and scrupulous about debt. "Friends are earnestly recommended not to extend their business beyond their ability to manage" is one of their quaint injunctions; one scarcely ever heard of a bankrupt among them.

But to leave out of this family story the burden our father bore for so many years would be unjust to his capacity to manage his affairs, and unfair to those who held up their end of the load and did it without bitterness; nor would our brother, if he were living, grudge this betrayal of Aunt Phil's unwilling confidence, for the sake of the tribute to her memory, that noble lender, cheerful giver, modest worker all the years of her gray life. She had one transient love affair which the family quenched; the man was not worthy of her. If she had married him, her life would have been wrecked — still it would have been life, and there might have been children. She was a trifle eccentric like her name, Philadelphia. There had been a Philadelphia in every generation of daughters on the Townsend side since a Quaker ancestress of ours was born, the "first female child" in the city of Philadelphia. Phil was the victim chosen in our generation; we said it was like her to take that which no one else wanted (even to a name!); also to plead that she might be the last "Philadelphia," and that no succeeding girl-baby be named for her.

All these trials were not crowded into a few paragraphs of living; they covered a long stretch of years full of love and laughter and lively talk and discussions of ourselves and our kin, and books we read together and visits we made apart to be shared in minute descriptions with those who stayed at home. I was the one who gadded most and talked most, very likely. I was in high spirits all through my unwise teens, considerably puffed up, after my drawings began to sell, with that pride of independence which was a new thing to daughters of that period. I did not of course launch out in dress and travel, but I made more friendships outside the family than the other sisters, and my work was a constant refreshment and striving and excitement while theirs was just work, the same from day to day. I had morning walks in search of "backgrounds" while they were sweeping the chambers upstairs, to save the time of floor-wipers in the basement, which was almost a house in itself to keep clean, as our mother understood the word. There was a certain joy in that work too, the satisfaction of perfect success: there is such a thing as a perfect spongecake — I have done pretty well in that line myself — but I never made a perfect drawing. My best work was mere approximation to anything like Art. If to begin was excitement and fresh hope, to finish was disappointment that often verged on despair. But one could always try again.

And what subjects we had about us! Those "fine big blushy lumps of gerruls" that passed through our kitchen, on their way to marriage or service in other kitchens glad to snap up a girl our mother had trained, were subjects for a Winslow Homer, for a Millet! We had his churning-women and spinning-women all about us doing other things, but just as big and simple, and in as startlingly beautiful light and shade. I must sing the praises of that basement that went under the whole house with windows set deep in the house foundations — windows at the level of a woman's head bent over a dishpan or kneading bread. Take a handsome creature like our Louisa with a tray of fresh-gathered butter resting on her hip, one bare and beautiful arm supporting a ten-pound churning as she carried it through the dark cellar passage into the milk-room, the light full on her fair upright throat and profile! I drew her so, but if I could have done her as she was, she would be as famous, with her butter tray, as the fishergirls with their baskets in Winslow Homer's "A Voice from the Cliffs."[1] I sold that drawing for a good price which made the matter worse. Those sales were too quick and too easy. It was the pressure at home which must excuse the plucking of such unripe fruit. We women were eaten to our souls with a horror of debt.

But there was the home, as I have tried to describe it; cleanliness and fresh air and tempers, for the most part, under control; food of the best and clothes of the plainest — this family agreeing with the Miss Brookes of *Middlemarch* that "well-bred economy made show in dress the first item to be deducted from."[2] John Sherman, who took a satiric joy in old clothes, seized this excuse to indulge in orgies of "well-bred economy" that verged on caricature. He was a noticeable person however dressed, not for his beauty but for the character in his harsh-featured yet gentle face and big sagacious head, and his bored yet whimsical expression. What romps I used to have with him when I was half a child still, at fourteen! — dressing up his medieval countenance in mother's garden hat, the strings tied beneath his short-bearded chin, or with a cloth bound round his head Arab fashion, the ends drooping on his shoulders. It was part of the game that he should be unmoved by these indignities, calm as Buddha, indifferent, withdrawn. He was really a consummate actor — all these depths of boredom lighted up with comic appreciations, all this reveling in old clothes, he had kept masked in the most perfect diplomacy (and exceedingly smart attire) in the days when he came a wooing, and would ask mother about her roses and listen to

---

[1] One of a group of drawings and watercolors that Homer did at Tynemouth, England, in 1881-82, "A Voice from the Cliffs" shows three sturdy, bare-armed fishergirls grouped on the beach, two of the girls with baskets on their arms. See reproductions in Albert Ten Eyck Gardner, *Winslow Homer, American Artist: His World and His Work* (New York, 1961), pp. 62, 80.

[2] In George Eliot's novel *Middlemarch, a Study of Provincial Life*, first published in 1871-72, the actual quotation is: "There was a well-bred economy, which in those days made show in dress the first item to be deducted from, when any margin was required for expenses more distinctive of rank."

Bessie at the piano playing airs from *Der Freischütz* or *Robert le Diable*.[3] And feed us on funny stories and the Victorian poets! He was a deep man — we were tremendous pals and I might take any liberties I liked with him until I was fairly launched on my "artistic career" and needed taking down a peg; he was distinctly the man for that job! I used to suspect he had a certain hid intent when he carefully put on his worst hats and most detached expression to meet at the steamboat landing my vaunted geniuses and best girls of the Old Families coming up to spend Sunday at the farm. They were an astute crowd, however, and they knew faces as artists do; he never but once succeeded in passing himself off for one of the hired men.

Sarah Walter was a perfectly healthy woman who suffered in specific ways, at times unspeakably, and got no credit for it. For ten years her marriage was childless; then a very fine boy was born but never breathed. She barely lived herself and suffered damage in that hour which but for the skill of a great surgeon and savior of women, Dr. Marion Sims, would have made her wish for death. This disaster happened at Milton in the dead of winter, the path to the burial ground packed with snow, the old graves inside the wall covered as with one mantle, and the little new grave the only scar on that whiteness of winter peace. We watched them from the sitting-room windows, father and son, take that path together with their light load — one was enough to carry it. More snow was falling softly; it was a scene to wring the heart, with the mother upstairs in the hushed birth chamber, sunk in delirium. Family incidents of this sort have more to do with family decisions than exact justice in material things.

How long it was after this I can't remember, long enough

---

3 *Der Freischütz*, first produced at Berlin in 1821, was an opera by Carl Maria von Weber, with libretto by Friedrich Kind. *Robert le Diable* was an opera by Giacomo Meyerbeer, with libretto by Augustin Eugene Scribe, first produced at Paris in 1831.

for Sarah to have recovered her strength for the ordeal — her courage was always ready — but it was summer, and on a certain uptown street in New York every house was closed except a boardinghouse which Dr. Sims kept filled with his patients.[4] I had been sent for to be with Sarah after the operation and felt it an honor, though I knew it was because I was the one at home who could best be spared. The doctor had his own staff of nurses, specially trained, who were very busy; one of them came in every day for certain services. Dr. Sims was a southerner of the prewar type, gentle and courteous, but not as talkative as most southerners I have known; he had no time for conversation. He would come rapidly up the stairs and usher me out into the hall to my place of waiting in my bedroom above. With the door open I could hear his call when he left: "Come down, Little Sister!" — and before I had reached Sarah's door his carriage whirled away. . . . Twenty-five years later when his name came up as a candidate for the Hall of Fame, Little Sister, who was one of that much-derided body the hundred electors, had the satisfaction of helping to put a man of great mercies in his proper little niche. The ironic gods of criticism who laughed at these elections could not laugh at him.[5]

4 Dr. James Marion Sims (1813-83), a pioneer in the field of gynecology, was born in South Carolina and practiced in Alabama, before moving to New York in 1853. His practice there was interrupted by periods in Europe during the American Civil War and the Franco-Prussian War. He was president of the American Medical Association in 1876 and of the American Gynecological Society in 1880.

5 Mary Hallock Foote was indeed an elector of the Hall of Fame, in four elections, but the records of that body do not show that Dr. Sims won election at that time.

⟨ 7 ⟩

In dwelling on our father's business anxieties it should not be forgotten the great peace and satisfaction he found in the work itself, that inherited pursuit which was bone of his bone; it fed his nerves with health and his patient soul with beauty. He had not words of his own to express his sense of it, but he listened to his old poets all his silent hours, read them aloud in the evenings to his children. It was the reading habit and the wide choice of books they read, which kept that breed of farmers sane.

As the price of labor continued to rise and prices of farm products went down, plain farming became a serious problem with holders of old land who were dependent on hired help. Our father met it by concentrating his skilled labor on the fruit crop and cider making and letting the upper farm on shares to one of his Irish laborers, his own share not materializing to any extent when the accounts were made up. Every year the farm absorbed capital which he supplied and every year it gave up its dead in losses recounted by Pat Clancy with a rich, rolling accompaniment of excuses and lamentations. It would take the authors of the *Irish R. M.*[1] to do justice to those interviews! But the farm did not suffer, the tribe of Clancys up in the fields steadily increased, and, as our father used to say, "They have to live." We all know how much more our Clancys

[1] "R.M." stands for "Resident Magistrate." The reference must be to either of two books coauthored by two cousins, Edith Œ. Somerville (1858-1949) and Violet Florence Martin (Martin Ross, *pseud.*) (1862-1915): *Some Experiences of an Irish R.M.* (London, 1899) and *Further Experiences of an Irish R.M.* (London, 1908).

required in order to live, after they had been in this country a few years. Bridget no longer "stepped" across the fields with a shawl over her high black head; she drove beside Pat behind a "nice little plan of a mare," bought by father, in a bonnet newer than mother's, and she made her boast that she was " 'Mrs. Clancy' to everyone in the neighborhood except the Hallicks."

Also the Crosbys had to live; they were the family in the Mill House — and John Crosby was the miller. . . . These old farms owned by the Hallock brothers were settled by Edward Hallock in 1762. The name had been on Long Island since Peter Hallock landed at Hallock's Neck in 1640, and it was his grandson, John Hallock, who married a Quaker girl and whose death and that of his wife Abigail is set down in the Westbury Meeting records, "both very ancient and in Unity with Friends." That would have meant disunity with the family of John. That Quaker branch was lopped off to start a tree of its own in Edward, son of John. He had been in the coasting trade with the West Indies, but lost his larger craft by privateers (there was always trouble enough in those waters) and having made a deal with an uncle, Foster Hallock, for some wild land up the Hudson, he loaded his goods and his wife and eleven children in a little sloop, the last of his sail, and landed them safely — "the river being mercifully clear of ice"— on the usual rock, the stepping stone of so many hazards of new fortunes in the wilderness. He seems to have done a good deal for a ruined man between the date of his landing and the Revolutionary War. He had built the mill, which ground flour for both armies, and a good stone house which General Gates made his headquarters on his march down the river after the battle of Saratoga. Our father remembered the burning of that house and the family's removal to the Mill House, the home of one of his married brothers.

The Mill place fell by inheritance to Uncle Townsend, a kindly but rather feeble person dominated by the pretty widow he married. He became involved in the affairs of a beguiling stepson, a member of the "great race" of borrowers, and the old place would have had to go if our father had not bought it in to keep a home for the aged couple. They ended their days in the Mill House peacefully, if somewhat querulously, in an atmosphere of shut-in warmth in winter, with sunshine through the south windows and the droning of the mill outside. I recall the pang it gave us to see that room and the whole place change its character after the Crosbys moved in, Mrs. Crosby being a very different class of housekeeper from Aunt Rachel. The mill suffered a loss too when the ancient overshot wheel had to go, with its dripping buckets that plunged and rose with a dashing spray out of the cool, thunderous wheel pit. Its work was done by a marvelous new invention called a turbine wheel, no bigger than the seat of father's armchair — wonders of efficiency replacing the joys of the beautiful past.

But the milldams were the same that Edward Hallock stoned up before the Revolution. They stood wedged fast between the hills, and the reservoirs they guarded had been settled so many years on their native mud they might have been mistaken, with their bordering woods and paths among old willows, for natural lakes; Long Pond, Old Pond and the Mill Head — linked by streams noisy or silent as the headgates were open or shut. The lane past the Mill House went up between old pastures to the Long Pond woods and that was our road to Arcady. That way we went for the first wild flowers in spring and the first skating in winter; we took our visitors up there, when we were girls, to stroll in the June moonlight — the young poets and artists of those lyric summers when sonnets were born overnight like the roses in the garden. You turned off from the hedgerows perfumed with wild-grape blossoms that lined the lane, crossed the upper dam by one of those old footpaths hid in willows, and directly you were in the perfect woods. And through them you came to the Old Pond, hidden, mysterious and lonely. You never met anyone and you could not hear the mill. It was "the dreadful hollow behind the little woods"[2] to me at the age when I first read Tennyson — but I have read him at all ages.

A steady stream of tribute came into the house from the mill which must have been a good part of our living; but there were the Crosbys and the Clancys and John the gardener who had a wife — an Irish wife with a troop of brothers and sisters who more or less lived on them — and the two "girls" in the kitchen and a choreboy and two or three men, and with our own double family, children and grandchildren as they came along, it will be seen the old farm had a load to carry for those hard times. Still, if our father could have controlled his debit column as he had done in the beginning, his books might have balanced to the end. But he would have had to be a different man altogether if he had been able to say "No" when his heart said "Yes."

"Best lovers but not best rulers" was a comment made upon our family life by one of our clever guests.

I remember a time when there were horses to spare for evening drives with city cousins staying in the house, when the happy ones gathered on the horse block after supper in their thin muslins and summer wraps and calls would be heard for Bessie — "Where is Bessie?" Bessie would be in mother's bedroom hugging a little sister of six whose lot it was to go to bed instead of driving on the river road in the moonlight, who had fled there to hide her babyish tears. Mother's hugs would be kept for when she had "got over it" and come forth with tears dried. There were horseback rides too when the youngest knew she couldn't go; but having seen the others mount, she rushed down to the ha-ha fence[3] below the fir trees to watch the long-

2 From Tennyson's "Maud."

3 A "ha-ha fence," also known as "ha-haw" and "haw-ha," was a boundary trench or sunken fence, intended to avoid obstructing the view.

skirted riders canter past and up the road; Bessie in a dark green cashmere habit made with a basque, a linen collar tight around her throat, and a long black ostrich feather in her beaver hat, such a hat as Rose Jocelyn wears in the old illustrations to *Evan Harrington*.[4] And here too the consolatrice would have said while she was changing, wistfully watched by the youngest: "Never mind, dear; thy time will come." It came, but too late for the trailing skirt and the hat with a plume!

My riding began with bouncing about in everyday clothes on the safest horse there was, which meant the oldest, beside Grandfather Burling who had been ordered horse exercise — he never walked; and it pleased him to think he was teaching a little granddaughter to ride. But it bored him — I don't remember that it lasted long. He lost his health very likely by going out of business and not having enough to do. He was a high-colored old gentleman with bushy black eyebrows over dark blue eyes which must have been very fine when he was young. He wore a stiff black satin stock supporting a good square chin — a fine old English type, bilious very likely. He read inordinately, in his chair by the window day after day, old books in ugly brown leather bindings, Burton's *Anatomy*, Plutarch's *Morals*, histories that he had read many times before, old novels and lives, and (we blush to say) chewed tobacco in defiance of the doctor's orders; it was his one sin in grandmother's eyes. She did more than blush for him; she dealt with him very faithfully after the manner of wives. Once a month he went to New York to collect the rents of certain houses he owned in what is now the tall-building district, and came back refreshed from meetings with old friends, loaded with the spoils of the city markets: pineapples and shell-fish and oranges and candy for the children. He loved the pleasures of the table, yet he was not a simple character — there was color and temperament in the Hull and Burling blood.

4 Rose Jocelyn was a character in George Meredith's *Evan Harrington,* first published in 1860.

Grandmother told us queer stories of old New York, when her brothers skated on a pond called the Collect on the spot where then the old Tombs prison stood, when the Lorillards kept a little tobacco shop and were not thought to be anybody, when Pearl Street was a fashionable neighborhood, when Elmore Sands was tried for the murder of Hope (what was her last name?), and Cousin Katie Ring was one of the witnesses for the prosecution whose testimony could not be shaken. It was the first tragedy of that kind we had ever heard of in everyday life and the incidents are as clear today as the headlines on the latest newspaper.[5]

Our Grandfather Burling had stepsisters older than himself who married, against their father's wishes, men whom he did not trust. He left their portions over their heads to their children, making his only son executor of his estate and trustee for these minors. Grandfather's own death occurred in the spring of 1861, the battle spring, when panic had seized the city and real estate could hardly be given away for the taxes. A mortgage had been put on his New York property to meet the last of these legacies — they were a great care and in the end a disaster. When his estate came to settlement, this mortgage would have had to be assumed by the heirs or paid off; there was a difference of opinion, but the timid one prevailed. Grandfather's holdings were not large, yet it is beyond guessing what those lots would have been worth to the heirs if they had summoned nerve to hold on for another generation, or even another twenty years. But no one knew then whether we should be a nation by another spring.

And so our proud and gentle grandmother had little left with which to indulge that bounty which was second nature with her and is the last gratification of old age. It hurts to remember how we used to laugh at her little economies and the

5 Some of the grandmother's recollections can be verified. The Tombs Prison was built on the site of the old Collect Pond; Pearl Street, once residential, became a crowded business street; and the Lorillard brothers, of Huguenot extraction, did become rich in the tobacco business.

meticulous care she took of her clothes. She brooded over the notion that in a way she was responsible, grandfather — by her advice — having refused some years before an offer for his houses which she thought was not enough, but by comparison with what they brought in the end seemed a fortune.

8

Up to this time women had been the dominant influence in my life. First our mother, sensitive little gentlewoman of the forties, who kept her Quaker speech but could not rule the color that would rise in her cheek instead of the hasty retort she had learned to suppress; who never argued about her Rights but knew how to get her way with "Nathaniel"; who taught us strict obedience as children and then left us to our own decisions and spared comments on some of their obvious results. Then Bessie, who was half mother as well as sister, "half angel" in my eyes. Then Sarah, who was society, as the Friends knew it, and the critic of manners and dress; whose own love of dress and society had been steadily crucified since her marriage to a luckless boy whose hopefulness was her hopelessness, as she said once (the only time I ever heard her criticise him), when one of his partial relatives praised his disposition. Aunt Sarah had been a great intellectual stimulus as we were growing up, but she was wedded to her causes, and we were weary of the Betterment of the World when there was all the World's Beauty.[1]

And then Helena dawned on my nineteenth year like a rose pink winter sunrise, in the bare halls of Cooper, sweet and cold after her walk up from the ferry. Staten Island was her home; a subsidiary aunt had taken me in that winter who lived on Long Island and I crossed by an uptown ferry and walked

[1] To avoid confusion, it may be well to point out that the first of the two Sarahs mentioned here was Sarah Walter Hallock, wife of Mary Hallock Foote's brother Thomas; the second was "Aunt Sarah," the reformer, who was the second wife of Mary Hallock Foote's uncle, Edward Hallock.

down. Across the city we came together and across the world in some respects. She was a daughter of Commodore de Kay and a granddaughter of Joseph Rodman Drake, and Henry Eckford, on another side; her people belonged to the old aristocracy of New York.[2] My people belonged to nothing except the Society of Friends and not to that any longer in good standing. She had spent her childhood abroad and spoke three languages, I "one, imperfectly"; she had lived in one of the famous capitals of Europe and walked its galleries among the Old Masters, while I was walking the "old green hills" of the Hudson and wandering through the Long Pond woods, and my longest journey at that time had been to Rochester, N. Y. She said she was a professional, but her friends were New York society girls and private pupils; she was in the painting class, I, in another part of the building, in Black and White, but we both stayed in the afternoons and had time for many talks, comparing our past lives and dreams for the future.

By spring we were calling each other Helena and Molly, and we sat together at anatomy lectures and Friday composition class and scribbled quotations and remarks to each other on the margins of our notebooks. I still keep one of these loose pages of my youth with "Let me not to the marriage of true minds admit impediments —"[3] copied in pencil in her bold and graceful hand, and on the other side in the same hand the words which began our life correspondence, not gushingly nor lightly; a certain hesitation was but natural on my side, which

[2] Joseph Rodman Drake (1795-1820), who took a degree in medicine but is better known as a poet, married Sarah Eckford, daughter of the well-known shipbuilder Henry Eckford. Eckford and Drake belonged to a little circle of very close friends that also included James E. de Kay, the naturalist and physician, and Fitz-Greene Halleck, the poet. Having married Eckford's daughter, Drake presently christened his own daughter Janet Halleck Drake. Janet, in turn, ultimately maried Commodore George Colman de Kay, younger brother of James. Helena was their daughter, born in 1846. The de Kays came of old New York stock. The Commodore won his title while serving in the Argentine Navy in the 1820s.

[3] Shakespeare, *Sonnet 116.*

might have had the effect of reserve, and on her side there were hosts of other claims. She already had a world of friendships on her hands. We wrote to each other for fifty years. She came up to Milton that following summer and every summer after till there was no more Milton for me — not that Milton! Her sharings in books and friends were the stored honey of my girlhood. The strings were tuned high for us in those years, but after we became wives and mothers, and had lost our own mothers (she loved mine and I loved hers), a settled, homely quality took the place of that first passion of my life. Salt is added to dried rose leaves with the perfume and spices when we store them away in covered jars, the summers of our past.[4] Coincidences have a haunting likeness to real meanings if we only knew what they were. On the day when I looked up Nadal's [5] first book of essays that he gave me in 1875 (the year when I first met him) to copy his description of the bay at sunset — that same day came one of his infrequent letters. It was hardly to say "written"; it was scrawled — in the wrecked remains of the clean, terse, literary hand that wrote the inscription in that book. He said that "something had happened" to him; he had just had his seventy-ninth birthday. Something more than that had happened, I guessed, but not till later did I learn that this letter was written soon after a slight stroke, the first warning. He had taken it with that gallantry with which he met the cost of high-powered living all his strange, vivid, half-revealed and subtle career.

I knew him through Richard and Helena first, but even Helena, the great interpreter, could not quite explain Nadal. . . . Here he was, what remained of him. There was one word in his last sentence which I could not decipher. It was hyphenated on two lines; it did not occur to me that it might be a name. "How often I want to say things to ———. Do you

---

4 See Introduction, pp. 7-9, on Mary Hallock Foote's lifelong friendship with Helena and, presently, with Helena's husband, Richard Watson Gilder.
5 See above, pp. 81-82.

feel so?" Later that same day I was suddenly possessed by a desire to look for an old photograph of Helena, to make sure that I had it safe. It was a special one put too carefully away. I could not find it then, but it was before my eyes during the fruitless search. I could see her as she is in the picture, her dark hair with the strong wave in it turned back from her forehead. It was taken shortly before one of her children was born, in her rich matronly bloom, yet the expression of her down-drooped eyes is grave — that look Nadal found words for when he called her the "gentle, profound Helena." His letter lay on the table and I took it up and returned to the undeciphered word. It was her name of course! She had been gone for seven years, I think, when out of the shadow of loneliness and old age came that simple cry — "How often I want to say things to Helena!" Helena who always understood.[6] It did not miss its mark.

Nadal was one of that group of young spirits with powers of expression and ideas to impart which followed Helena up the Hudson for a weekend now and then, after she had discovered us on the old farm. They might have stood for the artistic awakening in America, as the earlier procession stood for the national conscience and our duty to our neighbor's conscience. But these younger ones were much more amusing. They held no brief for any cause — if they died for anything it would be for Beauty; but they had consciences too. George W. Cable was one of them, incidentally, and George Macdonald, seduced up there to the old sidehill farm by Richard and Helena, who were his hosts in New York at the time, on his first visit to America.[7] Mrs. Macdonald was with him and of course they

6 Since Helena died in 1916 and Nadal in 1922, this episode helps to fix a date for the writing of these reminiscences. See also Mary Hallock Foote's comment on p. 398.

7 From the time of their marriage in 1874, the home of Richard and Helena Gilder became a magnet that attracted writers and artists of the new generation, many of whom published in Gilder's magazine *Scribner's Monthly*, presently renamed *The Century Illustrated Monthly Magazine*. George W. Cable (1844-1925), who became famous for sketches and novels of Creole life in New Orleans, was recognized and enthusiastically encouraged by Gilder at a time

loved it, even to the "small pillows" they found on the guest-room bed with a feather bolster underneath. They hadn't seen a small pillow, they said, since they came to America. He brought tears to our father's eyes reading Burns aloud, and he read his own "O lassie ayont the hill —." And Cable read a chapter from *The Grandissimes* — but this was a later time. In those early days the young poets were still on trial, the essayists and artists (except Vedder)[8] in the stage called promising. Helena, the First Friend, was the clasp in that chain of fortuitous comradeships. Reading of them later in far places where my life bestowed itself after marriage, I saw them — famous and bald and some of them fat — always as they were then; they had an immortality of youth for me.

In this procession of geniuses a certain young man, whom I had known since my adventurous Brooklyn visit, had no place; he was not one of the Expressionists. As a matter of fact he was in California working for the means to marry on, a form of expression which has had its appeal for a good many young women not wearing many willows at home.[9] We were not supposed to be engaged, but more and more through letters, as time went on, the tentative relation began to take hold upon one like an undertow. I wrote him, in defiance of fate, everything I was doing and all that happened to show that my life in the East was not made up of waiting, that it was going forward by leaps and bounds in a direction which did not point to marriage.

The year after he went away to "mak' his crown a pound"

when he was an unknown. George Macdonald (1824-1905), also spelled MacDonald, wrote poems and novels about Scottish life. He was born and raised in west Aberdeenshire, although most of his mature life was spent in England.

[8] Elihu Vedder (1836-1923), American painter, illustrator, and writer, who spent most of his time in Italy after 1867.

[9] The phrase "wearing the willow" means grieving for the loss of a loved one; here used in the negative.

the crowns came rolling in for me. Mr. A. V. S. Anthony, head of the Art Department of Fields, Osgood and Co., gave me a giftbook to illustrate, a new poem by Longfellow called *The Hanging of the Crane*.[10] It proved to be a business success, largely due to the fact that the House spared no expense. I saw my homely name in print — "Miss Mary A. Hallock" had flocks of pleasant notices.[11] Mr. Longfellow himself was pleased and desired to see the young artist's picture. The Anthonys asked her to be their guest in Boston on the business of another book, the invitation read, but in reality it was to give her the surprise of her life, a sort of curtain call before a select audience. Everyone knows how generous they were, those makers of American Literature, to all the young pilgrims who worshiped at their shrines. You went to Boston for the accolade and your shoulders tingled ever after.

And then my promoter, Mr. Anthony, came on to Milton and asked to see all my sketches and studies that I had in stock — my Louisas and butter trays; he wanted to buy them all and asked me to set a price on each one as we turned them over, my face getting hot — it was an ordeal! To ask any price seemed conscienceless, yet they were of value to me as studies for backgrounds or notes of details in many ways. He bought them to sell to anyone who believed I had a future. All of us were "sold" I fear! I parted with the only records I had of my old home; they were innocent of technique, but true to the subjects in a painstaking, dogged way.

[10] A. V. S. Anthony (1835-1906), a wood engraver, is best known for his long service (1866-89) in superintending the production of fine editions for the successive Boston firms of Ticknor & Fields; Fields, Osgood & Co.; and James R. Osgood & Co. Through this work he exerted a considerable influence upon the art of wood engraving.

[11] That most august of contemporary periodicals, the *Atlantic Monthly*, was enthusiastic about the illustrations: "It is in the conception as well as the execution of her work that Miss Hallock will delight the appreciative reader. . . . These ideas [central to the poem] Miss Hallock has realized with a delicacy and perfection worthy of the poem, into which she has entered not only with intelligence but with divination." "Recent Literature," *Atlantic Monthly*, 34 (December 1874), 745-46.

Every one of these incidents that gave color to my life, every pleasure and every triumph, I bragged of to my strategist in the West. It was ungenerous and crude of me, yet it may have been some latent instinct of Quaker prudence. . . . He stood the test — he remained calm and showed no trace of the begrudger. My companions in those days were some of the most brilliant and fascinating young people of their time, and I did not hesitate to let it appear that I was fascinated, flaunting these riches in the face of his poverty. But was it poverty!

He had been in the High Sierras, on work connected with the future of water power. He had been in a hot and dusty railroad camp on the line of the Southern Pacific, under William Hood, its greatest engineer, locating the famous "Loop" at the Tehachapi Pass. He had been in Sutro Tunnel, roasted, steamed out at a temperature underground that made strong men faint, and had come away with his life and a gold matchbox as a token of regard from his chief. There was no prospect of a home in any of these jobs.[12] But when, through the influence of James D. Hague and Hamilton Smith, he became resident engineer at the New Almaden Quicksilver Mines, an old and settled camp of a thousand persons, the event began to look possible.[13] He asked if I would come out and be married from his sister's house in San Francisco, and Mary Hague fulfilled her part in the invitation charmingly, but I should have needed far more nerve than I possessed for the adventure itself to have

[12] William Hood (1846-1926), the civil engineer, was assistant engineer first for the Central Pacific and then for the Southern Pacific Railroads in these years, and surveyed the remarkable Tehachapi Loop by which the railroad was carried over the mountains from Bakersfield to Mojave. After prolonged delays, Adolph Sutro (1830-98) finally completed his tunnel from the Carson River up to the Comstock Lode in 1878.

[13] For the career of James D. Hague, see Introduction, pp. 11-13. Hamilton Smith (1840-1900) learned engineering at his family's coal mine properties in Indiana and came to the Pacific Coast in 1869, where he soon won recognition as a major figure in mining engineering. Concerning New Almaden, see Introduction pp. 2 and 10. Mary Hague (1846-98) was the former Mary Ward Foote and had married James Hague in 1872.

entered another family in that way. Moreover I had a very good little job of my own that winter.

I was in the midst of a set of illustrations for *The Skeleton in Armor* — not a very Quakerish tale![14]— drawing Vikings in the back parlor where I had been invited to retire when it became a question of models at all hours cluttering up the sitting room. I had no studio — the whole house was my studio and any unoccupied relative of a suitable age and approximate appearance was my model. Just then I needed "wassailers" and we were not provided in that line, but I seized on the nearest male cousin, brutalized his type and rigged him up according to the best lights obtainable on the subject of "wassail bouts," and we muddled through. Then, out of the West, came word that the resident engineer (at that time residing at Mother Fall's boardinghouse in the Cornish Camp) was coming home to be married. He could come only when the work would spare him; it was now or wait another year. This was strategy of the first order.

He came — in a great hooded ulster belted around him, his field overcoat; his new one had been stolen by a hat-rack thief from the front hall of the house where he was a guest on the night before his journey — and that was a blow if you like! He unpacked his leathery luggage in the room we still called "grandmother's room" and laid his pipe and pistol on the bureau where her chaste neckerchiefs had been wont to lie, and he was as much of an anomaly in that house as if he had been a Viking himself or a man in armor. He came armed, in fact, with decision where indecision awaited him, and of course he carried the day.

14 Longfellow's poem, which in 1876 the publishers were promising would be "the most elaborate and beautiful gift-book ever produced in this country." When published, the *Atlantic Monthly* said of Mary Hallock's illustrations: "The latter merit, in the main, the highest compliments. Miss Hallock has not given us in her previous efforts the evidence of dramatic conception which these new illustrations disclose." "Recent Literature," *Atlantic Monthly*, 39 (January 1877), 114.

9

I REMEMBER how dark the old parlors looked that morning of the wedding [February 9, 1876], though they were white-painted rooms and the trees close to the house were bare. Rain had been falling with a southeast wind, which meant there would be no crossing that day at Milton Ferry; the spongy ice-beaches that lined both shores waited only for the next heave of the tide to crush into the treacherous mid-channel skimmed over with night ice and "go out." Cut off as we were, this meant a very small wedding, as it was a very hurried one. Richard Watson Gilder was one of the few who came up from New York, but Helena was preoccupied. She had a month-old baby. She sent me the red rose we called hers, her type and symbol, to wear inside my wedding dress — I have it still, a few petals empurpled with age pressed inside an old locket against the face of the man I went west with, taken when he was a boy of fourteen, a daring-eyed little rascal who would be sure by his looks to go somewhere far from home.

Our parents sat loose in what they deemed non-essentials to the stricter rules of Friends' discipline, but it was unthinkable that a wedding should take place in that house by any but the Friends' ceremony which places the entire responsibility on the parties who are assuming the chief risk. If it is a home wedding, the bride comes down the stairs unveiled and takes the arm of the man who is waiting for her and they walk up the rooms unattended to their places confronting the assembly, in a silence presumably given to prayer (I remember hearing the rain drip from the trees outside): then, taking each other by the hand, "In the presence of God, with these our friends as

105

witnesses," they pronounce the awful words which in their case are considered irrevocable. It is not a moment one is likely to forget.

I learned later that my husband's father, a staunch old-school Episcopalian, had his misgivings as to these unchurchly proceedings in which the youngest of his six duly baptised sons was to take a leading part; but, when a week from that day, in his own home where our short wedding journey ended, he inspected the formidable document we had brought with us, with its legal repetitions and "whereases" and the list of respectable signatures "thereunto affixed," and then he saw the name of God unflinchingly taken as the first of these witnesses, his mind was at rest. It had been done without benefit of clergy, but he "guessed it would hold." Those old Quaker marriage contracts usually did. I have gone into all these particulars because I have heard so many queer versions of the Quaker marriage ceremony, and there will never be another one in our family.

To great-uncle Oliver Hull, Grandmother Burling's only living brother, belonged the honor, it is deemed, of reading aloud the marriage certificate before it is signed. The witnesses were all seated in the front parlor; in the back parlor had gathered a group difficult to match even then, impossible now, for oddity, faithfulness as they understood the word, and length of service in one family — all the people who had lived with us in the house or on the farm who were still in the neighborhood. It hurts the Irish heart to miss a wedding or a funeral. Uncle Oliver took his place by a little mahogany table with pen and ink upon it, the parchment scroll in his hand, looking like an old portrait and filling the silence with his mellow tones and very pure enunciation. The old Quaker boarding schools, judging by results, would seem to have taken pains with their English in spite of the customary use of "thee" for "thou" which I have never heard satisfactorily explained. I noticed in Boston that Mr. Whittier said "thee is," which was some consolation — perhaps "thou art" would have sounded too apostolic and lofty. Uncle Oliver had mingled with the world in his business in New York for many years; he was dressed as any city man would have been for such an occasion, yet there was a clean-shaven, silvery neatness about him (in that be-whiskered period) which would have suited well the Quaker drab and high-collared coat. He and grandmother had the same oval line of face and high-bridged nose and finished mouth; both were exceptionally handsome, but with light-blue eyes deficient in brows and lashes; those pale, unadorned foreheads and quiet eyes, however, gave a Holbein look of veracity and calm.

Our grandmother would have been a gracious figure in this company, but she had been gone some years before. Older than Uncle Oliver and more Quakerish in her life, she put on the "plain, distinguishing cap" while still a young woman and wore the dress entire, making as much of its correctness as a nun of her convent garb. She sent to Philadelphia for her lusterless gray satin bonnets lined with white silk; there were no milliners in New York, it seemed, who could lay those crown pleats to her satisfaction. She lost her oval line in her later, sedentary years, but never the dignity of the full white throat that rose between the folds of her gauze neckerchief crossed over her bosom and pinned at the waist, while on either side fell the points of a soft silk shawl that came to the elbow and was finished with a narrow self-fringe. It was almost a matter of conscience with Quaker ladies not to make broad their fringes. But whatever they wore had to be the best of its kind in quality — that was their vanity. Grandmother's shawls and silks and cashmeres practically never wore out.

There were years before she died when her habits were as fixed as the march of the sunlight on the walls. It was difficult for her to mount the stairs, and when once settled in her chair by the sitting-room fire on the side out of the draft, she seldom went to her bedroom again till before the last meal of the day. After a certain hour in the morning it remained empty, in perfect order, warm and inviting. When the halls were cold, and little girls were told to stop reading, and it was too late to put on one's things and run out — before the lamp was lighted, one could take one's book and slip upstairs to grandmother's room and finish the thrilling moment — when the Knight of the Leopard, hurrying back to his post cheated and sick at heart, saw, as the moon broke out from the clouds, that the standard was gone from the Mount of St. George.[1] The last of the light looked in at the window towards the hills across the river where the East was bidding the West good night. The hard coal fire would be covered with a layer of cinders, and as these turned from gray to pink and the mass settled in the grate, a cinder now and then would fall tinkling on the ashpan beneath, a sound I have heard a hundred times in the silence of that room fraught with ecstacy; there was no hour in all the day like that — no place like that for reading!

Am I romancing my old Quakers, I wonder? seeing them across the years, as we looked over at the hills beyond the river after sunset, peaceful and alight with colors not their own. Again there is Charles Lamb who was the soul of truth as well as humor and could laugh at his "gentle Quakers," and yet said such words as these: . . . "The very garments of a Quaker seem incapable of receiving a soil; and cleanliness in them to be something more than the absence of the contrary. Every Quakeress is a lily; and when they come up in bands to their Whitsun conferences, whitening the easterly streets of the metropolis, from all parts of the United Kingdom, they show like troops of the Shining Ones."[2]

The Quakeresses whom I knew best in my childhood were our father's sisters, and they were not of the lily type. They

[1] From Sir Walter Scott's *The Talisman.*
[2] From Lamb, "A Quakers' Meeting," in *The Essays of Elia.*

were strongly made women with faces interesting and full of character but not beautiful. And they had humor which one does not associate with a description like the touch of poetry I have quoted. Aunt Phila had beautiful dark eyes and hair that was thick and curly, but she kept it packed away under her cap. Someone who saw her brushing it one day had no better manners than to remark: "Why, I didn't know thy hair was so coarse!" . . . "Yes, my hair is coarse," said Aunt Phila, "but I don't think any less of myself on that account."

Aunt Martha, whom I have presented only through her sorrows, had a ready wit of her own and was the bookish one of father's sisters. Discovered one summer morning, when she was about ten years old, hidden away under the currant bushes when she should have been dusting the sitting-room chairs, and warned of the consequences of idleness and neglect of duty, she looked her elderly monitress in the face and quoted dreamily: " 'I have been young and now am old; yet have I not seen the righteous forsaken, nor his seed begging bread' " — a rejoinder that must have been appreciated, for it was handed down as one of the family stories of our ancients who were better acquainted with the Scriptures than we were.[3]

3 Psalms 37:25.

Mary Hallock, ca. 1874

The Gilders at the time of their marriage, 1874

10

Two weeks from our wedding day my husband went aboard his overland train and I returned to the back parlor and my Vikings. Large sums must have been risked on those perfectly made giftbooks, as we should regard them now. The publishers of the *Skeleton in Armor* had prepared their advertising posters of the book "illustrated by Miss Mary A. Hallock"; they were not too pleased when she suddenly changed her name in the midst of the contract and rendered herself liable to other engagements. She might have finished the drawings just as well at New Almaden and something was said to that effect, but they made it plain that they expected them to be all in their hands before she went aboard the lugger, so to speak.

We had stopped in New York on our way back from our wedding journey that my husband might be presented to my best friend, who by some chain of coincidences had never seen him. It was the Gilders' second year in the Studio on East Fifteenth Street, where the Friday evenings began, where you rang at a gate instead of a door and the gate swung inward without hands, and you walked up a little paved court lined with flower beds and wondered where you were — in what foreign city, in what home of hidden charm not three blocks from roaring Broadway?

Richard received us and I ran upstairs to embrace Helena alone, and take a peep at the baby Marion. I thought I could see signs already of the change that told her girlhood was over. It went deeper than paleness and large eyes; it was the preoccupied mother-look I have seen in her expression so often when she was listening to one person and giving herself to

others at the same time — so many others! such millions of
things and people crowding into her not long life! . . . Below
the men were waiting — she went to the stair head and looked
down, her fate and my fate standing there side by side. "Tell
the Wretch he may come up," she said in her low, cordial
tones. My poor Wretch! he was so pleased — they were friends
from that word. When I asked him if he thought her beautiful
— if I had bragged too much? he said, "She is very handsome
— yes, she is beautiful, but not like anyone else." Not in
the American type he meant; not as his sister, Mary Hague,
was beautiful. When I saw the pictures of Duse in her prime[1]
(I never saw Duse herself), they made me think of Helena —
others saw it too, not a likeness in details, only the type and an
inborn sadness of expression which Helena's daughters defined
as "acquainted with grief." She was not acquainted with grief
at this time; her life had just been crowned with a woman's
greatest blessings. It was a foreknowledge she was ripe with
as a girl, and richly it toned with her brilliant mind and deep-
ened her life-giving temperament.

I might go on and make this chapter "one long sigh of articulate reminiscence," and most of it would be of her: Helena
teaching Bessie's little dark-eyed baby son [Gerald] to speak
her name — "Henena" was as close as he could come, making
it sound like an Arabian perfume. Helena reciting verses from
Omar — seated on the stone steps going up from our basement
hall to the level of the grass in sunlight; cherry trees along the
lane in blossom and a glimpse of the garden beyond. There
was no printed copy of the Rubáiyát in America at that time;
she had learned it by heart from a manuscript copy lent her
by John La Farge.[2] Helena in white, lying on the sofa in the
darkened back parlor listening to Katie Bloede playing Chopin
— light from one half-open shutter streaming in, perfect silence, and the bees and sunshine outside. I made a sketch of

[1] Eleonora Duse (1859-1924), the great Italian actress.
[2] John La Farge (1835-1910), the American artist and writer, a man of broad
cultivation.

her so, and the date is June 1874. It was Katie's last visit to Milton. Two years later she was Abbott Thayer's wife, in Paris; Helena was married to her poet and a mother, and I on my way across the continent. No girl ever wanted less to "go West" with any man, or paid a man a greater compliment by doing so.

He had asked me where I preferred to live: at the Hacienda, the seat of government at the mine, in the little official set where the manager had his handsome residence and gardens, where there would be more of what is called company; or up on the next hill near the Cornish Camp with only the miners for neighbors? He had his eye on a little cabin at the end of its own trail, he said, beyond that a drop sheer down the hillside to the tops of the live oaks and the valley — the Santa Clara Valley — and the Coast Range rising out of a belt of colored haze in summer, in winter out of a lake of fog. I knew nothing of small official sets nor of managers — the sunsets and the Cornish Camp for me! It was not a diplomatic choice, but it showed that our tastes were the same. When I had made a free decision, he told me that his office was on the hill; and if we lived there he could come home to lunch whenever he was not "underground." Home to lunch! What that meant to him who had had no home since he was fourteen, how could I imagine; yet he held back that reason till he knew my own mind.

The cabin was assigned him and he asked the manager for a few repairs, a decent place to live in being part of the resident engineer's pay. The answer was: anything in reason the company would stand for. Another official, unfortunately for us, had just had his house done over at a cost that exceeded the manager's expectations. He shut down on all further house repairs for that year. Work on the cabin had begun; it had to stop or go on at the engineer's expense. It went on, and it took all his margin of savings at that time. He had made a close calculation, but he had not calculated on the manager's changing his mind.

In those long talks I had with my husband's mother in the

short visit we made his parents at Guilford [Connecticut], she told me that her greatest difficulty in bringing up her youngest son was to get at "the rights" of his conduct from his own testimony when she herself was in doubt. He would take undeserved rebuke or punishment sooner than discuss the matter on a basis of excuses. So now he did not explain why he was short of money — so very short that his wife of four months paid her own fares across the continent when the cabin was ready and the Vikings were done. It must have cut him to the quick — it cut her too. But I think that wife should have remembered how she had made him come and get her in the only way she would consent to be married, when there was that other way Mary and James Hague had proposed which has served many brides as good as she. But it is true that young wives in my time were not proud of paying their own way and helping towards the home; they were humiliated by the necessity of doing so. But if I hadn't helped, I should have been a very expensive girl to marry on two hundred a month.

The servant question at New Almaden, I was told, solved itself usually by a Chinaboy, but I could not see myself domesticated in that way; and what should I do for a model without some young woman in the house, made as God makes them, to pose for me! I had taken an order, the most preposterous contract yet, to furnish, a year ahead, the illustrations for a Holiday Edition (strange description!) of *The Scarlet Letter!*[3] I took the order as part of my potboiling, and I can only offer by way of excuse for the presumption that I had to take what came into my pot, and if it had not boiled, I shouldn't have been making enquiries for a general servant whose first qualification must be youth and good looks. . . . It was a friend of the family, of course, who found us Lizzie Griffen, a young Canadian of English blood who had every requirement including

[3] When the book was published, the *Atlantic* remarked that although the publishers "have invited to illustrate the story the artist who perhaps unites more fine qualities than any other," nevertheless "the result is not perfectly satisfactory." "Recent Literature," *Atlantic Monthly*, 40 (December 1877), 753.

a babe in arms. The baby seemed almost providential: Hester Prynne must have a child. It was to be feared though that it might be something of a shock to the husband of four months, this patriarchal procession moving on him; but he took it calmly — anyone my mother approved would be all right of course; fetch her along!

It was now summer 1876, and the Centennial Exposition was inviting the world to Philadelphia to enjoy the big show and spend all the money it could spare. General "Joe" Hawley was president of the Centennial Commission. He was married to my husband's sister Harriet.[4] They were keeping open house, and they invited the sister-in-law whom they had never seen to pay them a visit before she vanished in the West. It was, in my untraveled experience, a unique opportunity, but I hadn't the nerve for it then; I was too deep in my own affairs. Perhaps Harriet understood, but I fear not. In the Foote family there were birds of long wing born among the farmhouse brood; packing trunks and saying farewell they took with as little expenditure of emotion as possible. When we left the old homestead at Mulberry Point, it was "Good-bye, Dad" . . . "Good-bye, Boy — behave yourself!" — the father of eighty to the son he knew he would never in all probability see again.

It was different with us; my trunks had been standing half-packed for days while a steady dropping-in of relatives came with last offerings as to a tomb. Mother had had the lunch basket on her mind for a week. There were no diners on those trains; you dashed across the tracks at meal stations and captured your food to consume in your section, or you bolted it at a counter with one eye on the conductor bolting his; but the wise and provident, and such as had homes, brought these

4 General Joseph R. Hawley (1826-1905), editor, politician, one of the founders of the Republican party in Connecticut, Civil War officer, governor of Connecticut, U.S. representative and senator from Connecticut, was president of the U. S. Centennial Commission in 1876. His first wife, Harriet Ward Foote, died in 1886 and Hawley married Edith Anne Horner in the following year. See below, p. 299.

huge lunch baskets. . . . The Overland Limited from New York to San Francisco reached Poughkeepsie somewhere about midnight, long after the horse-boat ferry laid off for the night. Our own ferryman had been chartered to row the family party up the river to see the youngest aboard her train. No one in the neighborhood had ever crossed the continent before.

It was a warm July night, like one of our rowing parties except that it was more silent and the parents were with us instead of waiting up at home. The trunks were piled in the bow. Lizzie with her boy in her arms sat on the forward thwart, committing herself to the blind authority of an ignorant young wife who knew no more than she what that dark stream of fate might be leading to — and without the means to come back. Then Caleb Wood, our ferryman, long and lean, with a cud of tobacco stowed in his cheek, took his place facing the eyes of his passengers with a countenance discharged of all expression. He pushed off from the old wooden steps, the dock receded, the familiar outlines of the hills faded in the starlit dusk; hemlock-wooded shores and little gray pebbled coves slid past. We watched the flare of the iron foundry at Poughkeepsie mount against the sky and the lights of the sleeping city draw near. Caleb unshipped his oars; in silence we glided up to the landing steps.

BOOK II

An Engineer's Capital
Is His Experience

DRAWN BY MARY HALLOCK FOOTE.

THE ENGINEER'S MATE.

ENGRAVED BY M. HAIDER.

❲ 11 ❳

THERE was no Bay Shore cutoff in 1876. The old single track of the Southern Pacific ran into its Oakland terminus around by the western side of the San Bruno Mountains.[1] We had left a little station called San Leandro and were putting on speed when someone came up behind me and leaned over the back of my seat and called me by name. Only one person on that side of the continent could have done that, and of course it was he. It was not as I had pictured to myself our meeting, but it served, and it was very good to have him there to see us into port.

We were a car-full of wives past, present, and to come. There was a young Scotch lady, quiet and sweet, who had done what I refused to do only much more; she had crossed the ocean as well as three thousand miles of land to keep her word to a young man whom she had not seen in over two years. There was my handsome Lizzie who had in her arms all that was left of her marriage and was fleeing with it away from her legal protector. There was Madame ———— of San Francisco, returning from her Paris where she had spent two years for the sake of her daughter's education. The Franco-American daughter was with her and seemed happy to be going "home." And there was myself, a wife of two weeks with a four months' separation between then and now.

We were crowded in the dressing room smartening our-

[1] Coming from the east, the railroad swung around a series of ridges, each with its local name, then paralleled the San Leandro Hills as it proceeded north through San Leandro to Oakland. There is a San Bruno Mountain, but it is across San Francisco Bay, overlooking South San Francisco.

selves for "shore." The San Franciscans were getting out their coats and furs, but I was as the shorn lamb: I had made the usual mistake of green easterners to whom California means nothing if not sunshine and July nothing if not heat. Indeed we had had plenty of heat, but now in my crumpled pongees and linens we were plunged into one of San Francisco's July fogs.

And there at the ferry entrance stood James D. Hague, my new brother-in-law, coolly waiting till the last handshakes and hopes to meet again were over — we made more of our fellow travelers on overland trains in those days. Crushed as I felt by my own appearance, I was the more impressed by his: I thought him appallingly well dressed and handsome. We broke the news at once that my wretched trunks were a day behind. He took me in with one of his strong penetrating looks and changed our arrangements at once, despatching A. up-town to borrow a tide-me-over outfit from his sister Mary, and he took charge of me and my domestic retinue himself as far as the Occidental where our rooms had been engaged. And when, that evening, I came into the hotel parlor to be presented to my lovely sister-in-law, I was dressed self-consciously in her own clothes, but her eyes met mine without a glance at what I had on. She had selected a black silk dress made in a fashion that commended her taste to my taste, adding a little black lace jacket to save the fit — and everything else a woman seven days on an overland train should need, with the fragrance of her bureau drawers included. Before I had seen her face I had breathed the "savor of her raiment." And the whole incident in its intimacy and awkwardness brought us together as nothing else could unless I had fainted in her arms.

Mary Hague and her friend, that other beautiful young New England woman, Mrs. William Ashburner, were both of the pure, transplanted English type that Boughton loved to paint in his Mayflower maidens: but who today will know who Boughton was, and who are left in San Francisco who can remember that grande dame, Mrs. Ashburner, when she first came out from the East![2]

There were more and unexpected greetings in that room at the Occidental where I first "took off my things" on the western side of the continent. The strong sea air through open windows smelled of roses, a sumptuous basketful Mary had sent, which stood on a little common table, but under it was a cover of woven grasses, soft and pliable, in the natural colors, a little gem of Fijian workmanship — great excitement when it was learned that this belonged not to the hotel but "us"! There was a Fijian fan to blow our fire with in the cabin I had never seen, and a strange, dark wood bowl which A. called a poi dish, hard as stone, polished with seashells and labor of Fiji women — I saw it was destined to everlasting uses. Above, on the hotel mantel, the usual mantel, stood a pair of Guadalajara water coolers decorated with bold swipes of a brush, made of that silky, pale gray clay which is the queen of earths for pottery. And around the bulge of one in rude black letters and peasant Spanish we made out — "Help thyself, little Tomasa."

All these things "not at date paying wages," as I remarked to A. in my role of the prudent wife, reminded him to tell me that coming up from Clay Street with them he had met an old pal, Harry Mitchell, and made a brazen show of his trophies and been called down with the ancient remark about the fool and his money. Even so, every useful thing we bought for that first home has gone down the stream of time, but Mary's roses never fade, the Guadalajara jars and the poi dish stand on the mantel in front of me in this the last of our western camps that became homes [i.e., North Star House, Grass Valley]. The little duck of a table cover perished, as the grass it was made of withereth, in the winds of Leadville years ago. But that was because we lent our cabin there to one whose gods were not our

[2] George Henry Boughton (1833-1905) was British-born and spent most of his life in Britain, but because he lived in the United States as a boy and young artist, he made early New England historical scenes one of his artistic specialties. Concerning William Ashburner, see below, footnote 7.

gods — he nailed it up for a window shade, where it flapped itself to pieces before his eyes. I believe he was a person we liked, all the same.

On Saturday we visited the Hagues in their house on Bush Street [San Francisco], and on Sunday, the trunks having come, we took ourselves off to the mine —to San Jose by train and by carriage to New Almaden, a hot, beautiful drive through a valley bounded by hills shaped like mountains where the native live oaks stood about parklike on harvest fields of gold. The prudent wife felt bound to say the stage had been good enough for her, but enjoyed herself all the same. As we begin in marriage, so we go on, it is said: I went on, all my life, rebuking extravagance and enjoying its results, as I enjoyed those wanton purchases from the far Pacific Isles when what we needed was pots and pans. As a matter of fact they could not be bought now in Clay Street, nor anywhere else, for many times what A. paid for them; but I don't seriously recommend this way of saving money to other young housekeepers.

We had a large, fat Cornish dinner (very good though) at Mother Fall's, Arthur's erstwhile home. The more she liked him the keener eye she cast on us, his female liabilities, especially Lizzie, the maid we had imported from the East. The good practical soul, who probably knew the amount of everyone's salary at the mine, must have wondered what on earth we needed of a maid in that little box of a cabin we were going to and what "the wife" was "able for" anyway. There were many and miscellaneous introductions, quite a little burst of publicity, before we plunged into the seclusion that awaited us down the trail. Hastings and Henwood, Arthur's "boys," went with us to help carry things, and I was given private notice that they must be our first guests; they had spent hours of their own time getting the cabin ready for its mistress.

We stepped inside and I looked around with great content;

beamed ceiling, redwood-lined walls, dark floors — we had left the glare outside; the little place seemed furnished already. He did know how to build for a woman! Yet, cool and dark as it was, the woman went to work on her curtains at once and was told by the man that he supposed if they lived in a cave with one hole for a window she would want a curtain over that; and she said certainly she would — "The Cat That Walked by Himself" had not been written at that time, or she might have reminded him of the Wild Woman who hung up the horse skin over the hole in her cave and said to her wild mate, "Wipe your feet, dear, when you come in, and now we'll keep house."[3]

We kept house in that redwood-lined cabin just one year and a month [1876-77]. A son was born to us there and prospered through the first four months of his existence; then we shut the door on its little histories and never saw the place again. It was not expected to have been more than a temporary home, but we should have been glad to stay a few years if we might have done so "without capitulation."

Wiser friends could have told us we were rash, making over a house not our own, perching aloof in an attitude of indifference to society, alone with the proletariat and the great valley at sunset. We were in the camp of labor, yet not of it. On the last hill above us the Mexican camp was the home of a more barren and hopeless poverty even than that which we had at our elbow; and as the shadow of that hill covered us at all hours except the morning, so, after the first few weeks of ignorance on my part, we lived in the face of all that natural beauty, conscious in our souls of an overhanging mass of helplessness and want.[4]

3 From Rudyard Kipling's *Just So Stories*.
4 As Mary Hallock Foote implies, at New Almaden the economic and social groups lived in separate communities. Thus the Spanish-speaking workers lived in a "camp" that was distinct from the settlement of the more highly paid Cornish miners.

The company stores were run on the ancient system of exploitation — not for the benefit of the company in this case but of individual owners, and in our time the policy was frank extortion. The prices were exorbitant and the men on the payroll were expected to buy nothing outside which the stores had for sale. A system of espionage kept the manager of the stores informed if anyone infringed this law of the mine. That man's name went on the blacklist, to be discharged without other reason. The policy, I believe, was common, but the mean and vengeful way in which it was carried out under L. makes it impossible to give his name, though he was but an instrument and owed his power to one higher up. With the Mexicans this rule amounted to peonage — they hadn't the means to move. The Cornish were thrifty and great "kickers" but home lovers too. They clung to their jobs and toadied to L. and hated him the more. An old miner who had worked for the company fourteen years had the temerity to bring in a piece of stovepipe from San Jose which he might have bought at the stores. He was made an example of. His little house, that he had built on company land at a rent of a dollar a year, was wrecked and carted away as lumber outside the lines, and notice given that whoever bought his stuff, his cow or chickens or anything that was his or assisted him in his flitting, would be treated as a sympathizer and meet the same fate.

We had supposed that we might live on our hill to windward of the camp smells and escape its gossip — certainly that we need not go in fear of visits from L., if we took no notice of him. But we had put ourselves within his sphere of influence and he could not brook a public snub. At the Hacienda the social issue would not have come up. We of course did not realize the importance of the incident nor of L. himself. Such men are not easy to replace when they are suited to the sort of work required of them, nor always safe men to discharge.

Everything, as I thought, was going beautifully; housekeeping and blocks working smoothly in harness. I was deep in

THE MEXICAN CAMP (WEST END) AND THE HILL OF GRAVES.

THE WATER-CARRIER OF THE MEXICAN CAMP.

my *Scarlet Letter* drawings (we drew on wood in those days; the engravers' blocks were sent me by mail), not neglecting the daily walk for exercise and in search of backgrounds. All the trails winding up and down between the two camps were as safe as our wood paths at home. In lonely spots deep in the chaparral, I used to meet our black-visaged Mexicans who looked as if they might have been pirates of the Caribbean — I didn't know them but they knew me: lowered eyelids, "Buenos dias, Señora!" — the gentlest manners, softest voices, those poor people of the sun whom nobody seemed able to help, yet so proud of a chance to help others! We were not customers of the camp *aguador* [water carrier], yet when he heard that the *Señora del Agrimensor* [surveyor] wished to draw him, he came with all his muchachos and donkeys and water kegs and wasted two hours in front of our gate — and so delicate about asking to see the sketch, which indeed I was ashamed to show him! He was magnificent, dressed in goatskin *chaparreras* [leather leggings] with the hair outside, a pink cotton handkerchief, bound round his head, showing beneath his hat. When A. would have paid him for his time at least, he looked hurt and murmured "No posíble!"

A notice had been posted in the engineer's office forbidding any person to smoke in that room, "by order of the manager." An office is not a club, still the manager saw my husband smoking there every day. The men of my family were not smokers, but I had not forgotten Grandfather Burling's state of mind when women and doctors attempted to wrest the tobacco from between his teeth. I was amused yet alarmed: "What if he should speak to you?" I asked, knowing that no attention would be paid to the notice. "He won't speak more than once," growled my dog with a bone. "He" didn't speak. Hamilton Smith had not only recommended A. for the work, he was the company's consulting engineer and the judge of his performance — *he* would have spoken fast enough if the work had been at fault. He was a man our boss did not wish to displease. Foote would not be discharged; he would be induced to resign. One little prod after another would be sufficient; the final hint came when A.'s salary was reduced and his work considerably increased.

Smith's interest in anyone he liked resembled the "softness" of Baloo [5] — you were liable to be all bruised with it. It was not wise as a rule for one of his junior assistants to say to him when at work: "Behold I will show thee a more excellent way"; yet if there were such a way that required to be shown, that young man would find it ill to dally with his message. They were sinking a new shaft and all the underground surveys at this time were critical; there was one most particularly so and Smith himself was at the transit.[6] He fumed and swore because the same angle would not read twice alike; the transit must be out of adjustment. It was taken on top and half the morning wasted finding nothing wrong. They were working in the bottom of a tunnel where a stratum of carbonic acid gas had been stirred by their movements; a ray of light passing through this variable medium was deflected as by water. Taking his life in his hands, Foote suggested that when *he* made surveys in that tunnel he found it necessary to place his lights by actual measurement, on a level with his eye, instead of sighting downwards through mixed gas and air. . . . "Why in hell didn't you say so before!" roared Smith, and for a few seconds there was more than carbonic acid gas, heavier (and hotter) than air, in that tunnel.

There was something high-minded and bracing in Smith's bluntness; he was a man my keen young husband loved to work under — he would have stayed and swallowed a few more hints if the work had remained interesting. What he called interesting was to breakfast by candlelight at 3:00 A.M. and go underground and remain there, stooping at a transit in

[5] The bear in Kipling's *Jungle Books*.
[6] Transit or transit compass: "a variety of theodolite with the telescope mounted so that it can be transited" (Webster).

low dark drifts, till after midnight of the following night, a twenty-hour shift, and crawl home nearly blind with eye-strain, and call it a day. The work underground had to stop while those surveys were being made, hence the long shift; but it seemed a little thoughtless of the manager to send down to enquire why Foote was not at his office at the usual hour next morning. He was in bed, his head bursting with neural-gia. He had very strong eyes, but they were astigmatic as well as farsighted and he used them mercilessly. . . .

They are all dead, that unmatchable group on the West Coast who were not only great engineers whom it was an edu-cation to work under, but remarkable men, cultivated, trav-eled, original; Hamilton Smith, the Janin brothers, William Ashburner (James D. Hague's close friend), "J.D." himself, that "beautiful man" as Louis Janin called him when they were both old and fat but no less charming. Often they had been pitted against one another in those famous mining law-suits with millions at stake, when the courtroom would be packed as at an all-star performance of a play or a field day in Congress. Many a gay bout they had in retrospect, those friendly rivals, the best experts of their time. England seduced some of them away from us after the gold discoveries in South Africa. Our last evening with Hamilton Smith was in New York, at a dinner the Hagues gave him on the eve of his sailing for London. "Over there," he explained largely, "they know how to treat an engineer." . . . "How to pay him," James amended.[7]

---

7 This was indeed a remarkable group. See Introduction, pp. 11-13. Of the numer-ous Janin brothers, at least three became mining engineers, with Louis and Henry receiving the same kind of cosmopolitan training by which James Hague prepared himself. That is, they went from Yale to the famous Royal Mining Academy at Freiberg, Saxony, then to the École des Mines in Paris. Similarly, William Ashburner went from Harvard to the École des Mines.

12

We HAVE worn out many a dry season since our first house-keeping began on that sunbaked hillside at New Almaden. I have grown used to them and learned to find a sort of content in their smiling, inscrutable monotony; and the overpowering light and emptiness of the sky by day is marvelously atoned for by the nights — the great nights of stars.

We opened the cabin in the middle of July, and three months of the same thing followed. The rains held off uncommonly late that year. There was only surface drainage in the camp and, as the dust grew thicker on the cinnabar-colored trails and sifted over the manzanita scrub and dulled the perpetual green of the live oaks, not distance nor aloofness could cut us off from that wind of our common humanity when it blew from off the hill. It was a population that said: "Moab is my washpot; and over Edom will I cast out my shoe!"[1] Edom was the back fence and Moab was the street or the front yard, and who could blame them! Bonfires were forbidden till after the rains and there were no sewers, not even open ones; the hill was all one sewer. We had bargained unknowingly for those smells when we chose to live among God's smelly poor. Also for a share in their grievances. They trusted us, and they visited Lizzie who could not be expected to keep to herself all that she heard. Some of it may have been lies, most of it was

[1] This phrase occurs in Psalms 60:8 and 108:9. Washpot means wash basin. Casting one's sandal upon property seems to signify taking possession, although apparently with an implication of defiance or contempt, in this instance.

disloyalty in return for exploitation — all of it was the Wine of Astonishment[2] to me.

I might have lived a long life shut up in that old sweet-smelling orchard farm and never have heard so much and such primitive gossip as came to my ears in one season in New Almaden — with that most heavenly view always there in all its changes. Every evening the lingering, deep-colored sunsets, every night the amazing rush of stars. But the beauty and shut-in intensity of the life (with my baby coming) made it worse. It bred a sort of nostalgia that was all one with the smells of a strange vegetation baking in the heats of a summer that never dies. If I opened a trunk and took out a dress that had hung in the closets at home, waves of a faint, sickish emotion went over me. I didn't wish to go back, yet I could have cried with the pang of those odors released from its folds. Visions and voices from another world as different from this as my life was now from that girlhood to which I had died: "O perpetui fiori!" . . . These are not earthly odors. I thought then it was New Almaden and marriage and the dry season.

In November there came a cool, gray afternoon, a sallow gray with a rising stir in the live oaks, a wind that we snuffed before it reached us, sending the dry leaves hurtling down the trail; dust whorls traveled ahead of it. We listened for the first drops on the roof — then dust and smells rose up together like battle smoke and all was drowned in the steady drumfire of the rain. It lasted only till sunset — but what a sunset! The valley was transformed. The dry season had broken.

There were hours of sudden darkness in the little familiar room when one couldn't sit still but walked the floor in ecstasy to hear the rain sweep over the roof; there were bursts of sunlight calling us out to look at the valley — and lo, the clouds were all below us and the valley a lake, with light and shadow marching across the mountains. Thanksgiving week we spent

---

[2] From Psalm 60:3. "Thou hast shewed thy people hard things: thou hast made us drink the wine of astonishment."

with the Hagues . . . and for years their friends whom we met at Mary's dinners, that exclusive and critical little group of professional exiles we remembered on the background of the windy, precipitous city, stood in my mind for San Francisco society. They were no more San Francisco than they were Boston or New Orleans or Freiberg or New York; San Francisco never was the West, even the West Coast, in any sense that has to do with society. It is always the City of the Unexpected. It was just as unexpected when we saw it twenty years later; but the old set we knew in the seventies, the Hagues and Ashburners and Janins and Thibaults, were scattered to the ends of the earth and beyond.

The twenty-nine *Scarlet Letter* drawings were finished by the end of the year. Lizzie as a model proved a rock of endurance and was grand to look at when not starched up in ill-fitting clothes. I saw ahead of me the embarrassments of my profession if I expected to keep it up in camps and cabins of the Far West. Costumes and accessories worried me more than when I flew the kites of childhood with any sort of rag tied to their tails.

Other matters besides engraver's blocks were taking their natural course. Lizzie's little Georgie could waddle all over the place by this time and his mother's methods in training him were natural too: a crash (of kitchen crockery) followed by a spank and a howl, then mumbled words and kisses to make up for mummy's abuse of her baby boy. About this time we had our first houseguest, whom neither of us had ever seen before — Mrs. Kirby of Santa Cruz, introduced by a letter from Aunt Sarah. They had been friends in their youth, not personally intimate but through their mutual causes and ideals.

Mrs. Kirby before her marriage was Georgiana Bruce, one of the Brook Farm transcendentalists, devoted to the improvement of society and the world.[3] She had not been with us two

---

[3] The famous Brook Farm cooperative community was established in West Roxbury, Massachusetts, in 1841, with George Ripley as its central figure. It at-

days before she saw a missionary work before her in the training of that embryo man who went by the name of Buster. He
was destructive, she said, because his latent tenderness had not
been appealed to; boys especially should play with dolls, to
teach them care for others and paternal responsibility —
brickbats and tiles they would find for themselves. She asked
for strong cotton cloth and rags. We hadn't accumulated many
rags as yet in our housekeeping, but enough were found to
furnish the vascular tissues of a large rag baby which she
placed in Georgie's arms with cooing words. Georgie looked at
it with patronizing interest but was pleased, and Lizzie accepted the gospel of gentleness with gratitude. There was a
gate near the kitchen end of our high piazza to keep Buster
within bounds. We heard it slam and the padding of bare feet
on the piazza floor and looked out just as the rag baby flew over
the railing at its highest part and disappeared amidst the chaparral, and there ended Buster's paternal responsibility and so
continued to end every time the object of it was put in his care
unwatched. And Lizzie was more than grateful — she was
tickled to death! it showed that her baby was "pure boy." She
had left his father because he was pure brute — but Lizzie was
not strong minded; she would have been called "pure woman." It was a quaint visit; I needn't have dragged it in, however, but for the link with Aunt Sarah, and for its results un-
thought of at the time.

Mary Hague came to spend a few days in the latter part of
February, when all over the hillsides wild flowers and mush-
rooms were springing and the trails were clean of dust and
smells. She thought the place ideal! The valley, changing from
hour to hour, battlefronts of clouds forming along the bases of

tracted a remarkable group of reformers and intellectuals. See below, p. 144.
Georgiana Bruce, a young Englishwoman of modest background, was allowed
to join as a worker-student. See Lindsay Swift, *Brook Farm, Its Members,
Scholars, and Visitors* (New York, 1900), pp. 75-77. She moved to California in
1850 (see below, p. 144). Transcendentalism received its most important expression in Emerson's writings.

the mountains, charging, breaking, scattering in tatters and streamers wildly flying; tops of the mountains seen with ineffable colors on them at sunset and the nearer hills like changeable cut velvet. She walked the piazza smiling to herself; she laid soft hands on my housekeeping and said I must spare myself now.

I think our simple routine rested her after the conventional perfection she had set herself to achieve in her five years' marriage to a man whose life demanded it; for she had been a farmer's daughter, too, and I daresay had to ask her husband what wines to serve with which courses, when she gave her exquisite little dinners. And all our childish extravagances excused themselves in her eyes when she came to see their fitness and shared their use. She helped herself at bedtime from our water cooler with the invitation to "Tomasita"; she shaded her fair New England face with our Fiji fan when "Pete," as she called her brother in the speech of their childhood, made too hot a fire at twilight, which he invariably did. She watched him, squatted in front of it, clean and fill his pipe from the poi dish now a tobacco tray. They sassed each other in the Foote-family way; and when she saw the artist-wife in her digging hours — more really at home than in the city where she was inclined toward excess of participation under the influence of evening clothes and evening company — I think whatever misgivings she might have come with were satisfied. She knew that, in the words of her father when he read the marriage certificate, "it would hold."

We did not, naturally, bring out our family skeletons for her amusement. A common tool like L. was not worth wasting words on; our manager belonged to the same clubs as James and his friends — he had an agreeable side, and his wife was one of the lovely women of the West and had showed me every kindness. So, leaving us in ignorance of our rash design, when Mary, a few months later, heard we had "resigned" — from that idyllic place — she thought her brother must be mad. True to his mother's report of him, he never fully explained.

James probably understood and liked him no less for preserv-
ing the silence of professional etiquette. It was not a good time
to change jobs; still we had saved a few hundreds — two to be
accurate — out of A.'s salary, besides that which we called our
self-respect, and had a baby too. Oh, yes; and my silly old
blocks had brought in $600 which was called mine. That was
not to be touched, except by the hands that made it.

On the twenty-ninth of April, on a Sunday morning, our
New Almaden baby was born, a ten pound boy, and the camp
said that was all right! Two weeks before the expected event
reinforcements had arrived from the East, the result of anxious
consultations by letter, and the camp was not sure that this
was all right. What did the missus need of more help with
Mrs. Griffin still to the fore? My husband was a great favorite
with the Cornish wives (" 'E'ave a way with 'im!'") and they
looked after our affairs pretty closely. It did seem a big load on
a young man's back in the first year of marriage, all those railroad journeys, and such a houseful of women and one with a
baby of her own cluttorin' up the place. The missus "could
picter anything," but what else was she "able for?" The missus
had asked herself that question and decided that she hadn't
enough experience either in picturin' or baby tending to do
both successfully; hence Marion C., from the East, lady-help,
to help take care of the baby when it came. Still, such is the
force of public opinion, I felt that we were a scandal to the
neighborhood when we took the trails on my first sketching
mornings after the baby was born. As he was dependent on his
mother he had to follow her in his pram wheeled by Marion,
who carried herself very well, and after her trotted my little
caddie with the sketching stool and big white umbrella. Never,
except in the heart of Old Mexico, have I gone forth for a
morning's sketching with equal pomp and conspicuousness!

When Boykin was four-months old (and the New Almaden
summer was old and very hot and dusty), his father asked me
if I felt strong enough to move. He knew I did, but it was a civil

question. For some time I had seen that he was only waiting: working over hours to finish up drawings of pump stations and such things — most wonderful, I thought them; and bringing up to date his map of the mine underground, all its years of development. Four months he had worked over it, coat off and pipe in mouth — that bone of contention! such a man and such a child! I was looking about me retrospectively, gathering up all I could by way of memories on paper of the strange, dear, horrid little place we were never to see again.

Scribner's Monthly (afterwards the *Century Magazine*) had said it wanted my New Almaden sketches, but what about the text? No one except the artist could supply it. I sent them my first shy effort in this way and two more articles followed as carriers for the author's illustrations. For some time I had seen the difficulties in illustration when drawings had to be ready on a certain date; if I wrote my own copy I could take my own time. But my first story I sent, as a precaution against self-deception and the perhaps too flattering encouragement of friends, to Mr. Howells, knowing how he would be likely to treat it and resolved to know the worst; and lo, he took it![4] And my *Scribner* friends said, "How's this?" — pretending to be quite mad with me for the inference implied in my excuse that I courted the sternest criticism and thought Mr. Howells would be the man for that. After this it was agreed, though without any pledges on either side, that the House that had brought me out should have the first reading of everything I wrote. I never crossed the cold frontiers of the *Atlantic* again till ten years later when invited by Mr. Horace E. Scudder — and by that time the *Century* company, though they were too polite to say so, were quite willing, I don't doubt, to share me with others. At least I gave them the chance.

In these days, but for the charming letters they used to write

4 William Dean Howells (1837-1920), the distinguished novelist and critic, for fifteen years was first sub-editor and then editor-in-chief of the *Atlantic Monthly*, to which Mary Hallock Foote submitted her first venture into fiction.

us, those editorial friends of all the contributors of that period
— R. W. G., Horace Scudder, Bliss Perry, Ferris Greenslet —
I should doubt that I ever had had a story accepted by any one
of them, so completely has my vogue passed away. I don't like
to put them to the trouble any longer of refusing the old lady
they have been so kind to all these years. Publishers have
hearts — at least they have very nice manners.[5]

Our neighbors in both camps knew now that we were leaving and humble tokens of regard and friendly speeches found
their way to the cabin and pleased the "missus," if not her
man. He never admitted that he had done anything for the
miners; he had treated them like men and enjoyed them at
times — there were rich studies of character among them.

"*I* know why you're a going, Mr. Foote, sir," said our neighbor, the fresh-butter man as we called him. He had the nearest little ranch and delivered his packets of butter on horseback, never forgetting to give Georgie a ride and to enquire of
Lizzie, as he set him down. " 'Ow's the missus and the Boy?"—
"I know why you're quittin' us," he said in his deep, double
bass. "A poor man is the same to you as a rich 'un and that
don't go around 'ere." This was the popular belief and there
was no shaking it. Another day, in the midst of our packing, a
young woman brought a gift of a crib quilt which her man,
she said, had pieced with his own hands; the hands that wield-
ed the pick and shovel had set all these stitches in their little
time for rest. She had to own that he had begun it for their own
baby and I was remorseful at taking it, but she would not be
denied: "E'll make me another one; this, 'e say, must go to Mr.
Foote's boy." And so I kept it — kept it dark for it was a fear-
some collection of colors; but the sentiment just then meant as
much to us as if it had been a silver service presented with a
handsome speech in the best of English.

5 R.W.G. was of course Richard Watson Gilder. Horace E. Scudder (1838-1902)
was editor of the *Atlantic Monthly* from 1890-98, and Bliss Perry (1860-1954)
edited that journal from 1899-1909, with Ferris Greenslet serving as assistant
editor and as editor during a long absence of Perry's.

Our last Sunday was Marion's "day" and we had been up on the hill, man and wife and child, in good Cornish fashion, to say good bye to Mother Fall — smiles from all the groups we passed to see Mr. Foote wheeling his own baby, as a man should do on a Sunday. And now he was doing his duty still, putting him to sleep, while I wrote my weekly home letter. He lay stretched on the Japanese lounge, Boykin's little white head cushioned in his daddy's hands, propped against his raised knees, while he jogged him to sleep to the monotonous chant of "There were three sailors of Bristol City." I looked at them without seeing them, for I had a difficult letter to write. What should I tell them at home, after months of boasting how happy we were, to explain this breakup? I could not go into details without indiscretion — "What *shall* I say?" I asked my husband, and his answer was the key to our code of living for some years to come: "Say we shouldn't have stayed long in any case; an engineer's capital is his experience." The family rose to the occasion and spared their surprise or condolences: I remember Bessie wrote: "Well, you've had one happy year anyhow — nothing can take that away from you!" But what a long year!

13

W<small>E MET</small> a young man at New Almaden whom we were to know twenty years later as Professor Christy, head of the Mining Department of the University of California, afterwards Dr. Christy. He was an undergraduate then, working with pick and shovel during his vacation for the sake of that practical experience underground which was part of the mining course. He lived at the boardinghouse and spent many of his evenings on our piazza talking of everything under the sun with great seriousness and conviction. He might have been twenty at this time. We were quite a bit older, with a few convictions of our own still unshaken by experience. When he took leave of us at the end of his vacation, his last words as he held us each by the hand were "Stick together!"—"Let you," as the Irish say, "stick together." We cheerfully assured him we would do our best to follow his advice; but the first thing we did that summer of 1877 was to part.[1]

A man in search of a job on that coast if he were an engineer would go to San Francisco; a woman with a baby, in search of health and economy, might be satisfied with good board in a kind family in Santa Cruz, and beauty would be added — beauty and climate second to none in the world. I should have known nothing of Santa Cruz nor of these advantages, but for Mrs. Kirby. Pride came into the decision too: we had friends in San Francisco who did not think us overwise in making this

[1] Samuel B. Christy graduated from the University of California in 1874 and served for ten years with the rank of instructor, before being appointed Professor of Mining and Metallurgy in 1885. He was a key person in starting the new College of Mining, of which he was the first dean, 1896-1914.

change but would have had us on their minds. In Santa Cruz
we knew no one but Mrs. Kirby, who had everybody on her
mind. She was an institution — you felt she might put you on
a list. I did not hesitate to consult her judgment in choosing a
boarding place for ourselves and a situation for Lizzie where
she could have her boy with her. Mrs. Kirby knew the answer
to both questions, and I have thanked her many a time since in
my thoughts — and Aunt Sarah, for introducing us. My husband did not enjoy her visit much, but he was always ready to
own she was "a great old girl."

Mr. and Mrs. Cutler and their niece, Miss Nelly, lived on a
street which the padres called the "New Street of the Little
Fields." When you came to the end of it, one block from the
Cutlers', all the town, the Monterey Mountains, and the sea
lay below — trees blowing, the roar of the surf under all, and
the great quiet sky over all. To reach the business part of the
town by the quickest way, you went down a long flight of
wooden steps with a landing and bench midway and through
an alley intersecting Pacific Avenue, and just before you came
to the corner you passed under a sort of Bridge of Sighs uniting
the second floors of the Pacific Hotel which occupied both cor-
ners. The effect was quite foreign and surprising. There were
no "Little Fields" on our street then, only city lots lately built
on and planted enthusiastically with everything in the way of
flowers and trees the new settlers never could have had in their
old homes. Mrs. Cutler came from central New York where
Lamarque roses do not live outdoors in winter. Her heart's
pride was a two-story Lamarque that garlanded the entire
front of her modest little villa and tossed a great blossomy
branch up over the eaves. They gave us their two best bedrooms and the freedom of the whole house.

Santa Cruz in 1877 must have been at a low ebb com-
mercially: there were many little homes where the wives of

defeated men were doing their own work and would have welcomed a boarder. Mrs. Kirby had a wide choice, but in our case she could not have made a better. She was equally clever in regard to Lizzie. The situation she found for her took her out on a ranch where she was cook and housekeeper and could do as she pleased about Georgie. Her employer, a middle-aged bachelor, respected and well to do, showed what he thought of her by making her his wife in the course of a year or two, and she ended her days in biblical fashion amidst the "alien corn." And Boaz, I believe, made a good step-father.[2]

The Kirbys were called rich; Mr. Kirby was a tanner in the days when tanners had their hands and their pits full of business, and if they did not make money, they must have been exceptionally stupid, which Mr. Kirby was not. Still, he was not at all a bookish man nor intellectual in his wife's sense of the word. They lived in a large house in a garden that filled a whole block. There was neither symmetry nor arrangement but much that was beautiful and botanical, and it gave you a sense of largesse, of crowding, of casting and giving away, in keeping with the climate. It had a grape arbor like a long green-lighted alley where I used to draw the Kirby girls, especially Georgie, who was the prettiest and the gentlest.

Mrs. Kirby's life, as she depicted it with her extraordinary gift of language, struck me as being somewhat like her garden, heterogeneous and crowded, yet there was room in it for great loneliness, one surmised. She was a difficult woman to be quite just to; she made a great appeal to me. Intellectually she was far in advance of the town, of any town of those days no older than Santa Cruz. Some of her theories that were new at that time and risky, to say the least (like birth control), she drove so hard that whoever did not agree with her was quite likely to hate her. Reformers are seldom tactful and she was incapable

[2] The allusion becomes understandable if one remembers that in Keats's "Ode to a Nightingale" it was Ruth who "stood in tears amid the alien corn," and that Boaz was the man who finally married Ruth.

of that wisdom which allows other people "to be uncomfortable in their own way." She made me at times excessively uncomfortable, not to say "mad," talking to me about my most private affairs with a view to a sort of enlightenment I should not have dreamed of asking from her. But when I came to wean my baby the following spring, she may have saved his life; she was the first person who taught me to beware of ordinary cow-stable milk. That was very advanced then. She gave me a formula for my baby's food which would not disgrace a baby doctor today.

She took me for many drives (I can't think of any kindness she did not try to show) along roads she had galloped over when they were cattle trails, telling me in her fashion of the monologue the early history of each home as we passed it. It was the truth as nearly as one with such a fatal facility in words could be expected to tell it, and she was bitter-shrewd! The life of the place had been rather cruel to her. She told me she owned the first copy of *Leaves of Grass* that ever came to that coast. There was one other person in Santa Cruz with whom she thought she might venture to share it and he was faithless to her injunction not to pass it on. Her laugh, when she described the sensation the book made as the consequence of that indiscretion, was about as cheerful as a stone dropped into a foot of water in the bottom of a well.

Aunt Sarah read Walt Whitman, my mother not — he was the subject of hectic discussion in bigger circles than Santa Cruz. He was of course an honored guest at the Gilders' Studio, where Madame Modjeska,[3] meeting him for the first time, leaned to Helena and studying him with her long, dark eyes, murmured, "Il est trés primitif." Harriet Hawley, a strong churchwoman and a hospital angel during the Civil War, could not bear to hear him mentioned. She had a horror of his untidy person and his irreligious talk at the bedsides of her sick and dying. He was to her worse than primitive, he was

[3] Helena Modjeska (1844-1909), the great Polish actress.

profane, and his genius could not save him in her eyes.[4] And there you were when you talked of Walt Whitman in those days!

Mrs. Kirby's maiden name was Georgiana Bruce, Scotch blood and harsh Scotch features. She never could forget that once she had wiped dishes with Margaret Fuller and sat on doorsteps on spring nights and talked philosophy with George William Curtis — young, then, and quite godlike in appearance as she described him.[5] The Brook Farm chapter must have been a short one, but it seemed to have altered the values of her whole subsequent existence and given her a slight sickness of the soul. What could come after the intensity of companionships like those! She had gone out to California at a time when every woman had to marry if she expected to live in peace. She would have been one of the plainest, yet she was beset with offers — "and I took the little tanner," she remarked with her usual irreverence and air of detachment. She did well, most persons would have said! They were married on horseback in a brief stop for the purpose in front of a magistrate's office. She had a great sense of story and used her own life as conversational material with a frankness that suggested an equal freedom with another's privacies. She was like Esmond's muse of History, "familiar but not heroic."[6]

4 Harriet Hawley, Arthur Foote's sister (See above, p. 116) did remarkably effective work in military hospitals during the Civil War. While in charge of a ward in Washington that was daily receiving combat casualties, she encountered Whitman, of whom she wrote in a letter of February 19, 1865: "There comes that odious Walt Whitman to talk evil and unbelief to my boys. I think I would rather see the evil one himself — at least if he had horns and hoofs — in my ward. I shall get him out as soon as possible." Maria Huntington and Kate Foote, *Harriet Ward Foote Hawley* (New Haven, Conn., 188?), p. 64.

5 Sarah Margaret Fuller (1810-50), despite her eccentricities, was one of the striking and influential figures of her day. A famous talker, she was also a critic, journalist, and reformer. George William Curtis (1824-92), who in his youth spent two years at Brook Farm, became a journalist and reformer and then for nearly thirty years was editor of *Harper's Weekly*.

6 Georgiana Bruce (see above, p. 133) came to California in 1850 to join her friend Mrs. Eliza W. B. Farnham, and the two women scandalized the local

Between the Kirbys' garden and the New Street of the Little Fields there was a great gulf fixed. It was crossed by me on a bridge of countless favors and kindnesses from both sides. It was a giddy effort and at times I wearied of carrying water on both shoulders, but too much can never be said for the kindness! Good "Auntie Cutler" was a consistent believer in "doing by others" — she never strained my faiths nor discussed our neighbor [Mrs. Kirby], though I know she distrusted her influence profoundly. She spoke of her quite sincerely, on her own account, as the direct instrument of Providence in sending us to them that hard winter when they hadn't known which way to turn. Mr. Cutler had failed in business, or been cheated — perhaps both. I doubt if they had any provision for old age, aside from their steadfast affection for one another and hard work from day to day. One must put the glare of the world and of great achievements out of one's eyes to see anything worth chronicling in lives like theirs. Their home life was narrow — and so was the New Street of the Little Fields till you came to the end of it, and then it was breadth and peace and beauty, and for me it was waiting, from day to day.

Waiting is part of the breaking-in of an engineer's wife. I did a good deal of my waiting on those steps that winter, sitting on the bench and watching the "vacant smiling seas" — waiting for my husband's train when he came down for over Sunday, which he couldn't afford to do if he had any work to keep him. But he hadn't much work. An engineer whom he knew named

people by wearing "bifurcated garments" while they did their own farm work and helped build their own house at Santa Cruz. In 1852 she married Richard C. Kirby, like herself a native of Britain, who had had a varied career on the Pacific Coast since he deserted from a whaler in 1845. Kirby ran a successful tannery in Santa Cruz. The couple had five children. The house on Mission Street, of which Mary Hallock Foote speaks, was built by the Kirbys in 1853 and was surrounded by trees and shrubs from many parts of the world. The phrase quoted at the end of the paragraph is from Thackeray's *Henry Esmond*, in which Esmond says, "I would have History familiar rather than heroic."

Hoffman had gone out of town on some expedition and left A. in charge of his office with a share of the fees; but few fees came in. It was a dull winter. One of Mrs. Kirby's kind thoughts for which we blessed her was to lend us her own pony phaeton whenever A. came down, saying she never used it on Sunday. With Boykin half asleep in my arms we would drive out to Moor's Beach just beyond the ranch where Lizzie lived and spend the afternoon loafing and sketching on top of those cliffs that were then as the Lord made them.

Santa Cruz, when we knew it, was innocent of jazz music and Ferris wheels and boom hotels and weekend popularity. Lonely peninsulas of yellow gray rock strode out into the surf, tunneled by the waves or worn through into natural bridges. Three miles of beach we looked down upon with seabirds flying over it and not a bathhouse in sight. The plover's sad, wild note was quite distinct against the long roll of the surf, like Boykin's little laugh — there seemed to be room in that vastness for the little things. And there were Sunday mornings we spent in the priests' garden, sitting on the curb of a pool set amidst callas growing tall, half hiding the water, or wandering about listening to the chorus that came in bursts from the windows of the new church overlooking the old mission gardens.[7] Two little altar boys in white gowns and scarlet stoles were there one morning playing about with their nighties tucked under their arms. They had escaped by some back way from the church. But gardens I could have on weekdays — it was the shore that called us.

There are stretches of wild pasture like the English downs along that coast that sink into hollows deep in grass or drop off into cañons that hide the course of a laguna running up from the sea. Such a spot we found one Sunday morning, and I said: "I wish we might stay here forever! What could be better than this!" That speech of mine in my recklessness might have been

[7] According to Leon Rowland, *Annals of Santa Cruz* (Santa Cruz, 1947), p. 6, the old adobe church building had fallen down during an earthquake in 1857 and had been replaced in the next year by a wooden structure.

ITALIAN FISHERMAN'S HUT ON THE ROAD TO THE LIGHT-HOUSE.—ROCKS AT LOW TIDE.

the beginning of our first dream — one of the many dreams that came true, but not in time for us.

We approached it we thought prudently, but like all dreams it was hard to hold. It ran away with us before the winter was half spent, the winter that should have seen us settled on a new job. There are cement works now in Santa Cruz using that same rock and clay which tempted my breadwinner — not that the idea had not occurred to others before him, but no one had found the right formula for combining these materials nature had provided into an hydraulic cement for which they were plainly intended. But it was partly for his wife's sake that he looked into this chance, because she had weakened on the long trail before us. He did not realize that that speech, which I had better have suppressed, was only a phase of new motherhood. I wanted a safe place to hide my offspring in, a hole or burrow of some sort where I could stay and watch it. The spirit of adventure was dead in me for the time.

He worked in San Francisco for weeks and he made the stuff. He tested it under fire and water and pressure and everything but time. He took it to the experts of Colwell and Davis, the great lime and cement firm, and they received it hospitably.[8] All portland cement was imported then. Our hopes were high. Mr. Kirby was enthusiastic; he said he had always believed that stuff would find the man who knew how to use it! He clapped my young man on the back figuratively and said if he had had any capital free he would have backed him in another fashion.

Then arose one Denis Kearney, with his Sand Lots Meetings and his slogan: "The Chinese must go." He bored a great many people and alarmed a few — he ruined us. Nothing short of direct action was threatened in those meetings and no one knew how far the propaganda might spread or mob politics carry the day.[9]

8 According to the San Francisco directories, the firm was Davis & Cowell.
9 Denis Kearney (1847-1907) emerged during the economically depressed years of the late 1870s as leader of the Workingmen's Party and demagogic orator against many presumed ills, notably Chinese competition with white labor.

Colwell and Davis had a wide area of investment open to disaster if the Chinese did "go" — if the mob should get out of hand and begin destroying plants where Chinamen were employed. They said they did not care to put up any more works just then. Capital is always willing to wait. But we couldn't wait.

We had picked out a heavenly point down the shore about three miles from the town for our future home (founded on cement). We might have bought the whole of that point then for a sum which as it happened I had at that time in a bank at home. That was a dream we might have realized more on than any fortune we could have made in cement. Santa Cruz "boomed" a few years later. . . . So, it was the out trail once more for "him" and the home trail for me. I had come to the end of my drawing money, and it was some satisfaction to know how much it had been needed in the kind little family [the Cutlers] where most of it was spent. I don't know why the times were so hard that winter? Perhaps it was the Sand Lots agitation, perhaps it was the break in bonanza stocks — more likely that. Men like Hague and Ashburner and the Janins were sitting in their offices chaffing one another with little else to do. The busiest camp just then was Deadwood in the Black Hills, 260 miles from Cheyenne by stage — and by flood and ford and mire at that season; there was work enough there, but that was not a trip for a wife and baby.

James Hague had accepted an appointment as Commissioner of Mines to the Paris Exposition [of 1878] and they were breaking up the home in Bush Street on the eve of their long journey, the entire family crossing the continent en route for London and Paris. (How little would be made of it today!) He offered me his convoy and my reservations were taken with theirs for the last of March.

The Mitchells in San Francisco, mindful of all these things, invited us to spend our last week with them in their large house where they said they lost themselves! (No more jokes from

Harry about the fool and his money!) [10] It was through them
Marion C —— found a new situation; going back east so soon
did not appeal to her. Being a good sport, she later struck out
for Honolulu, and there she settled her own fate by marrying
a Scotch widower — I speak as if they were a breed — a man
of some prominence in the Islands, and she made an admirable
stepmother to his large family of half orphans. But her people
in the East did not like this marriage very well because the
mother of those stepchildren had been of island blood.

"Let us build altars to the Beautiful Necessity!" It was a
necessity we did not see the beauty of at the time which drove
us away from that heaven of our hasty desires. To lie out there
on beds of mesembryanthemum in the face of all that beauty
in a climate meant for rest and listen to the waves and the
sound of a baby's laugh and the plovers' cry — we were young
for that sort of heaven; and my "companion" (as the dear old
Quaker ladies called their husbands) owned, in our last talks
together when we were facing the separation to come, that it
would have been hard for him to give up his future in the profession he had but half learned and settle down to making cement and ever more cement, even if it had paved the way to a
settled income and a home. He was not ready to settle in any
sense, just yet. And he told me too, for my comfort, that some
months before, a telegram had gone to a certain development
company far away — in South America, I think — signed
"Hague and Janin," in these words: "Foote wants chief engineer and superintendent entirely competent." "Entirely competent — Hague and Janin"! That was enough for me. We
could afford to wait. It was mere luck that he didn't get the job
— but Hague and Janin did not sign words like those carelessly or for friendship's sake. I hummed them over and over like
a song on the train going east, each day farther and farther
from our point of divergence, I for the shores of the Hudson at
the opening of spring — home and the hill orchards in blos-

---

[10] Perhaps Henry K. Mitchell, attorney and representative of mining companies,
whose home and office were in San Francisco in these years.

som and the garden beds made up; he to Deadwood City in the Black Hills, and well named!

All the rivers were in flood and all the roads were deep in mud and slush and he was thirteen days by stage reaching Deadwood City from Cheyenne when it should have taken four, a record trip for difficulty. When they came to the ford of the Old Woman's Fork of the Cheyenne River, the team refused it, but the driver, with less sense, forced them in, helped by two of his fares, A. being one and a man he had dubbed Montana the other. Montana rode the near-lead of the six-horse team, A. took the off-swing and they were soon beyond their depth, all six horses swimming, when it was too late to turn back. There was but one landing place they could have made and they made it, the other passengers, both men fortunately, on top of the stage holding on for their lives. If the current had caught them a little lower down, where it swings around the bluff, the stage would have rolled over and the team have been lost, and all lives of those who could not swim. But the riders had their worst job before them when it came to the bank where the wretched beasts, one by one, tried to lie down sooner than pull another pound. They leaped off and stood in the icy water up to their chests and clubbed their horses up the bank, and saved the poor beasts' miserable lives for more trouble. Thank heaven for our gasoline machines that cannot feel!

The Hagues in those years, and in other years to come, were always very firmly and beneficently mixed in with our affairs. Their house was the first home we entered on that coast. We made them our counselors when we needed counsel (and were willing to take it!). I have told how James's hand was the first one held out to me as he met us at the ferry, and how Mary dressed me for my first appearance! And now they charged themselves with my safety and eased my burdens when my husband was forced to leave me at the parting of our ways. So, about the end of March we gathered at the ferry, the Hagues and their two children and Peddie the Scotch nurse and I and my baby and thirteen pieces of hand luggage, a sight to make every Pullman porter grin. But J. D. [James D. Hague] himself was the most rewarding feature of the show to the experienced eye of that functionary; if the women and children were his convoy, he was as smart and handsome as a man-o'-war. No sign of the harassed pater familias about him! At San Leandro, I thought, "Just two years, less four months" — since that voice over my shoulder had spoken my name and I knew who it must be. One of the consoling things about living is the queer way we manage to accept what comes, after it has come! . . . It looked like going home defeated — but, "entirely competent!" — Thanks, "Hague and Janin"

I had written home that no one was to meet me in Poughkeepsie; for them it would have meant spending the night there beforehand — for me the very name of the old river city was a promise of perfect rest. To walk into the waiting room I knew so well, take a carriage up to an old countrified hotel, breakfast there, and bathe the baby in comfort for the first time in seven days without being hurled and knocked about the delicate task. Then a respectable hack with a citizen of P. as driver, to cross by the first boat and take the old road home from New Paltz Landing — every foot of the way I knew; I could smell the hemlocks in the glen and see the morning shadows lying across the old stony acres of the farms we passed.

All turned out as I had dreamed except the beginning — which was at 4:00 A.M. . . . James looked troubled as he left me at the platform alone. There was no carriage at the station and no one there whom I could send up town for one. He urged my going on to New York with them, but that was unthinkable. That would have killed my pride completely. The waiting room had iron arms dividing the seats which made it difficult, after I had walked my baby to sleep, to lay him down without waking him, and he was a nervous and tired baby. So it was walk and sit with him in my arms for two hours, until the door of the restaurant was opened by a sprightly young woman who showered wonderment and pity on the returned native, sitting there hungry and cold and happy because she was only four miles from home. "All the way from California — and with that baby!" The news had to be told to another young woman equally amazed and sympathetic, while the mother of the baby laughed and laughed — for the journey was over and the baby safe; she was utterly silly with fatigue and happiness.

Two hours more and I was pushing open the front door at home, big baby in arms whom my own mother had never seen. There seemed to be no one around. Telegrams for Milton were delivered by mail and the morning mail had not come. I set down his lordship on the old rug in front of the black-marble hearth, the twenty-two pounds of him, and straightened up for a first look around at the good old room again, when I heard a step that I knew and my mother's little cry speaking my name, "Molly" — the name of my childhood that never was in print.

IN THE PRIESTS' GARDEN.

14

THE FATE of the Maryland property comes in here as part of the family story on which other matters hinged. I can give merely the outstanding facts, which sound queer enough unless one knew the Fosters who were the other parties to the transaction. We had known them for years, but not in a business way; no one who knew them in any way could have doubted they were honest, though liable to be absurd. Mr. Foster was or had been an English dissenting minister who became an antislavery lecturer before the Civil War: it was he who asked, "Why do we 'ate the Negro? We 'ate the Negro because we 'ave wronged the Negro." He also pleaded for the Negro's share in "God's free hair." His children were now grown up and he had a son married who wanted to get out on the land. They owned a small place near Kingston which had those advantages of location Tom now desired, and he had the land — in its virgin state, waiting for just such a little colony of workers as the Fosters all combined. An exchange in short was effected; the deeds had been signed and made over; the Fosters had moved themselves and their all down on the glade lands and Tom was in possession at Kingston when it was discovered, though not at once I think, that a flaw in the title to that property made it of no more value as a medium of exchange than so much wastepaper. And there it ended, for Tom. Why it so ended I don't know — the law of caveat emptor may have cut him off from any legal redress, or he may not have sought any, knowing the Fosters to have been innocent as babes in the matter. It would not have been unlike our brother to have found it too hard to dispossess those unhappy partners to the transaction. . . . But now he was homeless himself. Father offered him the Mill House and the mill's small revenues to tide him over this fresh disaster.

The Mill House did not strain Sarah's housekeeping capacities much, and no doubt Tom chafed at the day of small things in the mill's petty round, but the old house itself took on an air of happiness in having them there; it was fulfilling what had been its family custom and use. It had sheltered misfortune and old age and, in the case of the Crosbys, incapacity. Now it seemed to have come into its own again. The long, slanting roof and wide gray eaves had a look of great comfort and resignation. When you opened the gate of the garden from the lane beyond the pollard willows, you felt a sunny wistfulness, and always there was a sound like spring of running water mingled with the steady hum of the mill. In these days too there was the laughter of children playing in the old dooryard. Sarah was never too busy to sit down and have a "crack" [conversation] with any one of us who wandered in. I trust that I never forgot it was largely through her encouragement and her father's hospitality that I had been able to start my own little industry while there were so few rivals in the field.

There appeared to be a demand for such stories as mine, and the impulse was on me of the unseasoned traveler to set down things about places new to me which now had the magic of perspective and like other vanishing things began to shine and call. When Mr. Howells took my first story, he had complained in his charming way that it was "too wantonly sad" (one never forgets the words of a first "acceptance"). Keen to win his entire approval, I set to work and added a second part ending in happiness and the rains! As at first written it was a dry-season episode, breaking off on a minor key as such an episode would in a place like New Almaden. He took the second part, rather gloomily — he said it was "good, but not as good as the first part." And that too was a lesson![1]

[1] It was characteristic of Howells to recognize and help an unknown writer who seemed to have potentialities. His high reputation as an editor was well de-

Milton was the port of home — but one's thoughts may go swinging outward with the stir of the restless tides. Deadwood City held half of my divided life that summer [1878].[2] It was one of those casual collections of houses, works, and shacks that are called a city as soon as they begin to function on the lowest plane of existence, and its general appearance was that of having been "shot out of a gun." All around for miles, and covering the mountains, stretched a forest of dead trees, black from the fires or naked white where the wind had stripped them of their charred clothing.

Arthur was doing field work in rain and shine — chiefly rain. I read his letters, sometimes [while] pushing the baby carriage along the upper lane between the peach and pear orchards in blossom, or pacing the long walk alone in the restful old garden, its beds made up for another summer's planting. He wrote of lying awake in his tent watching the weird picture the dead forest made at night when a storm struck his camp and the long rapid flashes of lightning kept the cañon in a continuous blaze of light with thunder pounding away on the mountains. A cabin where they did their cooking leaked rather worse than the tents and was muddy and moldy inside, but had that greatest of luxuries to civilized man, a table to eat and write on. . . . All those stark effigies of trees with silence in their tops rose out of a gay green jungle of young growths,

---

served. Like many of Mary Hallock Foote's later stories, this first one was written directly out of her personal experience. The hero was a young engineer from Massachusetts; the heroine a pretty young schoolteacher from Connecticut; the scene, New Almaden, where the girl felt "in exile." "In Exile," *Atlantic Monthly*, 48 (August and September 1881), 184-92, 322-30.

[2] Reports in 1874 that there was gold in the Black Hills of South Dakota led to a rush in 1875-76 and the creation of the booming mining camp of Deadwood, whose name was based on the natural phenomenon that Mary Hallock Foote describes. Although the initial rush was based on placer gold, lode claims (actually, replacement deposits) quickly began to attract attention, and in 1877-79 engineers were in the Black Hills investigating claims for men with capital, such as George Hearst of San Francisco, and supervising the beginning of development work. See Rodman W. Paul, *Mining Frontiers of the Far West, 1848-80* (New York, 1963), pp. 176-96.

birches and quaking asps, with wild flowers thick about their feet. In Deadwood City, I gathered, there were more moldy things than rain-soaked cabins and more sinister things than dead trees; there was, too, that inrush of youth and the hopes of youth that "ever presses on the footsteps of decay." He boasted of outrageous health and plenty of work to expend it on, but in speaking soberly of the actual conditions of life in Deadwood City, he never failed to bless our stars for the safe port of home where the "convoy" was peacefully moored — peacefully, but not as safely as we flattered ourselves.

It had not been a subject our forebears dwelt upon, but it was admitted (generally as a thing of the past) that to be acclimated to our neighborhood — possibly to the neighborhood of the millponds — one had to reckon with a turn or two of chills and fever. Undoubtedly the ponds when they sank low in summer were a menace, but I should never have thought of malaria as an objection to bringing my California baby home. We may have become immune as a family through generations of us living out our lives, and long lives, in that environment. But my little Californian was immune to nothing; he had never had a "temperature" nor a sick day in his life. And if he had had, the bite of a mosquito would no more have been connected with it in our minds than the evil eye. My baby was a big, fine fellow, a grand field for germs, and owing to his mother's conceit of her own opinion, he was the only one of the children who slept out in his carriage that spring and summer. He had done so all his life, I argued, and never had had a cold; the family shook its head: it wasn't safe in that climate. We were both right and both wrong. He was the only victim. His first attack was slight and easily cured, but the doctor said it might return.

In midsummer I took him to Mulberry Point, the old Foote homestead on the Sound shore [i.e., the Connecticut shore of Long Island Sound], to show him to the grandparents there and to give him the sea air. Father Foote was now in his eighty-third year; he was sick-abed never to rise again.[3] It was not acute illness — just wearin' awa.' Harriet Hawley had come on from Washington, or Hartford perhaps, if Congress had adjourned (General Hawley was now in the Senate); Kate and Elizabeth were at home, Mary was in Paris, Arthur in Deadwood City, Sam — I don't know where he was, Captain Sam, on the face of the earth or the ocean — but those three were never to see their father again. Hot summer lay outside; the great old maples by the entrance gate cast their deep shade where my little nursemaid camped on the grass beside the baby asleep in his carriage. Mother Foote never spoke of anything I did or did not do in managing my first baby: she was experienced as a mother-in-law and a wise woman in every way. One of the old farmhands, stopping to look at him as he sat up in his carriage, took the fat baby hand in his big, knobby one and examined it smiling to himself: "Ef thet aint the old Cunnel's hand!"

Harriet Hawley and I walked up and down under the maple trees and discussed infant baptism; I wished to have my boy baptised for family and sentimental reasons; she hoped to make me see it in a more serious light. One day I asked the grandfather to write in the family Bible the date of his youngest descendant's birth. He complied cheerfully, but when it was done he added, "I'd far rather write the date of his true

[3] In both this and her previous reference to the age of Arthur's father (see above, p. 116), Mary Hallock Foote seems to have been in error by a considerable margin. If the printed family genealogical book is to be trusted, then George Augustus Foote was born on December 9, 1789, at Guilford, Connecticut, and thus must have been nearly eighty-nine in this summer of 1878. He died soon afterwards, on September 5, 1878. In 1829 he had married Elizabeth Spencer (born 1812), by whom he had the following children: Harriet Ward, who married General Hawley; Andrew Ward; George Augustus; Christopher Spencer; Katherine; Samuel Edmund; William Todd; Mary Ward Shotwell, who married James Hague; Arthur De Wint; Elizabeth Elliott. Abram W. Foote, *Foote Family, Comprising the Genealogy and History of Nathaniel Foote of Wethersfield, Conn. and his Descendants* (Rutland, Vermont, 1907), pp. 203-04. Note that contrary to Mrs. Foote's comment, General Hawley had not yet been elected to the Senate but had served in the House. See also Introduction, pp. 9-10.

birth!" . . . . There was no further discussion — Old Dr. Bennett was sent for, who had christened all ten of Father Foote's own children, and the ceremony took place at his bedside. No mother, let her be a child of whatever faith or no faith, can resist the sight of her own child so pledged for and supported; one cannot have too many safeguards. Father Foote was a memorable figure propped on his pillows, with nothing of pathos or even weariness in his composed expression. Elizabeth had dressed the room with oak boughs and white summer lilies — I can see her in her white dress and fair hair of baby fineness, done in a Greek knot with little tendrils about her forehead. The girls were both unmarried then. Kate said Elizabeth must be careful, when she made her choice, not to fall below the proud mark set by Harriet and Mary. For herself, she was "not a marrying man," as she put it. And yet, for all her deep voice and rather brusque manner, she had the Italian madonna type of face, the full eyelids and mild, large blue eyes, and as a further incongruity she was the family wag! Harriet stood godmother to the boy, his grandfather and Uncle [Christopher] Spencer Foote were the godfathers — all were gone before he could read his own name in the prayer book his Aunt Harriet gave him.

In memory of those three who spoke for him and now were silent, we sent him to St. Paul's [School], and there in his fourth-form year he was prepared for confirmation by the school's great rector, Dr. Henry A. Coit, and was brought before the bishop — which we considered a very good start in life for a baby born in a mining camp and sheltered in his first slumbers by the folds of a Chinese flag. The flag is no figure of speech — it was a huge thing, twenty feet long, which the Chinese at New Almaden had made for their own glory and to represent their country in the Fourth of July parade, and the boss-Chinaman gave it to A. as a mark of extreme regard. We draped it around the hot corner of our piazza where the hammock hung, and many hours our little "native son" slept there in its glowing shade; it was chiefly red and yellow. . . . All our lives we have alternated in this way between the two sides of the continent, between safety in the East (where lurked unsuspected germs) and risks in the far places that we recognized and defied.

The one-man influence which we should have called the most sinister in Deadwood City at that time belonged to George Hearst.[4] He has apologizers in California and I suppose he had them then in Deadwood, though his life was quite open and unashamed. He was a characteristic specimen of that old "hard-boiled" set of capitalists who sowed in iniquity and sometimes, to the confusion of moral logic, turned and gave large parts of their harvest to the uses of philanthropy: everyone knows what George Hearst's money has done — and everyone in California, for his wife's sake, goes lightly on the subject of his past.[5]

Our industrial civilization uses these men, I suppose, to push some one purpose which a later and different type takes over to larger ends. Kipling's Sir Anthony Gloster, while making himself a million, builds the first steel ships and forwards the merchant marine of all the world, England getting her full share through such old sea sports as he.[6] They have good women for wives, usually, who try to steer their primitive instincts

4 George Hearst (1820-91) had experience in the lead mines of Missouri before coming to California in 1850. Further mining experience in California prepared him to profit handsomely from the new opportunities that opened with the rush to the Comstock Lode of Nevada in 1859. Although subsequently he lost his Comstock fortune, he recovered and went on to become one of the greatest mining magnates in the West, famous for his hard-headed knowledge of his field. See Paul, *Mining Frontiers*, pp. 62-68, 147-48, 180-85, and illustration.

5 Phoebe Apperson Hearst (1842-1919), much younger than her husband, became as famous for her good works as her husband had for his self-made fortune. Kindergartens, hospitals, libraries, schools, the University of California, anthropology and archaeology, and talented young artists and musicians all received substantial help from this remarkable benefactress.

6 Kipling's poem "The 'Mary Gloster' " is the deathbed monologue of a blunt, sometimes coarse ex-mariner who has made a fortune in shipping and shipbuilding; first published in book form in *The Seven Seas* (London, 1896).

and fail yet stick by them, and very often they have been cursed — and have cursed the world — with decadent sons. Almost all young professional men come up against them in the course of their legitimate work; many a one they have made rich, many another, if he insisted on being too legitimate, they have broken and cast aside.

Hearst gave Arthur his first job, running a ditch line to carry water to the old Homestake mill. A. worked for him on and off all summer; he was an easy man to work for; he gave you a free hand; but when it came to the usual question — "run her or open the bilge cock, precisely as I was told —," the younger man refused to do as he was told. It was a question of testifying on one of Hearst's lawsuits for possession of the Old Abe mine, and A. demurred: certain things he could not swear to. The men who could swear to anything were called "Hearst's affidavit men." Probably the "darn debts," as A. called the price of his cement dream, might have been marked off then and there. But that was not to be the answer: "I guess you don't need me on this job, George." . . . Nor on any other job![7]

A young man does not stay in a place like Deadwood City for what office fees he can pick up. There was no future there for my young man and no home for the wife and child. It cost him little to move on: he had but driven in the tent pegs of existence. All that he brought away with him were a few more of those lighthearted trophies which his friend Harry Mitchell would have smiled at: a pair of spreading elkhorns that required a packing box big enough for a piano, smaller pairs of deer's antlers poked in between, a stuffed and mounted stag's head with great wild eyes, and a bundle of beaver skins for his wife, which she prized but gave away in one of her desperate

---

7 The Homestake and the Old Abe were claims acquired in the early days of the Black Hills rush by the Manuel brothers, pioneer prospectors, and sold to men with capital. Hearst and his partners bought the Homestake and developed it into one of the greatest gold mines in the world. Paul, *Mining Frontiers*, pp. 184-85.

fits of elimination on the eve of a continental packing. The money we made in these tentative places we spent very soon, for some reason inherent perhaps in the places themselves or the state of mind they led to; but in each one, if there was the slightest personal link, that held, and curiously joined on to the next one, making a chain of human relationships which did not alter with the depreciation of our hopes nor the state of our bank account. In some cases they led to life friendships.

❴ 15 ❵

THE mining interests were unsettled that year [1878] like a swarm of bees excited and undecided where to alight. The fame of Leadville silver had eclipsed Deadwood's promises in gold and the new camp was booming at an altitude of ten thousand feet, close to the ridgepole of the continent; the men who went up there liked to speak of it as the Camp above the Clouds. A. was bound there and at Denver he encountered capital again, this time in the person of a queer old tightwad whose metier might have been that of a successful country storekeeper, hardly of a mine operator with a fortune reckoned in millions. The Iron Mine was said to be worth four millions; its product was not iron but silver, in the peculiar Leadville formation which was attracting all the foremost geologists as well as practical miners to the camp.[1] One need not mention the owner's name; he and his mine had a story of their own which has long been forgotten. The incident we remember him by was more characteristic of my husband's way of making a bargain than it was of capital in whatever guise.

The Iron Mine was in litigation, as good mines are apt to be;

[1] Concerning Leadville and its carbonate ores, see Introduction, pp. 2, 16, and Paul, *Mining Frontiers*, pp. 127-34. In terms of both mining operations and lawsuits, the key points were that Leadville's ores contained both silver and lead, thus requiring expensive smelting, and that they occurred in a form new to western mining men: as replacement deposits in limestone, rather than as veins. The Iron Mine was one of the first claims to be developed systematically and proved to be very valuable, but the mine was harassed by lawsuits instigated by its neighbors. A dispute started in 1878 led to armed conflict between rival crews of miners. The Iron Mine was owned by William H. (Uncle Billy) Stevens, a Leadville pioneer, and Levi Z. Leiter, a Chicago merchant prince and partner of Marshall Field in their famous Chicago store.

no one covets a poor mine. The defendant was in Denver when Arthur arrived and he asked him to go on the case for him and to name his price. A. was not quite a novice, but he had never testified before on so important a suit, with such large interests at stake. Charles F. Thomas, who conducted it for the defense, was a man of high character and a lawyer of distinction.[2] The trial would come off in Denver with the whole state, or territory perhaps it was then, looking on; in short he was keen for the job, and not knowing the extent of the work required, he merely stipulated for his expenses and the usual fee for expert testimony based on a personal examination. If a man's testimony was worth anything at all on such a case it was worth a good deal, but it was a "gentleman's agreement."

He spent two months at the mine, and in it, making his own surveys and maps, large and small — large, to show on the courtroom walls, and small for the judge and counsel to examine in detail. His glass model of the vein scored a hit with the jury who admired it like a toy; for awhile it became a quite celebrated little toy. The new expert worked away in his room at the hotel in Denver which was crowded all day with mining men discussing the suit. He went into court knowing his part rather better than the opposing lawyer knew his, and his cross-examination was "fun" for the defense. The Iron Mine won the suit and lawyer Thomas very generously (though he had laurels to spare) gave Foote's testimony, and the way he presented it, the honors of the case. The gentleman's agreement was settled by the owner of the $4 million mine handing his expert a cheque for $100. A good dishwasher could have made

---

[2] Charles S. Thomas (1849-1934), later governor and U.S. senator, was born on a Georgia plantation but came north after the Civil War and took his degree in law at the University of Michigan in 1871. Moving first to Denver and then to Leadville when the boom began there, he succeeded better than most lawyers in recognizing that existing precedents, which were based upon deposits found as veins, must be adjusted to the puzzling new replacement deposits. See the biography by his son, Sewell Thomas, *Silhouettes of Charles S. Thomas, Colorado Governor and United States Senator* (Caldwell, Idaho, 1959).

more at a pantry sink in the Clarendon Hotel, or washing tumblers behind a bar, as wages went (not to speak of fees) in Leadville then.[3] A. could not of course keep the story to himself. It added to the gaiety of the camp for a brief while; and he had his chance to get even later; but getting-even stories are hardly worth telling. My husband could never sell anything; *I* didn't mind his being "sold" so long as he had done the work and earned the respect of his ranking officer. It was always a pleasure to remember his relations with Charles F. Thomas.

Work flowed in. He was making money, he wrote me, hand over fist. I shall not attempt to describe a man's winter in Leadville that year [1878-79] when men were pouring in faster than the stages could bring them and many had not where to lay their heads. The road over Mosquito Pass[4] from the end of the track began to look like the route of a demoralized army; there was no road — there were wheel-ploughed tracks upon tracks and sloughs of mud, dead horses and cattle by hundreds scattered along wherever they dropped, and human wreckage in proportion. Many of the derelicts, men or cattle, would not have been worth fetching in where the climate selected the fit very surely and promptly; a man had to live right or he could not live long at that altitude, it was said. . . . Of those winter rides over the mountains to examine outlying claims, caught in blinding blizzards, often on precipitous trails where a horse's misstep would mean a lonely death in the snow, I heard little at the time; such tales were kept for the long safe talks to come. But the man did brag of his horse Dick, and of his other faithful assistant, Sam Clark, a tall Vermonter, son of a farmer and graduate of Dartmouth, who was as true at his job in the office as Dick on the high trails. As to where and how they ate and slept, that was one of the huge boyish jokes shared by thousands in the camp and passed back east where wives and sweet-

---

3 At least the Clarendon was the best hotel in Leadville! It boasted of 80 bedrooms, in addition to its "public rooms."

4 Elevation 13,600 feet.

hearts were waiting and mothers were holding their breath.

The fruit of our discussions in letters had been that Leadville at present was not a place for babies, but A. proposed that the baby's mother should come out for a summer's visit [1879] and leave his nibs in that "safest place in the world," with his grandmother and Aunt Bessie and the family doctor in Poughkeepsie. All the wives and mothers at home united in saying it was "the right thing to do." I wish to call attention to the unusualness of such advice from a set of conservative women at that time. American mothers did not do then as the English have done for generations, stay by their men and leave the children or send them home. It was considered unnatural to part a woman from her child, selfish on the husband's side and rather fond and feverish of her to consent to the sacrifice. I needed upholding and I got it, from my own people who were neither feverish nor selfish; they said it would be selfish of me not to go. I have always found those simple women in the right when it came to any unsimple choice in conduct.

Arthur had heard of a young couple who were setting out from New York for Leadville early in March and he desired me to come on the same train. He would meet me in Denver. He had never seen Mr. and Mrs. Dawes; he had merely heard of their plans and that they were "nice folks." There was not a wife in Leadville at that time — yes; I think there was one, the wife of a German miner who had walked in with her man over the pass and helped him carry their goods. It would be a German wife when it came to carrying goods.

On the morning of the day fixed for my starting, Boykin looked so ill, after a bad night, that we sent at once for the doctor. He pronounced his symptoms serious — the beginning of a long fever, it proved to be. There was no question now of his mother's leaving him. I was to have taken the westbound train at Poughkeepsie; the Daweses were on board expecting me to join them. John Sherman went up to explain my change of plan and to send my telegram to Arthur. For some reason he could not send it himself that night. He gave it to Mr. Dawes to forward at the first stop next morning, "collect" — we did not know the rates beyond Denver. Mr. Dawes decided, in the interests of economy, to wait a day and send it from farther west. That day cost Arthur the message which was to prevent his starting for Denver. He had given himself ample time, allowing for accidents on the road, and the dispatch came a day too late. There was no one for him to meet but the Daweses. I rather think he damned the well-meant thrift which had saved him a dollar perhaps, at the cost of $200 and the drive back, a cheated man. The Daweses had a comfortable ride, however, instead of going by stage as they had expected — the ill wind blew them some good. But that was the man's side of it: to have a piece of news like that handed him by strangers and walk out to the cabin and sit with it alone.

This was the first case of sickness I had ever nursed. I had never done anything for anybody — I was the "baby" of the family; everyone did things for me. And now my sister, leaving her own children to the care of others, watched with me day and night. Our orders were: every two hours a tablespoonful of milk forced between the fever-crusted lips, every four hours the shuddering dose of raw quinine dissolved in water. We took the watch by turns, but if this ordeal came during my watch I woke her, for my nerve failed. She had the quiet strength and gentleness to overcome quickly, and with the least possible excitement, the resistance of a half-unconscious child. And she never betrayed the impatience she must have felt with my helplessness and panic.

It was a white fever —deep-seated, and no one who knows fever cases need be told how critical was the convalescence. If it had been hard to leave him before, when his spine was like a willow withe and his sturdy legs bore him about the house on a steady trot, it may be guessed that it was no easier to leave my little two-year-old after that disintegrating fever. I marvel still at the nerve of those women who undertook the care of him and the responsibility of telling his mother when it was right and time for her to go. His father would not have asked me to leave him then; the decision lay with me. It was one of those invisible divides from which little streams of circumstance part which may turn into tides of fate.

On the run out from New York to Chicago something went wrong and we lost hours and I missed my connection. But the one person I knew in the city was at the station to meet me, Walter Vail, son of a family much esteemed and loved by us all, and a friend of my New York winters. His mother had written him the date of my journey and he was there to see me safe across the city. But as it turned out, there was much more than that for him to do. I wrote out a long telegram to A., which he reworded to save expense. He combated my idea of keeping on in a day train and taking the Overland next morning at Kansas City. But I could see that he considered himself my host for the time and he had no time — a young business-man with engagements he could not break offhand. So I persisted, and he helped me to carry out what he called a mad plan, to ramble through Missouri on the "Hannibal and St. Jo" [railroad] and spend the night in Kansas City. I confessed my childhood's impressions of Missouri as a state with a lost soul, inhabited chiefly by slave catchers and Border Ruffians.[5] He was much amused and said I might trust myself without hesitation to the Border Ruffian who might be in charge of that train, and take his advice as to my affairs. Which I did — and was treated like an official guest! There was nothing he could think of that he did not do for me, even to asking me to come forward and ride in the cab of his engine. No one had ever

5 A reference to the tumultuous days before the Civil War when men from western Missouri "invaded" Kansas in order to force slavery upon that region.

asked me to ride on an engine before, nor has anyone since; still I allowed this opportunity of a lifetime to escape me. I felt quite sporting enough going alone on the giddy Hannibal and St. Jo to spend the night in Kansas City. My conducting friend did not forget me next day; being at the end of his run he found time to call for me at my hotel and see me aboard my right and proper train, connected up with all the other overlanders.

Walter Vail I never saw again — nor any of his lovable family. That was one of the losses of going west. Families have their own histories to make, and there were six young histories in that family just beginning to shape their courses. It was Mrs. Vail, by the way, who secured us our first year of comfortable housekeeping, in finding for us Lizzie Griffen.

All down the years of change and journeys, looking back, I see those long continental trains coming in at their last stations, the dust of state after state upon them, and the waiting crowds in sight. Others jump off first, nor am I among those who are tall enough to be seen at a distance; but I see another person who stands in the crowd on the platform, a pair of attentive eyes that pass from face to face expressionless, till suddenly they change; it comforts one who has lost one's self for days among strangers to be recognized, to be waited for, as we hope to be recognized and waited for by one or two, when we come to the last terminus. . . . It had begun to seem like a dream that anyone could be waiting for me at Denver; I became half panic-stricken as the train pulled in, lest he should not be there. But of course he was there — for the second time he was waiting. He looked thinner than I had ever seen him; the high altitudes are not fattening. He did not look older precisely, but the year and more since I had seen him had done its work; I thought he looked like a man one might go to Leadville with. The absurdity of our going to a place like

Leadville at all struck me, yet it seemed the next thing to do, and I had resolved never to lay a finger in the way of hindrance on my husband's "legitimate work."

We left Denver by the narrow-gauge [railroad] that afternoon[6] and started out from the end of the track just at dusk; it was then a provisional sort of place called "Slacks." Trotting along with our light load[7] we very soon overtook the Leadville stage, packed with passengers and piled with baggage, and A. pulled out to pass when a voice from the driver's seat hailed him quite humanly: "Hello, hello! That you, Mr. Foote? How's the Old Woman's Fork tonight!" It was the ex-driver of the Deadwood stage on that record journey from Cheyenne — moved on like the rest of the mining population to the new camp. With the eyes those men have for faces and the memory they have for comradeship, he had recognized his passenger of the year before who rode his off-swing through high water at the ford. The Leadville stage with six fresh horses, making time while the night is young, does not haul up for idle conversation: he had a valuable piece of information to give us as to a bad place on the road ahead where we were liable to plunge on in the dark and be mired in a slough where a team had perished by a day or two before. Owing to this encounter we did not spend the night disastrously on the road to Fairplay, but

6 Many of the early railroads that were thrust up the canyons and passes of Colorado's mountains were narrow gauge, because it was so much less costly to build, equip, and operate them under mountain conditions. Frank Fossett's contemporary guidebook, *Colorado: Its Gold and Silver Mines, Farms and Stock Ranges, and Health and Pleasure Resorts* (New York, 1879), p. 80, identifies this as the Denver, South Park & Pacific Railway, which by early 1879 had been completed across the plains from Denver to Webster, where the rapid ascent of the mountains began.

7 Mary Hallock Foote's first letter from Leadville, May 12, 1879, to Helena de Kay Gilder gives a clear and vivid account of this journey. In details, the letter and reminiscences sometimes disagree. The letter states that they left the train at Webster, wound upward through pine forests and over a bad road to the magnificent South Park, spent a night at Fairplay, crossed two successive mountain passes, and reached Leadville "by lamplight."

reached it about midnight and slept there before climbing the pass.

The mountains of the Great Divide are not, as everyone knows, born treeless, though we always think of them as far above timberline with the eternal snow on their heads. They wade up through ancient forests and plunge into cañons tangled up with watercourses and pause in little gemlike valleys and march attended by loud winds across high plateaus, but all such incidents of the lower world they leave behind them when they begin to strip for the skies: like the Holy Ones of old, they go up alone and barren of all circumstance, to meet their transfiguration.

We spent the early part of the day steadily climbing; our horses had no load to speak of, yet before noon one of them was hanging back and beginning to show signs of that rapid lung fever which if a horse has taken cold in those altitudes has but one end. A. thought he might hold out till we reached English George's, but from that on, the drive was spoiled by seeing the gasping creature kept up to his work. On the last and steepest grade, before you got to English George's, a sharp turn with a precipice on one side narrowed the road suddenly. The view was cut off ahead, and here we met the stage coming down, all six horses at full speed — they had the precipice on their right, we had the bank and we had to go up the side of it if only on two wheels, for there was no room to pass. I felt that moment I would just as soon die myself as see my husband force that dying horse up the bank, but it had to be done. He stood out on the buggy step, throwing his weight on the upper wheels, and laid on the lash; we did not turn over and we did get by, with a few inches to spare. The two men driving exchanged a queer smile — they understood each other; and I am glad I have forgotten what I said to my husband in that moment when he saved our lives, and I hope he has too! The horse died after we got to English George's and there we hired another, or the remains of one, and he died the day after we reached Leadville. A. paid for both — and how much more the trip cost him (both trips) I never knew, but that is the price of Romance: to have allowed his wife to come in by stage in company with drunkenness and vice, or anything else that might happen, would have been realism.

We knew that we were nearly "in" when corrals and drinking places and repair shops began to multiply, and rude, jocose signs appeared on doors closed to the besieging mob of strangers: "No chickens, no eggs, no keep folks — dam!" was one that A. pointed out to me. . . . "Shall we drive out or walk? — there is a trail?" he asked. . . . "Let's walk, of course!"

We left behind us that disorganized thoroughfare called Harrison Avenue, with its blaring bands of music and ceaseless tramp of homeless feet on board sidewalks; if I remember, there was a moon to show us our way along the hydraulic ditch — which came to be in a year or two the fashionable promenade and was known as the Ditch Walk. Our cabin then was the first and only one on the ditch; there were woods behind us and on one side, and the lights of the town in Carbonate Gulch lay below and climbed and scattered on the flanks of Fryer and Carbonate Hills. And Sam Clark had made a good fire in the cabin, and no one was there.

Of the many details of that summer that come back to me there is no end — the foolish nothings that make "all the difference!" If I were to let myself go I should be writing a book soon which no one . . .

[At this point occurs one of the very few breaks in the narrative. Two pages of Mary Hallock Foote's original typescript are missing from both Versions "A" and "B" (concerning which see pp. xi-xii). Probably the explanation is that after the foregoing incomplete transitional sentences, she launched into a discussion of her husband's personal traits. Always fiercely defensive about Arthur, she must have concluded that she was being too frank, and thus must have crumpled up and thrown away two whole pages. But the concluding part of her comments on Arthur happened to be typed onto the same sheet that contained the start of the next chapter. Therefore she merely scratched out her very interesting final paragraph, in which she spoke not only of her husband but also of the position of any engineer in the West who was managing an enterprise for absentee owners in the East. The paragraph is here restored precisely as she wrote it. Mary Hallock Foote's remarks begin in the middle of a sentence. A reasonable guess would be that in the missing half of the sentence she was quoting Arthur's mother, who had a long and frank discussion with the bride shortly after their marriage.]

... were married, that he had a "devil of a temper" (exercised in disputing the authority of five older brothers). I shouldn't be surprised if he had; yet the day he lashed that dying horse up the bank he was cool, and when I screamed at him, he was too big or too busy to notice it. Perhaps it takes a devil of a temper to do things like that when they have to be done; he never wasted any of it sputtering around. All things he saw largely and men the same way, but if anyone handled him in a mean and petty way, he became what he would have called "ugly" and he was slow, when once deeply angry, to forgive. It was part of my content, wherever we went, to see him shoulder his job and take whatever blame went with it, and blame there is sure to be. Men in the Far West working for men in the cities of the East are exposed on a wide area of possible misunderstanding; they have to decide and decide quickly — they make mistakes, but they do not, if they are men, whine or sidestep when the blame follows the failure. And I particularly liked his way of choosing his subordinates and standing by them. His boys all loved him; almost every one of them who is not dead is counted a lifelong friend. I speak as if we were all dead — and in effect we are. No one could see in us now what we were then, or what we fancy that we were. All the above is merely to explain what I mean by the sort of man it was safe to go to Leadville with; it would have been a regrettable experience to have gone there, that summer, with some men.

AT THE FOOT OF THE PASS.

16

The Leadville scene, when it wasn't snowing or sleeting or preparing to do both, was dominated by a sky of so dark and pure and haughty a blue that "firmament" was the only name for it. Beneath that floor of heaven sat those Mighty Ones in a great convocation, those summits which turn the waters of the continent east and west. At sunrise or sunset, beholding their faces, you understood Ruskin's theory of the essential connection between spirituality and color: such rose, such blue and amethyst and topaz and purple! They were like great altarpieces (and often as unregarded) set up before the eyes of those who burrowed in gulches and built cabins on ditch walks. Indiscriminate houses dropped here or there did not count, nor smoking chimneys of smelters, nor brass bands every evening, if you lived far enough from the streets they paraded to get the sound softened with other sounds of the human surf beating on the flanks of those gulches.

A.'s first location for our cabin was jumped by a professional in that line of business who stood him off the ground with a shotgun. A. laughed at him and went back to the real-estate office where the lots were for sale and chose another and, as it turned out, a better one.[1] The land had not been paid for — even if it had, I trust he would not have wasted blood on a Leadville cabin site. . . . But there seems to have been this one jumper and he pursued his avocation too long. One evening, in

[1] A modern book about Leadville states: "Up on Capitol Hill at 216 West Eighth Street lived the authoress, Mary Hallock Foote." Don L. Griswold and Jean Harvey Griswold, *The Carbonate Camp Called Leadville* (Denver, 1951), p. 249.

The Leadville cabin

the face of one of those great, silencing sunsets, as we watched it from our cabin porch — down in the town where lights pricked through the twilight, this man, and a holdup thief whom the town was equally tired of, were at that moment being lynched by hanging in front of the prison door. A. knew it as he stood there beside me, but he did not speak of it — he never spoke of it till years after.[2] He saw no reason why a woman who had no business down there should break into that life which twilight covered, or question what was going on in those houses whose lights from our distance looked not unworthy neighbors of the stars. If I had any philanthropic or social duties in Leadville that summer, I have to confess that I wasn't even conscious of them. I went on with my little job — those engravers' blocks to cover with drawings — and my husband went on with his. For company he brought to the cabin such men as he saw fit, measured by his own standards, together with those between whom and ourselves there had been links in the past. And in that odd little room, in a place which, the year before, had been nowhere, we had guests who would have been distinguished anywhere — this being one of the well-known compensations which offset the perpetual changes and general unrest of the life of an engineer in the field.

Our cabin was built of round logs at a dollar apiece, and they were not very long logs either. It was all in one room, lined with building paper which had an oak-grained side and a reverse of dark brown; one width of the brown we used as a

[2] Two separate but similar episodes seem to have become confused with one another in retrospect. In August 1879 a crowd seized an alleged thief, put a rope around his neck, and twice lifted him off the ground by the rope, before being persuaded to turn the man over to the sheriff. This must be the episode of which Mary Hallock Foote is speaking, for the actual lynching of the claim-jumper and the thief took place on November 20, 1879, shortly after Mrs. Foote had left for the East. (She was in Chicago by November 12.) See Griswold and Griswold, *The Carbonate Camp Called Leadville*, pp. 154-56, 170-77. But Mary Hallock Foote knew about the episode soon after she had returned to Milton, for a letter to Helena Gilder from there, apparently written on December 19, 1879, mentions the lynching.

wainscot, and the walls were covered with the oak side put on like wallpaper, and where the edges joined, pine strips painted black were nailed over them with an effect of paneling. The open-beamed ceiling to the ridge pole was papered between the unbarked log rafters, like the walls. So our color scheme matched the woods and on this quiet background we added pinks and blues and greens by pinning up the Geological Survey's maps of the Fortieth Parallel.[3] When the geologists came out and were our guests, they stared around and laughed to see this frivolous use their brains and research had been put to: James Hague insisted that geology had never been turned to better account! They mocked each other gaily of the impertinence which they considered peculiarly feminine (it was in fact my own idea) to stick up Old Silurian and the Tertiary deposits for the sake of their pretty colors! We had no chimney that year: a man tempts fortune who builds him a chimney. There was no kitchen; there was no bedroom — the woman went to work on her curtains again and made a sort of drapery for her couch, which was called the bedroom, with hangings of printed calico bought at Daniel and Fisher's. They had purple velvet riding habits on show in their windows and pink silk peignoirs, but the choice in calico was very limited.

We had an iron fireplace, more homelike to sit by than a stove. The man broiled steak and made coffee on its coals before breakfast: he was a much better cook than his wife and he had the hardy unspoiled habits of a good camp mate. He leapt out half-dressed in the cold austere mornings and filled his pails with snow water from the ditch — let it not be confused with anything sluggish or muddy: it shot by us like something

[3] The Fortieth Parallel Survey, which Clarence King headed from its birth in 1867 until it finished its work in 1878, was one of the most successful of the federal government's scientific studies of the American West. Among the distinguished geologists who served with it were James D. Hague and his younger brother Arnold, Samuel F. Emmons, and King himself — all New Englanders from Harvard or Yale and all figures in these reminiscences. Richard A. Bartlett, *Great Surveys of the American West* (Norman, Okla., 1962), pp. 141-215.

chased, like the snow-born Arethusa, but I suppose there was not much it could escape after it reached the town. The woman washed up and tidied up after breakfast and lunched by herself out of paper bags and marmalade pots, and the man by himself, bolting his food on horseback after capturing it wherever he could find it, or going without. And we dined at the Clarendon with the mob — in a bedlam of male voices, a wild clatter of dishes, orders shouted, waiters rushing madly from table to table with heaped trays poised above their heads; now and then one came down with a crash. We smiled at each other and consumed our food.

In this uproar the Jacksons dined with us one evening; Helen Hunt and her husband.[4] He had a mining man's interest in Leadville, she was there for the spectacle. By sinking our voices below the storm key of sound and speaking almost in each other's faces we managed to communicate; she had a speaking face and a wonderful eye for meeting another human eye. She assured us earnestly — she warned us — that we could not stay; the place was too unnatural. Grass would not grow there and cats could not live. We smiled: we were not cats — nor grass, as yet! We were at that well-known phase of the altitude fever when the hopeful ones are sure that they are to be the exceptions — Leadville agreed with us, we said. In the back of my mind always, however, was a secret quake when I thought of our little boy.

It was through the Gilders "H.H." had heard that we were there. She had been told in town that ours was the only cabin on the ditch. She had walked out by herself and knocked at our

4 Helen Maria Fiske Hunt Jackson (1830-85), who often published under the initials "H.H.," was a schoolmate and lifelong friend of Emily Dickinson. After the deaths of her first husband, Edward B. Hunt, and two children, she became a professional writer, best known today for two books inspired by mistreatment of the Indians, *A Century of Dishonor* (1881) and *Ramona* (1884). Her second marriage, in 1875, was to William S. Jackson, a Colorado financier, promoter, and railway man. Thereafter she made her home in Colorado Springs. A letter from Mary Hallock Foote, Leadville, August 22, 1879, to Helena Gilder describes Helen Hunt Jackson's visit.

door. It opened directly into the only room we had, where I happened to be dressing at the time; the day was fine and I set out a chair for my unknown guest and asked her to wait a few moments — fancy asking Helen Hunt to wait on one's porch! But I left the door ajar and we chatted through the opening while I clothed myself. I might have gone behind my bed-curtains, but there was no light there to "do one's hair" — also my dressing tools were all outside. . . . Well! When I did open the door and took a good look at my visitor, if I hadn't guessed it already, I should have known by her face that she was the only one of her kind in America. She had waited to introduce herself till we were on a common level, as to clothing at least.

We were supposed to have about one month of summer in Leadville, but I don't know when it could be said to begin. A great soft snowfall was dumped on us out of a clear sky on the ninth of June — but about this time the Geological Survey made camp in the woods back of the cabin, and S. F. Emmons and his chief topographer Wilson, and others of their mess, became our frequent visitors.[5] Emmons wore riding clothes of Indian-tanned buckskin made by his London tailor; his tall, conspicuous figure in these beautiful white buckskins was a most agreeable sight whenever he loomed in the doorway of the cabin. He was always good tempered, always imperturbable; he prowled about all summer doing important things silently; when he talked he said little about his work, but what he did that year and in the summer following is now embodied in a

---

[5] Samuel F. Emmons (1841-1911) was educated at Harvard, the École des Mines in Paris, and the Royal Mining Academy in Saxony, before joining the Fortieth Parallel Survey. When the United States Geological Survey was created by Congress in 1879, with Clarence King as its first director, King at once sent Emmons to Denver and Leadville, with A. D. Wilson, late of the Fortieth Parallel Survey, as his topographer. Emmons' work at Leadville has been called epochal, because of its identification and explanation of the Leadville deposits. See Paul, *Mining Frontiers*, pp. 130-31. Emmons' first marriage, to Waltha Anita Steeves, ended in divorce, after a difficult experience; his second was to Sophie Dallas Markoe of Washington, D.C., in 1889, but she died in 1896. His third marriage, in 1903, was to Suzanne Earle Ogden-Jones.

book with a long title, usually spoken of as "Emmons's book," which grows steadily more valuable with time, I am told.

He was as fond of people as he was of rocks, which is saying much for an eminent geologist, and he was never weary of doing kind things for his friends. You might have but a small place in his life, but he never forgot you were there. His first marriage was a tragical failure — he bore its trials with great patience and dignity; then Miss Sophie Markoe of Washington rewarded him and made his home delightful to him and to his friends. But she died, a sweet woman of the southern before-the-war type, the old Washington set was her background — and, spoiled for loneliness by her memory, he married again, another lovely woman we were told. Men less susceptible to sympathy sometimes smiled at these frank domestic adventures of his; they were an essential part of that kindness and humanness in him that we all found so pleasant and dependable. He could not have lived without a home in which he might devote himself to a woman's happiness.

He was tall, spare, rather harsh featured but distinguished looking, a somewhat hawklike profile deficient in chin, black hair, marked eyebrows, an open-air color on his thin cheekbones. When he rode he was one with his horse and went cogitating along, rolling cigarettes and lighting them with the flint and steel in a little silver box that he always carried. His whole attitude towards Leadville and the life there was so different from the feverish states of mind around us, it made his visits a great rest. His interest was wholly scientific and theoretical, yet it pleased him to know that his big book was used as a guide by the gold seekers, even the practical miners consulting it.

We reached the height of our preposterous social brilliance that summer in Leadville when Clarence King arrived from Washington with members of the Land Commission in tow — huge Tom Donaldson being one of them. "He's such a unanimous cuss," King said of him.[6] To Hague and Emmons, widowed of their clubs, it meant delight of battle with one's peers which always marked the joining of talk in that rare group of friends. In the *Education*, Henry Adams, who probably knew King better than any of them, says: "No other young American approached him for the combination of chances — physical energy, social standing, mental scope and training, wit, geniality, and science, that seemed superlatively American and irresistibly strong."[7] This described King in 1871. In 1879 he had scored a great scientific and personal triumph in the passing by Congress of a bill uniting the two surveys under himself as director; not that he cared for the office, he was enjoying his powers as an organizer. Later, years later, Adams says of his friend's fortunes bitterly: "The result of twenty years' effort proved that the theory of scientific education failed where most theory fails — for want of money."[8]

An appointment to the Geological Survey under such men as King chose to head his divisions was a position any young man might have coveted for the sake of "scientific education," but if he had a family to support on the Survey's salaries, he could scarcely afford the honor. There was a proud wife in the cabin when such an appointment came to her man, and there was no thought of refusing it then, but she asked herself secretly, "How are we going to live on both sides of the continent

---

[6] Clarence King (1842-1901), a product of Yale and of experience with the famous California Geological Survey before he conceived the Fortieth Parallel Survey, was at this time serving in the dual capacity of director of the U. S. Geological Survey and expert member of a Public Lands Commission set up by Congress in 1879 to investigate the public lands and land laws. Thomas Donaldson (1843-98), who held many government positions in his very useful lifetime, served with the Commission and edited its great compilation of documents. For this visit, see Introduction, p. 19. A letter from Mary Hallock Foote, Leadville, August 22, 1879, to Helena Gilder described King as being very "agreeable," as "brilliant" as she had expected, but more gentle, and somewhat like her friend Nadal (concerning whom, see pp. 81-82). A subsequent letter to Helena, dated Leadville, September 8, 1879, described King as "charming."

[7] Henry Adams, *The Education of Henry Adams* (Boston and New York, 1918), p. 346.

[8] Ibid.

— winters to be spent in Washington — when it seems difficult enough to live first on one side and then on the other?" It
was the company "we" desired to keep, and professionally it
seemed quite a rise from running ditch lines under George
Hearst or "Sam" McMasters.[9] We could see that J. D. [Hague]
was pleased, and whenever he liked what we did we were apt
to think we were on the right track.

James Hague was in Leadville during the greater part of
that summer examining mines for eastern investors. We knew
of course how he and Mary lived: her health would not have
permitted her to hike about with her husband, even if she had
not had two children to consider. (They had left Peddie in
England and brought back with them a German governess.)
The more his affairs prospered, the less they could see of each
other. His office now was in New York, their home was in
Orange, N. J., and he was in Leadville! It always amused him
to look on at our fortuitous housekeeping, the casual way in
which we set up our family lares. Nothing casual would have
suited him in his own homes, but he was a charming guest in
ours — never more so than that summer in the cabin on the
ditch.

One Sunday morning a plain but agreeable-looking person
called on us who introduced himself as W. S. Ward, manager
of the Evening Star Mine, a rising star of prosperity in the
camp, already making a name for itself.[10] Its backers in New

---

9 Superintendent of the Homestake Mine in the Black Hills. See above, p. 161. A
letter from Mary Hallock Foote, Leadville, August 22, 1879, to Helena Gilder
explains that Clarence King had hired Arthur as a "mining geologist" on the
staff of the U.S. Geological Survey, and Arthur had gone off with A. D. Wilson,
presumably under Emmons' direction.

10 William S. Ward, born 1844, a graduate of Princeton and the Columbia School
of Mines, and a veteran of ten years in the U.S. Assay Office in New York,
came to Leadville in 1879 to take charge of the Evening Star, which he developed into a very profitable mine. Griswold and Griswold, *Carbonate Camp*,
p. 238. Mary Hallock Foote, in a letter to Helena Gilder, dated Leadville, September 8, 1879, described Ward as a cheerful, refined, "clean-souled" man who
"wears wonderfully well" and had known Richard Gilder in New York.

York were Watson Bradley Dickerman and his friends. He appraised us with a very keen blue eye — took in not only the beauty but the commercial possibilities of our situation: the Ditch Walk, he predicted, would in another year be the "fashionable residence quarter," and he advised us to lose no time but corral all the lots on it not already bought up, and sell only to our friends. It was excellent advice, but we had not the necessary funds just then to act upon it — he had. He bought up the whole neighborhood, so to speak, and became himself our first neighbor. And a very good one he proved to be.

His house was no cabin — I believe he gave it a name: "Cloud-rift Cottage" or something like that — it was ready in time to welcome as its first guests Mr. and Mrs. Dickerman, when they came out from New York.[11] . . . She was then in the flower of her beauty, Martha Dickerman, and she was as lovely as she looked. Of all places on earth to meet one like her with her tea-rose coloring and her "sweet eyes" — there she was, one summer morning, on the Ditch Walk, with those crazy gulches below her and those solemn mountains above, turned out as New York can do it, spick and span, to begin the day. (Bless her — as she blessed others — from her rising up to her lying down at night!) It was a friendship between us without a break, from that summer morning to her death; our lives never ran parallel, they were as different as two women's lives could be, but the links so intangible between us held, mainly through her own untiring thoughtfulness of others. . . . How we used to laugh together over her first sight of my husband — the way *he* was "turned out!" — dashing out of the little cabin next door in "pants" and undershirt before breakfast and stooping from the bridge plank, which was opposite her bed-

---

[11] Watson B. Dickerman was cofounder, in 1869, of the banking firm of Dominick & Dickerman, president of the Evening Star Mining Co., and presently of the Morning Star Consolidated Mining Co., the Norfolk and Southern Railroad, and in 1890-91 president of the New York Stock Exchange. He was born in Connecticut in 1846 and married in 1869.

room window, to scoop his morning pailfuls from the ditch! And she was clever enough to have noticed that he scooped with and not against the current.

After the Dickermans went east, Mr. Ward proposed that we unite our housekeeping at mealtimes; otherwise, that we mess with him in his bigger house which had everything ours waited for, including a cook. "Jane" was an old family standby sent out by the Dickermans, who was almost too much of a treasure for one man in Leadville to keep all to himself. So the wild Clarendon struggle for food we left behind with the things of youth, and very soon we became pampered and particular. In view of the briefness of our summer, Mr. Ward built a covered walk joining his piazza with our porch, and now if we woke up in a snow squall, the protected woman could go in to breakfast without her galoshes. Winter things were not put away in Leadville; we never knew what a day or a night might bring forth in the way of weather.

Eastern investors and promoters were now coming fast, following the geologists and experts: wives and an occasional daughter began to be seen. Our neighbor, now that he had a chaperon handy, could ask young ladies to dine with him. One might behold almost any day our Leadville cavaliers dashing through the woods beside tailored habits which spelled Chicago if not New York. I did very little dashing myself that year — my cavalier was riding a white mule in pursuit of knowledge (and a living) under Emmons. But our evenings in the cabin were gay with the finest sort of company. "What do you *do* with all those people," my mother asked, in one of her letters, "when you have only five chairs!" Five were more than enough to accommodate all the ceremonious guests we ever had — the others were just from campfire seats themselves and had no quarrel with the floor if necessary; or they were escaping boyishly from a hotel bedroom in the town. The altitude did, I suppose, go to our heads a little like wine, if one had a head (and a heart) for altitudes at all. When Rossiter Raymond[12] went back to New York, after his visit, to report on the Pittsburg and Chrysolite mines, he found the city full of grippe and became one of the victims himself; whereupon he sent us this merry little rueful "roofer."

> Let princes live and sneeze in their palaces of ease,
> Let colds and influenzas plague the rich,
> But give to me instead, a well-ventilated head
> In a little log cabin on the Ditch!

But the Leadville summer was soon over. The birds of passage flocked east again. Ross Raymond's report brought him to grief and his clients to worse grief. J. D. [Hague] came out and made his own examination of the Pittsburg and a second report which wiped out several of Raymond's "suppositious millions," as he rather airily called them. He [Raymond] took the blow to his reputation gallantly, in fact audaciously — Leadville "knocked" a good many reputations as well as a good many fortunes. There were those who thought Raymond rather too versatile, too brilliant and temperamental for a scientific investigator. But he was a man of many sides; a wit, an orator, an occasional poet, one of a talented family who mus-

---

[12] Rossiter W. Raymond (1840-1918), who was the single most influential person in shaping the development of mining engineering into a respected profession, was well known to Arthur and Mary Hallock Foote, because their lives so often intersected. He graduated from Brooklyn Polytechnic Institute and was very active for many years in Henry Ward Beecher's Plymouth Church. He studied at Heidelberg, Munich, and the Royal Mining Academy at Freiberg. He was a consultant to Cooper, Hewitt & Co., both in their coal and iron mines and in the management of Cooper Union, where Raymond often lectured. In 1867 he began his long career as editor of what presently was retitled the *Engineering and Mining Journal*, and from 1868-76 was U.S. Commissioner of Mining Statistics and thus editor of a notable series of annual reports on mining. He was a founder of the American Institute of Mining Engineers in 1871, its president from 1872-75, its secretary from 1884-1911, and editor of its *Transactions*.

tered among them an astonishing array of gifts. He was a rapid-fire gun but not perhaps a great gun.[13]

When J. D. went east that year for the last time, his sister-in-law went with him to spend the winter on the Hudson. . . . We had five or six hours to wait in Chicago, and it happened to be the day [November 12, 1879] of Grant's reception by the Army of the Northwest to welcome its old chief home, covered with glory after his royal progress around the world. The congestion in the streets and at every hotel in the city was appalling. James managed to secure to my use for two hours a room at the Palmer House bespoken by persons who had not yet arrived. But they did arrive while the interloper was hurriedly scrambling her things together to depart, and they eyed her with much disfavor. At the Palmer House there was a grand gathering of notables and we saw the beginning of the show before our train went out. This was my one chance view of General Grant, then at the height of his fame. That winter he took a house in New York and fell into the toils of Ferdinand Ward, the "Little Napoleon of Wall Street." He was a younger brother of W. S. [Ward], but a very different man — as different, to stretch a comparison, as Wilkes from Edwin Booth. "Ferd" Ward was the assassin of Grant's reputation; and the figure of the old hero in his last years paying his debit to inex-

[13] Both the Little Pittsburg and Chrysolite mines were developed too rapidly, too speculatively, and probably with an intent to deceive. Rossiter Raymond unwittingly aided the boom in stocks of both mines by his unjustifiably optimistic reports. His report on the Little Pittsburg was advertised as saying that the mine would yield $2,000,000. By contrast, after careful inspection of the mine in April 1879, James Hague telegraphed his clients in New York that "I valued the property at $500,000 — considered intrinsically and independently of stock operations." Similarly, at a time when the Chrysolite company was publishing enthusiastic reports about their mine by Raymond, Hague was writing privately to Emmons (July 25, 1880), "Chrysolite . . . is going to disappoint many people who bought at high figures. It is very weak." Hague Papers, Huntington Library. In 1880 the public not only lost faith in both mines, but temporarily lost confidence in all Leadville mines, in the belief that all were dishonestly managed.

perience and misplaced faith was tragedy enough to grip the heart of the world.[14] He was never held in higher honor than when day after day he sat at his task, a dying man using his last strength to retrieve his name and fortune for his children.

When we dined with the Dickermans that winter — or spring, perhaps it was, when A. came east again — the place plates were Royal Worcester and Mrs. Dickerman remarked they were a present from Ferd Ward. A year later I don't think she would have mentioned him — perhaps she would not have used the plates! Their sympathy with W. S. would have kept them silent, in bonds to that friendship, but men like James Hague were mercilessly outspoken as to those sensational pranks in Wall Street.

That winter I worked hard and took exercise towards dusk, walking the long path in the garden. As a child I had been smiled at for going off alone from the depths of a story and walking off the excitement of it in the open. This was probably the same sort of impulse, only now the make-believe was my own. . . . The first fruit of those walks and thoughts was a Quaker story called "Friend Barton's 'Concern.' "[15] And since I am so bitter about other people's Quaker stories, let me confess that my own first attempt fared little better with family critics of the blood. It dealt with an early specimen of the girl of today with a will and a mind of her own; but my father said no daughter of a Friend preacher in 1812 would have been pert enough to question her father's choice when it came to a conflict between family claims and the call of the Inner Spirit.

[14] Ferdinand Ward, a plausible, highly ingenious, conscienceless speculator, dragged down General Grant and Grant's son in the dramatic failure of the firm of Grant & Ward in 1884, a failure that left the general heavily in debt and with no resources save the nation's affection for him and his own determination. Mary Hallock Foote and her husband had become well acquainted with this son of the former president, U. S. Grant, Jr., when the latter was visiting W. S. Ward at Leadville in 1879.

[15] Mary Hallock Foote's memory must have confused two successive winters, for "Friend Barton's 'Concern' " was published in July 1879. Scribner's Monthly, 18 (July 1879), 334-50.

Quaker families were proud to have produced a preacher — they would not have tied him to the plow even if only a daughter were left in his place. Women preachers left their homes and young children — what were farms and mills and crops! I could not dispute the point, but if I had acted on it there would have been no story! I sent it as a thing of mere barter and sale to the editors who took it, and I took my cheque.

When the story came out it was amusing to see how the friends of the family reacted to the unwonted and rather shocking exposure, the exploitation in print of the faith of our common ancestors. There were two little maiden ladies of Marlborough Village, Cousin Mercy and Cousin Margaret Townsend, who had become Episcopalians but retained a Quaker consciousness which fluttered a little when the word was carelessly used. They were exceedingly dainty and "particular" and not without a touch of timid snobbishness. Cousin Mercy thought the picture of destitution the story gave was exaggerated: "I don't think the Friends were ever so reduced as that; they almost always had a *little* something to depend on!"

I am sure our church cousins, though they thought it hardly respectable to have nothing "to depend on," were not wedded to the things of this world. Particular as they were about their own appearance, they were not extreme to mark what was done amiss by others, especially the young. One day, when I was about eight years old, I was sent upstairs to dress "in a hurry" to go with father to call on the Townsend cousins and their father, about his own age, who had retired from business and lived on a modest income, nursing a few acres of garden and pasture. I loved to go there; the house and all about it were so finished and at rest and they had such pretty "things," different from our things. We were asked to stay to tea, and all the way home I was in a dream of content. But the instant mother's eye fell on me the truth was made plain: I had changed only one shoe and stocking — my feet were not a pair! And these little ladies of Marlborough had contrived to appear as if they had not seen: there had not been a spot on the sun of my happiness. I always did like those of our kin who went into the [Episcopal] Church; the combination appealed to one's "romantic" tendencies towards traditional forms and ceremonies, and what Friends termed reproachfully the "Outward comeliness which may rob the Inner Spirit" if not guarded against.

I don't dare to say, and I don't know, what we believed, as a family with little children to bring up, on the subject of prayer. Robert Barclay in his Eleventh Proposition concerning Worship says: "as to the outward signification thereof in Prayers, Praises or Preachings, we ought not to do it in our own will, where and when we will; but where and when we are moved thereunto by the stirring and secret Inspiration of the Spirit of God in our hearts; which God heareth and accepteth of, and is never wanting to move us thereunto, when need is, of which he himself is the alone proper Judge." [16] . . . But at three years old, the secret inspirations of the Spirit may be assisted by an impulse communicated from another spirit and supplied with a few words in common human use. I should have been extremely shy of anyone in the room with us, especially my father, when hearing my little son say his "God bless" at bedtime — nevertheless he did say it, and his superstitious mother taught him to add after his father's name the words, "and bring him home safe and well" — Milton being still the only place I could call home. There came a night, towards the end of February, when I said to him, "Daddy is in New York. Tomorrow night he will be here." We slept in grandmother's room that winter, Boykin's crib beside the wide four-poster where her nightcapped head had reposed for fifty years. There was the same hard-coal fire in the grate, the same iron saucepan on the hearth with warm water for a little boy's face and hands. He was ready for bed, but when he said his prayer, the last words, "and bring him home safe and well," were omitted.

16 Barclay, *Apology*, p. 231.

"Why was that," I asked? The logical answer was, "He *did* bring him — you said he is coming home." Why go on re-iterating a prayer already answered — why keep hurrying God and insisting, even to the last few miles!

As a matter of fact, never had his father more needed pray-ers for his safety than on that day of his homecoming, with the very shore in sight, where we were waiting confident he would be with us in an hour. . . . It was a day of east wind and drizzl-ing rain, like the day when we were married. Milton Ferry was a small way station;[17] there was no waiting room, nor any-one in attendance. Arthur had watched the river all the way up from Fishkill where people were crossing on the ice. The train conductor had no advice to give except "follow the tracks." The broken cakes of ice tumbled up near shore showed ample thickness; he followed the tracks out to the middle of the river, where he came to the first wide opening, and crossed it on a bridge of fresh black ice; it bent beneath his weight and water rose where he had stepped. The shores on either side were deserted; there was no one to hear his call, if he should need help. To go back was more dangerous than to keep on; the same bridge would not have borne his weight again. He crossed chasm after chasm, some of them thirty feet across, treading light and stepping fast. It was the sort of thing a man is "by with" before he realizes his danger, but he was in a cold sweat when he reached the solid ice that lined the Milton shore. There was no one to meet him; he carried his own suit-case up the hill, a happy man.

About half an hour after he reached the house, John Sher-man came in and was surprised to find him there. . . . "How did you get across?" he asked. . . . "Walked," said A. smiling. "Walked! but the river is clear, man! I've just come from the landing and the ice has gone out." A. might have seen it go out, if he had looked back from the top of the hill, and have

---

[17] Contemporary guidebooks explain that the Hudson River Railroad had a station opposite Milton from "whence a traveler may be set across by boatmen."

fancied himself going out with it in mid-channel, along with the crows and other black spots just visible from shore on the lonely waste of ice.

We said some words that night, Boy and his mother, which had to be said whether God cared or not. Silence and the voice of the Inner Spirit are the deeper testimonies perhaps, but there are times when they don't seem to "get you anywhere."

17

W<small>E WERE</small> open like others, of course, to the influence of salaries, but it was really the cabin at Leadville that lured us back there: the plans we had made to build on bedrooms and a kitchen wing and a stone chimney going up against the gable. We saw ourselves unpacking in a house of our own the boxes we packed at New Almaden with nowhere to go, and no job in sight. "He" left it to me: "Shall it be the [U.S. Geological] Survey or the mines?" I envisioned nothing connected with mines — I saw ourselves and little son in the cabin on the ditch.

If Arthur had stuck to the Survey he would have been with the California Division that winter, in the High Sierras. I should have stayed in the East or taken Boykin across alone and found a perch as near him as possible, perhaps in the Napa Valley. "What could be better than a little house in the Napa Valley?" Clarence King had suggested encouragingly. I know those valleys now — very lovely, but scenery is not everything; for a homebred woman, husbandless and divorced from her family and friends, pretty lonely! King was distributing these little homes with his genial smile — they had to be very small, on the salaries his appropriation allowed. Most of the Survey men were unmarried or, like Emmons, possessed of private means to make them independent.

But Arthur needed no urging: he was well satisfied to go back, though he must have known that he was in for a heap of trouble, as he would have put it. There is always trouble in the mining business; there is trouble in every business. It is only the men of theory who can do as Emmons did at Leadville, commune with Nature and enter into the counsels of Creation with souls at peace. *He* did not worry about the "outfit" at the Adelaide Mine when he went poking up Stray Horse Gulch; he could question the rocks which speak what is true and do not interrupt.

But young Fisher, Arthur's clerk at the Adelaide mine[1] at that time, had orders to eject a certain lady from the miners' boardinghouse, which she claimed it was her privilege to "run," and get her and all her possessions off the company's ground, and she was a person who did not always speak the truth and who did interrupt. A. had fired all her friends on the payroll — the whole place was to be cleaned out of its human messiness, and it was an unco [strange] job for those two young men, one with an unadulterated Boston accent whose middle name was Bowditch, the other a son of that pillar of the church on Guilford Green, old "Cunnel Foote." It had to be done or the new management would be discredited at the start. It took a boyish threat of dynamite to move the lady from her position, and if she had been clever or game enough to "call" his bluff, A. would have been in a queer fix himself. The success of that form of persuasion is all in the eye: Fisher had a fiery-cold blue eye.

This was the first act: the lady took refuge with her faithful knights of the Highland Chief [2] hard by; anonymous letters containing the usual warnings were hurled at our men through the mails. The shortest road to the Adelaide was by way of the one narrow street of the Highland Chief: to have

[1] While Arthur assumed responsibility for several different mines during this second stay at Leadville, his principal job was as manager of the Adelaide Consolidated Silver Mining & Smelting Co., which according to the *Colorado Directory of Mines* (Denver, 1879) had its headquarters at Leadville and Washington, D.C., and included among its trustees Senator John P. Jones of Nevada, the veteran Comstock mining man. It adjoined the Argentine mine, with which it presently had a fierce dispute.

[2] The Highland Chief mine, a consolidation of four claims, with most of its shares of stock sold in New York, was doing well by processing a large volume of low-grade ore.

gone around would have been to notice those threats. It was both theory and practice to ride at ease, lounging through the hostile camp, with a pistol ready. This was the absurd side of life in Leadville which made them all seem boys together; that the methods of schoolboys and savages should be the ones these grown men were obliged to use, who were not savages nor excited nor warlike nor angry with anyone. The Highland Chief continued to breathe fire and slaughter, but it helped to keep the actual peace that our men were known to be quick and convincing shots with a revolver.

The Mike and Star meantime,[3] our other baby, had nothing in sight but expenses and good indications, as they were called. This stage of infancy in mines does not exhilarate the owners much, and the Adelaide, although it was called a mine, would have been one of those described as "too poor to pay, too rich to quit." The last straw was stealing, on the part of a neighbor across the gulch, from our only ore-bearing ground. Such a neighbor we had in the Argentine Mine. This, as far as I remember, was the general situation about the time we went back, or possibly the stealing had not yet begun.

Our owners were New York men, in Wall Street most of them. We went down from Milton — Arthur to confer with his people, I to go with him to the pretty dinners they gave us, he to go with me to the little companies our old friends were giving for us both. All that time was flooded with gay talk. Nobody feared the future.

From New York we went on to Guilford and talked everything over with the family there: the wise, placid mother in her black dress, with the fold of gauze over her delicate old head and the soft, grayish curls in front, saying little, comprehending everything, surprised at nothing! At Nutplains near Guilford, the other family homestead, we seduced a young niece of Arthur's into going back with us to Leadville, the ad-

---

[3] The Mike and the Star Gurnee were listed as mines under Foote's care. Griswold and Griswold, *Carbonate Camp*, p. 189.

venture for her (she was scarcely nineteen), for us the help
and company she would be, especially with an active little boy
to watch over and the ditch running close by our door.[4] They
are always ready for adventures, those little New England
nuns, cold-mannered, self-effacing, but doing such a number
of things so remarkably well. . . . So that was fixed, and on the
strength of Lily Foote I ventured to take on myself another
book contract, the most preposterous one yet. Imagine illustrating *Lucile* for an edition de luxe in Leadville — I who had
never been abroad in my life and didn't know even what sort
of chairs they sat on at European watering places! (Where was
it those highly sophisticated Victorian lovers met — to part?)
But it wasn't so ingenuous of me as it was sheer commercial.
Publishers perhaps are commercial too: it could not have been
in the interests of pure art that my well-known House was
issuing an expensive holiday edition of *Lucile*. They probably
knew something about the book market.[5]

Milton was all fruit blossoms and May winds when we said
good-bye. A belated gift from one of the aunties had been
added at the last moment to our luggage; one of those huge
down puffs which lie at the foot of the bed in cold country-
houses and are pulled up to one's chin when required — it
looked queer to take such a thing with us in the month of May,
but we rolled it small and crowded it into our shawl straps and
it saved our little boy an illness, I believe, for we arrived at the
end of the track in a howling blizzard and we had to keep right
on. Sam Clark was there to meet us and we had thirty-five
miles to drive. The railroad had advanced that far towards
Leadville. We bundled little son into this down thing and his
father held him in his arms, taking a look at him now and then

---

4 Lily Gillette Foote was the daughter of Arthur's brother Andrew Ward Foote,
  "a farmer of the well-read New England type," as the family genealogy book
  puts it (Foote, *Foote Family*, p. 336). Since Lily was born March 2, 1860, she
  must have been twenty, not "scarcely nineteen."

5 *Lucile* was a narrative poem by "Owen Meredith," the pseudonym of Edward
  Robert Bulwer-Lytton, first earl of Lytton. This edition was published in
  September 1881.

to see that he did not smother. How Sam could see to drive was his affair — we got through. We stood Boykin on his feet in the cabin sitting room; the clumsy wrap fell off — we gazed at him in rapture to see him safe there, rosy and undisturbed. He and his cousin Lily had taken their first blizzard precisely alike, smiling and saying nothing. He steadied himself on his feet and looked up at the raftered ceiling — not much like grandfather's house! "They have logs on the walls at Leadville" was his general observation.

The freight boxes arrived and we laughed and crowed over the old things as we set them up in their new places. The chimney had a high mantel and a face of rough gray stone and a fireplace so big that our Irish mason pronounced, when it was finished, gazing up in it, "Ye'll not have a bit o' hate in the house." We took down the curtains of the false bedroom which James Hague always referred to as "upstairs," and the big foreroom was all in one. We built bookshelves into the recess on one side of the chimney, the door into my new bedroom opened from the other. But the most popular feature of the room was a hammock slung across one end cornerwise where one could read and keep warm; where one's man could smoke in the evenings and little son take his daily nap while his mother went on with her desk work and Cousin Lily went down town to do errands; we didn't go far from the Ditch Walk — there was no strolling through the woods in Leadville. We lived on the crust of much that lay beneath. But we thought we were so lucky and so happy! Soon we should be having our meals under our own roof; for neighbor Ward had just married, in Chicago, one of the riding-habit young ladies I had chaperoned the summer before. He did not want us now as table-boarders.[6]

---

[6] A letter from Mary Hallock Foote to Helena Gilder, Milton, apparently December 19, 1879, described this lady, Kitty Ward, as "a handsome girl of the (I s'd fancy) English countryhouse style. Admirable on horseback — beautiful hands and feet and head — thorough-bred looking." Descendant of distinguished New England stock, Kitty Ward was in Leadville because her father owned the Little Giant mine.

We were finishing off our kitchen, hurrying to get ourselves out of the way of the bride's homecoming, when a crisis struck us where we might have expected, which our doctor at home indeed had warned us of. Those old sleeping germs our little boy had left in his system which he had brought with him from peaceful Milton, from his grandfather's ponds, woke up in the strange mountain heights and made a last stand which brought him pretty low as a battleground. It was not the fever alone but the bronchial inflammation that set in with it. And we had not our home doctor now, nor Aunt Bessie in the night watches. Lily would have watched, but she was doing other things, and I could not have slept — I was too rattled and convulsed with fear. It wasn't the illness so much as the strange climate and the strange doctor that tormented me. There was no fault to find with Dr. D'Avignon[7] personally, but his doses of mercury and jalap affected me very much like the methods of a Sioux medicine man. My nerves were undone for the rest of the summer and my sleep destroyed by the panic-terrors of that illness.

It was a late spring even for Leadville, the weather diabolical. Storm upon storm came howling over us and drove the snow in under our new doors, where it lay unmelted all night even with a fire kept up, in the room where my little boy was ill; taking fresh cold would have meant pneumonia, and with the doctor we had I knew we should lose him. A. was obliged to leave us, on one of his mountain trips, and good old Sam Clark came and slept on a cot in the sitting room, in case of need. He couldn't have been called company for he never said anything — he couldn't have talked, as Fisher talked, a steady stream of anecdote and personal experience; he wasn't enough of an egoist for that, but he did whatever was required of him in sober earnest and was not amusing but he was faithful. He was a chunk of Vermont granite, which can take noble shapes under the right chisel of fate and all the necessary polish —

---

7 Dr. Frederick D'Avignon, described in an 1893 publication as "a genial and generous gentleman, liberal in his ideas."

some people don't care for polished granite. I could not help speculating a little about him and Lily — they were not of the same class in their generation quite, but Sam had come of good blood, the Men of Grants, makers of history. . . . They were a pair, when it came to valiant, impenetrable reserve.

How many different types of young Americans we met — I often take account of them, all so true to their own backgrounds, so true in their work and personal relations — so young in experience but morally so sound! Why do we hear so much of the deterioration of the youth of this time; we heard the same thing then, but if any better stuff for a race to build on than we found knocking about in all sorts of places could be asked for, I think the demand unreasonable to say the least. They were being tried, these boys, and well they stood the test.

I don't remember how many days the fear was acute — how long one carried about inside one a sickish lump which made food impossible to swallow. Good old Jane was as kind as she could be — also as busy, getting ready for the bridal pair. They arrived — and one had to put on a cheerful face not to cloud the happiness next door. . . . Then Fisher came to say good-bye: he was "quitting" at the Adelaide and going off prospecting on his own. He left his photographs and keepsakes and his home address in my care — needless to say why. He was not sentimental about it, but he took a long look at his pictures — they were lovely faces, types of the very best sort of people anywhere.

On one of those days during a week which I remember as all one blur of misery, I was in the hammock in the sitting room, resting but not asleep, when Maggie, the new cook, showed in from the kitchen-way a young man who loomed up six feet or so and said he was Ferdinand Van Zandt[8] and he didn't wish to disturb me but would I tell him where the kitchen stove was to

[8] Concerning Ferdinand Van Zandt, see below, pp. 251-253. In a letter to Helena Gilder, dated Leadville, June 12, 1880, Mary Hallock Foote described Van Zandt as "an extremely goodlooking and debonair youth like 'Quentin Durward' who tells me his sister knew you."

stand? I sat up bewildered, having forgotten that our cookstove and the kitchen stuff were to arrive that afternoon. . . . It was all taken off my hands at once, however: Van Zandt was Fisher's successor — "soldier and sailor too." "Leave it to me," he said. "There can't be more than one place for a stove to stand." Quite true, in a kitchen the size of ours with only one stovepipe hole! When I went out, after he was gone, to inspect the job, I found Maggie beaming and speechless with admiration; she was ready to believe that Saint Michael in reefing jacket and leggins had come down from that hardware wagon on purpose to straighten out her kitchen for her.

Van Zandt's next appearance was some time later, through the front door this time, bringing a new young man whom he introduced as his "wife." Bob Booraem[9] had just arrived to fill the assayer's place at the Evening Star, and he and Van were setting up housekeeping together in one of Mr. Ward's cabins on the lot behind us. Booraem was a fresh-faced, well-dressed young man of the same old Dutch blood as Van Zandt's, rich in color, dark eyes and beautiful simple manners, with anything you choose to imagine as to a Patroon or Knickerbocker family past. And in Bob's case there were fat bank accounts — and later, boxes from home filled with good things which he passed around and dispersed among his neighbors. A bottle of his precious Old Port found its way shortly into my possession to buck up the little boy's appetite. The nickname "wife" gave the key to the domestic relation between the two young men. Van by temperament would take the initiative, Bob would do the worrying and cross all the bridges they hadn't come to.

Leadville was one of the wildest and also one of the most sophisticated of the mining camps; its fame had come hard upon a time of extreme financial distress,[10] and a surprising

9 Robert E. Booraem (1856-1918), who was educated in Germany and New York and took his degree at the Columbia School of Mines in 1878, began at Leadville a long career in western mining and petroleum that lasted almost until his death.

10 The great depression of 1873 did not begin to lift until the latter part of 1878.

number of diplomaed and highly specialized men were crowded in there desperately in need of a job. At the time of General Vinton's funeral, twenty-eight graduates of well-known technical schools rode in that extraordinary and motley procession — following the son of Dr. Vinton of Trinity to a Leadville graveyard.[11] Each little group gravitated toward some chosen fireside. Mr. Ward's back lots were filling up; the Duvals of San Francisco lived in one of his new houses; we observed that the Young South and San Francisco enjoyed themselves together. Our own little set came chiefly from New York or around New York Harbor. Van Zandt's home was on Staten Island. He had lost his father while still a boy. His mother told me that he became her caretaker when he was fourteen; he was but twenty-three in Leadville that summer, but he had settled a few points with himself and on those he was immovable — one of them was drinking. Every month he sent home to his mother a third of his income, which wasn't large. He was every kind of a "good sport," but not any kind of a young fool; it didn't affect him in the least, for instance, that he was called the handsomest man in Leadville. He was shrewd yet generous, a warm-blooded, light-hearted boy, and his huge laugh shook his vest buttons so low down that we used to warn him: "Take care, Van — you'll be fat before you are forty!"

It is these little things that stick in one's memory now that time has sifted that confused mass of incident. That summer was crowded with people coming and going in and out of our lives, but a few figures, these whom I speak of, remain. We had the experts the first summer, studying the proposition Nature had hidden there on deposit; the second summer brought the

[11] Actually the Rev. Francis Vinton, the Episcopal clergyman who served with great success at Trinity Church, New York, was the uncle of Francis L. Vinton (1835-79), but because of the early death of the boy's father, the uncle raised Francis L. Vinton. Young Vinton graduated from West Point, attended the École des Mines, Paris, 1856-60, won the rank of general in the Civil War, and became the first professor of civil and mining engineering at Columbia School of Mines, 1864-77, before moving to Denver to begin a consulting practice. He died at Leadville while on a professional trip.

younger men who were to work out those problems in practice. We knew them in our homes because of the little homely ways that tied us together; the stovepipes and kitchen fixings, the offerings out of boxes from home, the fetching of the horses for a ride in the valley with a message from one's husband saying, "too busy to go to-day — take Van." I didn't believe he was always too busy. I fancied it was his way of giving Van a little breath of change from the office grind; the amusements in Leadville for a boy who has settled points with himself were not many.

But there was another reason back of that thin excuse. The men with any responsibility were more than busy — they were some of them worried by strikes and bad luck underground, and they were all of them tired. Those who had been there as long as my husband were very tired. The effect of those high altitudes is cumulative as well as searching. It is safer in some cases to be one of those who succumb at once. There were days when after a long morning in the saddle A. could scarcely crawl up his office stairs. . . . The men talked of their work with certain significant omissions when we gathered, each little group around its own council fire. When the summer — what we called summer — was but half spent I knew that a miners' strike was brewing, and the glum silence on some matters connected with it, and sundry grunts and sarcasms, meant things which they were not ready to speak about. The operators had to hang together outwardly. Years afterward I was told that it was an operator who brought on the strike, who had a selfish reason for wanting an excuse to shut down his mine. He gained time to sell his own stock in it before the price went down. When the strike was over and the truth came out that the mine was done for — by that time he had made his pile. This is the sort of business which corrupts labor unions and kills legitimate mining.[12]

[12] In support of Mary Hallock Foote's comment as to the origin of the strike, C. C. Davis, who was editor of the local Leadville newspaper at the time, later said that it was "generally believed" that two mine operators, W. S. Keyes of the

The riding in the valley was not for pleasure only; it was the one safe panacea I knew for sleeplessness, in a place where no woman could walk alone. Sleeplessness from having been a tendency had become a fixed habit — starting with those night watches when Boykin was ill. My work suffered and my eyes gave warnings, and in the end I broke the *Lucile* contract, and my publishers most handsomely insisted on paying for the drawings I had made. But I never took a time order again, not for even a single illustration. That is how I came to illustrate chiefly my own stories: no more giftbooks for me! Our good doctor, whom I quote so often, had warned me in that matter of sleeplessnes never to tamper with the bedtime dose. Sleeplessness for a constitution like mine, he said, was no killing matter, but doses can kill a soul.

There was a young Englishman who spent his evenings rather often in the cabin, whom Arthur called Pricey. His name was Hugh Price. He had no "wife," no pal, no special fireside unless it was ours. The other boys teased him about being always in our sitting room, always silent and buried in a book; they called it a "free reading room for Pricey"; and he defended himself candidly, to everyone's delight, with the badgered apology: "A man can't sit in his bedroom, you know!" He was a public-school boy, an Oxford man, a student in Germany, a traveler — an impecunious younger son; if he had any remittances, they were small ones. He was a doleful duffer when it came to handling things in a laboratory or stepping about

---

Chrysolite and George Daly, had deliberately precipitated the strike in order to serve their own temporary speculative purposes. Carlyle C. Davis, *Olden Times in Colorado* (Los Angeles, 1916), pp. 249, 261. This bitter strike for higher pay and the eight-hour day, by a miners' union that had been formed in 1879, began on May 26, 1880, at the always controversial Chrysolite mine. It lasted more than three weeks, paralyzed life in Leadville, and closed down all mines. The mining companies hired armed guards, which further embittered the workers, formed a citizens' committee, enlisted volunteers for semi-military service, and successfully appealed to the governor for arms and militia. This show of force presently broke the strike. Arthur Foote was one of the managers who signed the rejection of the union demands.

among coffeepots and frying pans at a campfire, but he had read enormously, and when alone with one or two who could catch what he was trying to say in his shy, hampered fashion, he was awfully good company.

Every evening in the cabin he took the same chair in the corner by the bookshelves (unfortunately it was a rocking chair) and read and rocked until all the others were gone. The rocking annoyed Arthur who was sensitive to little personal habits; he did not hesitate to correct this habit in Pricey in a somewhat crude manner. One evening when Pricey was deep in a book and the chair in full career, A. stepped behind it and slipped a book under each rocker. It surprised Pricey and caused a general laugh, but he took it with touching good nature; he was not thin-skinned in such ways. We had many long quiet talks when the merrier part of the company had left. His mind was the most abstruse and cultivated and the least available of any of the younger men's in Leadville.

Yet he had his happy moments — never indoors! Once when we were riding in the valley — the valley of the little wild Arkansas near its source, with that towering and stainless sky resting on the mountain peaks, he looked up like a worshipper and said in his fine Oxford accent:[13]

> 'O tenderly the haughty day
> Fills his blue urn with fire —

Who in Leadville could have done that but Pricey, or would have thought of doing it! But alas! he was one who stayed in Leadville too long. It was the winter after, when we were in New York, A. received a letter from him and laid it down with a queer look, "Either Price was drunk when he wrote that letter or he has gone out of his mind." It was the last he feared, and drink had nothing to do with it. When Emmons returned from Washington in the spring and Van Zandt from his wild trip to New Mexico (of which more later), those two took care

[13] From Emerson's "Ode Sung in the Town Hall, Concord, July 4, 1857."

of poor Pricey and sent him back to his relatives in England at their own expense. He had been taken up on the streets wandering about insane and lodged in the common jail for mere safety, lacking every comfort or even decency. No one knew him and he could give no account of himself — so quickly the little fireside groups dispersed in that senseless, rootless place. "The altitude of heartbreak," it was sometimes called.

The case between the Adelaide and the Argentine had been pending in the courts, but on the ground meantime it looked like war. A. had been summoned east for a conference of the powers, and fearing trouble ahead, he took his family with him. We were on the train midway when the Argentines, carefully choosing that time, broke into the bottom drift of the Adelaide, the territory in dispute, and set up a barricade with a door in it. The door was not an invitation to the Adelaides to drop in any time to tea — it was a sallyport against the hour when they [the Argentines] should be ready to try the law of possession. The time of course was then — with orders hung up between East and West. But robbery under arms did not succeed that time. The Adelaide had a dauntless foreman named Steve Fleming who went down the shaft alone and waited for them in the dark drift; one man, with a Winchester, held up the gang, man by man, as they came through and showed against the light. The story was never forgotten while any of that crowd was left in Leadville. When charged with what looked like personal courage, Steve had passed it off with, "A Winchester is mighty comprehensive."

Their next attempt was on top, but an armed shaft house is no ill place to defend, and Van Zandt was ready for them with a better lot of men than the Argentine's "ten dollar fighters." This was the news he wired east (with boyish glee) asking further orders. "Hold the mine in spite of hell" was the answer he expected — and got, from his equally boyish chief. But it was not sustained by the head office. The owners were weary of the Adelaide's freakish favors. When it came to shedding blood in her defense and a lengthy lawsuit in any case, they preferred to shut down. It hurt the young men on the spot who were all ready for action, and struck them no doubt as a lame conclusion; which is the difference between realism and romance. The wife in the case agreed with Wall Street and was thankful to hear of the end of that job.

And now we were back to our bold beginnings once more and the tale of our last campaign sounded like a wild and silly dream told to those quiet faces at home. The cherry trees were all yellow up the lane, a few pale leaves drifting down on the dooryard grass that was still green. We were eating ripe peaches off the tree and baked sweet apples jellied in their own juice and smothered in thick cream and Bessie's sponge cake, the ten-egg kind. I lay on the old lounge in the sitting room and chortled over *The Grandissimes* just out of press, with Richard Gilder's welcome penciled in front, a book to grow fat on.[14] Yet Louis Janin, whom we prayed to read it, did so offishly — not his New Orleans, nor his Old Creoles! He was as difficult about them as I am about my Old Quakers when those not of the blood aim to describe them in modern stories. But we could not be shaken as to our *Grandissimes*. Art is Truth.

We were feeling fit once more after our wasteful altitudes, when the next call came of fortune or adventure. Whoever takes a trip to Mexico may be sure of the last. How A. managed with his syndicate (that was sending him down there to report on mines) to take a wife along, I don't remember and it doesn't matter. But I daresay friendship had something to do with it. Drake de Kay was head of the Michoacán Syndicate, looking for an engineer to report on their mines in the province of Michoacán, about the time A. was in New York looking for a job.[15] Not necessarily a job for his wife too, but the *Century*

---

14 George Washington Cable's novel, published by Scribner's in 1880. See above, p. 101.

15 Drake de Kay was Helena's brother. He was secretary of the Chrysolite Mine Company, owners of the Leadville mine of that name. Michoacán province is in central and western Mexico.

people, hearing that she was to go, said they would be glad to consider for the magazine whatever she might bring back in the way of illustrations and copy, which gave a color of practicality to her side of the affair. As a matter of fact A. said he would not go without me, and I am not sure but he took the job for its romance side for us both. We were no longer so very young, but we were still foolish. It came into our lives without plan or prevision and led to nothing in the general course of events, if there can be said to be such a course in the life of an engineer. There it glows, a spot of intenser color in memory's painted windows that look toward sunset, riveting the eye amidst lower tones of burnt-out forests and dry deserts and old, fenced-in farms.

The question of Boykin was settled as usual by the family, which meant Aunt Bessie to mother him at night and keep watch by day over one of the young Clancys, being broken in as temporary nursemaid. And his rambling mother got together her sketching tools, packed a steamer trunk with a layer of thin things underneath, and was off for the "gulfs enchanted where the siren sings." Her only preparation for travel in Mexico was having read Prescott's *Conquest* when she was about ten years old.

BOOK III

Romance

$\mathfrak{C}$ 18 $\mathfrak{D}$

A. HAD played around Nassau one winter with a rich cousin, sailing his boat and sharing his acquaintance with the pretty girls, and he had raised oranges in Florida, but travel and the tropics were both new to me — travel, meaning latitude not longitude.

We crossed the river on the ice at Milton Ferry, in a sleigh, buried in rugs, to take our southbound train. It was hard January weather up the Hudson but beginning to rain as we left New York harbor; and I hung over the rail till the land was lost and the great sea roll took hold of us, stood it as long as I could, and then the usual eclipse followed abolishing all forms of consciousness but one. A storm lashed us down the coast, but after Cape Hatteras all was bliss. We dug out our thin clothes and awoke one morning in a harbor where it was summer and saw the "palm green shores" and the white walls of a sixteenth-century fortress and the shipping of all nations with their flags at rest.[1] Little awninged boats flocked out to us from the pink and blue houses crowded down to the quay, and I knew that we never had been anywhere before — we had merely romped about a bit in that "historic vacuum" of the Far West. Here was an old color-washed city that was called the Key of the New World[2] before we had been discovered, that had been sacked and burned and plundered when we were nothing up the Hudson but night-dark forests and Indians dancing their feast-dances on our rocks at low tide.

[1] Havana harbor. The fortress was Morro Castle, built 1587-97.
[2] A royal decree of 1634 so declared.

211

I got out my drawing things and made a note of the Casa Blanca and asked the name of the black trees massed against its lower walls, and a fat little gentleman with no collar and a thick profile and a Scotch cap, with ribbons floating out behind, said softly, accenting the last syllable, "Laurél." . . . Not four days from New York and we heard people speaking of us as "Los Americanos del Norte!" The continent was not ours any longer.

We lay off Progresso (which I learned was the port of Merida) and lighters came out to us, and a native woman was hoisted aboard in a boatswain's chair at the end of a yard, a row of strange faces watching from the ship's side as she rose in air a spectacle. She was strongly Indian in type, unpretty but not uncomely, and she lost no more "face" for being waved aloft like that than if she had been seated on her own doorstep. She had no pretensions to face to lose; she kept her patient composure, as her race had done for centuries under the alien observation of its conquerers.

There were nights of magic moonlight crossing the gulf. A group of Cuban girls who came aboard at Havana sang the songs of the country with their peculiar languid, halting rhythm, in the intervals of cigarettes, seated along the rail with their men companions, faces in shadow, blanched hands in the moonlight. The harsh jar on certain low notes made one shiver. We heard those songs again one stifling night off Yucatan, sung by half-naked convicts in the steerage who had climbed the hatchway ladder for a breath of air. They were put ashore next day with a guard of Mexican soldiers to be left to slow death on the government works; it was the yellow-fever coast. A number of our own American boys of miscellaneous sorts were on board, seeking work on the two railroads then building in Mexico; jobs were not plentiful in the States. At the captain's table we were introduced to a young Swedish engineer who discovered that we had heard of his great poem of the North, and on deck, on those tropic nights, as we watched our phosphorescent wake spread and gloom and flash behind us, we sat in a little group apart and heard it recited for the first time in its own tongue by one who was an enthusiast — Spanish love songs and the Frithiof Saga![3]

One morning at daybreak, before there were any shadows, we saw a rose-colored mountain peak shading down in delicate gradations of color to the pearly fogbank it appeared to float on, and were told that the mountain was Orizaba and the fog was land mist covering the *tierras calientes* [coastal plain]. In a few hours we passed the fortress of San Juan de Ulúa and entered the harbor of Veracruz.[4] It was easy to believe that Cortes and his helmeted soldiers, or even the modern French, might have assisted history in this place, but that we in our sober senses as a nation should have come in here with ships and cannon and bombarded this theatrical-looking old pile, on the still more theatrical errand, a march on Mexico City, was hard for U. S. citizens of our time to conceive. But we found that every Mexican citizen we were able to talk with was well posted on that war, and however politely he may have listened, it was evident he could not credit our assertion that all the *Americanos del Norte* of that period were not of one mind.

That evening in the shadowy plaza opposite our hotel we sat and listened to the band and watched the ladies of Latin American society, in volantes or landaus, parade their powdered charms.[5] Along dim footpaths the brown-skinned mestizas passed and repassed us on our bench, looking as if they had forgotten to put a dress on, though an embroidered chemise and a petticoat, and a rebozo cast back from one's shoul-

---

[3] Usually Frithjof or Fridthiof, the hero of an Icelandic saga composed about 1300, and the subject of a famous Swedish poem written in 1825.

[4] Veracruz was the traditional gateway through which foreign troops had invaded Mexico. Cortes founded it in 1519 and used it as his base for invasion. Winfield Scott, who captured it in 1847 during the war between the United States and Mexico, marched from there to the conquest of Mexico City and indeed of the Mexican nation. The French seized it in 1861 at the start of the military invasion that put Maximilian on the throne as emperor.

[5] A volante was a two-wheeled carriage; a landau a four-wheeled one.

ders, we thought a prettier dress than any we saw in the carriages. Some had their black hair crinkled its full length, falling below their waists, and a red rose stuck behind one ear through a band of ribbon. At the railroad station at midnight, Arthur and Lingren, the Swedish engineer, managed to fill the remaining seats in our carriage with their pick of the first-class passengers, which was not saying much for the class. And so we were off, through the fever-haunted lands around Veracruz, for Mexico City. After that, except in little asides between ourselves, we lost touch with real life till we stood on the dock in New York again and handed our keys to the custom officer.[6]

In the drama, we are told, "there are minor actors: there are no minor roles." In Mexico, which is the land of living drama, we were unable to feel the importance of any of their chief roles, while all the actors, "Lords, gentlemen, officers, murderers, attendants and messengers," were stars! If you stopped at the door of a hut on a long day in the saddle and asked for a drink of water (the last thing you should drink, but at times one became desperate), the peon's wife offered it held out on the flat of her small brown palm and the act became symbolical. If the señora, your hostess of the Creole caste, led you to a seat beside her on the sofa at the top of the room and the gentlemen present, according to the rules of precedence, took the armchairs lined up on either side, you felt that here was a ceremony that had been enacted thousands of times, a thousand

---

[6] When the Footes visited Mexico in 1881, that country was under the de facto rule of Porfirio Diaz, who was temporarily out of the presidency because of a law that prohibited consecutive presidential terms. With one of Diaz's associates as president, Mexico continued the Diaz policies of inviting foreign capital to build railroads and open mines, while at the same time suppressing banditry and enforcing domestic peace. Since these policies did little for the bulk of the population, the very large gap between the rich and the poor persisted, as Mary Hallock Foote's narrative suggests.

years before you were born, and if these people were perfect in anything, they were in manner. They might have better or worse morals than yours or mine, but in these gestures and observances they could not make a mistake.

From the city of Mexico to Morelia,[7] at that time, there was only one public conveyance and one road, the camino real [highway] — which might turn into a quagmire or a mountain pass; or, when you struck a section of the ancient pavement laid some two or three hundred years ago and apparently never mended since, you might think you were on the bottom of a dry torrent lined with loose stones. And, speaking of stones, a man with a leather sackful sat beside our driver and pelted the lead mules with small pebbles to keep them up to their work. He never missed his aim, an ear or the root of a tail or a projecting hip joint. The eight mules were hitched as two wheelers, four on a swing and two leaders, and the ordinary stagecoach rode no easier for being called by a name that would scan like poetry.[8]

We crossed that proud valley of the capital in the early morning light, all its shining network of canals and waterways steaming up into the sunshine. Chapultepec, in the distance, lifted its light arches above the cypresses in the garden of Montezuma. We rattled through Tacubaya, a suburb of country seats with glimpses of flowery patios framed in archways of shadow. Our driver put on speed whenever we entered the marts of men; he could have done no more for the capital and he would do no less for the meanest Indian village. On the back seat beside me sat a little black-eyed señorita traveling with her father who was third man on the front seat opposite. Our acquaintance ripened into intimacy through being much

7 Morelia, capital of Michoacán state, is about 130 miles from Mexico City and is on a fertile plateau, at an altitude of more than 6,000 feet. Founded in 1541 as Valladolid, it was renamed Morelia in 1828 after the patriot priest who was a leader in the revolt against Spanish rule.
8 Presumably "diligencia."

thrown together, for sometimes her head was on my shoulder, and sometimes mine on hers and my hat brim in her eye, as we bounced over the broken pavement or were hurled from side to side.

For many of those first miles the road was a moving market — cargoes for Mexico City, on donkeys and pack mules and in bullock carts with wheels of solid wood; cattle and hogs on the hoof and Indians on their sandaled feet who had come over the mountains from that interior we were going to, loaded with frails [rush baskets] of fruit and bundles of camote [sweet potatoes] and wooden trays and toys and dulces [sweets], rolls of matting, live fowls in wicker crates (fowls above and eggs below), and masses of pottery woven together with cords and towering above the bearer's head — a pair of live hens never came amiss dangling by the legs from a corner of the load. Whole families were on the road, staff in hand and cooking pot or baby slung at their backs. Many of the Indian huts we passed had an entertainment set out for the wayfarers, such food as they could afford spread on a clean cloth held down by stones, and a rude platform near to rest the backloads on. Women came out to gossip with their guests and take payment, or to say in their soft, apathetic voices, "Nada, nada!" [nothing].

My señorita knew a little English "as she is spoke" and I could patch up a few sentences of Spanish in the newly arrived American manner. The men smoked while the women got together as usual through their tongues. But we kept to the trite and the obvious. As we climbed the sierra at the Mountain of the Crosses, I pointed questioningly to the monument to Hidalgo,[9] and the señorita said he was their Washington and the place of the white crosses was their Bunker Hill. But the daughters and wives of those patriots went up the mountain after the battle and buried their dead with their own hands.

9 The patriot-priest and national hero, first leader in the Mexican war of independence, executed in 1811.

When we reached the summit of the divide and looked back at the great valley below us, Popocatepetl and the White Woman[10] mere incidents on its skyline, I made a rather tactless remark (considering the complexions of the majority of our traveling companions) about Cortes and his men. This was a republican period — the señorita was proud of the fact that she had those eyes of hers (*los ojos negros*) [dark eyes] from an Indian ancestress. If I understood her, the old lady was one of that remnant of a tribe unconquered in the heart of Michoacán which had helped deliver the province into the hands of Hidalgo.

We were on a main thoroughfare of the country, yet all the way we were escorted by soldiers of the *guardias rurales* [rural police] changed at various outposts. Any one of our fellow travelers could have told us they were probably ex-bandits themselves — they were Diaz's good bandits now, or the stuff bandits were made of if left lying around loose. Everything was grist that came to the Diaz mill. They looked interesting on the road ahead, lounging in their saddles, each man with a bright serape[11] twisted round his pommel and a carbine swinging at his knee. On later days of the journey as we plodded along at dusk towards our night station, they would ease their souls of melody that might not have been music to the musical — it sounded like improvisation which the common people drop into as naturally as a bird utters its cry.

We slept at Toluca[12] the first night — incredible city of 8,000 inhabitants that you find up there alone, with no approaches, nothing to tell you you are coming to it at the foot of

---

[10] Two famous mountains with Aztec names that are even harder to spell than to pronounce: Popocatepetl, a dormant volcano, is south of the twin volcano that is variously known as Ixtacihuatl or the White Woman or the Sleeping Woman.

[11] In Mexico, a serape was a narrow blanket worn by men in lieu of an overcoat, or, when not in use, carried across a rider's saddle, as Mary Hallock Foote here describes it.

[12] Toluca, founded in 1530, is situated at an altitude of about 8,600 feet and is perhaps 45 miles from Mexico City by road.

its burnt-out volcano. It has an ancient Toltec past, burnt-out also, but full of fiery records before the Spaniards took it and made it over into the likeness of a city of their own. We crashed into its streets of silence at the hour of the siesta; no traffic stirring except drowsily on sandaled feet or unshod hoofs of donkeys pattering by. From our balcony in the Hotel de la Diligencia we saw at early bedtime the new moon setting over a blue mountain line which we knew was in Michoacán. The city's sixteenth-century profile rose in the flush of that marvelous afterglow, for which this part of Mexico is famous — white bell towers, terraced house roofs, tiled domes, and cypresses. At three in the morning we were groping along a cold corridor guided to hot coffee in the dining room by a shock-headed mozo [manservant] with one candle. But as we looked down into the patio, there was a scene worth sitting up all night for! Torches on long iron staves planted in the pavement lighted the place like a stage for the figures of men who were dragging out the coach, piled with baggage, from under the arches and harnessing the mules. The coach might have been built in Concord, N. H., the mules were just ordinary mules who had seen life, the men were not dressed as one would expect on such a background, but we found it always so in Mexico — nothing conformed: you could have your medievalism, but it would be mixed up with French aniline dyes and American missionaries and German drummers and English railroad engineers.

We settled into our old places, the eight mules took hold on the pavement, and we crashed out of the archway into the dark street, our erstwhile stone thrower now carrying a torch made of agave rope soaked in pitch; and so we flared and thundered forth and were swallowed up in a dim country seen in flashes. These old Indian cities had no suburbs; one road led into them, the same road led out through a half-ruined gateway that never would be repaired. Not even a smoke cloud hovered above their sun-warmed azoteas [roof tops].

At the first change of mules after daybreak we crawled out and stood around and snuffed the morning air. If it looked all right ahead A. would toss a piece of silver to the driver and we walked on a mile or so in the open country, blessing the stillness after the wheels. It was spring — in January — and as we went down the great plateau the season advanced by leaps and bounds. One morning we met a peon going afield, his woman trotting behind him, a sleeping child rolled in the folds of her rebozo. She had broken a branch of a shrub and held it to shade her eyes from the low sun as she stared at us amazed. There had never been a tourist then (not that we were tourists) as far as that in the interior. Maximilian[13] and his retinue had taken that road on his progress to Morelia; Madame Calderon de la Barca[14] took it in 1843, as the wife of an ambassador travels: they were part of the historic scene — we were anachronisms, but as we were not seeing ourselves we were able to remember those grand and simple sweeps of country unmarred by any but the figures that belonged there.

One day it was droves of black swine, and their Indian drivers wore capes made of a thatch of palm leaves that rustled like cornstocks in autumn. Another day we stopped at an old worn-out hacienda where we lunched, attended by its people, all Indians, and a woman brought us tortillas on the palm of her hand and laid them in a neat pile on the tablecloth; the leperos[15] swarmed about us, the refuse of humanity but bold as hungry dogs. And here in all this poverty there was a fountain almost pure Greek in design and a beautiful little chapel,

[13] The Austrian archduke who was persuaded to become emperor of Mexico during the period when Napoleon III's French troops were in fact the controlling power. He was executed by the Mexicans in 1867.

[14] Frances (Fanny) Erskine Inglis was born in Scotland, raised partly in France, and became a well-known figure in Boston literary circles before marrying the Spanish minister to the United States in 1838. With her husband she was in Mexico in 1840-41, and in 1843 published *Life in Mexico*, which Mary Hallock Foote had apparently read.

[15] As used in Mexico, this Spanish word is roughly equivalent to "beggar" or "rabble."

closed, hard by the stone bath for the horses. There were no
horses — whatever had been the life of the place, or its grandeur, had gone like a dream: there were only Indians and
leperos, and a country that made you take a deep breath as you
gazed. On all that journey the only four-wheeled conveyance
we met was a private coach drawn by four mules, two men in
straw hats and serapes on the box, two more, mounted and con-
spicuously armed, riding behind the coach; inside on the back
seat alone sat a fat old lady with a brown complexion and a
black shawl over her head. One would go far astray in Mexico
who judged a woman's class and condition by the way she
dressed.

We had brown complexions on the seat in front of us, sharing it with the father of our señorita, who introduced himself
as a *licenciado*[16] of Morelia and looked more like the Creole
type which holds itself above all others except natives of Spain.
The Indian ancestress whom the señorita boasted of may have
been on her mother's side. The near-whites were decorous persons with those good manners we met everywhere in every
class; they scarcely spoke except to murmur "gracias" when
one gave another a light for his cigarette. Don Antonio, not
having a card to present with his name, wrote himself down
with all his assets and liabilities in the way of family in my
sketchbook and there I have him to this day: "Lic. Antonio del
Morál, padre de la Señorita Soledad," (our pretty neighbor)
"de Concepción, de Manuel, de Antonio, de José, y marido de
la Señora Antonia Perada — Morelia." It seemed to give him
pleasure to hear these names which summed his existence repeated slowly by a stranger in her strange American accent.
The Señorita Soledad followed my pronunciation of the *d* in
Perado [sic] and the final *d* in her own name, with a little
lesson on consonants, just touching it with the tip of her
tongue, making it the mere breath of an expiring *d*.

There seemed a certain frivolity in our starting at 3:00 A.M.

[16] A colloquial title given to lawyers.

on the morning of our third day, just to lay off at Maravatío at high noon. But it was the Feast of the Conversion of St. Paul and we were expected to celebrate it by going to the bullfight in the afternoon. I think everyone in the town went, even to the leperos who got no further than the barriers. We sat in the deserted plaza and heard the shuffle of sandals like dry leaves drifting through every street towards the plaza de toros. We had seen the parade of the toreros [bullfighters], a very pretty show, and we had seen Don Antonio and his daughter depart with sober elation to join themselves to the crowd. . . . It was sunny and charming in the plaza, the silence and the distant music and the shouts — and we said, "Why don't we go too — why sit here and be prigs!" I had said I wouldn't go in Mexico City where the thing was as well done as anywhere out of Spain, but we went in Maravatío, hypnotized by the sound of those sandals. We stayed long enough to see what a bullfight in the provinces is like! We had seats in the front row — room was made for us beside Don Antonio and his daughter. The seats in the sun were packed by those who couldn't afford seats al sombra [in the shade]. There came a moment when A. put his hand suddenly before my eyes, and as we rose to go, the señorita said tolerantly: "It is too strong for you."

It was late the next night when we got in to our cold lairs at the hacienda of Tepetongo and walked its corridors at moonset until doors were opened to us by sleepy servants and beds made up in the bare rooms reserved for strangers on the road. Tepetongo was one of the great estates far apart on those rich tablelands where travelers were given such entertainment as the public which travels by diligence could generally afford to pay for. The lands of Tepetongo marched with us next day for miles and were a study in the ancient methods of cultivation. We had seen how wherever the padres waved a hand cathedrals uprose from villages of hovels at their feet, with flights of stone steps and twin bell towers and sculptured doorways — but here also, deep in the country, stone dams, buttressed as for a city reservoir, held back water for the fields; there were granaries of stone built like round towers for defense, pillared arches led to cattle corrals, stone bridges crossed every arroyo and each had its carved niche for the Virgin's image. Every old dreamlike city we passed through had its fountain and stone seats in the plaza for people in rags to sun themselves on; Hotels de la Diligencia had wrought-iron railings to their corridors and balconies and courts fit for an embassy. The cost in unpaid human labor gradually weighed upon the spirits with a sense of complicity in an ancient wrong which the beauty could not pay for. One knew that one would soon become used to it and love it inhumanly, if one lived there one's self.

We crossed the line into Michoacán on our second day, going down through a broken and beautiful country of wooded hills into a warmer valley where the road lay for miles between hedges of nopal [prickly pear] and organum [organ] cactus. There is a valley of Maravatío and a valley of Morelia, but these valleys are tablelands 6,000 feet above the sea. On the afternoon of the fourth, our last day, we were among low meadows where breezeless pools reflected the sunset and the flight of wild fowl in flocks crying over them. Twilight came and the last divide was still to cross. We walked a long distance that evening, taking to higher ground above the stretch of muddy road where the coach toiled along. The heart-stirring tread of the cavalry horses kept beside us; they were a younger, smarter set of men on this detail who we surmised might be the sons of rancheros joining the mounted police for the sake of the lark and the gray cavalry uniform; but what did we know! And what did they know of us — but they were curious; no Mexicana not a peasant would be tramping alongside her husband in the dusk of moonrise! One of them drew rein beside me and asked the needless question, "Una Americana?" "Si, señor; una Americana del Norte." Had I been walking on stilts or dressed in bearskins, that answer would have been sufficient.

In the middle of the night, it seemed, we stopped to water the mules at an Indian village and in talk overheard around the fountain we learned that we were "cerquita" [close to our destination]. We looked out and caught only the view of a dim country falling away below us to an infinite shrouded distance: we were then on the last divide. . . . At length came the shocks of that burst of speed which always announced our approaching landfall; by the light of a single lamp we passed the pillars of a gateway; arches of an aqueduct strode into sight and were swallowed up in trees and darkness. "San Pedro!" our Morelians murmured. It was not an invocation — only the name, thankfully pronounced, of their city's beautiful park that we had just left behind us. The lamps became continuous; we climbed a roughly paved street and rolled into the court of the Hotel Michoacán.

The card of Señor Don Gustavo Gravenhorst was handed us and we learned that our host, having waited for us till midnight, had ordered a hot supper and beds to be ready and tactfully gone home. Our room opened on the corridor — plants, arches, and starlight — and had French windows and balconies above the street. We dragged one shutter open and stepped out. Over across the square with its mass of dark trees rose the cathedral towers. We were used to great churches and little villages — this was a city, by its very shadows at night. The bell tower spoke — it was two o'clock; we counted the four quarters, then a deeper note struck the hour. Twenty-three hours' staging since we left Maravatío by torchlight the morning before, and our first day in Morelia had begun.

ON THE ROAD TO MEXICO.

COURT AND STAIR-WAY OF A MEXICAN HOUSE.

❲ 19 ❳

AFTER that journey, shaken up with our fellow republicans, brown and white, we found ourselves guests of one of the proudest and most exclusive houses in the city. Bankers if they are proud are usually discreet: Don Gustavo was a Prussian banker who had lived twenty years an alien in the heart of Mexico; how discretion had prospered with him the Casa Gravenhorst bore witness. This is not to impugn his sincerity as a Prussian or any other kind of banker; he had a high reputation in business, and he was frank enough in speech with us to say, speaking of the wife he had lost in her youth — he said she was no Mexican but of the purer race allied with his own (this was one of his naïve boasts) through those gentle ancestors of his, the Visigoths. She had been a blue-eyed, brown-haired daughter of Old Spain.

He was then not over forty, but set in the customs and use of two generations ago which were as well suited to the tastes of a Prussian banker as of a Mexican grandee. His wife's sister, the gentle Emelita, our hostess, was young as a woman in her thirties may keep her youth through never thinking of herself at all. She managed his great mansion and retinue of servants, looked after its economies and its hospitalities with equal magnificence and thrift, and mothered his only child, Enriqueta, a little girl of thirteen. This was the family who took us in — inhabiting a house built for a priests' college; they were not pressed for room even with a guest or two.

Twenty rooms opened on the corredor[1] of the Casa Graven-

---

[1] Closer in meaning to "gallery" or "arcade" than to the English word "corridor," even though Mary Hallock Foote uses "corredor" and its English cognate interchangeably.

horst which was open to the sky. You looked down through its vine-wreathed arches into the main court as into a church crypt, stone pillared and full of shadows and romantic sounds. A brace of young bloodhounds chained there at night wakened us at sunrise baying to be loosed; gamecocks shouted from their gallery above the rear court; Isabel, the coachman, led out the saddlehorses and a pair of big white carriage mules from their stalls beneath the arches to water at a stone tank in the sunny corral. He sat on the curb while they were drinking, and tall bamboo stems, leaning over the pool, sprinkled the pavement and Isabel's shoulders with flickering lights and shadows. A little later, sandals shuffled past our bedroom door and we knew they belonged to Ascensión, in a white jacket and black trousers and scarlet sash, who would be sweeping the corridor and watering the plants and giving the doves and parrot their breakfasts. When all the life and colors of the corridor were assembled there of a morning, including Enriqueta and her white poodle (her namesake, "Enrique"), it was a most lovely sitting room. Enriqueta would come springing out after lessons with a German governess whom no one ever saw, and call in a voice singularly deep and sonorous for a child, "Enrique, mi alma!" I used to wonder what pent up form of power or emotional capacity that remarkable speaking voice betokened. The whole plan of the house was perfect for the life of a secluded woman with resources which most intelligent grown women manage to find, but for that secluded child I should have had my fears, if she had been mine. She had a small, pale, oval face between masses of golden brown curls, and the dark blue eyes that must have been like her mother's — Emelita had the same eyes, while Don Gustavo's were black and irritable looking and his hair was straight and black, and pomatumed.

Much work must have gone on after the house was awake of a morning, but there was no bustle. There was no mechanism but hands and feet. If the señorita wished to call a servant, she stepped into the corridor and clapped her small hands —

skilled in every task allowed a doña of her station. She took me into her linen room one day, and if I had been a true house-wife, I should have fallen down and worshipped in that shrine. We were shown the saddle room also. It impressed one with the fortunes of a house that could own those museum pieces whose worth and workmanship I had not the knowledge to evaluate, but for riding I would sooner have had my little old Whitman, price fifty dollars!

The rooms of ceremony were furnished according to European taste of that time, or a little earlier; this was only ten years after the Peace of Paris — Germany was the proud man of Europe,[2] and a Prussian of wealth buried in the interior of Mexico might be excused a certain amount of swagger. The salas[3] were rather offensively gorgeous to be sure, yet interesting if you thought how everything in them from the grand piano to the lusters on the chandeliers had come over seas and over three mountain ranges by the ways we had seen. But no artist would have paused in those rooms! The small artist I was went through them to the balcony and drew that corner of the square below it in the morning sunlight. The leaves were coming out on the trees in the Plaza de las Martires; there were always beggars squeezed into the niches of the monument to Morelos which stands at the entrance where paths and street diverge. Morelos was one of the martyrs to whom the square had been dedicated by a populace in arms. The old name of the city, Valladolid, had been changed in his honor. But that did not prevent it from being the last stronghold of Catholicism in Mexico at that time, nor change the nature of its aristocracy. The Creole families were all Monarchist and would have handed over the country to Maximilian for the titles and honors he promised them.

It was Lent, and below the balcony women with their heads covered with shawls or rebozos were flocking along the street

---

[2] I.e., the triumph of Germany over France in the Franco-Prussian War of 1870-71, and the proclamation of the German Empire.

[3] A hall, drawing room, or other large formal room used for entertaining.

towards the cathedral where bells were clashing for services at all hours. Across the street I could read the first of a string of letters on a sign: "Del Ferrocarril" [railroad] — which meant the Anglo-Saxon was there with his inventions — the barbarians were over the wall. In the room behind me a flat-backed Mexican girl went stooping across the carpet, sweeping it with dustpan in one hand, whisk broom in the other. She would not have used a carpet sweeper or a long-handled broom if you had given her one; no inventions wanted in that house! Eight servants were paid about what we paid our one in Leadville, and she was about the poorest servant we ever had.

Being Lent, there were no entertainments to interrupt the charming, secluded routine. Don Gustavo gave a grand breakfast to the engineers on their departure for the mines, but that was a business affair and I suppose it was only through courtesy to me that the ladies of the casa were present. The cooking was French and Spanish, worked out with German meticulousness; and Morelia must have had one of the most fascinating markets in the world. If we had read Kipling in those days we could have said: "With . . . rice and red pepper, and little fish out of the stream in the valley, and honey from the flue-like hives built in the stone walls, and dried apricots, and turmeric, and wild ginger, and bannocks of flour, a devout woman can make good things."[4] . . . There were better things than these in the marketplace at Morelia, and there were devout women in the Casa Gravenhorst. Emelita, I am sure, had inherited recipes in her old Spanish cookbooks that went back to the expulsion of the Moors — so mysterious, so recondite were some of the dishes on that table.

It was a far-flung company in its nationalities: Don Gustavo (as Herr Gravenhorst liked to be called) spoke English to me on his right and to a young Scotch engineer, Mr. James Simpson, on his left. He too was going up to the mines, and he may have been our hated rival, but I did not know it: he seemed

---

[4] The quotation is from "The Miracle of Purun Bhagat," in *The Second Jungle Book*, first published in book form in 1895.

much more like an ally, and he made a third in those little
English-speaking asides that were such a comfort as the plot
thickened and things became almost too good to be true! And
he rode with us back to Mexico [5] when we made the journey
on horseback, sharing the finest time of our lives.

But the scene of scenes in Morelia was the departure of the
engineers for the mines, outfitted for mountain trails and
weeks in camp as if they had been royalty. Don Pedro Gutierrez, who had a large interest in the expedition, escorted
them and furnished the retinue of servants. The ladies of both
houses were up in the corridor of the Casa Gutierrez, which
has the finest staircase in Morelia. About twenty-five horses
and pack mules were clattering in the court and mozos were
saddling and packing them with unlimited stuff piled on the
pavement: hampers of fruit, cases of vintage wines, down
pillows covered with silk, linen fit for the trousseau of a
duchess — I saw what they called a camp bedstead — of solid
brass — taken apart and strapped on a mule's back to go over
the trails as steep as ladders, worn by human feet in the solid
rock; all went up on the packsaddles roped and balanced with
the skill of a mozo de camino.

The men in riding clothes, "our men" as I called them to
myself, our plain Saxons, came clanking up the staircase to
make their shy farewells, and Don Pedro, a figure for the
stage, bowed over one's hand and murmured the phrases that
matched his costume; tight leather trousers embroidered down
the seams, and I wot not of togs and silver buttons and velvet
embossed work on his brown leather jacket, and a wonderful
hat of white beaver, with a brim like a halo, silver braided
and wound around the crown with silver cord; soft leather
boots and immense silver spurs and a serape of price folded
narrow and tossed over one shoulder. When we saw him at the
breakfast in ordinary dress, he was a little dark-visaged man of
fifty who looked as if he might have sold dry goods on Sixth

5 I.e., to Mexico City.

Avenue; but he was one of their grandees, of a family that went back to the Conquest, owner of great ranches as well as historic mines — he probably did not know (and did not wish to measure) the extent of his own lands. The Señora Gutierrez (y Salarzono) was another illustration of the fact that you could not judge a lady's rank in Mexico by the way she dressed, especially in the early hours of the day. Her manner, hampered as she was for words between us, was charming. It clothed her with graciousness and courtesy.

When the men were gone we took up our dreamlike routine again. How much lay beneath that was anything but a dream for my hostess I could not know, nor how my habits may have disarranged her. One idea possessed me and one-ideaed people are always a nuisance. I wanted to draw — to let nothing escape which I had the power to preserve the least hint of on paper. Inside the walls of the mansion, Emelita, as she wished me to call her, opened every door; the house was mine. But in the streets of that fascinating old city, no lady walked. To go sketching in Morelia meant the family coach with Isabel and the white mules, and Leonarda, and a chair for the *niña Americana* [6] to sit on, and an umbrella for Leonarda to hold over her head, and *la niña* herself, in afternoon dress — in the morning! I had made what seemed a simple request, to be spared Leonarda for a couple of hours to go with me alone, on foot, to the park of San Pedro to draw a certain corner of it in the morning when the native women were fetching water from the fountain in the *glorieta*,[7] the arches of the aqueduct crossing the grass — this was all I asked, and that was the result! If I had made a point of walking, Emelita would have walked by my side — in black silk or cashmere that dragged in the dirt; no power on earth could have induced her to hold up her skirts, nor have prevented her doing her duty to a

6 Literally, "child," but in Spanish American customarily used by servants in addressing their superiors.
7 An arbor or bower.

guest. I never saw San Pedro again except at the proper hour when ladies, dressed and powdered for the regular parade, smiled and fluttered their fingers at one another from the windows of their carriages and bowed to the young bloods of society on tall English horses who met them on the bridle path.

There were not many English thoroughbreds nor many carriages, but those who owned them did this every day of their lives; they were the old exclusive set who could not change though kingdoms and cities were lost, who intermarried, generation by generation, and called each other by their first names like royalty. I shall never forget the little scene as they passed and repassed under the black ash trees in that ordered, stately simplicity that knew no other way of life — that almost persuaded you there was no other. At a certain turn Don Gustavo met us after his walk for exercise — which we were not supposed to need. By this time the sunset would have gone out, and we drove home through the dusky streets brightened by little charcoal fires in braziers where Indian women along the sidewalks were doing a little cooking.

Then conversation and chocolate in the corridor. Words between Emelita and her guest were limited of necessity, but Don Gustavo spoke English by the book fluently and was keen for social practice with English-speaking persons. He talked with astonishing freedom; a man accustomed to be listened to by women, who did not stint his ego. In fact he had written a poem about himself in Spanish called "Yo," [8] which he translated for me into English prose. It were ill done of me to laugh at him here, even though we are all dead, so to speak — one must be civil to ghosts, and he was more than civil to us.

I would have given a good deal to know just what Emelita thought of him. I had no chance to judge her mind by her conversation, but its results in practice showed she had a mind. She was not pretty except for those dark blue eyes, and she

[8] Meaning "I."

never was well dressed though she went in silks and had treasures of old blond mantillas and fans and jewels in quaint settings; these she was keeping for Enriqueta. Her own hopes of children she had sacrificed to this child death had left her, and love of that kind is its own reward; but something more was her due from the child's father, I thought, whom she served and comforted. Don Gustavo had made a vow in the freshness of his grief — all his world knew of it — never to put another wife in his dead lady's place. He was so in love with his attitude of constancy and so vain of it that as long as he could be sure of Emelita's constancy I don't suppose he would ever have given her more than the right to go on living in that wealthy house waited on by his servants, herself the best servant he could have had.

I thought about Emelita a great deal and continued to think about her for years. There was a possibility that we might have been neighbors and she, my first friend in Morelia, teaching me how to manage my life there as she taught me Spanish in the corridor mornings while Enriqueta was at her lessons and all the gentle stir of the house went on about us. If the sale of the mines had gone through, A. would very likely have been sent back there to manage them, a long and difficult and hazardous job. It was fortunate we did not get it; but it was the master dream at that time, and for the wife it would have had much charm. It would have meant a house in Morelia — not a doge's palace like the Casa Gravenhorst, but a one-story white-walled house around a patio such as one we used to pass on our way to the park. It stood on the edge of it, between the sunny street and the park's vistas of light and shade. I could have ridden there mornings with little son beside me and an old Rubio or Bonifacio attending us. I turned my eyes away from it as we passed its gateway, for we were growing hungry for a home of some sort.

It wouldn't have done for me: I should have yielded to the enervating charm of that life — a woman not used to it. Even on this short visit, after the first restlessness wore off, I gave up walking too easily, except after dinner in the corridor where the doves were asleep and the flowers awake in the moonlight. Out there I would go and prowl by myself alone. From one of the rooms where lamplight streamed through a half-open door, Don Gustavo's monologue could be heard and Emelita's low infrequent replies, having their family talks — discussing their American guests perhaps, as A. and I discussed them when we were alone together.

But one walk we did take which shall be set down for the sake of what came of it. I had determined to go, once, to the marketplace with Rubio when he did his purchasing, to examine for myself the native pottery on display; for we were ready to pack and I wanted bits of the best, since we couldn't take much, as *recuerdos de Mejico* [souvenirs]. This could not be done with carriage and mules, I thanked my luck! and for once I did not scruple to put Emelita through the ordeal of a morning stroll. She went with me of course. We had made the rounds of the stalls and the groups [that,] under matting umbrellas, [were] camped around the fountain in the plaza, and were going home under the *portales* [porches] that line the square, chatting together, my voice in the ascendant no doubt. A gentleman happened to be walking behind us who knew there could be only one woman in Morelia who spoke English like that. It was Maurice Kingsley, just arrived with a party of railroad engineers. He had heard about us from Colonel Fergusson (whom I haven't mentioned), the syndicate's agent in the capital.[9] Who we were did not matter; it was the English-Speaking Union in the heart of Mexico. He called at the Casa Gravenhorst, and when he learned we were to ride on our return journey and that A. was looking for a mount for his wife — something better than the horses for hire which

9 In reporting this journey for *Century Magazine*, Mary Hallock Foote identified Maurice Kingsley as being "chief of the Morelia division of the railroad." In speaking of Colonel Fergusson as agent of "the syndicate," she was probably referring to the mining syndicate that had sent Arthur to Mexico.

are called "regulár" — Mr. Kingsley saw to it that the thing was done! But it took more than the "hire" to secure the favorite saddle horse of a private owner for a strange lady to ride six days away. He was a friend of Mr. Kingsley's and I hope that he got his horse back in proper condition. The "Rosillo," as the mozos called him (a strawberry roan with a blonde mane and tail), was the saving of my life on that six days' ride.

And Emelita saved my complexion. With her needlewoman's skill she made me a little black silk face mask and persuaded me to wear it — over a coat of powder which was a mask in itself. The sun of Mexico, she warned me, was "muy fuerte" [very strong]!

One morning there was an earlier and more than common clattering of hoofs in the court; I put on my old Colorado habit, the smell of pine smoke still clinging in its folds, hung my mask over one wrist, and went down the staircase for the last time. The entire household assembled in the court. They made a little scene of our farewells. Emelita embraced me in the fashion of the country, not lips but cheeks touching, first right then left, and a little pat on the shoulder completing the gesture. Don Gustavo with his short military step walked at my horse's bridle; Rubio and the second porter took off their great hats and stood at attention, one on each side of the arch. There were many graceful gestures and adios as we looked back — and that chapter was closed.

20

W<small>E HAD</small> Mr. Kingsley's company for the first hour of the
ride; after that we were the two Americans and Mr. Simpson,
our Scotch cousin, and at the last moment a Mexican colonel
of cavalry had been added unto us rather unexpectedly. I am
sure we did not want him, but it seemed best not to allow the
fact to appear. He and Mr. Simpson rode knee to knee, a striking racial contrast, Simpson being as tall and blond and ruddy
as the colonel was dark and lined and sallow and sinister. One
was carelessly a gentleman, the other was one of Diaz's
colonels but what he had been, *quien sabe!* They rode the same
sort of brutes of horses and their shoulders kept the same motion in time to the clink of the bullets in their Winchesters
hung at each saddlebow. The colonel called his black bronco,
derisively, "Napoleon Tercero." Don Pepé always rode behind
me, I observed, to be ready with his "Si, niña," if anything was
wanted from the packtrain. Don Pepé was his title as acting
commissary in charge of the whole outfit. He was a veteran of
the Mexican War and a trusted retainer of the Gutierrez family, loaned us for the journey. José Maria, another picked man,
rode ahead on scout and to announce us at the haciendas where
we were expected for the night. Then came the queer, sullen
little packtrain, two loaded mules and two led mules and a
pair of spare horses, in charge of Rafael, whose assistant did
the work while Rafael sat his mule very close to the tail and
did nothing that we could discover but shift the angle of his
hat according to the shadows.

Thus for hours we tramped and jingled and shuffled along,
sometimes changing partners as we rode from one high valley

to another by miles of sun-baked highway. We met no one but Indians; once it was a young man who had given his strawhat to the woman behind him and went bareheaded, his coarse thatch of hair shining like shoeblacking in the sun. She carried a sleeping child swaying heavily in the folds of her rebozo. Behind her marched one of those straight-backed girls with the peculiar thick aquiline nose which gives a sensuous look of pride to their dull profiles. She carried nothing but her shoes of light-colored sheepskin, and a rude guitar at her back, and stared at us fixedly with her great black eyes, lifting one corner of the blue cotton headcloth she wore. A. had taken my bridle, and as we passed these Indians I happened to be riding with hands clasped behind me as a rest from holding in my Rosillo, who was a much freer traveler than the broncos. I may have looked to them like a captive masked and bound, being led away to the mountains.

How much of all this is worth retelling? Many books on Mexico have been written since then, and there is a general belief that nothing down there ever changes; yet, are there still such homes as Queréndaro and Tepetongo and Tepetitlán, within sound of a locomotive whistle? The new railroad was hard upon our tracks — another year and such a ride as that would have had no excuse; even diligence travel was on its last wheels, nor could anyone traveling by diligence without letters have seen the inside of those walled mansions as we saw them on our return. It was when we came back in our temporary grandeur, like knights and ladies, that the seneschal met us at the outer gate, and our host the lord of the castle at the inner gate, and vassals and serfs knelt to unbuckle the knights' spurs, and we sat at the head of a feudal board with retainers silent below the salt, and there was minstrelsy after the feast in a bare hall opening on a court lighted by torches.

Talk of drama! It was a pageant in which we played our parts, conscious of one another's amusement. Our host at these great estancias would not have been the owner as a rule; he would be merely the *administrador* acting for his principal, who might have been in Paris or the capital. We were taken in at an hour's notice, with our six servants, twelve horses and four mules, and we caused not a ripple apparently on the surface of the peaceful routine. Our mozos knew their duties; they "waited in hall" with the servants of the house. Bonifacio was an excellent cook, and when no ladies were in residence, he prepared my meals and served them in my room, and his comforable, gutteral "Si, niña!" answered every requirement. He saddled our horses and packed our huge leather rolls called *maletons*, made up our beds in the great bare chambers assigned us; his hat came off if you looked at him; he slept on the stone floor of the corridor outside our door rolled in his serape, ready at a word to spring, as man-at-arms or lady's maid — in short, a mozo de camino!

Queréndaro, twenty-five miles from Morelia, was the first stop to break the stage to Maravatío. We came upon its cream white walls and gateways at two o'clock. The outer court, surrounded by one-story stone buildings, had no shade, but crossing a long bare room with glass doors, we stepped into the cloisters of a lovely inner patio turfed and planted with young orange trees. When the introductions and efforts at conversation were over we went to our rooms, closed out the afternoon light, and slept — as I was beginning to sleep again. It was bewildering when we woke a little after sunset to find it the same day. Dinner, at eight, was such a baronial feast as I have mentioned, with the visiting lady in the host's place, he and his wife on her right, the engineers on her left, the Indian colonel somewhere down the board between the top and the bottom. It was an evening like June. Lighted torches burning in the patio sent a Christmas glow about on the summer greenery. We sat out in the cloister and heard the *grito* [sound] of the crickets, as I had listened to them a thousand times from the front piazza steps at home.

Queréndaro was beautiful in the early light as we rode

across its lands. Our host rode with us to his boundaries, between the tilled fields where men and cattle were going to their work. The landowners said of the Indians, "They have no aspirations" — perhaps not. And in some cases they seemed to have a strain of brutality not to be wondered at considering Aztec sacrifices and Spanish bullfights as part of their educational history. The muscles which encircle the mouth parenthesis-like in many of their faces have a thickened rigid look like a Medusa or the tragic mask. The men's faces are not pleasant when they laugh. Our Mexican colonel had those lines which spoiled his smile and gave his dark face a cruel look. He may not have had aspirations either, but he appeared to have sentiment. . . . Beyond Zinapécuaro we left the camino real and took one of the many trails that finally merged and grew steeper as we climbed that last divide which we passed in the night going in. Now we saw what we had missed! the whole valley of Morelia, looking back from the highest point of the trail, lay below us: white cities, long-walled haciendas, the lake of Cuitzeo, green young crops, plains, woodland and water. We sat our horses and no one spoke — till our colonel murmured, lingering on the vowels with a cadence like a sigh: "Adios, Morelia, y Morelianos, y Morelianas!" He spoke for us all — we rode on saying to ourselves, "Adios Morelia!" It would have hurt us then to have been told we should never see that view again!

We lay at Maravatío that night; but all Hotels de la Diligencia were much the same whether you came as ordinary travelers or clothed with the prestige of two great provincial houses. Only this time we did not get up in the dark and crash out of the patio by torchlight. . . . At Tepetongo, the next estancia, we took up our medieval roles again. The outbuildings and dependencies made a small village in the solitude of the plain, the only travelers' rest for miles. A company of about twenty Indians arrived within the hour and camped across the outer court against the wall; each man hoisted his bundle of camote [sweet potatoes] onto the wall, stood his pole beside it, and sank down on the ground beneath his burden. There they sat motionless (I was at least an hour sketching them from the corridor) except when the *administrador* rode past with his little son on a pony beside him — then each silent figure lifted itself from the ground, took off its wide straw hat, stood till the riders were past, and dropped down again. And when the voices of the Indian children were heard at Vespers chanting in the chapel, another stir passed along the rank of dark figures as each one crossed himself and murmured his Aves. At moonrise they were gone. They carried seventy-five pounds of camote apiece, we were told, and had nine miles further to travel that night.

This was our last moon of Mexico. It rose big and splendid and we needed no torches to light us when we made the rounds of the outbuildings which are the pride and history of the estate. We were shown the threshing floor where centuries of harvests had been trampled out by the feet of cattle, a great circular area slightly concave, over a hundred feet across, sinking towards a flat stone in the center. From the threshing floor we went up a stone gangway, where ten men might walk abreast loaded with baskets of the trampled grain, to the winnowing chamber. Here was another vast circular pavement, not of stone but large tiles set in mortar, and all around it ran a low parapet pierced with loopholes for shooting when the crops and the mansion were in danger; property in Mexico has seldom not been in danger. On this parapet rested short heavy pillars supporting the great timbers of the tent-shaped roof open to all the winds of the tablelands. The name of this round tower of the fields was the *aventadero* [winnowing place].

The next was our fourth and most beautiful day's ride, and the longest, before we saw the sheer gray walls of Tepetitlán sweep round the crest of a distant height bristling with nopal cactus. Tepetitlán has a beautiful little church within her outer court where we were shown an image, carved and painted by the Indians of the estate, representing its patron saint as a laborer plowing with a team of oxen, a long, lancelike goad in his hand and a nimbus around his head. This image was carried about the fields in procession at planting time to bless the future harvest. During the year offerings of fruit and flowers and little sheaves of each new crop were laid before it. We visited the milk and cheese rooms and the granaries and another vast threshing floor, and last an old garden where pansies were blossoming under a giant pear tree near the wall. As we returned to the patio through the corral, a troop of fine young horses was being driven in for the night. One three-year-old, which was openly admired by Mr. Simpson, our host at once with a gallant gesture placed "a la disposicion de Usted" [at your service], Simpson rising to the occasion and accepting the compliment in its figurative sense, and all were pleased with the incident.

All the bells of Toluca were calling for Vespers on the last night of our ride as we trailed along the level road which seemed so long in reaching the city. My Rosillo was lasting well, but the men's horses were suffering. Twilight brightened into moonlight; three mounted men passed us with a wary exchange of salutes. Something in the colonel's manner as he looked at them led to the question: "Buenos hombres?" "Si," he answered; "buenos hombres, con Winchesters — sin Winchesters, quien sabe!" [1] He smiled his wrinkled smile and patted his rifle.

Our letters awaiting us when we reached the capital had nothing but good news of everybody at home — little son safe and well. Sharp upon that half-satisfied sigh of restlessness came the shock of a grief to persons who were strangers to us, yet it bound our thoughts to them and is the one thing I remember vividly about those last days in Mexico City. A. can't remember that he met Mr. Schuyler — we had never seen either of them in our lives — but Mrs. Schuyler wrote me an

[1] "Con," with; "sin," without.

impulsive note asking if she might send her carriage for me to come and take tea with her alone, as she was not making calls. She might have heard of us through Colonel Fergusson who knew everybody — that we were at the Iturbide, and she wanted to talk to another mother in her own tongue. She had just lost her little son, the age of ours. He too was a California baby, never sick a day in his life when they brought him down to a house like a little palace, and there he died, with all they could do for him, of one of those lurking fevers that are in the very soil the city is built on. No one could ever forget such a visit, even if the house had not been so strange and alluring and the young mother in her stricken beauty so quiet and so brave.

Among the engineers in Mexico at that time, no man would have seemed to us more enviable than Eugene Schuyler. I am not quite sure of his first name but he was the elder brother of James Dix Schuyler, whom we knew afterwards in California.[2] He was down there to work out the fulfillment of his great dream, the Mexican Central — that long line of road which was to connect the capital with the Southern Pacific lines at El Paso. He had strong backers and he was his own chief engineer and general manager. He had fitted up for her that beautiful home where I saw his heartbroken wife — even so, she had not come to the end of the price that was to pay for that dream's accomplishment. It could not have been more than two years after I saw her that we read of the death of Eugene Schuyler, found murdered by the trail on one of his lonely and fearless mountain journeys. He traveled often with only a mozo riding behind him. He had been shot in the back, and the theory nat-

---

[2] Mary Hallock Foote must indeed have been mistaken. Eugene Schuyler was a well-known diplomat and scholar, much in the public eye in the 1870s and 1880s because of his negotiations in the Balkans, his translations of Tolstoy and Turgenev, and his life of Peter the Great. James Dix Schuyler, his cousin, became famous for his work on railroads and water systems, especially in California and Mexico. The person referred to here must have been still another member of this distinguished New York family.

urally was that his servant had done it — for the value of his horse and saddle and what he had on him. Some of those soft-spoken fellows like our Bonifacio would give their last breath for you, others would shoot you for a dollar. There are ways enough by which a man, preoccupied and unsuspicious, may be stopped in his work in Mexico.

BOOK IV

Birth of a Scheme,

or

The Vision in the Desert

⚭21⚮

LIFE seemed good to us that summer in spite of continued uncertainty as to the next job. We were living on the previous jobs and my own gleanings in the wake of the man's harvest in Mexico. Another summer at his grandfather's we did not think advisable for Sonny. We took him up to Deer Isle in Penobscot Bay [Maine] and buried ourselves in a little village at the mouth of the inlet which cuts the island nearly in two. The island we never used except to sleep on — our faces were always set towards the outer bay.[1]

We engaged rooms in a house we had never seen, on the word of a respectable New Yorker who with his wife were the only other boarders. Arthur knew him slightly in a business way; he came up for over Sundays, and his wife, a stout lady with a silently curious eye, always seemed to be knitting or darning her husband's silk underwear. It was a house too big and expensive and modern for the place and for the home, one would think, of an old man who sat in the kitchen and his daughter who did her own work. She did it well with few words — not a happy looking woman. Yet if beauty could mean happiness, she might have had her share, twenty years before. We ate our eggs at breakfast out of silver eggcups; on the walls of our bedroom there were steel engravings after French painters unknown to us. They were pretty, but scarcely

---

[1] For a splendid photographic essay on Penobscot Bay and the islands that Mary Hallock Foote mentions, and a detailed map, see the Sierra Club publication by Eliot Porter, *Summer Island, Penobscot Country* [San Francisco and New York, 1968].

art, nor what Dr. J. G. Holland[2] used to call "vehicles of moral values," the subjects being chiefly on the order of Susannahs and Dianas and other ladies of good character taken at a disadvantage in the matter of clothing. It was hinted the house had a history, and it did look somewhat as if we were surrounded by the spoils of a queer past; but evidently it was past — long past, and we were very comfortably warmed by its ashes. Our days were spent on the water or on the lovely, empty islands farther out in the bay. The sailing was perfect — still water, with at intervals that great ocean roll coming in like an infrequent sigh. We had an open fire in our sitting room (speaking of ashes), and there was a big unfurnished room at our disposal where Sonny made all the litter he liked on rainy days, and the men cleaned their guns. Arthur had found Van Zandt in New York, waiting as we were, and instantly annexed him as a second "gun." Sport is poor business all alone. We hired Captain John Scott and his boat, the *Blue Bird*, for thirty dollars a month, the pair, and what Cap'n John and the *Blue Bird* didn't know about the inlet and the bay and the mackerel runs, nobody on the island could tell them.

Every day of sailing weather we were off as soon as we could get the guns and tackle and sketching things together; but when we were on the hunting grounds, and the steep fronts of Bradbury [Island] and his neighbor, Big Pickering, began to repeat the note of the guns in echoes back and forth, or when the bottom of the boat was one shining mass of flopping, gasping mackerel, sport was too much for me! — we left the young barbarians to their play and had ourselves set ashore, Sonny and his mother, to kill nothing but time, loafing on the island beaches or strolling over the sea-bitten moors, eating blueberries as fast as we could pick them. They grew among the

[2] Josiah Gilbert Holland (1819-81) was well known in his own day as a writer and as the editor of *Scribner's Monthly*, where he was Richard Gilder's immediate superior. Holland's death virtually coincided with the transformation of *Scribner's* into the *Century Magazine*.

rocks, mixed with sweet fern and juniper bushes and wild roses. Every day we were cleaner of our malaria germs and every night I was better of my Leadville sleeplessness — though the Mexican journeys had pretty much finished that.

Of all these sea nurseries for land babies, the perfect one was Big Pickering. Why such an island as that should lie there untouched, with but one house on it and that a fisherman's shack, who knows? Islands had not come into use as playgrounds then, except on the grand scale of Naushon.[3] This was a poor man's paradise; we might have bought the whole 400 acres then for $3,000. We did buy Little Pickering (with the price of one of my drawings), the little island joined to it at low tide, when you could walk across to the big island and all its beauties were your own — sea pastures and cranberry swamps and pinewoods on the sheltered side where the great blue heron breed. Little Pickering was a toy and we were children to buy it, when we had not an idea what we should do next or whether we should ever see it again. But there were four white birches on it which someone might have cut down; they were almost human in their maidenly beauty. We put them and the island in Captain Scott's charge and dreamed that we might come back someday, when we had made the price of a summer holiday in the East, and build a fishing hut on Little Pickering and be independent of silver eggcups and Susannahs. Every year, wherever we were, Captain Scott's report of his stewardship followed us. He named his next boy, born after that summer, Arthur; and when Van Zandt made his first big mining purchase he named his mine the "Blue Bird."

But in the evenings, when the games of chess were over and the last pipes were being smoked, our talk ran on Mexico and the medieval doings down there. Van's experience of that people was very different from ours. We had heard rumors of

---

[3] Naushon is one of the Elizabeth Islands, a small chain that separates Buzzards Bay from Vineyard Sound, Massachusetts. For generations members of the Forbes family have made it their summer home.

a wild chapter in his affairs since he was last "under arms" in defense of the unlucky Adelaide. He was always running into romance — now we heard the whole story in his own words, mixed as it was with friendships and loyalties and frank horror through it all.

A cousin of his, Charley Potter, as he was known to society in the East, had been in Leadville the last summer we were there, staying with Van and Booraem at their cabin and making himself agreeable all up and down the Ditch Walk. He was good looking and well bred and bored apparently with whatever his life had been; or that may have been merely his mood at the time. He wanted something to do quite different, and Mr. Emmons was able to gratify his wish. He procured him a job on the government census work which took him down to New Mexico and gave him lonely journeys rounding up a scattered and picturesque population, and then he disappeared. He had set out at last accounts for a little pueblo, alone, on horseback, and was not seen again.

It took some time, in the irregularity of the mails, for the absence of all word from him to alarm his friends; then they sent Van Zandt down on his trail. His uncle, Governor Van Zandt of Rhode Island,[4] used his influence at Washington, and a posse of soldiers from the nearest army post went with him to save him from disappearing too, and to protect him in whatever he might have before him. They were under his command. Young Potter's death was a case of cold-blooded pursuit and murder such as neither our government nor the Mexican over the border seemed able to deal with. Van Zandt dealt with it out of hand by the methods of wild justice. He brought home his cousin's body, with a few of his personal possessions found upon the man they captured, proving that they had hanged the right man.

4 Charles Collins Van Zandt (1830-94), long a member of the Rhode Island legislature, was lieutenant governor from 1873-75 and governor from 1877-80.

A strange story to listen to in that little island harbor of the far North — and with our own so different memories of Mexico still warm in our hearts; the gentle voices, the flower-lined corridors, the doves asleep in the moonlight, and Emelita's dark blue eyes with tears in them when we said farewell; yet, turn the page and there was our amigo, Colonel Zapato, with his cruel smile, whose friendship you could purchase for fifty dollars; there was the germ-soaked soil which those Moorish courts and corridors were built on; there was the cool and frivolous taking off of Schuyler in his prime, and Van Zandt's nightmare journey with its ghastly end — "Viva Mexico!" Should we have gone back if fate had given us the chance? — I suppose we should, and it was well that we were thwarted.

We saw Van Zandt the following spring, and for the last time. We were able to remember him at his best, if that means success and happiness. We were "on the bough" in New York, before starting for Idaho on the longest and wildest of our schemes. He had just returned from England, fortunate in the business entrusted to him and engaged to the woman over there whom he loved at first sight — a whirlwind wooing of a girl above him in one sense, perhaps in more than one, whom he might never in the course of events have met again. She was one of a party of distinguished guests at Dalmeny Park where his business took him for a few days; a young widow of twenty-four, a daughter of Sir John Lubbock, highly educated (which of course Van Zandt was not), an heiress, which made no difference to either of them.[5] There was youth and beauty and the force of dynamic natures on both sides; they rode to hounds together — and were engaged in two days.

That strong element of drama that turned its light on Van's

---

5 The London *Times*, March 20, 1884, reported the marriage of Ferdinand Suydam Van Zandt, eldest son of the late Charles Van Zandt, of New York, to Amy, eldest daughter of Sir John Lubbock, Bart., M.P., and widow of Andrew Mulholland. (Sir John was later raised to the peerage as Baron Avebury of Avebury.)

life at this age put out some of the finer shades of his nature
which time had in its keeping. The hero roles were thrust
upon him, and to help him carry out the part he had a wise
old Chiron [6] to push his affairs and introduce him to the world.
"Old Sam Ward," "Uncle Sam" Van called him, "knew more
of life than all the departments of the government put together," said Henry Adams.[7] His rooms in New York were
free quarters for Van, whose stories of his patron were as
amusing as anything on the French stage. It was "Uncle Sam"
who sent him to England on the mission which took him within the sphere of young ladies like the one he chose, but when
it came to winning the princess and carrying her off to his
fastness in Montana, the Blue Bird mine, it was not Uncle
Sam who did that.

We continued to hear of this romantic pair on occasions
like the birth of a daughter and then a second daughter, then
silence and rumors of troubles at the mine that I don't recall
in detail — an ugly strike and an expensive lawsuit. Van had
remembered his Leadville friends: Bob Booraem was there
as superintendent, I think, and Steve Fleming had a share in
Van's prosperity while it lasted. But now he went to England
on a different errand and his mission did not prosper. He was
ill with influenza alone one night at Brown's Hotel in Dover
on the eve of crossing to Paris, and in a fit of delirium at the
acute stage of the attack, he shot himself — but no one who
knew Van could have believed that he was responsible. Nothing could have been less in character — Van had too much
humor to do a thing like that, not to mention all he had to live

---

[6] Famous as the teacher of Jason, Hercules, and Achilles.

[7] Samuel Ward (1814-84), often known as "King of the Lobby," came of good
family, was the brother of Julia Ward Howe, and an author in his own right,
but is best remembered as an influential lobbyist in Washington from the later
days of the Civil War through the administrations of Johnson and Grant. His
friendships included not only politicians but such unlikely figures as Longfellow, Thackeray, and the Earl of Rosebery (who gave him the nickname "Uncle
Sam"). The quoted phrase is from Adams, *Education*, p. 253.

for, and his life not half spent. It was unfair of fate to play him that trick after petting him up and trying to spoil him for years. That of course was the point about Van Zandt — he was not spoiled. He was a very strong and steadily developing man. On every side of his life the best was yet to come. He was blown out like an unspent torch in a blast of wind.[8]

8 Van Zandt's Blue Bird mine was near Rocker, Montana, which, in turn, was a few miles from Butte. British capital financed the mine, including construction of a large stamp mill in 1885 or 1886 and a brick house for Van Zandt and his bride. Mary Hallock Foote heard that Mrs. Van Zandt's money and that of her friends in England had been sunk into the venture. She compared Van Zandt's disastrous mining scheme with Arthur Foote's equally unhappy irrigation project, in that both dragged down with them whole families and their close friends, because in each case an ambitious man had made a typically American bid for success. Mary Hallock Foote, Boise, March 7, 1892, to Helena Gilder. News of Van Zandt's suicide had just reached her (his death occurred March 2, 1892).

22

Everything hinging as it does on something else, it was Ross Raymond's disastrous report on the Little Pittsburg which crippled the Michoacán Syndicate in placing its mines; it was a shock indeed to all mining ventures based on the judgments of high-paid experts. There was another, more to blame than Raymond, mixed up in that affair who made no mistake — who lied to his old friend and fellow student with an eye to personal gain. But Raymond would not shield himself behind this other, nor did he accuse him. The fact was guessed by one who knew them both and put it up to Raymond. He admitted it with humility and without bitterness; "I was there to see for myself; I had no business to take the word of any man."[1]

Arthur went out to Leadville that summer [1881] to close up our little matters there. It was well that we didn't build cabins to sell! Real estate values had shrunk since our gay days on the Ditch Walk, and no one ever gets his price who is in a hurry to sell. . . . Wife and boy fell back on their old base line at Milton and the man took a room at the Collonade Hotel on Astor Place [New York City], where she could visit him occasionally [during the winter of 1881-82]. Between these visits, and sometimes during them, she kept her own little industries going. 'The Led-Horse Claim," my first attempt at a novel,

[1] Mary Hallock Foote may well have confused two very similar episodes with which Rossiter Raymond was connected. As indicated on p. 187, footnote 13, Raymond misjudged both the Little Pittsburg and Chrysolite mines, but the details cited here correspond precisely with the circumstances of the Chrysolite affair, where Raymond seems to have been misled by W. S. Keyes, a fellow graduate of Freiberg and a well-known mining engineer, who was then superintendent.

ran as a serial in the *Century* that year and was published in book form, with the author's illustrations, by my old friends in Boston, James R. Osgood and Company.[2] It told of things that interested the writer and was called a success; if it was, it was a most ingenuous one.

Nothing that could have come to us in the way of luck to send us west would have compensated for the friendship that began that winter with the Rockwell cousins through hanging around New York waiting for a job. They were living in Boston but came on to visit the Hagues who never failed to put in our way any good thing they had to share. To dine with the Hagues meant crossing the ferry and taking a train to Orange, with our slippers in a bag, and preening ourself in Mary's bedroom, to be introduced to these new cousins on our husband's side. He had lived with them in his college days, Colonel Rockwell being then professor of mining at Yale — *that* invitation was for the family's sake; but now he was to know them as himself. For me, I would not have missed meeting them for all the jobs in the United States or even Mexico.

The relationship was on the side of Mrs. Rockwell who was Katherine Virginia Foote,[3] and went back (we come now to my husband's early Episcopalians) to the marriage in 1772 between Eli Foote, who was Tory as well as Episcopalian, and Roxanna, daughter of the old patriot general, Andrew Ward of Nutplains, Guilford, Conn.[4] He was the great-grandfather

---

[2] Serialized in *Century Magazine* from November 1882-March 1883; published by Osgood in 1883. Mary Hallock Foote's statement is confusing, because, as she correctly points out on p. 262, she was only writing the novel that winter.

[3] Katherine Virginia Foote (1839-1902) was the daughter of Captain Samuel Edmund Foote (1787-1858) and thus cousin to Arthur De Wint Foote. In 1865 she married Alfred Perkins Rockwell (1834-1903), a mining engineer who had studied at Sheffield Scientific School, Yale, and at London and Freiberg. During the Civil War he rose to the rank of colonel and was brevetted brigadier general. He was appointed professor of mining at Sheffield Scientific School, where he remained until 1868, when he took a similar position at M.I.T. In 1873 he gave up teaching to enter business.

[4] Arthur De Wint Foote's grandmother, Roxanna Ward Foote (1751-1840), was the eldest daughter of the revolutionary general Andrew Ward (1727-99), who

of that unusual group of first cousins, the children of George Augustus Foote and of Samuel Edmund, his elder brother. Eli Foote acted as secretary to General Ward throughout the war. (There were two Revolutionary generals named Ward.) He was said to have been a personable young man, not unlikely to have found favor with the general's daughter, but it seems strange he should have been his private secretary. They were both Episcopalians, however, and his Tory sympathies may not have been more than a matter of sentiment and early training. General Ward had known him from a boy and his people before him.

He died in early middle life, and Nutplains became the home of his widow and her children. There were five sons, The two elder died, leaving Samuel, aged fourteen, to take his grandfather's place, at his death, as the accepted head of the house.[5] Roxanna was said to have been a great reader, a very clever woman, witty and with great store of quotations at her tongue's end, but with no head for practical affairs. In Samuel there was that which demanded scope; a year later he arranged with his younger brother, a sage person of twelve, to relieve him of his family responsibilities and he was set free. He took his life abroad on the high seas and made a story of it and a great experience. He became that sort of fairy-tale uncle no family of homebred boys should be without.

At eighteen he was captain of a full-rigged ship. Soon he was sailing his own ships and carrying his own cargoes in partnership with his brother, John, backed by an uncle in New York, a shipping merchant who had taken John into his

---

is not to be confused with the more famous revolutionary general Artemas Ward. Roxanna married Eli Foote (1747-92) on October 11, 1772, and at his death twenty years later moved to her father's farm, "Nutplains," near Guilford. It was at General Ward's death in 1799 that his young grandson, Samuel Edmund Foote, became "accepted head of the house."

5 The three surviving sons were John (see next footnote), Samuel Edmund (1787-1858), and George Augustus (1789-1878), but Mary Hallock Foote did not have their ages quite right in relation to their grandfather's death.

business.[6] Maritime trade must have been a wild romance in those times, but it took hard sense to make it pay. Samuel Edmund became known as a merchant captain of unusual shrewdness and daring. All this time by study and practice he was broadening his education: he spoke French and Spanish and Italian fluently and made profit of these acquirements in Europe's old wars and suppressions of rebellions in the New World. He took his ships past their guns into sealed ports — once into Callao, blockaded by Spain during the Peruvian revolution. That voyage must have been worth to him nearly the capture of a gold ship in the days of Drake and Hawkins. There were many gallant stories of Uncle Sam Foote's seagoing days, and no doubt his fame did not die stifled in the breasts of his farmer kin. An uncle to brag about by the family fireside, and to awaken the ambition of dreamy, inarticulate half-grown boys. He made fortunes and lost them with the same equanimity; the last one he kept; and after these years of boyish risks, his work became technical and constructive — he was called one of the best-equipped men of his time, through reading and study and varied experience.

George Augustus, the farmer of twelve, went on with the work to which he was called, stayed unmarried until nearly forty and then took a wife, Eliza Spencer, aged seventeen. Their acquaintance began one summer morning as he was passing her father's front fence and saw her seated on top of one of the square white-painted gateposts, gazing at the world. The world was pleased with her, and the man whose life she was to share stopped to ask: "Whose little girl are you?"

That little girl bore him twelve children [7] and governed his

---

6 John Parsons Foote (1783-1865), elder brother of Samuel E. and George Augustus Foote, was adopted by his uncle, Justin Foote, presumably at the death of Eli Foote. Justin Foote was a merchant in Brooklyn and with his nephew formed the firm of J. & J.P. Foote, Merchant Marine, of which Mary Hallock Foote here speaks. When Samuel retired from the sea in the 1820s, he and his brother John moved to Cincinnati, where Samuel made and lost several fortunes before deciding to return to Connecticut.

7 The family genealogy book lists only ten. See above, p. 158.

house where often twenty persons would sit at table for weeks at a time, Nutplains being the seat of family hospitality as in General Ward's day. The aged and infirm and childless (and childish) came there to be nursed in their last illnesses; smoothing pillows in last hours being the duty of every woman as long as her strength held out — and bearing children as the Lord sends. The autocrat and head of the house was not ungentle, albeit a man was a man in those times, nor was he idle. Five years he sat in the state legislature as Whig representative from Guilford, many years he was colonel of militia and senior churchwarden of Guilford church which he gave largely of his means to build, resigning from both military and church duty only on account of old age. He added Mulberry Point to Nutplains and made it his own home, leaving Nutplains to his eldest son.

But he kept guard over the family burial ground which his grandfather laid out before his own death. There were no hearses at that time; the dead were carried by their friends and neighbors, in relays when the homes were too far from the churchyard for one set of bearers. General Ward's two eldest grandsons, youths of sixteen and fourteen years, had been chosen for this duty one midsummer day, and did it like men and died shortly after as the result of sudden illness brought on, it was thought, by heat and excessive strain.[8] The sacrifice of these two fine boys nearly broke the old man's heart: no young men, he said, should carry him in his coffin three miles to Guilford churchyard. He dedicated the family acre with his own body and there they lie, the generations of homekeepers and wanderers, under the oaks on a little hill in sight of the fields their forefathers won from the wilderness. The dead of Samuel Edmund's line were not many but too many for the number that was left.[9] His second son lay there,

---

8 These two boys were Andrew Ward Foote and William Henry Foote, elder brothers of Samuel E. and George Augustus Foote. They died, respectively, in August and October 1794 at ages seventeen and sixteen.

9 His children were: George Augustus (1829-34), who did not survive childhood; Frances Elizabeth (1835-75); Katherine Virginia (1839-1902); and Harry Ward (1844-73).

George Augustus Foote

Harry Ward Foote, unmarried, at twenty-nine; his eldest daughter Frances Elizabeth, wife of Edwin Lawrence Godkin, and two of their three children — only one grandson left to carry on that branch.[10] Reading Mr. Godkin's *Life* years after, we came upon that reiterated cry from the heart of a lonely household: "Lawrence will not marry!" All the future was in Lawrence who was taking his time.

But up to that winter the Rockwells, with their double family inheritance of means and three fine children,[11] had gone unscathed, and one honored post after another General Rockwell had held since he won his youthful laurels in the Civil War. It would take a long sentence to list the notable things he had done. In any roomful of company which they entered, eyes turned to them as the most conspicuous pair: Kate, a tall white lily of elegance beside the general with his soldier's eye, his handsome beak and moustaches, and his crest of dark hair which turned snow white, and then he was more striking than ever.

This was the family background shared by that highly individualized group of first cousins. The girls all married exceptional men.[12] Elizabeth [Foote] did not lower the mark, nor Kate [Foote], though she was a long way past girlhood

[10] Frances Elizabeth Foote married Edwin Lawrence Godkin (1831-1902), a journalist who was born in Ireland of English stock and who became one of the most influential American editors of his generation. He edited the *Nation* from the date of its founding in 1865 and was editor-in-chief of the *New York Evening Post* from 1883-1900. The *Life* to which Mary Hallock Foote refers is *The Life and Letters of Edwin Lawrence Godkin*, ed. by Rollo Ogden (New York and London, 1907). The surviving child, Lawrence, was born in 1860.

[11] The children of Katherine Virginia Foote Rockwell and Alfred Perkins Rockwell were: Mary Foote, who was born and died in 1868; Frances Beatrice (1872-86); Samuel Edmund (1873-84) and his twin, Katherine Diana Ward.

[12] At this point, confusingly, Mary Hallock Foote shifts from discussion of the Rockwells to a broader reference to that whole generation of cousins to which Arthur Foote and his sisters Elizabeth and Kate belonged. Both sisters married late. Elizabeth, born 1852, in 1885 married Edward H. Jenkins, a chemist who had studied at Yale and Leipzig and became director of the Connecticut Agricultural Station. Katherine, born 1840, married Andrew J. Coe in 1895. Coe, a Wesleyan graduate, was an attorney, farmer, member of the Connecticut legislature, and judge of a local court.

when she made her choice. We played with the Hagues and
Rockwells that gay winter of suspense while fortune played
with us. On my side we saw much of the Gilders and of their
literary and artist friends. There was a dinner one night
to meet Henry James who was Mr. Godkin's houseguest —
"*Hamlet* with Hamlet left out," as our host ruefully announced on greeting us, Hamlet being upstairs in bed with a
headache in consequence, as he explained next day at the
Gilders, of a "flirtation with coffee."

The evening lacked nothing to us who had never seen
"Hamlet" and could not ask more than we had. And at its
close there was an invitation from our host and cousin-in-law
to come and stay with him and bring our little boy. A week's
visit in that house, that winter, would have been a chapter
by itself. Arthur left the decision to me — why did I refuse!
Helena said it was the Quaker Negative acting automatically
from generations of habit. It may be; there was something in
me which knew as a rule when it was time to stop. Certain
combinations of intangible joys would go to my head and
cause my color to rise and my tongue to run, and a little of it
was good — very good for my work, but not too much: "Tune
ye the zither neither low nor high." It was time to go back to
Milton and submerge again and put away one's best clothes
and prepare for the baby that was coming in the autumn.

But one evening of that winter time has left us undimin-
ished in memory — others have had thousands of such evenings, but not I! A party of us which included Mr. Godkin and
the Hagues went to the first night of *Patience* in New York.[13]
It was the English company — the original, the unrivaled
Bunthorne, the dresses that Du Maurier caricatured in *Punch*,
the players in high jollity at such a welcome from a house
packed with the city's best. Encore followed encore, with

[13] Of this first season of *Patience* the comment has been made: "The Gilbert and
Sullivan satirical operetta was a raging epidemic in the season of 1881-82, only
a trifle less devastating to other theatrical ventures than had been *Pinafore* in
1879." George C. D. Odell, *Annals of the New York Stage* (New York, 1939),
XI, 452.

tears of laughter from the audience and a frolic response on the stage. With a geologist of high repute on one side of you mopping his eyes and a formidable journalist mopping his on the other, and a poet-editor talking witty nonsense between the acts and two of the sweetest women you knew leaning to exchange looks with you — better fun and better company were not to be had in New York at that time — not by casuals like ourselves dropped down there by an oversight of luck.

Towards spring [1882] Arthur went out to the Wood River region — the darkest part of darkest Idaho — to manage a mine, not thinking much of the mine nor of the job as the basis of a future home; but the present we had to think of now.[14] I was at Milton finishing the last chapters of "The Led-Horse Claim" — rewriting them to make the story end well. It was assuming rather too much for that little romance to make it a tragedy. But I always knew it should have been, as far as the "love interest" was concerned.

14 The Wood River, in the central part of southern Idaho, flows southward from the Sawtooth Range to join the Snake River. A boom began there in the summer of 1880, following earlier discoveries, and by the time that Arthur Foote arrived in 1882, mines and smelters were in operation; railroad service began the next year.

⟨ 23 ⟩

THE doctor had been having John Sherman under observation for some years. He was much more to us than "the doctor" — he was an old friend who knew the family's physical history and idiosyncracies, root and branch, and he must have divined silently a good deal more of its inside life and problems than anyone had ever told him. He said John must go away; he needed a change. Even a change for the worse would be better than none. That was something Arthur could offer him on the spot; he was starting for the Wood River and he asked John to go with him and camp around while he was opening the Wolftone Mine. The savagery of these dark-colored names did not deter the Quaker farmer of the Hudson. He never was really meant to be a farmer, though he couldn't help being a Quaker. So they went together at a few days' notice and the summer was a good one for John in many ways. He even made a little money in clever ways of his own, taking advantage of the opportunities such as they were. He did not make mistakes. He came home without Arthur, who had drifted down to southern Idaho on some new adventure not yet developed in his own mind. He had resigned from the management of the Wolftone which did not look good to him in any respect.

In September our little daughter was born — son or daughter, it made no difference to me: I had wanted this baby for two years. Nature sometimes takes care of the mother first in making up her vital accounts — now the books that had barely balanced showed a good surplus and this baby weighed eight pounds and had not a blemish on her. I had given away my baby things to someone in Leadville (when my own hope there was lost), someone in urgent need. Mary Hague's little Billy was going into short clothes just as my Betty arrived; she sent me his entire first wardrobe — what a haul! everything much finer than I should have been able to buy. My little daughter was presented to her parents' world dressed much above their circumstances at that time. . . . Other things went along with the nursery schedule because they had to. The galley proofs of the first installment of "The Led-Horse Claim" (my daughter's "twin") arrived by mail on the first day I "sat up," with a polite request that they be returned promptly. The doctor found me stewing over them with a hot face — he did not approve of writing mothers.[1]

But that which did send me back to bed and turned my face to the wall was a letter about this time from my husband. It was written carefully, but the news could no longer be delayed: he was not coming home till after Christmas, because of this new scheme just looming for us in southern Idaho. He had work to do on it which could not wait. I had thought we were committed to deep mining, and here we were turning our backs on the experience and the friends we had gained in the last six years and beginning all over again in a new branch of engineering. What did "we" know about irrigation? — and not on an assured job, but as authors and projectors from the ground up. The ground indeed! — three hundred thousand acres of it, in an unknown region, the great attraction of which seemed to be that it needed water. It was a desert to be reclaimed, a scheme so vast that millions would be needed to carry it through. Who were we that we should think we could influence capital to that extent! There it was in

---

[1] Elizabeth Townsend Foote was born on September 9, 1882; "The Led-Horse Claim, a Romance of the Silver Mines," began running serially in the issue of the *Century Magazine* for November 1882, which explains why the printer would have wanted his galley proofs returned in September. William Hague, whose clothes Betty Foote inherited, had been born March 31, 1882.

a nutshell as it looked to that "eternal misbeliever," a man's own wife. The mother of a two weeks' baby has had all the adventurousness taken out of her.

I gave a night of waking if not tears to that portent of a scheme. I thought of my unlucky brother and his gallant barks of no return; and Sarah's words: "His hopefulness is my hopelessness."[2] It was the family fate apparently. I had thought to escape it, having a market for my goods and marrying a man who had the goods if not the market. But I had not reckoned on the schemes. He had risen, poor wretch, in obedience to his own inheritance, from the ashes of all the jobs that gave out, the cement dream that failed, the men you couldn't work for and be a man yourself, the climates we could not live in; he had resigned from the Wolftone with not a tangible thing in sight: I couldn't count this appalling undertaking as anything more than the stuff of wakeful nights for mothers of young babies. It was exactly like his Uncle Sam, only his gallant barks came into port with colors at the peak — when they did not go down! No doubt his wife, the fair Elizabeth Elliott, had her wakeful nights.

And a girl baby! Boys for the frontier, but with the arrival of this little downy head next my heart, that foolish part of me turned back to the East of my own girlhood. This meant farewell music, art, gossip of the workshop, schools that we knew about, new friends just made who would forget us, old friends better loved than ever and harder to part from — all the old backgrounds receding hopelessly and forever. Mexico had not been farther to the imagination than this — and what compensations! You reached it by the gulfs enchanted, by moonlight nights in old Spanish-American cities, by strange, medieval roads. But — darkest Idaho! Thousands of acres of desert empty of history. The Snake River had an evil name — the Boise, the source of our great scheme, emptied into and was lost in it and carried out into the Columbia which I knew

2 See above, p. 97.

was Bryant's "Oregon" that "hears no sound, save his own dashings."[3] I felt adrift, as it were, cast off on a raft with my babies, swept past these wild shores uninhabited for us. My husband steering us with a surveyor's rod or some such futile thing — and where were we going on this flood of uncertainties? I was in that frame of mind and body that if my dreamer had been Moses I should have tried to stay his hand lest the water when it followed his stroke might become a torrent and overwhelm us. . . .

He came back in February [1883], and in one evening's talk upstairs by ourselves he convinced me that he was not mad. He was as quietly assured of the worth of what he was doing as I was of my own little scheme of a six months' baby asleep in her crib beside us. No one could have convinced me that she was not worth a lifetime of pains and all the money we could scrape up to bring her to womanhood.

He had that recklessness of time and cost, with absolute conviction as to the worth of the undertaking, which makes it possible to unfold a country or bring up a child from the cradle. I no longer quarreled with his imagination, though I held my breath; the wonder was that he should so soon have found other men with imagination! Not shysters, but men in big business of their own whose names commanded respect. I asked to be told about General C. H. Tompkins, the president of his new company called the Idaho Mining and Irrigation Company;[4] I could see that my husband already loved him as a brother in the scheme. He was another Civil War veteran

3 As Mary Hallock Foote indicates, Arthur Foote was planning to build his irrigation system in the cañon and valley of the Boise River, which is a tributary of the Snake River, which in turn empties into the Columbia. The quotation is from William Cullen Bryant's "Thanatopsis."

4 The double title, Idaho Mining and Irrigation Company, reflected Arthur Foote's belief that in addition to achieving its primary purpose of delivering water for irrigation, the company could use its water supply to work the Snake River gold placers, which had defeated experienced placer miners for twenty years. The Snake River placers had a very fine and widely dispersed type of gold ("flour gold") that had defied profitable operations.

and, like General Joe Hawley and General Rockwell, a comparatively young man when the war closed and left him worked up to his highest efficiency with all that gallant temper unexpended. General Hawley had gone into politics and was a party man, General Rockwell took hold of a fire department and a dying railroad, and General Tompkins had built up the American Diamond Drill Company and was its president.[5] It sounded like the rose of capital or near it; there was the same solid family background too and conservative training. General Tompkins' sons were St. Paul's boys; his eldest, just graduated from the Boston Tech, I heard, was going out to Idaho in the spring to run canal lines under my husband in the Snake River desert.[6] It was all incredible; and these good names connected with us added to the pilot's responsibility; still, it looked less lonely on that raft! I was able to sleep of nights again and did not even dream of lonely rivers that hear no sound save their own dashings.

All things going ahead, as it seemed, and the Shermans being still in the valley of decision, I sounded Bessie on the question — would they, could they, take the Long Trail with us? — let this scheme, wild as it sounded, be the way which might lead to other and safer opportunities for them? She not only considered it, she was keen from the start. My sister was timid about horses — it was an idiosyncrasy, for she was our best rider — but I don't know of anything else on earth she was

---

[5] Charles H. Tompkins achieved the rank of colonel during the Civil War and was brevetted brigadier general. New York City directories of the later nineteenth century listed him as a civil engineer and head of the American Diamond Rock Boring Company.

[6] "Boston Tech" of course meant Massachusetts Institute of Technology, and "St. Paul's" referred to the well-known Episcopal preparatory school at Concord, New Hampshire. The scant alumni records at those two institutions show merely that Charles H. Tompkins, Jr., the "Harry" of these reminiscences, attended St. Paul's from 1877-79, graduated from M.I.T. in 1883, and died June 22, 1914.

afraid of except snakes and debt. She and John must have been longing for years to be free, to live their own lives in their own way. The Old Things and the Old Faiths have their price. They had been faithful, and they were no longer young. But the cost to our mother! Partings like that are a kind of death — "un peu la mort."

The scheme seemed to have taken on organic life and to propagate itself; more and more people were on the raft committed to those currents of fate! The Hagues I am sure were doubtful, but James never was one to prick another man's bubble. General Tompkins had a most lovely wife — one of the Carrs of Baltimore — and two young daughters just ready for society, worthy of their breeding. Their home was on Staten Island; but the dinner they gave for us on the eve of Arthur's return to Idaho was at an hotel in the city. Mrs. Tompkins asked me what we meant to do about lessons for our young children if the Thing did go on, and I told her of a little arrangement made a few years before with Nelly Linton, a friend of my girl days and daughter of my old master, William James Linton:[7] that when the need arrived for a governess in our family, wherever we might be, she would come to us and take the place in the sensible way the English understand it. Mrs. Tompkins mused upon the name and smiled: "I hope she's not too pretty?" And one of the sisters laughed and said: "Mama means that Harry is very susceptible." Harry was the brother going out to Idaho. That was only a sister's jibe. . . . No, our gallant little Englishwoman was not too pretty, not too anything for the place she filled in our midst, on all our rafts, on all our currents of fate, for thirteen years from the

7 William James Linton (1812-97), while best known as a wood engraver and illustrator, became famous also for the fine printing done at his Appledore Press in Hamden, Connecticut, and for his poetry and participation in political reform movements. Coming to New York from his native England in 1866, he taught wood engraving at Cooper Union during the later 1860s, and there had Mary Hallock Foote for a student. Among the many books he illustrated was an edition of Bryant's "Thanatopsis" in 1878, twice quoted by Mrs. Foote.

time she joined us in Idaho. And if ever a cog slipped (to change the metaphor) in the order of things (and there was order where she was in command), its name was not Ellen Wade Linton.

It struck me, looking at the Tompkins family that evening, that they were, one and all, much too nice and too secure in their present happiness to be risking anything of this actual prosperity on a scheme. According to the history of most big schemes, what we needed was at least one old, tough business pirate (I don't say that we wanted him!) with no conscience to hinder him from smashing through any scruples he might encounter on the road to victory. But my man would have replied, if I had jested with him in this way, that our scheme was an endurance test; the end was as sure as spring after winter or grass after rain; and we should need our principles, if we had any, for that side of human contacts which must be the basis of any land scheme. We must have the confidence of the homemakers.

The new irrigation company's first report came out in great form, printed by De Vinne, with an Egyptian hieroglyph on the title page signifying Agriculture in the desert: fellaheen in loincloths carrying "pots" slung from a pole across their shoulders and emptying them on the land; underneath, from Psalms: "I have removed his shoulder from the burden; his hands were delivered from the pots."[8] When Clarence King saw this report — he probably went no deeper into it than the cover — he said, "That quotation ought to build the canal." The engineer's wife read it somewhat as a work of fiction, all

---

[8] Psalms, 81:6. The biblical quotation appeared on the cover of the second of two reports by Foote: *The Idaho Mining and Irrigation Company. Report. 1884* (New York, 1884), printed by Theo. L. De Vinne. The earlier report had been entitled *Report on the Feasibility of Irrigating and Reclaiming Certain Desert Lands between the Snake and Boise Rivers . . .* (New York, 1883). Both reports contained the introductory description by Foote that is quoted by Mrs. Foote in the next paragraph, although the precise version quoted here is based upon comparison with the original.

history in the making being fiction to the majority in its day. It was an assembling of facts to show the feasibility of the enterprise, these facts having been collected in Idaho since the idea took root in my husband's mind.

There were columns of estimates which the reader skipped; there were interviews with farmers and desert settlers, and statistics of crops and analyses of soils, and maps of the entire canal line, from the spot where the river was to be turned into it down to the gold-bearing sands of the Snake River, seventy-five miles, and in all that distance it crossed no man's land. My husband saw in this no claims for damages, no conflict as to rights-of-way; to me it meant a land without life, not dead, perhaps, but unborn. . . . Then, with a restrained ecstasy, he begins:

The lands which are the subject of the following report . . . may be roughly described as lying in the form of a triangle, the apex of which is the confluence of the Snake and Boise rivers; its sides are these rivers; its base the line of the canal necessary for the irrigation of the lands. . . . These lands lie in immense benches or broad plateaus, which for long distances slope gently toward the meeting of the rivers; at intervals the general slope is broken by a sharp mesa or bluff, and dropping fifty feet, they stretch out again as before.

The author of this scheme was thirty-three years old. He had lost two years of his technical training which never could be made up quite to his own satisfaction, though he was always at school, the school of self-training. What he wanted was opportunity, like the days of the early discoverers, or the rise of the American merchant marine, or the Civil War which had taken his older brothers and tested them and wrung them out. And if a man desires to be wrung out to the last dregs and take the risk of failure and years of work with no return, a better job than this could not be found. Only one-half of the tale can be told by me, but it should be remembered that there was always the eastern half where the money had to come from, and that endurance test lasted as long as ours did, and was borne in silence by our partners and allies there.

Arthur left us that summer [1883] for Idaho, taking John Sherman on the promise of a job, with the understanding that Bessie and I and the children should follow our husbands in the autumn. We had gone to the South Shore, I and my two, when the heat came on at Milton; we were living in a little summer cottage near one the Hagues had, at Point Lookout, on the same boardwalk.[9] Mary and I were thus close neighbors for weeks and she observed me with a sisterly eye — burning the candle at both ends, as she called it. My baby was ten months old in July; we never weaned our teething babies in summer in those days. I expected to keep it up — with baby and with writing and drawing (the cottage being a little beyond our means) till the autumn and the end of the Idaho journey — and then rest. But I hadn't allowed for a miscarriage which had nothing to do with my general health but which had to be made up for in various ways. I was indeed cutting it pretty fine.

But the cottage season was over; I went back to Milton with the children and began my packing; and then James and Mary broke their rule of noninterference and made the trip to Milton on purpose to change our family plans. It was the first and last time I can remember either of them offering unasked advice. I was so impressed that I took it — but not until we had argued the question hour after hour of that lovely October day. It was so warm that we sat out on the piazza, and the home folk discreetly let us have it to ourselves. Mary gave me the history of some of her own imprudences and the result to her health, and reminded me of the years of journeys I probably had ahead of me. James said, with a peculiar earnestness

9 Point Lookout was on the southern coastline of Long Island, near the town of Long Beach and within commuter distance of New York City by railroad, as James Hague's diaries make clear.

which made me remember his words though they were simple enough: "There is no hurry about your going to Idaho, Mary; nothing is so slow as a scheme like this. There is plenty of time!" There was ten years of time!

He did not doubt the value of irrigation to the lands that needed it, yet he would not have risked money of his own in any irrigation scheme at that time nor have advised his friends to do so.

Seeing the coil I was in over this recreancy at the last moment, James offered to send the telegram breaking it to Arthur himself, over his and Mary's names, and I allowed him to do it and felt more recreant than ever. But it was done — and my husband, being in bed when the message came, head and eyes and stomach all on strike together, was cross with his relatives and mystified by me. He wired, "Telegraph me about it." He wanted more details, but by the time these words reached me, repeated from office to office, they read "Tell grandma about it." He had never called my mother "grandma" — and the message was absurd! I saw no occasion to wire again and wrote a second long letter; and for a week or two we were "islands shouting lies to one another across seas of misunderstanding." Which was cleared up soon, and the wisdom of James's advice showed when A. found himself obliged to come east again in the spring [1884]. But Bessie and her children arrived in Boise on the date set in October [1883], and on her descended that flood of first calls, the unanimous welcome given each newcomer in the hearty pioneer fashion which the city had not outgrown. Her first general observation was subject to revision but quite true in the main: "This is a city where the ladies say 'ma'am' and the servants don't."

We had planned to keep house on a two-family arrangement at first, and A. had rented and furnished the house, on the outskirts of the town in a big dooryard planted with fruit trees and poplars along its fences. It had been built by an old French priest with some of the increment, not spiritual, of his cure among the Indians; it was called the Father Mesplie house.[10] Trust an old Catholic priest to plant a garden and make himself comfortable when he rests from his labors in the vineyard of the Lord! This was the home we had in our thoughts as we started on our next adventure — our longest and hardest campaign, and the last one we ever attempted on our own initiative.

[10] Father Toussaint Mesplie was sent to the Boise Basin in 1863 during the gold rush to Idaho. He was reported as holding Catholic services in Boise City in 1867. He left Boise in 1882.

❨24❩

W<small>E KNEW</small> it must be a long parting when we left for Idaho,
taking the last of our possessions with us that had been
stored in the family garret. Our father was eighty that spring
[1884].[1] The youngest grandchild, born in his house, we had
asked him to name and he gave her his mother's name, Elizabeth Townsend, hoping, he said, that she might make as good
a woman as her great-grandmother. She was now a volatile
person, a year and a half old, much pleased when it came to
being cloaked and capped for the journey — all roads being
alike to her. She laughed and jumped in his arms and kissed
him casually when told to, and he carried her out of the house
for the last time and put her in her mother's arms. We knew
he was thinking, "I shall never see this child again."

After that farewell there was nothing to speak of connected
with the journey except that Sonny had a chill — his last
clap from our old enemy, searched out by the altitude when
we climbed the Rockies again. His father carried him across
the tracks at Granger, where we left our Pullman on the U. P.
and took the crowded day car on the Oregon Short Line (in
which we spent the night), the only passenger car on the train.
It was a construction train loaded with material for the new
road farther down the line. But of course everyone was as kind
as possible, giving up two seats for our sick boy's bed, to sleep
off his fever on. And the next morning he was up and taking
notice of things at Kuna.[2]

[1] Since other sources give his date of birth as 1802, Nathaniel Hallock must have
been 82.

[2] During the years 1881-83 the Union Pacific Railroad built the Oregon Short
Line Railroad across southern Idaho, starting from the Union Pacific's main

No one remembers Kuna. It was a place where silence closed about you after the bustle of the train, where a soft, dry wind from great distances hummed through the telegraph wires and a stage road went out of sight in one direction and a new railroad track in another; but that wind had magic in it. It came across immense dry areas without an object to harp upon except the man-made wires. There was not a tree in sight — miles and miles of pallid sagebrush: as moonlight unto sunlight is that desert sage to other greens. It gives a great intensity to the blue of the sky and to the deeper blue of the mountains lifting their snowcapped peaks, the highest light along the far horizon. As to foreground — we were the foreground, bowling along in our light livery rig. We did not go over to Boise by stage, and there were no protests from the family economist this time.

But what a morning! Meadowlarks were springing up all about us — it was April and we knew there were nests and wild flowers hid in the sage beneath those jets of song. John Burroughs says that along the Platte and Yellowstone rivers we have a genuine skylark (Sprague's lark), and if I had known as much about birds then as my youngest eastern grandchild knows today, I could say if these birds were skylarks or just the common pipit.[3] Their note was a brief song, sad and sweet, that rained down to us from the sky. It haunted us, that song, every spring of all our years in Idaho, as it welcomed us that April morning. The birds and the wind filled the vast, brooding silence — the desert wind that talks, that whispers, that brings messages from the infinite filled with whatever each human soul that listens can put into it.

From time to time the front seat looked back to see how the back seat was "making it," and how we liked it on the whole.

---

line at Granger in southwestern Wyoming. Kuna, about 15 miles southwest of Boise, was the nearest station to Boise.

3 John Burroughs in fact identified this as "Sprague's pipit, sometimes called the Missouri skylark . . . which from far up . . . rains down its notes." John Burroughs, *Birds and Poets*, in *Works*, (Boston, 1904), III, 22-23.

We liked it very much! Over there, we were told, was the Saw-tooth Range where the Boise River heads up in southern Idaho; War Eagle [Mountain] and his brethren of the Owy-hees might be fifty miles away — there was no guessing dis-tances in that pure light and featureless perspective.[4] We were driving "straight across the drainage," and the wife of the new irrigation engineer marked the phrase as part of the language she was expected to know. We came out on the last long bench above the valley of the Boise and saw, across a bridge in the distance, the little city which was called the metropolis of the desert plains, the heaven of old teamsters and stage drivers crawling in at nightfall; saw the wild river we had come to tame, slipping from the hold of the farms along its banks that snatched a season's crops from it as it fled. Multiply that in-constant water a hundredfold, store it in those reservoirs the man talked of building up in the crotches of the hills, cover the valley with farms, and even to the mind of the misbeliever, here was a work worth spending a lifetime for, even the one life that is man's in this world. Confucius says: "I can find no flaw in the character of Yu. . . . He lived in a low mean house, but expended all his strength on the ditches and water-chan-nels."[5]

We sported with these quotes from the ancients, suspecting them of being deep humorists; and the humor was obvious be-fore another spring: Yu had "nothing on us" in the matter of his dwelling place. We were the inheritors of fat old priests no longer. We were seeking caves and holes in the rocks as it were — in the rock garden of Boise Cañon. The scheme had met with its first jolt.

We lived all together in the Father Mesplie house only one

4 As the Footes approached Boise from Kuna, the magnificent Sawtooth Moun-tains loomed up ahead (to the northeast). while the Owyhee Mountains were behind them (to the south), with War Eagle Mountain (altitude about 8,000 feet) standing out prominently.

5 *Confucius and the Chinese Classics*, ed. A. W. Loomis (San Francisco, 1867), pp. 112-13.

year — in a green dooryard with a trickle of little ditches running through it and the rustle of the old priest's poplars in our ears at night. Across the sagebrush common beyond our street we heard the bugle calls from Boise Barracks, and after taps, when the children were in bed, Bessie and I had our long talks as we used to talk at Milton, only now we had this new world to speculate on. We two in Idaho! That was the miracle that most affected me.

The day the news struck us from the East I thought my husband seemed uncommonly cheerful; he was reacting as he always did to a sudden blow. It was merely his usual "come back." The work had shut down temporarily; we were to give up the house and entrench ourselves in Boise Cañon, the headquarters of the engineers — to save expense, to watch the location and see that the measure of work required to keep up the water right was steadily performed. The "force" had been laid off but the organization must continue, for we might start up again at short notice. It had been a campaign of work; now for a campaign of waiting! A firm in the East named Pope and Cole had been our "angels." They had failed,[6] or there was strife among the angels, and we had passed as an asset into the hands of the Keysers of Baltimore. Steel and iron people allied in business and by family with Robert Garrett, president of the Baltimore and Ohio R. R.[7] They would be sending one of the firm or an agent out in the course of the summer to report on us, not being sure if they cared to carry us alone. The scheme, we were told, had merely paused — but

---

[6] By bad luck, Foote and General Tompkins had launched their company at an unfavorable moment. Conditions in 1883 constituted a recession, which in 1884 slid down into an outright depression, characterized by panic in the money market, declining prices for stocks and bonds, and failures among bankers and brokers. See Willard L. Thorp, *Business Annals* (New York, 1926), p. 134.

[7] Robert Garrett, son and grandson of men who created the Baltimore & Ohio Railroad and many another successful Baltimore enterprise, was a vice-president of that railroad from 1879 until 1884, and president 1884-87. On the Keysers, see below, footnote 12.

other things went on which we had started on the basis of optimism, which was the only permanent basis we ever had.

Nelly Linton — unsuspecting because we could not reach her to forewarn her — was coming by stages of farewells to friends on the way, from France to London, from London to New Haven, Connecticut, and was on her train crossing the continent when these orders came, which sent us up into Boise Cañon to be neighbors to coyotes and wild young mares of the range. She had been living in an old chateau on the coast of Normandy, an artist's paradise, teaching the children of an American artist, W. J. Hennessy (whom nobody knows today, but he was known then).[8] Rouen was within less than a day's journey. When we heard of this we had said no more about our little arrangement — we did not class ourselves with French chateaux nor thirteenth-century cathedrals. But Nelly had written early in the spring to say her hour had struck; the Hennessys were going to Paris; their children had outgrown her teaching, she modestly put it, and we shouted back, "Hurrah!" — the hour had arrived with us; our children were ready — come as soon as she could. But then we had a house with chimneys, not a board shack with a stovepipe hole through the roof and a tent for a dining room, a men's camp, in short, taken over to the uses of women and children.

I don't believe that any warnings would have stopped her; when you have that North Country blood and such names as Wade, Linton, Carthew back of you, other things go with it. She had never seen my husband when we made that compact, but she knew Milton and she knew Bessie — and, as far as that went, she knew me. And the daughter of William James Linton could not be very easily surprised. Still, it was amusing to contrast the stages of that journey with its end. She had stayed in London with her brilliant stepmother, Mrs. Lynn Linton,

8 William John Hennessy (1839-1917), painter and illustrator, was born in Ireland, trained as an artist in New York, where he first made his reputation, but spent much of his mature life in France and England.

who was then at the height of her fame. She was the author of
that much discussed diatribe "The Girl of the Period," showing that all periods have had that girl![9] Mrs. Linton had been
a close friend of Nelly's mother and was a faithful guardian of
the trust when she became stepmother to her many children.
They were all grown now and she had her work and her own
life in London. Mr. Linton was at a low ebb in his fortunes.
There was no breach affecting their regard for each other
when she declined to go with Mr. Linton to America: his
daughters understood and defended her decision. Nelly bade
her father good-bye at Appledore, his home near New Haven
which was his workshop; she left him buried in his magnum
opus, *The Masters of Wood Engraving*, which had cost him
years of preparation for the task. He was a many-sided man;
he was a Chartist, a Brother in Mazzini — his art was not
more to him than "Libertà! O bella Libertà!" He spent nearly
all he made, and he must have made a great deal by his noble
craft, on lost causes and brothers in exile. He never feared the
future nor counted the price of true feeling. His generosity
crushed one at times. When *The Masters of Wood Engraving*
came out — hand printed from the Appledore Private Press,
an autographed edition of five hundred copies not to be reproduced — he sent me a copy at Christmas as it were a
Christmas card! Every copy is now a collector's prize.

Nelly never saw her father again. He frankly neglected her
in material ways, but she knew he loved her and she worshipped him — with clear eyes. She kept a bunch of our
Cañon wild flowers in their brief season beneath his picture,
his old leonine head of tumbled hair, saying how he would
have loved the places where they grew. The hills above the
bend which shut in the river above us made her think of the

---

[9] Eliza Lynn Linton (1822-98), novelist, essayist, and critic, wrote her controversial essay "The Girl of the Period" for the *Saturday Review*, March 14,
1868, but it was reprinted in book form, with other essays, in 1883. She was
Linton's third wife. A reason for the failure of her marriage is suggested by
her autobiographical novel, which deals with a woman who turned into a man.

walks about Brantwood, her old home in the Lake Country, the place Ruskin bought when Mr. Linton "went broke" and came to America. One of the greater hills she said was like Coniston Old Man and took something of his colors in the blush of our pink sunsets late in summer. Brantwood and Boise Cañon! [10]. . . The world is an amusing place to live in if you live with the right people! Nelly's unpacking of her English traveling cases in the new pine-board bedroom we gave her in the old shack in Lytell's Gulch was a quaint bit of biography. And she will forgive me for turning out her things for inspection — it was a lonely place and we all shared our personal belongings. We pored over her fat photograph album full of remarkable faces and some beautiful ones, like those of the Hennessy children, while she gave us hints of the stories that belonged to each group. It touched and troubled me a bit to see how she had burnt her ships in this packing for such an unknown port. The trustfulness it showed went to my heart as she brought out, one after another, her family lares and set them up in our poor dwelling scrambled together for a season's waiting. Here were her old books treasured since childhood, some of them rare and out of print; her father's drawings of the English wild flowers engraved by himself, her own set colored by her eldest sister, the adored "Gypsy," her father's favorite child, the wild flower he lost from his English garden. She was the genius of the family, and the sacrifice to her father's genius and his love for his political exiles. He took one of them into his lonely home at Brantwood and trusted him as he would any handsome young English boy — but Slavic exiles are different. And there was a photograph of an elder brother in London, a shy, unnoted man on a bank clerk's salary who never married but devoted his life to the broken flower — in the asylum of her living death where she was put away for years. She had lost her mind over that cruel little

[10] The Old Man of Coniston was a mountain in the beautiful English Lake District, North Lancashire. Brantwood was on the shore of Coniston Water.

tragedy of girlhood shut up in lonely Brantwood and speech-less, as an English gypsy would be.

On the mother's side there was the traditional training of the English gentlewoman which Mrs. Lynn Linton had car-ried on. Nelly had brought her mother's workbox along with her father's watercolors, a gem of Victorian marquetry inlaid with ivory and ebony and satinwood, all fitted inside with little trays and lidded boxes which Nelly had filled with an assortment of good English pins and buttons and "reels" of cotton and silk and yards of linen tapes and bobbins enough to last for years, besides those "real" lace edgings for the neck frills she washed and pleated herself as she sat teaching our children, year after year, with that workbox before her. She had come provided with everything a stouthearted little Eng-lishwoman needs, with her prayers at night, to keep her self-respect and be at home wherever her fate might lead her. Her record in our family for thirteen years with scarcely a break — the family of a writing mother and an engineer in the field — would look as beautiful hung on a wall as one of her father's water colors in pure wash. In that medium he loved, her life would fitly have expressed itself, had it been a work of art instead of conscience. If we had raked the earth to find a teacher for our children in these places where we dared to take them, we could have found no one more quaintly suited to our needs — who might have been thought on the face of things more unsuited!

I should like to take the members of our little ditch crowd and lay a suitable wreath at each one's feet, or hang it on some wall — not for any great and conspicuous action, but —

> Is it small and mean? — nay, hard and long,
> To be but kind and clean, and sometimes strong.

And I should prefer to call the young men by their first names: but they were Tompkins and Wiley to their chief — to the mothers and children they were Mr.————, that was household discipline in a time when we were not so free as now with one another's given names, and especially when living on the "work."

A. J. Wiley, the junior assistant, outstripped us all on the road to success, yet so modestly and in ways so technical and unadvertised that I think only the profession knows him outside of Idaho, his chosen field, where he outstayed failure and came into his own as one of the country's great hydraulic engineers.[11] He was a boy of twenty-three that summer in the Cañon where he worked on faith, and without salary, for a cot under canvas and a seat at the camp table, and such satisfaction as a man may get out of sticking by his own crowd.

Harry Tompkins, another diplomaed engineer with his future before him, stayed by his father's orders to await the event. All salaries had stopped except the chief's, and that was a waiting not a working salary. For me and my work, all places were alike — but when I talk of "my work" it should be remembered that in these uncanny places I had always unusual helpers, not only sister and lady-help but strong arms to swing a child up to a tall shoulder and prance her up the trail from the beach at bedtime, or a patient reader, hours and hours — that was Wiley — to a group of insatiate children sticking to him like burrs or squatted round his knees in front of his tent on the dry and windy hill.

11 Andrew Jackson Wiley (1862-1931) richly deserved this praise. A poor boy, he attended Newark Academy, Newark, Delaware, and in 1882 graduated in engineering from Delaware College. After a year with the Baltimore & Ohio Railroad, he went to work with Foote's irrigation company in 1883, had to shift to the Union Pacific Railroad for 1886-88 because of Foote's financial troubles, then returned to Foote's company and spent the remainder of the century on Idaho irrigation projects. By 1900 he was noted for his reliability as an engineer, his integrity, and his kindness. From about 1900 he began a thirty-year run of notable irrigation and power projects throughout the West, and served for most of that time as consultant to the United States Bureau of Reclamation and the Department of the Interior generally. His home remained in Boise. He never married.

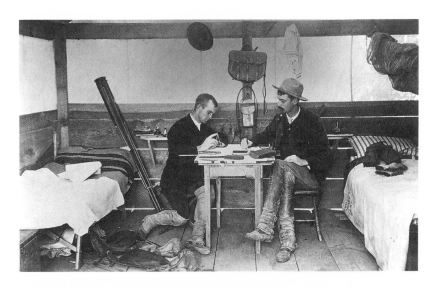

"They were Tompkins and Wiley"

The Victorian gentlewoman in the Boise River Cañon

These might be dreamlike scenes but for the book of our old Cañon photographs in evidence; here we have C. H. Tompkins, Jr., St. Paul's boy and graduate of Boston Tech, in flannel shirt and corduroys, pipe in one hand, hoe in the other, pausing to be taken while tending ditch along the slope of our new kitchen garden; here is A. in his white helmet and leather jacket and boots — if ever there were boots! — gathering the reins on old Dick's neck ready to mount and ride up the hot trail behind him. And there should have been a picture of our fishing camp that summer on the beach below the Atlanta Trail, where the Indians' Arrow Rock crowds the trail, a sheer shaft split down the middle. Into that dark crack the Indians on their hunting or war parties would shoot arrows to discourage the intentions of any evil spirit watching them from that crack.

And here, twenty-five years later, the great Arrow Rock Dam went in at a cost to the government of $7,000,000, to complete that very irrigation system our men sleeping in their blankets on the beach were planning that summer of a false dawn. When this heroic piece of engineering was finished and the water backed up against the dam, 350 feet high, at that time the highest dam in the world, Mr. Wiley wrote a description of it to his old chief, but he neglected to mention that he was himself on the government's board of consulting engineers who designed it and saw it built. We had to watch the engineering journals to get news of his great jobs, as they followed one another in those years when we were all scattered but never forgetful of the past.

Our packer and camp cook on that trip was a Swede who called himself John Brown. He was born on an island in the Skagerrak and the river was play to him. The West had caught him young and taught him about horses and camps and trails and teaming; gardening and cooking came to him by nature — he always came into the kitchen and saved our lives if we lost our cook. We trusted the children to him anywhere they could go with him in a wagon or a boat. He never raised his eyes in taking an order, yet orders were obeyed and there was nothing our way of life required that he did not know how to do. When that life broke up he followed my husband on the Government Survey by ways known only to the elk and the bighorn, and in places where any day a man might be called on to choose whether to save his own life or stick by his campmate. He would have given his life for the boss as simply as he would saddle a horse or strike a tent for the next day's journey. A wreath belongs to that Unknown Soldier, John Brown, whose real name we never knew. And another to Ed Marnell, the little Irishman down at the gate of the Cañon, moving stone off the future canal line day after day, seeing that each day the work required by law was faithfully done by the little handful of men under him. Going down to Ed's cabin to "count the force" was one of the little jokes in the Cañon.

The Keysers' examiner came out in June and proved to be a son of the House, R. Brent Keyser, a very young man then — he looked scarcely older than Harry Tompkins, and had been one of the class a few years ahead of him at St. Paul's.[12] We photographed the three men as they sat their horses before riding away; Wiley being at the camera is not in the group. How young they look — in this old, yellow print, full of the sunlight of the gulch — their chuck wagon in the distance crawling up the grade — what boys to have such a business as that in their hands! He was taken down the whole length of the canal line. They showed him those vast light-struck areas of dust and sage and the same soil with water on it in patches along the river bottoms, growing crops and feeding families and fatting cattle. They tempted him with the assays of the

[12] R. Brent Keyser (1859-1927), attended St. Paul's School from 1875-78 and then went to work for Keyser Brothers & Co., iron and steel merchants in Baltimore. In 1883 he shifted to the Baltimore Copper Smelting and Rolling Company, where he remained until 1910 and of which he became president. He was prominent in business and public life in Baltimore.

gold-bearing sands of the wicked old Snake River. They interviewed farmers and desert settlers as to water contracts; they took him up into the hills whence came that water and showed the natural reservoir sites for storing an almost unlimited supply, and incidentally they gave him some superlative fishing. No need to expatiate to that young man on the wonderful playgrounds there were up in the heart of those hills! They came back browner and more boyish looking than ever, obviously pleased with one another, and Mr. Keyser's last words when he said good-bye were: "I suppose you'd like me to hurry back so Mr. Foote can get to work?" No ifs about it!

As the wave climbed so it sank, and we waited for the next wave. The young envoy was taken ill directly after he reached home and for a time his life was despaired of. No business could be done with the house of Keyser then. Late in the autumn [of 1885] Robert Garrett came back — who was the kingpin of our hopes. The Keysers had waited on his decision and he washed his hands of any more heavy investments, some of his own not at that time giving him much comfort. Whenever a squall struck big business in the East, the ground swell rocked our boat. It meant exit the Keysers, to us.

BOOK V

The Endurance Test

25

THE Cañon was a howling desert if one depended on company and social events or small politics and poker. Such things were to be had, and better things, only ten miles away. We were just so far from town that no one came to visit us whom we had not asked, and so near that Harry Tompkins had his washing done there and our new cook, a little Chinese dandy (and a dandy cook), could ride down and get a shave on Saturday night and return polished and powdered to serve the late Sunday morning breakfast. His name was Charley Moy and little Betty called him the Pretty Chinaman.

Now and then a star visitor dropped down on us from some outer track beyond our field of expectation. I can't account for the appearance of those Fortieth Parallel men in our quarter of the heavens, but they were there, that summer — Hague and Emmons came to see us from somewhere, and I know it was not to "report" on us, and they did not come together.[1] On separate dates, which were white nights in the Cañon for us, they came and sat on our river beach and talked geology musingly and watched the stars, and when the company had reduced itself to a safe number we gave ourselves up to unsafe personalities and wild general talk. Our delightful brother-in-law was a wise as well as a safe gossip, whether we talked in

---

[1] James Hague's diaries show that he visited the Footes from July 30 to August 2, 1885. A letter from Mary Hallock Foote, The Cañon, August 9 [1885], to Helena Gilder reported that Hague brought family news and general news of the outer world that to them was as fresh as if a ship had just called at a desert island. A letter from her to Helena, dated Boise, August 26, 1887, described Emmons' visit and his discussion of his own very unhappy married life.

a cañon lighted by the rising moon, or by the lamps in a cur-
tained drawing room in the cañon of a city street. He only
said, in a cleverer way, what everyone was saying in the world
we were out of. He knew his wit was not wasted — that the
one thing we perished for was the speech of one's kind on some
other topics than one's own.

After Nelly Linton arrived, the Sherman family went back
to Boise, partly to put Gerald in school, partly to start their
own modest experiment which I shall speak of later. No wonder they expected no help from us! They had tried riding in
our Chariot of Hope, and when neither faith nor works would
move it any further, they got out and walked. Brave and sensible people. They allowed us to keep little Mary Birney to have
lessons with her cousin, and they quite innocently (by putting
Gerald in the public school) acquired merit in a town very
proud of its schools, where there was a strong sentiment
against sending across the world for an Englishwoman to
teach American children.

I hardly know how to keep a true balance between the two
sides of that Cañon existence — the life of dreams it fed in the
beauty around us, and the grimy attention it demanded every
hour of the day to insistent realities. The children were never
really safe without a grown-up eye upon them — not until we
found we could trust their blessed little words not to forget and
to obey orders, eye or no eye. There were the high places on
all their walks; there were rattlesnakes lurking in holes in the
rocks; there was the wire bridge, a nightmare to mothers —
there was always the river. . . . And now it was time to be getting in wood for winter and the river brought it to our door,
or piled it as driftwood in wild heaps on the point above us
when the freshets were loosed. In the matter of fence posts
there was more premeditation. A certain number of logs were
ordered of Goodwin, and when his log drive came down at
high water, followed by his lumberjacks in their sharp-prowed

boats, our boys went out in the black boat they had named the Parson and picked their logs, each with Goodwin's brand on the end, and harpooned them with pick and rope and towed them inshore. Even a wire fence which begins in that gay fashion is not without its thrills. But no thrills were connected with splitting up those logs for fence posts.

Lytell's Gulch had been chosen for the camp because of a little stream which came down it intermittently from the mountain pastures above us. On our side of the river a horseback trail hugged the shore at the base of the lava bluffs, but the wagon road climbed the bluffs themselves, a longer and steeper grade for teaming. We used the better road on the other side of the river; hence the boat — to reach the stable and our transportation base. But, when ice clogged the river, the crossing could not be made that way. The men set their wits to work to build a suspension bridge, as cheaply as safety would permit. Three men cannot do the work of the Roeblings! They used the natural rock abutments where the future dam was to go in, anchoring two wire cables to these bridge piers, crawled out on their knees to lay the footboards and fasten them to the wires; a handrail of one rope went along one side only. "They" slammed across it without touching the rope while the wires pulsated sickishly to their tread; barrow loads of stuff of all kinds were wheeled across it tilting from side to side. It turned a mother weak to watch her little girl carried over it in her father's arms — it really could not be borne as a frequent thing! As for Sonny — it was a case, as I have said, of a man's word at seven years old and we trusted that word. This was one branch of education in the Cañon.

And now autumn had given warning. The wild geese were flying south; the sun set earlier in a brooding intensity of color and a longer, more marvelous afterglow followed, calling us all out of the house to watch it deepen and flood the world above us. It was a three-story place: the river and beach floor, the hill where we said we should build if ever that came to pass, and the bluffs that rose to the level of the mountain pastures. Twilight sank first upon the river floor; the dark fronts of the bluffs took strange colors scored by shadows like the sculptured doorways of Petra, rock city of the desert. The shadow mounted, the rose pink turned purple and greenish and died out. . . .

Waiting salaries leave no margin for house building, but about this time we began to realize that we should need a house if we spent the winter in the Cañon. And also about this time a *Century* cheque blew in for the serial rights of "John Bodewin's Testimony."[2] The men were gallant enough to say that "J. B.'s Testimony" built the Cañon House. It may have paid the bills — but there were so few bills! The work of all their heads and hands went into it. A. was the architect and made his choice of material on the spot, those wasted rock-slides only a short haul from the hill where we chalked out our ground plan. As the fruit of that winter's experiments with Santa Cruz cement, he made a perfect wall plaster out of the native earth we stood on, of its own soft color and a better cement than any we could have put into the walls themselves. They were two feet thick and the mason's orders were to roll in the rock and spare the hammer, mud being cheaper than labor. And so we had our deep window seats, and the house when finished looked as if it had stood there a hundred years. It had grown out of the hill as it were.

The trench for the walls was dug in September and we were moved in by Christmas [1885], and the Shermans came up to dinner in the house, thereafter to be known as the Stone House in the Cañon. The prospectors and men of wild habits who went up and down the gulch trail, their backstairs to the mines and the mountain pastures, named it so and wondered what the ———— we were doing there or what we came to do!

[2] Published serially in volume 31 (1885-86) of *Century Magazine*, beginning with the November 1885 issue.

Of all our wild nest building this was the wildest and the most improvident and the hardest to leave. We might have called it Beth-horon which means "the house of the hole, or cave," or "the house of liberty" — we used to call the road up from Coston's, the last ranch on the river below us, the way "that goeth up to Beth-horon."[3] Low ceilings are cheaper than high ones; ours were just high enough to allow for doors that Tompkins, who was six feet four, could pass through without stooping. Open fires in three rooms that opened into one another kept the little den from being stuffy; we could be one family or divide up into groups. All our old plunder, as we unpacked it once more, fitted those rugged, homelike rooms. The chimneys were built of lava rock and above the sitting-room mantlepiece hung a photograph of the Virgin in Titian's *Assumption*, alone in the clouds in her amazement and rapture. The fresh and delicate Linton watercolors went beautifully with our fawn-colored walls and sage green woodwork. From my desk by the sitting-room window when the working light began to fail, I could look through into the dining room and see the children at supper and Nelly reading aloud to them, her English profile against the deep-toned west. The long casement window behind their heads gave the whole gate of the Cañon, like those detailed backgrounds in miniature which the early Italian painters put behind their Saints and Virgins. There came a moment in those short winter days, the sun halfway down peering over the top of the bluffs, when the light suddenly changed and became like the light during an eclipse. It was very strange — a pause before the passionate moment of the afterglow to follow.

Because of my new hope[4] for June, I did not go out of the Cañon again. I was forbidden to get on a horse or cross the

---

3 Joshua 10:10. While the etymology of the name Beth-horon is uncertain, the name has commonly been taken as signifying "place of caves," which is reasonably close to Mary Hallock Foote's version.

4 I.e., she was pregnant again.

"CHEER UP, CHILDREN, AND EAT YOUR SUPPER," SAID THE NURSE.

wire bridge or ride in anything we had on wheels. I had seen Bessie for the last time till my event was over — unless something should happen: I was sure to see her then! That V-shaped notch where the river went out and the sunset looked in bounded our world towards the valley; the bend in the river above us where the hills interlocked shut us off in that direction. It was narrow but it was not unbearable. We were not waiting for anything that could be hurried, Nelly and I; our work went on — it was the men we were sorry for. Wiley had left us, after the house was built, to find a new job, but for Harry Tompkins there were but his orders. Perhaps the one who had no home remittances and no orders was the lucky one of the two; but each, as his lot was given him, took it and made the best of it.

We continued to put up the house all winter [1885-86]: "we" stained floors and made seats and cupboards, and bookshelves with closets beneath for children's toys and old numbers of *Punch*. The engineers' office was like a ship's cabin with all its stowaway places. They made a workshop of the old Lytell house, and down there in the winter days those prisoners of hope did their tow picking: working at their inventions mostly bearing on the one idea. Together they made a new thing called, for short, the "flop-gate." It came out in *Transactions* honorably mentioned as an "automatic waste-weir" and was used in Colorado where irrigation had got the start of us in Idaho.[5] A. was the author also of a measuring box to determine the exact amount of water delivered through a certain sized orifice in a given time, water for irrigation being sold by the miner's inch. The pair of them [i.e., Arthur Foote and Harry Tompkins] would be seen striding up the gulch in silence to look at their models working, tested by our little water supply. They were pretty toys to watch, and the meas-

5 Arthur D. Foote, "An Automatic Waste Weir," American Society of Civil Engineers, *Transactions*, 18 (February 1888), 58-60.

uring box came into very general use, but was too easily copied to be worth patenting.

But Nelly Linton conferred the greatest boon when she taught them bookbinding at second hand, her own instructor being no less a person than her father. They "ate it up," the monkish craft. I dare not say how many books they put into covers in the course of those frustrate years. Harry Tompkins read and *read* — like a man who has been four years at Tech when no man can read. He sent for what he wanted in the good old Tauchnitz editions and searched the saddlers' shops in town for leathers to put them into soft covers.[6] They did not do so much in the way of "boards." The next Christmas [1886], when he had got to be an expert, he gave me a Wordsworth in two volumes, perfect in stitching and lettering, bound in cream white lambskin with robin's-egg-blue paper lining and even a blue bookmark. It goes, when I am gone, to my Betty who loves the *Sonnets* and loved "Tomkin' " — though she can hardly remember him, her slave as he was!

My ditchdigger was loaded up with precious pamphlets and reports, the key to his thoughts and dreams. These he sorted and indexed and put into permanent shape, and we all read them — mighty stories of "kingly boys" doing the work of potentates, great systems of modern irrigation in France and Italy and Egypt and India told by their creators, such men as C. C. Scott-Moncrieff[7] or Colonel Baird Smith — Captain, when he wrote his two-volume *Report on the Agricultural Canals of Piedmont and Lombardy* as the trifling result of one of his furloughs![8] It is addressed to "the Honorable the Court of Directors of the East India Company" — but the

6 The German printing firm of Tauchnitz became famous for its paper-covered editions of works by British and American authors, supposedly to be sold only in Continental Europe.

7 Colonel Sir Colin Campbell Scott-Moncrieff, born 1836, had a distinguished career as an engineer officer and irrigation specialist in India, Burma, and Egypt, before retiring to become under-secretary for Scotland.

8 Colonel Richard Baird Smith (1818-61) was one of the heroes of the Indian

dedication made one choke up as one read: "To my Brother Officers in the Irrigation department of Northern India, because I respect and love them." What lay back of those words one might guess by reading, for instance, the report on the breaking of the Kali Nadi Aqueduct.[9] The records of rainfall for years had been destroyed in the last Indian mutiny and a mistake was made in the size of the wasteweir which cost the British government lacs [a great deal] of money and hurt the men who built it more than death. But they did not shoot themselves through the head nor lay the blame on the next man. They did the work again and did it right.

Mutiny and a remarkably effective engineer in matters relating to water supply in India. His great report on Italian irrigation was published in 1852 and reissued in 1885.

9 In 1885 the Nadrai aqueduct on the Kali Nadi River, a tributary of the Ganges, was swept away in a flood. *Imperial Gazetteer of India*, 14 (1908), 309-10.

"IT TOOK NO NOTICE OF ALL THE CHILDREN'S CARE."

(SEE "THE LAMB THAT COULD N'T 'KEEP UP.'" DRAWN BY MARY HALLOCK FOOTE.)

Spring had come; doors and windows were open to the river's mounting cry, louder in the nights when it seemed to fill the silent house. The freshets were loose in the hills — the men saw it all go by while they sank a sad little water hole and planted a homemade windmill above it which whirled and plashed and paused and whirled again to a sort of tune of its own. It fed their little ditches along the slope of the gulch where they had sowed a few seeds and stuck out a few hopeful trees. In May the sheepmen crossed the gulch above us going up into the hills with a band of 5,000, and every drop of water disappeared for days except that which our men had saved by their digging, and the 5,000 mouths cleaned every living thing off the hills where the first wild flowers were blooming. The herders gave our children one of their lambs which "couldn't keep up"; it proved a tragic gift. They hung over it with offerings of warm milk and brandy that it could not swallow; they carried it to the shady spot under my bedroom window where it lay all day on the patch of grass. At sunset it struggled to its feet with that last instinct of a wild thing of the herd which knows it will be trampled if it falls — it fell and died. And I made capital out of my children's tears and wrote a story called "The Lamb That Couldn't Keep Up" — and posed the children themselves for the illustrations and sold it to *St. Nicholas* for a good round sum to put away for my own lamb that was coming in June.[1] It was part of that remorseless prac-

---

[1] "The Lamb That Couldn't Keep Up," *St. Nicholas Magazine*, 16 (September 1889), 803-06.

ticality to which we hitched our dreams in the Cañon, lest we be trampled ourselves.

And every day and all day the wood doves up the gulch were calling, calling, hid in the willow thickets. . . . And we knew that Harriet Hawley was dead, and Spencer Foote and his wife were dead, and their little Margaret, whom her Aunt Harriet had adopted a few months before, was motherless a second time. . . . And the Rockwell's little Fanny was dead, the second child they had lost since that happy winter in New York — could such winters ever come again! [2] They were abroad somewhere, wandering about heartbroken in the midst of everything the world can give, with nothing that they wanted. . . . The air was heavenly soft and sweet, wild roses scented every breath of wind from up the gulch and all day the patient, maddening doves kept saying something we could not get out of our heads and could not understand.

Three times I had lost a hope so early as to scarcely seem a reality and under circumstances which made it more of a fear than a hope. Once in Leadville, where babies did not thrive; at Point Lookout, when we had the Idaho journey before us — that was why Mary and James, at her insistence, interfered. And at the Father Mesplie house — it took all winter to get over that, and the doctor said this baby would make me or break me. He put it more professionally, but I went softly all those days.

We had sent for our nurse in order to play safe. She had been in the house a week and had used her unoccupied time to overeat or overdrink (being a giddy old thing weighing about 175 pounds) and was taken with the frankest symptoms in the night before my date, with her patient as nurse. She was taken back to her friends in town next morning, and the man who took her brought back the doctor. . . . A., meantime, put Dick

---

[2] Harriet Hawley died March 3, 1886; Spencer Foote had died May 28, 1880, shortly before the birth of his daughter Margaret (born June 12, 1880); and his widow, Hannah, died May 7, 1885. Fanny Rockwell, daughter of the Alfred Rockwells, died March 25, 1886.

before the Bradley cart and tore over the bluffs by the road on our side to get Bessie — there being no other way and no other vehicle left. He snatched her from the midst of her family and carried her off to our fastness in the hills, much as a lawless Doone might have descended on the valley town and stolen a burgher's wife to help one of his women in her need. She came of course — and A. did his best to bring her safely, but the road was a mere track through the sagebrush; Dick stepped on a cobble and went on his knees; A. pitched over the dashboard when the shafts grounded and landed on Dick's neck. And Bessie, who was saving our lives, sailed out in some miraculous fashion in company with the seat cushion and found herself *on* it, seated in the sagebrush "as tranquil as an angel on a cloud," said A. when he dared to tell the story. "A hard cloud," the angel herself added, to be strictly accurate.

The day had been stifling hot with showers around us on the mountains cutting off our down-cañon wind. The baby came at sunset,[3] and out of the window of my room, they told me, a double rainbow could be seen spanning the hills where the river enters the Cañon. A sight so beautiful that he, who did not know that he had another daughter about two minutes old, came to the door and begged them not to let me miss this welcome to our Cañon baby. I laughed to think of it afterwards — how Bessie held the door against him and said sternly, "She is not thinking of rainbows!"

Heaven and all its rainbows could not have sent me greater peace than I owed that night to my tired sister on the cot beside me. Not a word had she said about her descent upon the "cloud." She had given its first bath to the new baby that lay cradled between us in that trancelike sleep which ushers in the troubles of this world. The wind rose in the night and came rushing past the house with a sound of mystery in the air. . . . It was Midsummer Night; the fairies might have been abroad on that wild, soft wind bringing dreams to our little Betty,

3 June 23, 1886.

asleep in the next room, of long-haired princesses such as she loved to draw on galloping horses fleeing through the dark.

Two little girls and one boy saved from our schemes and wanderings in the deserts of desire! I had thought that in our uncertain way of life we needed another boy rather than another girl — queer how even in our family, where all the women were self-supporting, that old tradition still held; that boys are sure to be an asset and girls a liability.

We named the new baby Agnes, a name of remote but honored associations on the Hull side of the family. She was smaller than the other two, smooth and well proportioned and with a vital bloom and color that promised health and a fair skin. Cut out for the rosy little thing she became, and more like my mother than anyone else — quick on her feet, resilient in spirit yet reticent in speech and full of a mysterious lonely joy, as if the fairies of her birthnight still kept her company, and double rainbows that no one else could see stood in her dreaming skies.

But there was no fairy luck for her that first year. The nursing body came back and took Bessie's place, and did as her kind usually did, and it was her best. Many generations of babies have survived those methods — our baby survived, but her rightful food was injured by her mother's constant anxiety during those first three months in consequence of the old dame's ignorant practices. One really cannot have babies in a cañon with perfect impunity! The next ordeal arrived within the year in the form of measles. My little nursemaid, Elma, good and pretty and invaluable, went to town at Christmas [1886] and brought it back with her and had it herself first, and by the time she was over it all the others came down — my three and little [Mary] Birney Sherman, and Aunt Bessie came up to our assistance as usual. She and *War and Peace* — I never shall forget — came into the Cañon House together. We had nights of watching over restless children when going to bed was a waste of time. We sat under the lamp at the dining-room table, surrounded by measles in the rooms adjoining, and Sonny asleep on a cot in the sitting room hard by, and there we read half through the night — Bessie with one volume, I with another — that mightiest novel of the time. The children's cases were normal — any amount of discomfort but no danger. Sleep was not for us, but we had a wonderful time — the lights burning till all hours and we two in the silent house awake, entranced over the great Russian epic. . . .

It was a year of poignant memories. It began to be evident towards spring [1887] that my teething baby was not gaining, that she was not holding her own. My orders were not to wean her until the heats of her second summer were over; that was a mother's religion in those days. I was sitting with her in my lap, brooding over her alone, one day, when Nelly passed through the room and stopped to smile at the baby. She studied her a moment in silence and then said softly, deliberately, in the North Country speech she sometimes used, as we use poetry for greater effect in the fewest words, "Little, wist-faced baby!" It was enough — she had spoken her thought, which matched my own. I shed a few tears over that phrase, but it gave me nerve to disobey orders, and it was high time. . . .

I can't be sure of the date but I think it was that spring, our letters from the East brought us the news that Henry Villard of the Northern Pacific had taken us up in connection with a greater scheme of his own.[4] Any map would show why the

4 Henry Villard (1835-1900) rose from penniless beginnings as a German immigrant to become first a successful journalist and then, sometimes with the help of German investors, the dominant figure in a complex of northwestern land and water transportation that utilized the Columbia River route and had its headquarters at Portland. Out of fear that the Northern Pacific Railroad, which was supposed to build to Puget Sound, would divert too much business from the Columbia region, Villard was led to buy control of the Northern Pacific, serve as its president from 1881-84. and work out agreements to harmonize the competing interests of the Columbia forces, the Northern Pacific, and a new element, the Union Pacific Railroad. which had just advanced into the region by building the Oregon Short Line Railroad across southern Idaho to Oregon. While Villard fell from power in 1884 and suffered a nervous breakdown, in 1887 he was drawn back into activity in a new attempt to produce peace between the rival interests.

president of the Northern Pacific should want a canal on those Idaho lands to open them to farmers and farmers' freights, with the Oregon Short Line as one of his feeders pushing across them. He was working for control of the Oregon Navigation Company which would have completed his dream of an ocean to ocean northern line. We were told to expect a visit soon from one of his head contractors who would go over the maps and figures, and work would probably begin within a few months. We put up our flag, as it were.

The man of estimates came. There were long talks in the office and long columns of figures; the engineers were admired for the finish of their work, which made his work that much easier, he said. The meals went off with a controlled cheerfulness on our men's part — they were slow to let go their hold on suspense. The contracting person remained inscrutable. He went away and there was a pause which became anxious, and then — exit Henry Villard. We hauled down the flag once more — our celebration was over. I don't know why I attempt these figures of speech — it was a stupid business, but it had to be put through. . . . At a reception in New York, a few winters later, we met Mr. Villard and he told Arthur in a man-to-man straight talk that he had not been playing with us; he had fully determined to finance the Idaho canal, but he himself was beaten. The Union Pacific combination under [Charles Francis] Adams was too strong for him.[5] We had accepted our fate by then and our wounds had begun to heal, and Villard had scars of his own; I dare say the two men understood each other.

We were four years — or was it longer? in the Cañon [1885-

5 Charles Francis Adams (1835-1915), of the Massachusetts Adamses, became noted for his investigations of railroad abuses before assuming the presidency of the Union Pacific Railroad in 1884. After Villard's return to power in northwestern transportation in 1887, Adams and Villard at first worked in harmony, but in the spring and summer of 1888 moved into uncompromising opposition to one another. Cf. James Blaine Hedges, *Henry Villard and the Railways of the Northwest* (New Haven, 1930).

89] — always on the brink of success, always remanded for
further waiting, and but for the Cañon mailbag I should think
our souls might have dried up like tumbleweed and blown
away. Twice a week it came, whenever a man could be
sent to town. It brought our home letters from four families;
it brought me letters from Helena which were as constant and
almost as regular, supplementing Richard's gay little post-
scripts in his own hand at the foot of a typed acceptance or a
suggestion for some change pending acceptance. He drove
his contributors with a light hand, but he kept us on the track
where the magazine with its million readers was tacitly
pledged to go. "Don't know what the moral is — don't know
as it needs any?" he wrote after accepting a story of the Wild
West called "The Rapture of Hetty," based on the time-
honored theme of Young Lochinvar.[6]

Helena said little about my work directly; she left that to
the shop. Our friendship was on bedrock by that time; it took
in everything vital to our lives, so joined yet so contrasted: our
children, our housekeeping problems, the new friends on both
sides, our individual hurts and griefs and our home people's
troubles. She told us who were in New York from the world of
arts and letters, who was coming into fame and who had arrived — Modjeska, Duse, Paderewski, Aus der Ohe, Kipling,
Clemens, Saint-Gaudens, Stevenson, Wyatt Eaton. . . . They
were in the heart of the international copyright fight[7] and
committed to all the civic reforms and charities, besides being
host and hostess in the name of the magazine to its visiting
contributors from abroad. I know these letters were written
often in a roomful of brilliant talkers, all trying to drag her
into the light war of words. It costs, this sort of giving out in
so many ways at once; she hardly ever had any time to herself
— she had no Self. Her manner of arranging flowers or

6 Published under that title in *Century Magazine*, 43 (December 1891), 198-200,
and with a dramatic full-page illustration by the author on p. 201.
7 The long battle to stop pirating foreign authors' books culminated in the act
of Congress of March 3, 1891 (the so-called International Copyright Act).

making tea was the same; you couldn't interrupt her or dis-
compose her, but it takes intense concentration and never-
resting sympathy to be always ready in that way.

About this time too there were long distance hails! — voices
in the air that I did not recognize; letters, in short, in the
Cañon mailbag from readers whom I instantly loved but
knew I should never see. Most of them were in men's hand-
writings with queer postmarks, forwarded by the Century
Company, from places as out of the world as the Cañon itself.
They followed every serial or short story dealing with the lives
of our engineers in the field, and they came from mines and
railroad camps on the far-flung lines of work, pushing new
enterprises from Honduras to Manitoba.

The men of all trades have been heroes of fiction, even
tailors, but the Sons of Martha[8] seldom saw themselves in
print in any aspect not connected with the paycheck or the
announcement that the work didn't need them or had shut
down. Here they were making love and winning at it — "The
Fate of a Voice" met with an almost pathetic response.[9] They
took these stories with delightful seriousness, not bothering
about my technique but jealous for their own. They watched
every term I used, every allusion where a pretender might
slip up, when I undertook to speak the language of the sacred
profession. These letters would be signed sometimes by a
group of names from the "Old Man" to the "Kid." The Old
Man, they said, had just been reading aloud to them the last
story (or installment of a serial) under discussion, there being
only one copy of the *Century* in camp; and would I please tell
them how I came to know these things which the eye of wo-

---

[8] A reference to the biblical Martha, who was the embodiment of the energetic,
practical approach to life, as contrasted with the spiritual Mary. Kipling's
poem, "The Sons of Martha," first published 1907, republished in *Twenty
Poems* (1918), sympathetically describes the engineering labors of the Sons
of Martha.

[9] Published under that title in *Century Magazine*, 33 (November 1886), 61-73,
with a full-page illustration by the author on p. 60. The story was set in an
engineers' camp in the West.

man hath not seen? I answered delightedly and told them that I had married one of their lot and knew *them*, in their remotest hiding places, but my technique was all borrowed, and I washed my hands of any mistakes they might find. Sitting beside my own smokers in the restful silence of the Juniors' room, often I thought of one of their phrases, "the angle of repose," which was too good to waste on rockslides or heaps of sand. Each one of us in the Cañon was slipping and crawling and grinding along seeking what to us was that angle, but we were not any of us ready for repose.

Signs were not wanting that our little world that had looked on at our years of futile waiting thought that the end of the New York Ditch[10] was near. We went on unconscious, each with his or her own job, each seeking his own angle of repose. Nelly Linton was "approached" (as I learned many years later) by a friend and guest of ours at the time, who assured her that it was known that the New York Canal would have to shut down. She was from the East and had a little daughter whose schooling was as much of a problem to her as our children's to us. It might be a convenience to both sides, she said, if a change could be made that would leave us free and not chuck Nelly out in the cold. She offered her, in case she should lose her home with us, the same position on Nelly's own terms. It was a timely offer if it had been made to a different person. Nelly's answer was that she would wait until she heard this general news from the family before considering the future for herself. She was not worried in any case; our children would have to be taught by some one and no one would do it cheaper than she, for she would stay with us for nothing but her keep, she said, if we continued to want her. I never knew of this incident till her work in our family was done — in one of our long, last talks before she left us finally to go home. The tears came into her eyes as she spoke of those days. . . .

[10] The "New York Ditch" was one of the major component parts of Arthur Foote's proposed irrigation system.

⟨ 27 ⟩

A BILL had been passed by the Congress of 1888-89, fathered by a senator from one of the arid states, providing for a government irrigation survey under the same head as the Geological Survey. Major Powell was director of the survey and he made Captain Dutton, U. S. A., chief of the new department.[1] About this time Kate Foote wrote to Arthur that at a reception in Washington she had met Captain Dutton, who said, "I have just been writing to a Mr. A. D. Foote to get him on our irrigation work. Is he any relation of yours?" "I told him," Kate wrote, "that he was a connection on both father and mother's side — he was my youngest brother."[2] After which characteristic opening, she proceeded to urge upon Arthur this appointment which was much coveted, she said, and would not go begging. It was the plea of the whole family that he would take it and come east now and then.... He was very cool about it, like a man awaking from a dream. He replied to Captain

[1] Senators Henry M. Teller of Colorado and William M. Stewart of Nevada initiated the action that culminated in authorization by Congress of the Irrigation Survey on October 2, 1888. The head of it was to be Major John Wesley Powell (1834-1902), the largely self-educated geologist and anthropologist whose dramatic western explorations had won him national attention during the decade before he was appointed director of the United States Geological Survey in 1880. One of Powell's principal assistants was Captain Clarence E. Dutton (1841-1912), a Yale graduate and Regular Army officer who by self-study and field work made for himself a national reputation as a geologist. For details of the survey, including Arthur Foote's typically ambitious thinking, see Thomas G. Manning, *Government in Science: The U.S. Geological Survey, 1867-1894* (Lexington, Kentucky, 1967), pp. 168-203.

[2] Katherine Foote was for fifteen years Washington correspondent for the weekly *New York Independent*, a fact which would explain her presence at a Washington reception. She did not marry until 1895. See p. 260.

Dutton that if his division of the work could be made to cover the Snake River Valley surveys, he would accept it. The matter was referred to Major Powell who "made it so," and was kind enough to add that Foote was one of the men he must have on this work. He gave him his own country, only a great deal more of it.

He remained with the old company without salary as consulting engineer and Tompkins took his place as chief — which meant staying on the sinking ship while we put off in the last boat. We had our excuse that there were women and children in the boat; but it was hard saying good-bye to old comrades and telling faithful servants we should need them no more. My husband took John Brown with him on his exploring trips, but our perfect little Chinaman we had to let go. He put his sentiments into washing all the blankets and cleaning the whole house as we stripped room after room, piling away pictures for boxing, sorting papers, and sacrificing old letters and the children's dead bouquets of wild flowers in the ashes of our last fires. Tompkins boxed his library of hand-bound books, took down his pipe rack from over the mantel in the Juniors' room and locked the doors of the Cañon House. His headquarters were to be in town.

Bessie opened her extra rooms and took us all in, the disjecta membra of the scheme (that had taken them in!). Her own little scheme was the usual resource, taking boarders, but she did it in a way of her own difficult to describe without making her out too perfect, whereas she was an eminently practical woman and saw things in their true proportions. She did the only thing she could have done, or any woman, in those days when women were not trained to a profession or for business. She had had the training of a perfect housekeeper in a house which lived by sympathy and service. Those things are always in demand. She took Nelly Linton "home," as it were. Nelly fell on her feet and found she could take her choice of pupils from the "best families" in forming her little class; she had made a reputation without stirring in the matter.

For me, since I could not "march with my beaten man," I preferred to march alone somewhere down to the sea level and have my children to myself for a little while and learn to know my silent boy of eleven who was to leave us in the fall. He was ready, thanks to Nelly, for the first form at St. Paul's.

It shows on the map how temptingly the island of Vancouver lies where Canada trails the fringes of her garment in the Pacific by a network of waterways. Victoria, at the southern end, looks across the Strait of Juan de Fuca to our own Olympians, blue on the horizon, with their heads always topped with snow. I knew the northern twilights would be long and the summer short and cool, and I thought it probable the Victorians would be cool to a stray American woman without letters, and with no money to spend. All of which would tend towards that angle of repose which one finds and loses from time to time but is always seeking in one way or another.

I told my little nursemaid (the same Elma) that I should have to get on without her for the summer. I could not afford wages and traveling expenses too. But seeing her face fall, I asked how she would like to go with us for the trip only and do what she felt inclined, in the way of help with the children — I knew she would take no advantage of that agreement. She had never been out of Idaho before and she jumped at the offer.

At the last moment I found myself chaperon to one of the nicest girls for that purpose one could possibly find — whom I didn't want in the least, but it would have been a distinct loss to our summer if I had evaded her.[3] She was going home to Boston in a cool open-eyed fashion, by way of the little city of the strait — down the coast by boat, touching at the California cities and landing at San Diego and so home by the Santa Fé. Quite a little plan for a girl of twenty-four, in those days. She had expected to leave me at the dreary hotel we went

3 Maud Ahern.

to on the inner harbor and go on her virgin way alone; but we found ourselves so happy grumbling together and so congenial in our wants and distastes that I asked her if she would care to stay longer and be one of us in the little cottage I took out by the strait, in the James Bay district, ten minutes walk from Beacon Hill Park. She was tempted and she stayed and was one of us in every sense: the best of pals for my tall lad on the long walks and rows they took together, the least of encumbrances to a chaperon whose main object was to be alone. I don't know if she had ever traveled much in "foreign parts," but she was a cosmopolitan born. The English we met were much struck with her and could find no better way to express their admiration that to assure me they never should have taken her for an American girl! She made her own independent terms as to expenses, and "Maud's money," as we called it (which I considered clear gain), was used each month as an amusement fund. It gave us our jolly extras — our boat on the Arm in the long twilights when all the little gay city was out on the water, or a carriage now and then to explore the long roads along the shores or through Ferndean Woods — beautiful names out of the city's fascinating past. I could chant those names — if I could only remember them! The cottage itself was on a little street called Bird Cage Walk, and our Scotch landlady, Miss McCandless, might have come out of Jane Austen's pages.

It was not a great journey — by the Oregon Short Line to Portland and Tacoma, and across Puget Sound — and then we were under another flag. And a gray-haired little Englishwoman who had been head nurse in the family of Colonel Ponsonby of the Grenadier Guards [4] — erstwhile quartered in the casemates of Windsor Castle, eyewitness to the comings and goings of royalty and gossiping with royalty's ser-

---

[4] Sir Henry Frederick Ponsonby (1825-95), equerry to the prince consort and later private secretary to the queen, commanded a battalion of the Grenadier Guards in Canada during the American Civil War.

vants, but now come down to general service in the colony —
came to us for twenty dollars a month and cooked and minded
the house. All because she too had followed a man with a
dream. He and their son of fourteen were in the forest felling
trees and building a cabin on their wild land, while she went
back to service to pay the bills.

Victoria, as the capital of a Crown Colony, had been in love
with her aristocratic past, her own governor and castle set
and the pomps of her little provincial court: the naval station
at Esquimalt gave her a sprinkling of noblemen's younger
sons to decorate her playing fields or race the town on the
waters of the Arm; but British Columbia had lately been
united to the Dominion and was feeling rather pettish about it,
more particularly its women. The Victorian-English, I observed, held themselves a trifle above the Canadian-English,
while the Americans, needless to say, did not count socially at
all. . . . Even so, a lady who was English-English, not a native
born, and as remote from the local point of view in her way as
we were in ours, called upon us one day without any introduction, and I saw that here was a woman worth crossing the
sound or the world to meet, if friendships were made that way.
After this first visit we were friends. We both knew that the
experience was exceptional. There is a touch of the miraculous about every meeting like this.

We said good-bye at the end of my stay, not speaking of the
future; she was as completely entoiled in the life and temperamental adventures of her husband as I in mine, as helpless to
direct her own course and as fatalistically unconcerned, on
the whole.[5] She was in America only because of him and his
people. She had married into a strong Scotch house, bankers
and retired cotton spinners. We met two or three of the older
members, living on fixed incomes, very well taken care of,

[5] He was an alcoholic. In view of Arthur's own drinking problem at this time,
talks with Edith Angus may have had a considerable effect upon Mary Hallock
Foote. See Introduction, p. 31.

immensely respectable — good to put into a story, but no
such brain among them as Edith Angus had. She was the
daughter of a Liberal writer and journalist, for many years
connected with the *Manchester Guardian*. Leaving out the
universities, he had given her such an education as he would
have given a son. Edith Angus might have lived anywhere
and not been bored nor have starved mentally. And that she
found a high spiritual stimulus in meeting the demands of
fate in deeper ways than mere residence, I could well imagine.
A straitened life for so large a soul in the shape of a small,
clear-brained, high-hearted woman. I wrote to her on my
return to Boise, expecting no more than a farewell wave of
the hand. I might have remembered the English are faithful
— her letters have never been absent from my desk for more
than a year at a time, since that summer on the straits. I shall
always feel that I went to Victoria to meet Edith Angus.

28

Our father and mother had spent their golden wedding day, April 1886, with all of the family who were left in the neighborhood around them. He died the following year. A mortgage in John Sherman's name had been put on the property when he and Bessie went to Idaho, nominally to cover what might have been their claim against the estate, if they had made any: but it was non-interest-paying and its only object was to protect the home, in any contingency, from being sold over our father's head in his old age. It remained for our little mother to bear it. The contingency had come, and on Tom's report of the state of affairs John sent back the mortgage, and the greater part of the land, including the house and home fields, had to be put up at auction that all might not later have to go. Father had given Tom a deed for the Mill place before his death, and that was left out of the sale, for him and his family which now included our mother.

Sarah, who was a good reporter, told us the story of that day. Cousin Townsend Sherman[1] had been present, to do what father had done when the Mill place was put up at auction years before. It was the custom with neighbors, when an old home is going like this and a member of the family steps in to save it, not to "bid against the widow." There was one man present who was not influenced by this consideration. He raised every bid with a cool determination to have the place at any price. Our mother, in the house awaiting her fate, was told of the little drama outside which threatened to involve Cousin Townsend too deeply on her behalf. She sent out word: "Let it

[1] John Sherman's brother.

go." It held the last meaning the word *home* had for her, but how wise to let things go! and how dear of Cousin Townsend — like his saying to Aunt Martha when the news came that her last son was dead in the war: "I will be thy son, Aunt Martha." And he was. . . .

The man who outbid him was one of that class of farmers who are not affected by the rise in wages. They work their own land, as our forefathers did; but they were not unlettered hinds, those old Quaker Hallocks and Townsends. Our mother remembered him as the first chore boy on the place when she came there a bride, and all the old things were new. She remembered his unmannerly curiosity as to the rooms he had never entered. The windows of the back parlor opened towards a path which the hired men took to their work after meals; it offended her sense of propriety to see the gawky lad planted in front of one of those windows gazing in, his face nearly touching the pane. They were good old rooms for that neighborhood — like none that he had ever seen, very likely. He married and raised a family of sons who were rough young fellows, but he taught them to work, and he knew how to save. While the old farm went on lending money without interest and piling up debts, he was piling up a bank account. He was well able to buy the place, to own the house where he had eaten in the kitchen. It might have been his youthful dream — to be master in a house like that. He might never have seen or spoken to our mother since she was young, and quite a little martinet, no doubt, in her new housewifely pride. Mistresses were mistresses in those days, and she had the ideas of her time as to behavior proper to his class. . . . It was a house not suited to him and his family — but it was no longer suited to us. This public sale and the parting with the deeds marked the passing of our branch of Hallocks from that neighborhood where five generations of us had lived on the same land. Other Hallocks remained and Tom's family were there for a few years more, but after that visit[2] I never went back to Milton. For our

[2] I.e., the visit referred to in the next paragraph.

mother a greater change was not far off; her losses here did not affect her long.

We had sent Arthur east that summer, consigned to dear Mrs. Tompkins who had offered to outfit him for school and send him up to Concord by John, her youngest St. Paul's alumnus. He was invited to spend his first Christmas at the Rectory. We went on soon after the new year [1890], A. reporting to his chief in Washington, I to join him there after stopping at Milton and going up from there to our boy at St. Paul's.

Eh, that Milton visit! I knew, when we said good-bye, that the foundations were broken, that I should never see my little darling mother again. She had accepted everything — her life ending as her own mother's had, without independence, without means of her own. It was not very often so in the history of old Quaker families. Grandmother Burling ended her days in her own daughter's house where she and grandfather had spread their bounty for years; but our little mother, dowerless and penniless, was now the perpetual guest of her daughter-in-law whose ideas in little daily matters were — better perhaps, but not her ideas. Without openly jarring, they were not happy in speech together. Our mother took refuge in repression, and repression was not natural to her. Being nervous and sensitive, when she spoke, conscious of a critical listener, she did not always give perfect expression to her thought, and her words would be picked up as they sounded, not as she had meant — which she took as a lesson in further silence. Hence a life that lacked air. Her own daughter (whom she could have with her but a few days amidst the years of separation) was forced to silence also, to keep back the passion of sympathy she felt, not to seem unjust on the other hand — for how could the wife of one dreamer tread on the heart of another!

My husband had extended his business in ways that must have looked like madness to many of our friends and kindred; only his profession saved him — and mine, my little arts and crafts that women in Sarah's youth were not trained in. Sarah would not have been an artist, but she might have been a doctor or a woman of affairs in public service as her daughter became, who inherited the best of both parents' qualities. Nature, with time, worked out the equation in that family; but our father and mother were caught, in their last years, in the wheels of change. Father belonged to the last of his breed of thinking and reading American farmers, working their own lands which they inherited from their fathers.[3]

At St. Paul's I talked with three persons who had our son's welfare in their hands: Dr. Coit, the keeper of his soul and mind and conscience; Mr. Hargate, who looked after his "incidentals," his physical health and amusements; and the comfortable matron of the first-form dormitory with whom I talked over the little things and the characters of his playmates. Dr. Coit was the only great religious teacher I had ever met and he remains in mind an apostle of boys — future men.[4] Before my train left next morning there was time to hear him read prayers in the beautiful little chapel and see the fifty choirboys march in. From where I sat in the cold and nearly empty gallery I could look down on the smooth crowns and white starched surplices, and I recognized on the decani side of the altar one whitey brown head as my own and I went away happy.[5] That much we had brought to pass in spite of the schemes! Dr. Coit said he did not take bad boys to make them

[3] Mary Hallock Foote's mother died that summer, 1890. A letter to Helena Gilder, dated The Mesa, August 31, 1890, spoke at length of her mother's death and of the mother's unhappiness in the closing phase of her life.

[4] Henry Augustus Coit (1830-95), the Episcopal clergyman who was rector of St. Paul's School for thirty-nine years, from its founding in 1856 until his death. Although not an educational innovator, his moral and religious influence dominated the school and helped to make it a successful and widely imitated institution. Since young Arthur actually lived in Dr. Coit's house for considerable periods of time, it is worth noting that although Mrs. Foote worried that her son was too "silent" and withdrawn, the fact is that the boy's mentor, despite his success with the school, lived much within himself and seemed to avoid contact with the world beyond the school's limits.

[5] The decani or decanal is the south side, as contrasted with the cantorial, or north side.

good — he took good boys to make them better. The school was not a reformatory. If the boy-material sent him was found to be tainted, it was quietly returned. . . . It was told of him that once when a visitor of some political notoriety, wishing to flatter the Rector, remarked that the senior class as a group bore a certain likeness to himself, showing whom they had taken as their model, he answered patiently: "There is an 'image and a superscription' which I should like to stamp upon them, but it is not my own."

So the first parting was over; the boy had stood his test in the big boy world. We had hauled him about the continent in wild places, and still the Doctor, who knew boys, had written, after the visit to the Rectory at Christmas was over: "Arthur is a good and gentlemanly child." (We delighted in that phrase!) And now we left him with all the safeguards we knew of to help keep him so.

There were short visits to New York and long talks with beloved Hagues and Gilders, making up back chapters, the things that can't be told in letters. The Gilders had moved into their new house, a spacious old one of a good period beautifully done over by McKim and Stanford White.[6] The rooms looked lovely on the evening of a reception they gave while we were there. The Hagues were in an apartment they had bought in a new building called the Navarro Flats. Everybody seemed affluent — the Dickermans were always a little more splendid every time we went east, but always the same. The Rockwells we could speak of only with awe for their sorrow — that lovely group of children, the harvest of their lives, dashed to pieces! In large families we part for years and come together fearfully — it doesn't do to go too deep into these reckonings with the past. We were told that in Washington we might expect to meet the Hawleys, which would mean "Joe"

[6] The famous architectural firm of McKim, Mead & White, formed 1878-79, and very much sought after as designers of both private and public buildings.

and the second Mrs. Hawley, Harriet's successor. Little Margaret Foote Hawley by the will of God had now a third mother.[7] The family were stunned at first, as families will be, but it was a fate that justified Providence in the sequel. The Foote family owe a debt of gratitude to that last mother who carried on her trust from the dead so ably and in so fine a spirit.

We were the guests of the Emmonses in Washington, although we had never met the second Mrs. Emmons, and I had never seen Mr. Emmons out of buckskins, so to speak. He enjoyed himself very much out of buckskins, and so did all the Survey men when they came back from their western wilds. They did us beautifully, of course, and it was all enormously interesting, with a flavor of the old South before the war which went with Mrs. Emmons' background.[8] She was Miss Sophie Markoe, and her elder sister, Miss Markoe, lived with them; and in an upstairs chamber I had a glimpse of a wonderful old aunt whom these ladies were taking care of, a grande dame in her day, who had lost every male relative she could claim in the war and all her means, and now sat up there tended like a child by the last one left of her house slaves, paralyzed, old, and defeated. In her chair by the window she looked out with sunken, piercing eyes at the new Washington of the postwar period, and to every visitor she gave her delicate, withered hand with the patient courtesy of an exiled queen.

All these visits were food for wakeful nights — the home visit the most poignant. We say good-bye in one look at a beloved face and there are few words — none that we really dare to speak. Then a multitude of faces and of words rush in from outside, but the little mother's face waits for the nights when we think of all the things we didn't say. . . . And on all the

---

[7] See above, p. 299. Spencer Foote having died in 1880 and his wife in 1885, their orphaned daughter Margaret was adopted by the Hawleys and given their name. Then the first Mrs. Hawley died, in 1886, and in November 1887 General Hawley married again, this time marrying an English lady named Edith Anne Horner, who assumed responsibility for the little girl.

[8] See above, p. 181.

visits one had to be so careful *not* to say things! In every life there was some sore spot to be spared.

Our last visit was to the family of General Tompkins — who had had our scheme on his back all these years, since that happy dinner together on the eve of our going to Idaho. We were together still in our sentiments towards one another — all in the same boat, the canal-boat! It was a beautiful sort of visit between the women of the scheme, much too subtle to be described in this hasty fashion. Harry had given me, as men say things, a sort of realization of the mother and sisters who were in his thoughts so much, who had given him his gentle training and made him so nice to live with; but we were almost strangers in the sight of one another. And all of us helpless as women are in the grasp of our men's determinations. And then one day the two husbands came back from the city and each told his wife the great news, and half shyly we women ventured to rejoice together. It was hardly time to hang our banners out, yet the news could be relied on, we were told. The general and his associates had done the deed — the scheme had been placed at last. The final deal had been made between New York and London with a group of English capitalists through their solicitor, Mr. Enoch Harvey; they had bought our bonds or whatever our "paper" was called.[9]

When we were beaten we had been the last to know it, and (speaking for one's self) we could scarcely trust our triumph now. Suspense had become our normal state of mind. With me it took the form of an intuition that something else would go wrong, that there would be a price to pay for this attainment of our hearts' desire. I knew that there would be a telegram if anything went wrong in Idaho; but I could not rest — I longed to get back in the shortest possible time. Yet we stopped over in Denver on more business of the scheme; there were contracts to be drawn up with a Mr. Bradbury to whom the

[9] Enoch Harvey (1826-90) was a solicitor in Liverpool from 1849 until his death.

job of "moving the dirt" on that seventy-five miles of canal line was to be given.[10] While the men were busy over their endless specifications and precautions on both sides, Mrs. Bradbury drove me around the shrill new city — and I hated it all, and the altitude made me breathless, and a host of vague, sickening fears kept me sleepless at night. We were snowbound and sidetracked on the Oregon Short Line, but that longest of journeys, measured by feeling, was over at last. There might have been a touch of foreboding in it, for there was reason for haste; but we were in time.

Our little Agnes lived through many shocks from outside causes to a wonderful physical endowment; she came through this one. I have no remembrance of anything that happened for a month after this, outside her sickroom. Our doctor was young and she was a baffling patient; she ignored sickness and pain because of some mental preoccupation that possessed her spirit. I made him come in the middle of the night when her fever ran highest (it was a cold settled on her lungs) and see what I meant by danger. She would then be almost unconscious, her blue eyes open, her cheeks deeply flushed — a racing pulse, panting like a runner, smiling to herself or to the images of her dream. Her look was angelic; she might have been in a heaven of her own foreknowing — and her mortal mother on one side of the bed demanding of the harassed little doctor on the other if he intended to do nothing with a fever like that! I called it nothing because he was a homeopath just shaking loose a little from his school. But we liked his hesi-

---

10 William C. Bradbury, born in Taunton, Mass., in 1849, went to Denver in 1871 and served as a draftsman and merchant until poor health caused him to seek outdoor work. He began by operating freight teams between Colorado Springs and Leadville in 1878, then added a stagecoach line over the same route. He shifted into cutting and hauling lumber and ties for railroads then under construction in New Mexico and Colorado, and presently began contracting to build irrigation systems in Idaho, Wyoming, Colorado, and New Mexico. His great hobby in all these years was collecting birds' eggs and nests. His wife, who spent so much time showing Mary Hallock Foote around Denver, was the former Hattie A. Howe of Boston.

tations better on the whole than the clumsy confidence of the
other doctors who were brutally "regular."

Our little one recovered; we called her well, but her lovely
color was gone, she could not walk — her dancing step was
still. I did not care what sort of a house they were building on
the Mesa so they got it done.[11] We were Bessie's boarders and
thankful to be so, but I longed, for my little one's sake, for the
great sun-warmed spaces I remembered and the dry soft
winds, as we were driving across from Kuna that April morning full of song. My prophet had said then that here, on this
bench of land above the valley looking out through the gate
of the mountains, should be our home — in the day when the
land was ready that he had come to reclaim. He had taken up,
alongside his preemption claim, a tree-culture and a desert
claim, making in all near a thousand acres. The government
price was three dollars an acre. Such a tract as that with water
on it, three miles from the capital city of a future state, might
easily be worth a fortune that would give us all the freedom
of choice we needed.[12]

The Shermans had wisely made their stake before the irrigation boom set in. They had bought a corner lot opposite the
capitol grounds, and out of his enforced leisure at that time,
Harry Tompkins had made the house plans under Bessie's eye
and with John looking after the budget.

The money to build it came from John's bachelor brothers
— they who would have stepped in to buy the old home for

[11] I.e., Arthur has raised the money to start building his family a new home on
a tableland or bench that the Footes called "The Mesa," from which Boise
could be seen two and one-half miles away.

[12] Under the preemption laws, a settler could acquire 160 acres at the "government minimum" of $1.25 per acre. By legislation in 1878 and 1880 preemp-
tors and claimants under the Homestead Act were placed on virtually the same
footing. The Timber Culture Act of 1873 and 1878 permitted the acquisition
of a further 160 acres, in return for planting trees, and the Desert Land Act
of 1877 permitted the purchase of 640 acres at $1.25 per acre, in return for
irrigating within three years. Roy M. Robbins, *Our Landed Heritage: The
Public Domain, 1776-1936* (Princeton, 1942), pp. 89, 218-19, 285-86.

mother.[13] That would have been family piety — this was business, a loan paying better interest than they could have got in the East. The house was not too large to be homelike, yet large enough to pay its way and enough over to make it a safe venture financially, and when it rose on that choice corner in the heart of the city, we said admiringly, "A Tech man can do anything." That was one for the architect, but still more we admired the quiet nerve of the owners who were making this new start not early in life, and one of them more handicapped in point of health than any of us realized.

By the first of June [1890] the irrigation boom was well started. New people were coming in, and many of our old friends who had been kind but skeptical were filing now on desert land themselves, copying our confidence. The engineers were not inventing work for themselves, in these days. The Cañon House was open again and every room a Junior's room, windows gloriously unwashed and floors printed all over with boot nails. Above Coston's ranch (the last one on the river "along the way that goest up to Beth-horon") there was a huge contractor's base camp — their lights were like a little city at night. The canal which had been a matter of diagrams and cross sections and dotted lines on paper (when it wasn't a subject for ridicule and pity) was now the great show of the countryside. An unroofed gallery eighty feet across the top, fifty on the bottom, swept in a mathematical curve round the shoulder of the hill; fifteen horsemen might ride down it abreast "nor be pressed." When the sloped walls were finished they kept their alignment, twelve feet high, and where they were not finished an endless procession of scraper teams crawled up and dumped and slid down to load and crawl up again.

All the summer before, my man had been with his little party on horseback hunting the Grand Teton Range for reservoir sites on both forks of the Snake, through Jackson's Hole up

[13] Isaac and Townsend Sherman.

to the Yellowstone and Henry's Lake, while Mr. Wiley, who had taken a job under him on the Government Survey, was running canal lines preliminary to opening millions of acres to settlement in the Snake River desert. That was the plan of the whole work in outline ready to be completed in details. A junior engineer was now put in Wiley's place on the Survey while he went back to the old canal crowd, and the old chief had both jobs under his eye in a general way.

⧼29⧽

My man of the future had been shut up with his theories so long in the Cañon that an outburst of practical energy now might have been expected: it was the release of all his cramped powers when the embargo on the work was raised. The Mesa was his private stake, and here he let himself go. It was useless to quote to him (as I did more than once!), "The Lord hates busybodies and people who do too much." We were digging holes for hundreds of baby trees, putting up a windmill and a tank tower and outbuildings, laying out ditches and plowing a fifty-acre field to be planted to wheat; a scraper team was grading around the house for a lawn, and when those soft dry winds I had pined for came tumbling over us they left a quarter acre of dried desert on the floor of our forty-foot piazza for the next pair of feet to track inside. And why have such a great piazza? — I suppose because we had no other shade. We had lined our half mile of avenue with poplars and set out a group near the house to rise like a spire, a landmark, in the future — in the present they were little waving switches watered with a hose cart from the windmill. . . . In order to lose no time!

We seemed to be spending money like water to get ready for water which was not even in sight. I wanted to know where it all came from and how long at this rate it could last? The answer was that the Rockwells had bought a good big chunk of A.'s canal stock.[1] He looked at it as an ordinary exchange of values to come for value received. He said Cousin Alfred had long been watching the scheme and had always believed in it.

[1] Concerning the Rockwell family's relationship to the Footes, see above p. 255.

I believed that the values involved went much deeper than the future of desert lands. There are many ways of taking an incurable grief; they had sought ease from their immortal pain in trying to do things for others, and they did big things just as often as little ones. I knew they believed in my husband personally, whether they did in the future of the canal or not. They were risking their money to give him his chance after he had waited so long. All that I could see in these furious activities was the Rockwells' money going into our wild land. I loved the land and I loved the Rockwells, but I would have had them kept separate.

And why put all this money in the ground at once! Why not wait and see? The answer to that was, because everyone else would wait and see what Foote was doing. If he held back, who was on the inside, or if he went ahead in a creeping and doubtful manner, everyone would copy his creeping example. There would be no land taken up under the canal, no purchasers for the water and no rise in canal securities. It was but keeping faith with the purchasers of the stock to go ahead and show what the land could do. There must be risks, of course, and we were the ones to take them — into the front rank of settlers we must go in this charge on the desert. Ours would be the pioneer ranch: behold our poplar avenue, our orchards, our fifty acres of wheat — if it came up. It was "fire, fire, burn stick — stick, beat pig — pig must go!" All of which was unanswerable so long as you believed that pig would go. But I was not happy that summer on the Mesa. I had seen so much trouble in families from mixing business and affection. The Rockwells did not need our scheme, but we needed them . . . useless, useless, and too late anyhow! The deal had been made and the money was half spent already.

Mr. Harvey came out to us in the height of the season [1890] when strawberries were ripe, raised on the little river ranches and displayed in the Boise market — there as an advertisement! He was a beautiful old gentleman, accustomed to be waited on, who took everything as it came with the gentlest courtesy, and it came very queerly at times.[2] We couldn't take decent care of him: there was no man, nor woman either, to brush his clothes and polish his "boots"; he never was sure of his tea at any hour; we childlishly feasted him on strawberries, and he took them as they came — such strawberries as they raise under glass in England. But first there were some hours spent in the office of our best lawyer in Boise going over the territorial land laws and the U. S. law as to water rights; sure of these things he was ready to dream with any of us. Arthur took him to a high hill beyond Kuna from which he could see almost the whole tract, from the head of the canal line above Boise to the meeting of the rivers, a province of 350,000 acres given over to jackrabbits and coyotes and meadowlarks — one must not forget those early poets in a lonely world. Mr. Harvey said the company that owned that water and could control its delivery to those lands need have no fear for the future of its investment.

Englishmen are patient, and they don't look back when they have put their hands to the plow, not Englishmen of his type; but there are other types, and there are several types of the American promoter. The one who had placed the scheme in London came out with Mr. Harvey, flushed with triumph, excited by what he saw on the ground without being able to grasp the half of it; in him our men recognized the fly in the ointment. Mr. Harvey took him lightly for what he was; he had no influence in New York, nor would have had in London if Mr. Harvey had but lived. . . . Fate, fate! He lost his life,

[2] Mary Hallock Foote's letter to Helena Gilder, dated The Mesa, June 15, 1890, described Enoch Harvey's visit, which came at an awkward moment when they were still painting the new house and hanging curtains and pictures. She found Harvey to be a charming, gallant, white-haired gentleman who was not "tiresome and common English." She stated that while with them Harvey made his decision and cabled London to complete the negotiation so that work could start.

that autumn following his visit to Idaho, by an accident so senseless, so wanton, it seems a disrespect to talk of it. He was very absentminded, he needed a servant at his elbow — had just parted with his man and was crossing the tracks at his own railway station in the country, with his eyes on his newspaper — and then he was gone, trampled out in an instant by a thousand tons of iron.[3] This was the end of that life so trained and guarded and perfected to the threshold of a beautiful old age. Barely acquainted as we were, he was one of those who are never forgotten. The canal could not have had a heavier blow. His influence with the group of City men in London who were putting up the money was absolute; when he was gone they were open to any wind of doubt or suspicion from any quarter.

It would only drag out the tale to explain all our troubles in Idaho as the ditch plowed its way along; the dissensions between New York and London were a story by themselves, which we could know only in part, but they finally wrecked the scheme. Our liaison officer was gone. When the Englishmen refused to put up the money they had promised, the Americans could not carry the scheme alone, nor get back their prestige that was lost.[4] Mr. Bradbury, the head contractor, was patient, but after a few months he could wait for his

---

3 He was killed at Mersey Road station, Liverpool, October 1, 1890.

4 By the spring of 1891 a disagreeable and many-sided dispute had developed between the several different parties interested or potentially interested in the irrigation project. General Tompkins and his son Harry, Wiley, and the Arthur Footes came to regard themselves as a little group that was standing loyally together against the intrigues and divisive tactics of selfish interests in Britain and New York who were seeking to get control of the ill-starred project on advantageous terms. Meantime Arthur's salary went unpaid until the arrears totaled thousands of dollars. Mary Hallock Foote was fearful that her eastern friends might be hearing false accounts of Arthur's role. Harry Tompkins was suffering what seems to have been a nervous breakdown, during which he experienced waves of faintness that robbed him of the ability to use his muscles, even though he did not actually lose consciousness. The strain was proving a "close call" for all of them, Mrs. Foote wrote. See her letters to Helena Gilder, dated The Mesa, April 8 and June 2, 1891.

money no longer; he took the whole property on a lien and it became the burden of his life for years. We were far ahead of the times on the subject of irrigation in this country. Mr. Harvey knew its history in older lands; he had been prepared to expect delays and reverses and mistakes in judgment. All schemes must learn, but the fundamental causes of our failure were the lack of teamwork between New York and London, and the meddlesome impatience of little-minded men.[5]

On the Mesa we learned also. The year following our first planting on the Mesa was fated to be one of the dryest on record. The wheat did not sprout, for there were no spring rains. The canal stopped two miles above us and we died — slowly, keeping up the fight to the last. Our orchards were the greatest tragedy; hundreds of little nursery trees struggled along watered by hand from a hose cart making the rounds from tree to tree — but that could not go on. It was the year of our private ruin and nothing was lacking to us in the way of

---

[5] Relying upon the promises of the British interests that were to purchase the company's bonds, in the spring of 1890 Arthur Foote and the two Tompkinses, father and son, had started Bradbury on a contract to build two canals: a small, short one known as the Phyllis, that would reach already established farms and the Snake River placers, thus returning immediate revenue; and the main New York Canal, which would take much longer. Foote and the Tompkinses somehow managed to advance $116,000 to get Bradbury started, and when this was gone and the promised British funds had not materialized, Bradbury advanced $184,000 of his own funds, so as to complete the Phyllis. Bradbury started work on the New York Canal but soon had to stop, taking a lien against the company for the amount due him. After waiting several years for his money, in April 1893 Bradbury had William E. Borah, then a young Boise attorney, file a mechanics lien against the company for $208,000. Through Borah, Bradbury then acquired both the Phyllis and New York canals at the resulting sheriff's sale held on February 8, 1894, which happened to fall in the midst of the severe national depression that had begun in 1893 and that had wiped out any remaining chance of rescuing the property. The later history of the project continued to be tangled and unhappy until finally it was absorbed into a bigger scheme planned and financed by the federal government. (Information supplied by two memoranda prepared by Dr. Merle Wells of the Idaho Historical Society, Boise, for the present editor, October 1971 and March 1972.)

conspicuousness. An old pioneer capitalist of Boise who drove out to look at the grave of our folly remarked to the man in charge of what was left, "*I* could have told him he'd find it cheaper to buy his wheat than raise it."

Wheat was not the commodity in question, however; it was faith we planted and that did not die — not with him who planted. It took twenty-five years for that crop to show above ground! The Reclamation Bureau under [Theodore] Roosevelt built the New York and Idaho canal following the old line our poor men laid out and left behind them. We did not leave our bones on that battlefield, but we left pretty much everything else we had. My husband left the crown of his years and the greatest of his hopes, the dream that satisfied the blood of farmers and home-makers in him, and the brain of the constructor he was born to use.

As for losses, our own were not a circumstance beside the losses of our friends — on the Mesa they were one and the same; but we came to know the Rockwell cousins as we never should have known them had we made a great success in Idaho. It was the road of humiliation for us, but we were not too old to tread it, and it led to sustained relationships with those dear friends which have been a better legacy for our children than many mesas in full bloom. . . .

But even now, on our continental journeys, when we have reached that country of the high valleys and the old lava flows between the knees of the ranges; when we halt at some lone junction or water tank in the sagebrush and step out to breathe that air again and listen to the "essential silence" after the roar of the train — it is there, that whisper of the desert wind — it all comes back, the shiver of an old longing and doubt and expectancy. . . . We see the long, low house stretched out on the Mesa raised above the valley, we see the ring of mountains lifting and lowering down to the great gate where the sun is setting in a storm of gold. Then purple shadows darken in their cañons; the color mounts to the zenith and the plains are flushed with light. I remember one evening when we sat out there with Mr. Harvey and the glow was in all the faces that stared into the future of that valley. He pointed where a railroad station should be on the lands he had picked for a colony of young Englishmen whom he dreamed of planting there; not wasters, whose people would gladly be rid of them, but nephews of his own and younger sons of those upper-middle-class families which I remember Edith Angus said were the backbone of England. There were long futures in his mind. And many things of the highest importance would have been altered for our children had we anchored them there.

The Congress that winter refused to appropriate for anything that looked as frivolous to them as the Irrigation Survey, so that died too. We shut down the Mesa as tight as we could without throwing it away; we stripped our rooms once more, sold our more rational belongings to Bessie who was furnishing her new house, and stored our fads and collections in her clean and empty attic. An attic that spoke of a house that has no history; it began to accumulate history very fast.

BOOK VI

Anything for Business

30

THE SHERMAN House opened its doors in the autumn of 1890 and might have been called the "Pension des Exiles," so many birds of passage took shelter there, to say nothing of birds with broken wings. That summer Gerald [Sherman] went east to stay with his father's people at Milton before entering Columbia, class of '94. It happened that an old friend of the family, Mrs. Howard Crosby, should be their guest while he was there. She looked over this nephew from the West, pronounced him "too nice a boy to be turned loose in a New York boarding house" and wrote to his parents asking to have him with them the following winter. No invitation from any source could have given the Shermans greater satisfaction; they were very happy in the boy's good luck. Never afterwards could this chance have been his: Dr. Howard Crosby died at the end of that winter, and one of the kindest, most cultivated homes in New York, distinguished for its graciousness and breeding, was broken up. Gerald's father died that same spring — in the new house in Boise City. His first thought was to drop his studies and go back at once to help his mother, but she would not permit the sacrifice; she sent him word to stay and go on with his college course.[1]

We had many thoughts ourselves in those days about the long consequences to our sister and her children of that move to Idaho for which in a measure we might have been held

[1] John Sherman died on April 3, 1891. The Rev. Howard Crosby (1826-91), in whose home young Gerald was staying, died March 29, 1891. Crosby was pastor of the Fourth Avenue Presbyterian Church, New York City, to which he had been called in 1863.

responsible. In our old age I asked her once how it had affected John himself, whose health had been one if not the chief consideration. He died of a long, slow illness which she thought due in part to the depressing situation at home which lasted so many years; seeing the property waste away while nominally under his care, when his hands were tied. The change to Idaho, she believed, prolonged his life "for those seven happy years — for they were happy," she added, "in spite of the worries, and the happiest time of all was the few months we spent in the new house together." He lived long enough to know that the venture was bound to be a business success, and he had seen his son begin his university course under the happiest auspices. He was a tired man — tired of doing his best with nothing to show for it. He was in bonds to his wife's devotion to her parents, and it was one of the long thoughts that haunted her after his death that she had sacrificed him to that first law of her being.

John was the youngest of his family, the only one who married. His sister and brothers wrote at once urging Bessie to come back to them with her children, who were all they had to live for. There was houseroom and heartroom waiting. It must have been a temptation, stunned as she was — the end had been sudden at the last. I remember the long silences when she sat and went over her past and balanced the opportunities for her children, east or west; their futures were in her hands. Her own life did not concern her, though it was hardly more than half lived; but she could not part with her independence. Her decision tied the master knots of fate for another generation.

In the house that had lost its head, no one was incommoded; meals and service went on the same, and in the town where John had many friends there was a sentiment of championship for his widow who would not go home beaten, who stayed and quietly adjusted herself to the unshared burden. Her business friends advised her, since she was turning away applicants, to skim the cream of the market, put up her prices above the reach of young schoolteachers and young men on vanishing salaries. She had what she considered the cream, but she kept her schoolteachers and her young men too. If one whom she liked lost his job he was invited to stay on till he had found another, and he paid when he was able to. But she chose her household wisely, and a sense of personal consideration for each one was included in her share of the bargain. We were there, and others who had been dumped from their chariots of hope through the exigencies of politics or schemes. The discontinued Survey dropped a nice young man or two from good eastern homes. The Wilds were there — Henry Fearing Wild and his wife who was Rosamond Dana.[2] He had been superintendent of the U. S. Assay Office under Cleveland. Now, under Harrison, he had lost both his post and the comfortable residence in the Assay Office building which went with it. His short-lived connection with the New York Ditch did not help him much — nor the ditch. The happier side of that acquaintance was through her — nothing could have been more gallant or more misplaced than Rosamond Dana Wild in Boise City. It takes a highly organized, highbred woman to be the perfect sport that she was. . . . So they were living at the Sherman House that winter, and we bowed and smiled to one another across the dining room at breakfast — they with their

---

[2] Daughter of Richard Henry Dana, Jr. (1815-82), who is best known today as the author of *Two Years before the Mast*, but in his own day was prominent also as an authority on maritime and international law and as a member of the antislavery movement. When Mrs. Wild first appeared in Boise, Mrs. Foote found this Boston aristocrat clever, charming, and worth knowing well. But presently Mrs. Foote came to feel that Mrs. Wild was erratic and irresponsible, was misplaced in the West, and was disturbingly "superior" toward Bessie Sherman because the latter kept a boarding house. See Mary Hallock Foote's letters to Helena Gilder, dated The Mesa, June 12 and August 8, 1891, and, apparently from Bessie's house, November 4, 1891. Mrs. Wild's attitude becomes more understandable if one notes her famous father's remark when Rosamond was born. He had hoped for a boy, but consoled himself with the thought: "I feel as though four generations of prominent & successful men, following each other, is as much as one family can expect." Quoted in Samuel Shapiro, *Richard Henry Dana, Jr., 1815-1882* (East Lansing, Mich., 1961), p. 41.

little daughter Rosamond enisled at one small table, we with our children at another. . . . It was farewell to something unique in Idaho when we saw her go east again.

I look back to that third-story bedroom at Bessie's, where my writing was done, as the best place for the purpose I have ever known, and my work in that room was blessed, if it be blessed to "sell" — I am not so sure about that! The themes were the best that ever came to me, but if they had been returned and kept for ten years till they had ripened and settled on their lees, I might have poured a purer wine. But quick sales were very needful at that time. The ceiling sloped down on one side of the room where a broad dormer window opened on a view of the sky and the treetops in the capitol grounds across the square. It was the grenier [attic or garret] of the poor artist with its atmosphere of solitude and concentration. Sounds of a busy household came from a distance and at certain hours the children's feet trooping up the two flights of stairs. A young high school teacher whom they adored had a little end room on the hall below us, and there were romps and ambushes in the long upper passage as twilight came on and shrieks of ecstasy over a surprise and capture.

This was the year when the Kipling letters began — a phenomenal event not lost on little daughters just old enough to read him — some of him. Their faces shone with wonder at the marvel of his very own handwriting (he who wrote "My Lord the Elephant"!)[3] — on a letter to mama, in Idaho! It was no more than a business order, in most enchantingly unbusinesslike language, for two drawings for the western chapters of *The Naulahka* — to be published, regardless of the trade, as his personal tribute to his dead friend and collaborator. The sorrow for young Wolcott Balestier was still in the air.[4] In this work I was to collaborate with Mr. Lockwood Kipling of La-

3 First published 1892.

4 In 1892 Kipling married the sister of Charles Wolcott Balestier (1861-91), who was an American publisher and author and Kipling's collaborator in writing *The Naulahka* (1892). Balestier had a brief but brilliant career in the London

hore who would do the Indian part, and he now took up the matter in letters almost as charming as his son's. "The drawings have come," he says (the western drawings) "and find me in dumb, conscience-stricken despair. For I have tried to do things for the Naulahka and failed utterly. . . .

"Meanwhile, my son, meandering about Japan with his wife sending us the gayest letters — three sheets in the wind with pure happiness — won't understand that I am a broken reed — and I don't know where to reach him with an emphatic telegram." . . . The project was finally given up, but the letters went on in an unbelievable way — sometimes from the father, sometimes from the son — sometimes from Lahore, and again from Brattleboro, Vermont, where the young pair were settled temporarily on a piece of family property belonging to the Balestier estate. Much must have been happening, but the letters lasted into the time when their little Josephine was born;[5] and later, her father writes, "This house and the next farmhouse is run by and for my mother-in-law's baby, a three-toothed little maiden of fourteen months and much dignity. She is not quite well — a cold or something — and you can distinctly hear all our hearts beating all down the road when she sneezes." . . . Speaking, later, of writing and drawing combined with motherhood (Mrs. Kipling had asked how we managed to write and draw and have babies in Idaho —), he says, "I can well see how there must be a big tug now and again between those gifts you own unto you, and those other gifts common to all mothers. I've a notion however that sometimes giving up is accounted as more than giving out." It is a special sin to quote from letters where all was so delicately shaded and balanced, and of course the context is everything. But I must add these few words — he was so enchanting about that little first daughter! "Our babe has approached litera-

literary world from 1888-91. Curiously, after dropping out of Cornell he had gone west to Leadville and used that region as the setting for some of his better fiction.

5 December 29, 1892.

ture" (this of course being some time later) "in a large and serene spirit; arguing from the Jungle books she assumes that all the books on my shelves were written by 'fa'ver' and the pictures to them were drawn by 'gran'faver' — all for her. It's a good view to take when you come to consider it, and I grieve for her awakening. She is a great child and the delight of our days."

From Lahore, April '93, comes this rare bit from Mr. Lockwood Kipling, so packed with autobiography.

> We go, my wife and I, in the "Locksley Hall" on the 17th prox. for Europe from Karuchi [sic]; she leaves the ship at Marsailles for London overland (if there is no cholera quarantine) while I go on to L'pool and thence, having landed our old dog Vixen — to New York & Brattleboro — to make the acquaintance of "that baby," that "international kid" & also the new little house on the hill side.[6]
>
> A gay lookout, when once the gate of the East is passed; but at present for us two, — who leave in Calcutta a daughter of the kind you wot of, that flushed as a child with the music of a "couch of snows on the Acroceranian Mountains" — and leave too, more than could be understood out of India, a most serious and saddening outlook, it is more like a dream of decease than anything else. My wife says "It is time; — I came a bride, and I go a Grandmother."[7]

Mr. Kipling Senior was a man of the widest knowledge and observation of men — and beasts. His letters were bursting with interest, and he could read more into any human book than the author or a million ordinary readers could get out of it. This I had occasion to note in regard to one or two books of my own published about this time which I made bold to send him. The whole, extraordinary correspondence illumined a

6 Called "The Naulahka," the new house built for the Kiplings at Brattleboro was ready for them to move into during Lockwood Kipling's visit, August, 1893.

7 The elder Kiplings had gone to India immediately after their marriage in 1865. The anxiety expressed here must have been for the psychological stability of their daughter Trix (Rudyard's sister), who was showing increasing signs of the mental turmoil that produced complete collapse in 1898. Charles Carrington, *Rudyard Kipling, His Life and Work* (London, 1955), p. 284.

gray and rugged passage in our lives as only the miracle of human sympathy can, yet we were not even acquainted except where our minds touched on paper. We never saw the younger Kiplings, and the father I saw but once in a conventional way that didn't count. He was a man to sit beside on a steamer's deck or on a summer piazza as an honorary member of that Society of Perfect Leisure which he said he founded in Vermont, with the baby as president and himself as secretary: "There could not be a more permanent staff! . . . but," he adds sadly, "one can see that leisure is rare." The American woman afflicted him (after twenty-eight years in India) with her "wild eagerness to be up and doing, ranging round for things to learn and talk about. . . . And they all seem to me to work too hard. That terrible New England conscience seems to hound them on to all sorts of painful endeavor." . . .

We had been moved on, when these later letters came, to our next post of painful endeavor, or fatuous waiting.[8] We were in the North Star Cottage at Grass Valley, and the little daughters who danced about the third-story bedroom at Bessie's in ecstasy over the first Kipling letter were now reading *Barrack-Room Ballads* in the English edition, autographed and presented by Himself. . . . More and more amazement and joy incredible when he sent their mother a letter all about *The Cup of Trembling* (which she, trembling, had laid at his feet) — and it wound up with the following: "P. S. If you wouldn't think it impertinent I'd like to have three (3) copies to send over [to] the other side with an eye to reviews and if you'd care to have me write to my literary agent A. P. Watt, with a view to pushing it and making new English contracts, I'd be even better pleased."[9]

8 This must have been late in 1895 or early in 1896.

9 Alexander Pollock Watt, Glasgow-born and Edinburgh-educated, claimed in the British *Who's Who* (1901) to have been "the first to conceive and put into practice the idea of the literary agent acting as an intermediary between authors and publishers and editors." *The Cup of Trembling, and Other Stories* by Mary Hallock Foote was published at Boston and New York in 1895. *Barrack-Room Ballads* had been in print in the English edition since 1892.

It was easy to know that my books were not best sellers, and from those mutual friends the Gilders he might have heard a word of our losing fight in Idaho; everything connected with the day's work appealed to him and all through his books he shows that feeling for the work that is "broken"; he was the poet of Unsuccess. I took him at his chivalrous word and he forwarded the books — which meant one letter more to A. P. Watt, and another faultless letter to the author who by this time was beginning to realize what she had done! He said, "Now that our insular ice is broken you should make a big splash." Nothing of that sort followed, but that letter — *all* the *Cup of Trembling* letters — were splash enough for me.

This fabulous correspondence did not break off at once; he did not drop me because there was no splash — rather he made a point of keeping on. But all ended with that fatal winter in New York, and life could never have been the same to them. The world of his readers felt it a personal sorrow when he lost that child; all the greatest people in it laid their sympathy at the parents' feet, but words seemed preposterous — they had words enough. . . . I remember one early nightfall in San Francisco that winter, the lighted streets shining with wet, when I stood on the outskirts of a crowd jamming its umbrellas together in front of the Chronicle Building where the latest report from Kipling's sickbed had just been chalked up. I asked the man in front of me if he could see what was written, and he repeated the words, ending with " 'Kipling sleeps' " — his first natural sleep — while the wife who watched kept from him the loss of his child that would have killed him then.[10]

[10] The entire Kipling family became ill during a stay in New York City in February 1899. Rudyard, desperately ill with pneumonia, very nearly died on February 28, but surmounted this crisis, fell into the natural sleep that Mary Hallock Foote mentions, and thereafter began to gain, so that by March 4 he was regarded as being out of danger though exceedingly weak. News that his little daughter Josephine, likewise gravely ill with pneumonia, was sinking, was kept from him; she died on March 6. The outpouring of sympathy was worldwide. Carrington, *Rudyard Kipling*, pp. 287-90.

Many in that crowd went their way saying to themselves, "Kipling sleeps." In every white man's city of the world they were saying it, and praying God to help him bear the awakening. Is that merely fame?

⟪ 31 ⟫

O NE MORNING [in July 1892], Nelly's knock came early on
our door (I take up my tale again where I left it, at the Sherman House) — Agnes slept in our room and Betty in a cot in
Nelly's room, so we knew the knock had reference to her. She
had been sick in the night and showed signs of a temperature.
The children were kept apart until the doctor had seen his
patient, and by that time there was no room for doubt: it was
a case of scarlet fever.

There was but one place we could go to. In less than an hour
we were packed for a six weeks' quarantine on the Mesa, and
we scuttled out of the house with our sick child bundled in her
father's arms, avoiding and avoided, but followed by sorrow-
ful looks. And what a trail of hard work we left behind us! —
clothes and bedding to be disinfected, rooms to be fumigated
in the old way with pans of burning sulphur — but we took
some work with us to the Mesa. We thought it very loyal and
decent of the Pinningers, our caretakers, not to pick up their
children and flee at our coming. What should I have done
without them! They put their trust in the doctor's orders and
in me to keep them. The kitchen end became their refuge,
leaving me the freedom of the wide, dismantled house, and
the long veranda was our hall of communication. Mrs. Pin-
ninger cooked and George fetched and carried and we kept
apart through a system of bells and signals.

The case was a blessed mild one — what a doctor calls mild.
I had my days and nights of fear, but when they were past and
we knew there were none of the dreaded "sequelae," the work
itself became a tonic — I hardened under it and grew strong,

342

because I trusted the hands I was in. . . . There were mornings "proud and sweet" when I carried out my pails (which were neither proud nor sweet) to empty in the ash pit over the bluff, and, straightening up to look across the valley — lo, beautiful upon the mountains the feet of sunrise! Another night safely over, and across the valley little sister just waking had not taken it, the devilish thing — we never knew how we had got it. Germs walked abroad in the streets of Boise and sailed upon its dust-laden winds. We were used to wind and dust, but not when so highly charged with humanity. The dust of a clean wide mesa, or a boxed-in cañon with the river for its floor, is not the same as the sweepings of a city that had then no health board.

And now came our evenings when the little convalescent could sit outside; when we watched that empty plain for the dust of a single rider from the west, a pennon lengthening fast in our direction, struck through with gold from the low and friendly light behind the hills of Boise Barracks. Then we could not see our rider but we heard his horse's hoofs, the hard quick stride up the steepest part of the bluff, and then he was there, clanking towards us in his spurs — keeping his distance, telling us his news, turning out his letters and parcels on the wooden parapet between us. Such letters!

The Rockwell cousins had heard that Arthur was not to go back to St. Paul's — they knew what that meant, and they thought it "such a pity" and wrote to say so. These boys were the family future they said; they must have their chance. We thought there might be other chances that we could better afford, but they asked as "a happiness to themselves" — who could do no more for their own son — to be allowed to help with ours. That letter was burned with everything we could live without when we broke up quarantine on the Mesa, but its words have been kept in my heart ever since. It was from Kate to me, but Arthur answered — they were his people, and he said "No." And I don't think it was pride.

Then Helena wrote, who had heard the same news, and begged me to take a little legacy she had just come into that was lying in the bank at a trifling interest — take it at that interest if in no other way, she said, but take it anyhow — not to break up our plan for the boy's education. Both mothers felt that in sending the boy so far away from us at his age we must make sure what hands we put him in. These were the all-important years. That letter I answered myself and I said "No." And that was not pride, but jealousy for our friendship without a flaw. . . . And then came the last of that beautiful flock of messages, and this offer was not ours to refuse: the boy had earned it himself. Dr. Coit wrote, promising in his delicate way, "if you feel satisfied with what the school is doing for Arthur," that he should come back — his place was "waiting for him" and would be kept for him and should cost us nothing for tuition and residence.

My poor man, on these evening visits, would ride from our lonely gateway where no one ever entered, through half a mile of dead hopes, dead trees and fields he had planted, but he brought these letters! And he brought himself — everything he had to give, including his patience and indomitable pluck. When he had a salary, it was "ours" — when he had debts, they were "his," and he paid them doggedly, year after year, as his life and work allowed. The cost of that six weeks' quarantine on a dry hill three miles from town, with fresh milk and ice and eggs and service and everything we needed, had taken his last cent and stopped an important piece of work he was finishing at the time. In one of his moments of prophecy he had located a reservoir site at a place in the backlands called Ten Mile or Indian Creek. It would be his legally as soon as the application papers had been recorded at Washington, water rights being in the gift of the government. One little detail necessary to perfect his title remained unfinished which required another day's work and the hire of one or two men. He said there was no hurry; the regulations allowed time for a locator to finish his preliminary work, and no one knew of the place who would see it with his eyes or know what was there.

The next news from Ten Mile was that he had "placed" his little scheme with an engineer in town who had come to him asking for something in the line of irrigation "about that size" to sell to an easterner who was out there in a coming-on humor. He was the promoter and asked A. to name his price. The work itself was all A. asked — to build his own dam, on the salary of a chief engineer. He showed his maps and drawings, laid out the whole scheme in detail, including the weak point in his title which waited for that last day's work. It was another gentleman's agreement, and the other party to it in this case (as I propose to take away his character) I shall call Blank. He said he would be obliged to leave town for a short trip east; on his return the deal would be closed on the basis of this verbal agreement. A. put no watch on his partner's movements. The journey east was a ruse to gain time. We were busy on the Mesa breaking up quarantine.

Blank kept out of the way and went secretly to the spot he had never seen except on paper, pulled up the original locator's stakes and put in his own, using A.'s surveys to supplant him on his own claim. This was done on the basis of knowledge obtained through a business confidence. When the final interview came off, A. was informed that he had nothing to sell; his partner's application papers had gone on to Washington and were on record by that time. All of which, he was informed, was strictly "legal."[1] A. would have tested that legality if he had had the money to go on to Washington with his maps and papers and a few affidavits — but the fact that he hadn't was

[1] Two letters from Mary Hallock Foote, in Boise, to Helena Gilder, undated but apparently written, respectively, in November and December 1892, give a full account of this episode, but place the site as Black's Creek and give the name of the cheating engineer as Clark. Still another of Arthur's schemes that failed in this black period was a proposal to build a new water system to bring into Boise supplies that could compete with the existing monopoly. Described in Mary Hallock Foote's letter to Helena, dated Boise, November 11, 1892.

common knowledge and entered, no doubt, into the scheme in the first place. From those who have not shall be taken away. Such tricks are abhorred in new communities where "gentleman" is a relative term, but to each man his code according to his trade. There are in most little western towns gentlemen and engineers and claim jumpers, but you seldom have to deal with all three in one and the same person. Thereafter, in the case of Blank, we omitted the "gentleman," and A. swallowed with dry grins the "engineer."

He took A.'s idea for the dam and left out the essential feature, the "core walls," and the dam went out before the reservoir was half full. In other ways the scheme was mangled beyond recognition, and the whole piece of bad sportsmanship rankled with my husband the more that he had been fooled by a man of his own profession. This was the last piece of property of the imagination left him in Idaho that could be lost or stolen.

Meantime we had three good and happy children — they were property of the imagination which we were pretty sure would pay. Sonny's chum at St. Paul's was an English boy whose home was at Yarmouth, Nova Scotia. His father owned a steamship line between Boston and Yarmouth and gave Sonny free transportation when his friend asked him to go home with him, and Dr. Coit advised us to let him go. We were glad enough to have him go, the lucky boy! I dare say we were cross and cranky in those days, but I am sure we were not in the least downhearted. We had all the fundamentals of life unchanged.

32

A NEW irrigation district was opening for settlement in one of the hottest valleys of California which had need of an hydraulic engineer and also of advertising. The corporation's business agent wrote to A. inviting himself and wife to come down and see what the company could do for us both in the line of our associated work. Apparently he thought we collaborated. He had read a recent book of mine, published as a serial in the *Century*, called "The Chosen Valley," and it had struck him as a bright idea for booming a new section of country in want of settlers. They needed settlers and he thought their valley might supply me with themes while my husband ran ditch lines and built reservoirs.[1] We laughed and groaned over this artless suggestion which pointed to our lying in one grave — the grave of our little reputations — and tried not to be too haughty in reply. Presently we heard more of the matter from one who knew the heads of the company and said they were "all right" — no offense had been intended. It was a friend of A.'s who had taken the trouble to write and persuade him not to be hasty. The job itself he said was well worth considering and the collusion plan between authorship and advertising was merely a flight of the businessman's imagination.

A. knew the country — knew there was nothing there we should be likely to love and most things we should hate, but if

[1] Since Mary Hallock Foote speaks of Bakersfield and mentions "Kern Valley" in one of her letters, the area in question must have been the hot, dry region at the head of the San Joaquin Valley, where for some years San Francisco capital had been developing a canal system. A letter from Mary Hallock Foote to Helena Gilder, dated Boise, March 27, 1893, describes both this possible job and the start of the venture with Emmons, and thus dates both episodes.

we could go uncommitted to any foolishness, it was not for us to be choosers. He went prepared to take the job but before the matter was concluded came a stay from an unexpected quarter. Once more a friend had remembered us. S. F. Emmons wired from San Diego to ask A. if he would be interested in the job of opening an onyx mine in the Lower Peninsula [Baja California]. If so, he would find him, Emmons, at the [Hotel del] Coronado and they would go down the coast and look at it together. Such a call just then came like wind to a flapping sail. We had parted for two weeks — it was nearer two years before I saw my job hunter again.

In the heart of the Lower Peninsula, two days' journey inland from the coast, is a region of horny reptiles and goblin vegetation where Nature has worked out some of her wildest freaks in the likeness of trees and creeping, crawling things that are found nowhere else on earth. It had a history once, connecting the Indian population with the Spaniard in the usual manner fatal to both. The last visitation of wrath had been smallpox and that was supposed to have ended the chapter. At all events the inhabitants at this time were as scarce as the water and possibly as bad. To ride across this country and study it in company with a man like Emmons was a very different proposition from Bakersfield.

On his way north by way of San Diego, leaving my husband on the job, Mr. Emmons found time to write me a detailed account of that weird journey, as if he might have been working up his notes and then had decided to share them with the woman whose husband he had commandeered at such short notice. But it was more than that — a good deal more to me![2] He spoke of him as "Arthur"; he made a point of naming over the various qualifications of his new executive whom he had evidently been studying on this journey. He praised his energy and decision, his handling of men, his technical knowledge of

[2] Since Emmons published a monograph on the geology of Lower California, in 1894, he may well have been "working up his notes."

such widely different kinds — of boats and trails and machinery and agriculture and construction, his Yankee inventiveness and resourcefulness — he said those things no man can say of himself, not even to save the faith of the woman God gave him to lead through the world subject to his decisions. I think Emmons realized that another strain upon that faith might be awaiting the woman he wrote to; he knew, as I could not (and A. would never have told me), the dangers and difficulties of the new job and the chances it held of another failure.

A road to the sea was the first requirement — always the white man builds a road — and a port of shipment for the onyx. This is a wide-open coast. They made choice of San Carlos,[3] for here the sea has bitten out a little bay sheltered from the offshore winds by a steep wall of rock twelve hundred feet sheer from the beach and flattened on top; the sailors who approach that unlighted coast use it as a landmark and call it El Sombrero.

The onyx was not jewel onyx, not the biblical "onyx stone," but beautiful stuff. It cropped out near the surface in layers resting on a softer, amorphous substance like itself in composition but uncrystallized. It was easily mined; the problem had been to get it aboard the coasters at their anchorage outside.

The company's office was in San Diego. Here A. came upon a 500-ton lighter built to carry Pullman cars across San Diego Bay to Coronado beach from the Santa Fé terminus during the Coronado boom — which had died — and the lighter was for sale very cheap. He had her copperbottomed and fitted with anchors fore and aft and towed her down the coast and moored his floating wharf just inside San Carlos Bay, where the steamers could load from her decks — to the disgust of the smug-

---

[3] San Carlos is halfway down the peninsula, on the gulf side, opposite Guaymas. Arthur Foote sought a loading point on the gulf side after it proved almost impossible to unload supplies and ship out onyx over an open beach, and through pounding surf, on the ocean side of the peninsula.

gling trade in that vicinity. Every man of them would have been happy to see the gringo and his lighter go out to sea and never come back. . . . If we had had a Conrad in those days, here would have been material and a setting for one of his tales of mixed centuries and mixed races in those latitudes. Letters from the Lower Peninsula came like triremes rowing home with cargoes of "apes and ivory" translated into terms of horned toads and half-breed smugglers and loads of pink-veined onyx hauled by sixteen-mule teams.[4] As for my letters — A. knew when he got the first one, scorched and smelling of sulphur, what had happened to us! Even the grim little doctor looked as if it hurt him to tell us we were in for it again — another scarlet-fever case, this time Agnes: twelve weeks in quarantine within one year! It was the last of March [1893]; we had fled with Betty to the Mesa in July the summer before, but now there was no Mesa, no wide empty house, no daddy to ride out every evening of the day, no George and Mrs. George. But there was Bessie and the little schoolhouse.

The three fathers of Nelly Linton's little school had built this classroom, literally one room, in Bessie's back garden soon after we came in from the Mesa: Captain Murray of the Fourth Cavalry, acting Commandant at Boise Barracks,[5] Mr. Cobb, proprietor of the *Idaho Statesman* (a new and advanced

---

4 A few of those letters have survived. They are the letters of a courageous, lonely man struggling against massive difficulties in a harsh physical setting and greatly missing his wife and children. A letter from Arthur to his wife, dated Onyx Landing, Baja California, April 23, 1893, says frankly, "Thee can hardly imagine how hard life is here at present." His farewell letter to his wife from San Diego, April 5, 1893, movingly says: "I am sick for thee tonight. It is hard to go off without a word or a hug from thee." Toward the end of the venture, after Arthur had succeeded against immense odds, only to have the price of onyx collapse, his letter to his wife, from San Diego, September 13, 1893, concludes with the confession, "If thee were around I would not feel so blue."

5 The Murrays became close friends of the Footes. Cunliffe H. Murray graduated from West Point in 1877 and was commissioned a 2d lieutenant in the Fourth Cavalry. After service in many parts of the West, he was commissioned captain in 1890 and was stationed at Boise Barracks from 1890-95. His later career included service in the Philippines, at San Francisco, Washington, and

influence in the town),[6] and Arthur. The pupils were Annie May and Jessie Murray, Margaret Cobb, and our two. For a short time Rosamond Wild was one of the little group of exiles — and we thought them a picked lot. We took the schoolhouse for ourselves and our germs, and the Sherman House did not have to be quarantined. Here we lived and looked out of our prison windows, and again the case was a mild one and we felt like old hands at the job. And again I had the best of little patients. There was no imprisoning my little dreamer — she had magic casements in her soul.[7] Bessie looked after the other part. Three times a day she came to the side window, bringing her delicious trays of rich broth and junket and cream, and gave us our mail and the sight of her dear face; and my little one began to put on flesh and color and came out of her old skin more blooming than ever. When she was well enough and needed exercise, Captain Murray gave us the freedom of the Reservation within certain bounds, where we could wander amidst the clean sage and meet no one. Sometimes a little figure we knew waved to us from a porch on Officers' Row; and on a certain trail there was one big sage bush which the little parted friends used as a post office. We left nothing we had touched, but we found and took — with fingertips — letters out of the clutches of the old crooked bush and went chuckling home with our wayside secret.

---

elsewhere, and ultimate promotion to colonel and command of the Seventh Cavalry, Custer's old regiment.

[6] Calvin Cobb (1853-1928) was editor and publisher of the Boise *Idaho Statesman* for forty years, starting in 1889, a year before Idaho achieved statehood. Under his leadership the *Idaho Statesman* became the principal Republican newspaper in Idaho and an important force in the development of the new state. The Footes and the Cobbs became good friends. Mrs. Cobb's unfailing kindness and generosity overcame Mary Hallock Foote's instinctive reservations about people who came from Chicago, where Mrs. Cobb (the former Fannie Lyon) had grown up. The daughter Margaret, who is mentioned here, succeeded her father as owner and publisher of the newspaper. She married James F. Ailshie, Jr.

[7] The phrase is, of course, from Keats's "Ode to a Nightingale."

April and half of May we spent in the little schoolroom and came out blinking into the sunlight of congratulations and welcomes and a houseful of friendly talk. Open windows and summer dresses were the rule. The Falkes and Schainwalds of Boise were showing the new suits just out from the Falkes and Schainwalds of Chicago and San Francisco.[8] The milliners were ready with the latest styles from the East, designed for the western trade. Our eastern ladies thrilled us now and then with new and authentic models from Hollanders or Marshall Field's. Mrs. Cobb had a mother of means and discernment who had known Marshall Field's when it did not require a palace for its home. She dressed little Margaret Cobb, to the admiration of all the mothers. My chicks were dressed by mail from Best's, the exile's friend, or our old standby, Lord and Taylor — which sounds reckless, but it would have been more reckless to have spent my time sewing for them (though I can sew) and the wolf at our door. Darling Aunt Bessie was a very gentle wolf — but think of the work we made her! Consider what those two cases of scarlet fever in one year meant to the mistress of a house like that!

Betty had written to amuse her little sick sister "The History of Ronto," an imaginary kingdom the two had invented and ordered according to their fancies, aided by a little growing knowledge, when it did not interfere, and now she had begun "The Legends of Ronto," where she could give herself free scope unhindered by any casual acquaintance with history or geography, and illustrating it in a large, untrammeled style to match the text. That child, I wrote her father, was too strong winged for Cousin Nelly's teaching much longer. We began to talk of the future once more. The times were bad for tourist travel; the management at the Coronado was offering astonishingly low rates to families who would live there the

---

8 Boise directories show that "N. Falke & Bros." operated one "general merchandise" store in Boise, and "Schainwald Bros." another. Mary Hallock Foote uses these two local store names as generic terms.

year around. We dreamed of that spectacular place as a temporary meeting ground where he could be with us for a few days once a month when he came up the coast to attend to his office work. We had lived in various ways and places but never had set up for anything quite in the line of the Coronado! It sounded like a huge joke.[9]

The times grew worse. Shadows of the business eclipse that ended in the panic of 1893 were creeping over us. Chicago, a year behind with her Columbian Exposition, went on building her White City on the Lake. That achievement in that place was regarded as one of the marvels of the time. Henry Adams (pondering on the steps beneath Richard Hunt's dome) called it "a breach of continuity — a rupture in historical sequence."[10] — That Chicago should have known how! She barely understood herself what she had done, but she liked it all, and she gave a magnificent free hand to those who did know how. The favorite sons of the Beaux Arts whom she set to work on the shore of the lake were rather stupefied by her nonchalance; they were on very good terms with Chicago but much amused at being there (they talked their own language among themselves) — wizards in the grasp of a cheerful industrial giant who told them to make their best magic and be quick about it.

[9] The famous Hotel del Coronado, which was built as part of the ill-justified San Diego boom of the 1880s. It is still in business, as one of the few surviving examples of the massive Victorian resort hotels.

[10] Adams, *Education*, p. 340.

33

THERE was a famous Board of Lady Managers in operation at Chicago the year of its World's Fair [1893]. The fair president, Mrs. Potter Palmer, could have anything she asked for in the line of Woman's Participation. The Board was an experiment but not the social influence of ladies like Mrs. Potter Palmer.[1] She decreed that on each of the juries of selection and awards a woman should be appointed by her Board to serve with the same honors and emoluments as the men. The men did not want us on their juries and some of us did not value highly the privilege of being there, especially a woman buried in Idaho who would have had to be bribed before she could have considered such an appointment. Well, I was bribed! I have to confess it. I had very naturally declined to serve on the jury of selection in Black and White which sat in New York early in the spring (I was in quarantine at the time), and I was about to do the same with the subsequent appointment as juror on awards; but neighbor Cobb said: "Hold on! nobody refuses a thing like that." And he set before me what it meant. I certainly could not refuse $500 and expenses to Chicago and a chance to see my boy after two years, with two more years of absence to come. Fannie Cobb had planned it all in a flash of *her* Woman's Participation.

There were hostesses in Chicago who stayed in town all that

1 Mrs. Potter Palmer (1849-1918), whose given name was Bertha Honoré, married Palmer, a merchant, in 1871, and displayed judgment and executive ability in helping her husband when he had to rebuild his business after severe losses suffered in the great fire of that year. By the time of the Exposition in 1893, she was not only the unquestioned social leader of the city, but also a person whose capacity and determination were universally recognized.

hectic summer and kept open house to the east and west — a continuous tide of guests pouring through their doors and feasting at their boards. Every one of them deserved to be crowned with a "civic wreath." Mrs. Cobb's mother, Mrs. J. B. Lyon, was one of these smiling, weary, imperturbable hostesses who spared neither herself nor her servants nor her horses nor her husband nor anything that was hers which could be dispensed in the city's honor. Though it may be said for Mr. Lyon that he could have withstood any tide of people or events that invaded his life: he was one of the bulls on the Chicago stock market, used to being stampeded if not slaughtered.[2]

Ever since we came to know her daughter in Idaho, Mrs. Lyon had been, through that daughter's connivance, our between-trains hostess. She had made Chicago another city to us. Instead of a huge wet slippery warehouse that one banged across in a transfer bus from one clanging terminus to another, her carriage was there waiting for us at the track gates — going west it meant several hours in a charming atmosphere of luxury and home, a bath, a delicious dinner, and a caressed feeling all along, and being taken to your eight o'clock train by the dear lady herself. But now by that same daughter's arrangement, she had us on her hands, both mother and son, for two whole weeks of that crowded summer — daily sessions for the mother with her committees at the Fair, numberless pleasures for us both tucked in between, evening drives along the lake and through the parks or over to the fair to see its courts and palaces illuminated, or by moonlight — better still. And finally a little reception for the committeewoman and the friends she had made in the course of her fraudulent work.

The jurors were naturally expected to know a little some-

[2] John B. Lyon, who was born in Canadaigua, New York, in 1829, but grew up in Ohio, moved to Chicago in 1858 and purchased a membership in the Chicago Board of Trade, then a young institution. As the Board of Trade matured into an internationally important grain and produce exchange, Lyon's business grew with it. By the time of the Exposition, he was said to be one of the most senior members of the Board.

thing about the special technique they were there to vote on. Technique had always been my weak point, still I had had some experience in Black and White and some of the best wood engravers in the country had cut my old blocks. But, owing to a slight mistake on the part of the ladies who appointed me, I found myself assigned to the Etchers' group which had its woman juror already and a very distinguished choice. They did not need me — to vote on men like Whistler and Zorn and Legros, for example.[3] There was a general laugh — we were all Americans and we might laugh — with the exception of our chairman, Frank Short (Sir Frank Short today), who only smiled discreetly and left the giddy Americans to settle their own affairs.[4] My own modest little group said: "You belong with us — come down from there!" But how to get down? It would mean an unthinkable amount of fuss, I was told, to bring the matter up before the Board, annoying busy people by showing them their mistake. It was time we got to work. And the etchers, not being peacocks, did not view me with proud eyes because I was in borrowed feathers. They said, "Stay with us and don't worry. Your vote will be honest as far as you know and where you don't know we will coach you." Which is a free translation of what they did say. . . . "But how about taking full pay for a 'prentice vote like that?" I asked my sponsors and guardians. . . . "They have bought your time which is not that of a 'prentice — if they don't know how to use it, that's not your fault." So spake Emily Sartain, woman of the world of art and of business.[5] I put myself in her hands,

3 James Abbott McNeill Whistler (1834-1903), Anders Zorn (1860-1920), and Alphonse Legros (1837-1911) were, of course, internationally famous as etchers — and were of, respectively, American, Swedish, and French origins.

4 Sir Francis Job Short (1857-1945), usually known by the nickname Mary Hallock Foote uses, was a distinguished etcher and engraver who had studied at what was later called the Royal College of Art, South Kensington, and from 1891-1924 taught his two specialties at that institution. He was president of the Royal Society of Painter-Etchers from 1910-38, and in 1911 was elected to the Royal Academy and knighted.

5 Emily Sartain (1841-1927), daughter and sister of engravers and artists, was herself an engraver and painter, and from 1886-1919 was principal of the

and with her and our chairman, Frank Short, I walked the galleries of the Black and White exhibit and learned more in one week about etchers and etching than I have been capable of remembering, and enjoyed being the greatest fraud I have ever consciously been in my life. We were friends in the manner of those who have no past and expect no future to their chance companionship. There was a later chapter in the case of Emily Sartain, but that belongs rather in the life of my daughter Betty than my own; though the Chicago episode led up to it.

The Exposition lost money on the woman from Idaho. Woman's Participation, till we get used to it, is apt to cost something. It must have doubled the expenses of the Fair Commission at Chicago. Education pursued one there till the mind became glutted and one longed to go away and look at the Javanese dancers. The pistons of the great Corliss engine did not slide with more certainty down their fearful grooves than those childish arms performed their play — so soft and silken smooth, a man might break them with his hands, yet, so far as the application of natural laws can go, the Corliss engine could not teach one more. I walked the Halls of Machinery with my firstborn listening to what the babe was saying — stooping his head to mine, and his understanding even more, when he talked of these mysteries and their principles of action through all the whizzing and whirling. All their bewildering mechanisms, and still more their heaped up products, made one long to go away and sit in a corner with one's head on one's hand like Dürer's *Melancholia*.[6] It takes from one's power to assimilate Things, a mass of Things, to have lived with a few persons intimately beside the voice of a river year after year, or listened to a wind from beyond half a million acres of desert

---

School of Design for Women, in Philadelphia. Mary Hallock Foote's daughter Betty later studied at this school.

[6] The reference is to the famous copperplate engraving by Albrecht Dürer, in 1514.

plain — you rest from details there, or you invent your own details.

But I had had what is called a great time and seen my big boy, and I went home praising Woman's Participation, shamelessly content with my ill-gotten gains, and with a French hat from Louise's, which my astute hostess seduced me into buying, to wear to the jurors' supper which the head of the Fine Arts Committee gave to the crowd of us on the breakup of the whole business. The supper, and the motorboat groups on the illumined lake afterward — all these shifting combinations of minds and manners exhibited at the fair were worth I daresay my little flirtation with fraud. My legitimate work seemed to go better for the change and thorough shake-up. Still, it went better also after my two quarantines, one on the dry Mesa and one in Bessie's backyard.

It drew on towards the darkest hour of that business eclipse which punctually supplied the next collapse of our hopes and plans. It was about time we were disappointed again. Henry Adams, whom I quote so helplessly because one cannot forget his way of saying a thing when trying to say the same thing one's self, in speaking of that summer wrote, "Men died like flies under the strain, and Boston grew suddenly old, haggard and thin."[7] The wave spread, and a bank in San Diego where my man had deposited his last-earned little pile broke, as it were, in a single night, and he heard of it as he was going down the coast to his work again, happy that he had been able the day before to send his wife her first draft since his salary began, and another to pay what he called a debt of honor. Both drafts were worthless when received. Old teamsters on the plains have an expression which he quoted in speaking of this news: "That time the wheels went over my neck." There was no more talk of getting together as a family once more, on re-

[7] Adams, *Education*, p. 338.

duced rates at the Coronado. But there was that letter from Mr. Emmons which I hugged to my soul, as I had, years before, the telegram signed "Hague and Janin." He had done the work — the rest was fate or finance or what you will. "Entirely competent" satisfied me as far as he was concerned, and I still had my own little job. Darling Aunt Bessie did not have to keep us for love, as she surely would have done, and never let us feel anything but the love through it all. My work at this time was potboiling which is "all right," Kipling remarked in one of his letters, "if it boils the pot."

To shut down a mine in that forgotten region, to shut down any mine, is to invite decay and destruction to come in and take possession — to "let in the jungle" in this case. All the costly machinery goes to rust; the great lighter, my husband's pride and the child of his resourcefulness, was now junk. The smugglers of San Carlos Bay were very tired of seeing it there attracting the attention of traffic — presently it wasn't there, and there was lifting of shoulders and spreading of dark hands. A storm they said had torn her from her moorings and sent her out to sea. The man who had her anchored there knew better; any storm capable of doing that would have driven her on the beach. A Pacific Mail steamship reported her a hundred miles down the coast and the last ever heard of her she was a derelict wandering about Oceanica, off Christmas Island at the time.[8] That blind and blundering hulk seemed the last mockery of our hopeful plans. That was the outcome of my husband's campaign on the Lower Peninsula. To outsiders not acquainted with the facts it looked like another case of failure.

He was still in San Diego settling up the company's affairs when he received a wire from James Hague asking if he could go up to Riverside, California, and examine an electric power

[8] More commonly Oceania. Christmas Island is one of the Line Islands, in the Central Pacific.

plant lately installed near there, and report on it to him in San Francisco. Electric machinery of all kinds was in its infancy at that time, a mighty infant dangerous in its cradle. No one felt sure of it underground in a wet shaft, and most mines are wet. There is not much likeness between an olive branch and an underground pump, yet when I heard of that order and whom it was from, I hailed it as a sign that for us the waters were receding.

I⊤ was all of two years before dry land became visible, so to speak, yet during those years of suspense we never quite lost sight of the harbinger of hope in the person of J. D. Hague. He was, if not the embodiment of capital himself, the mightiest power we knew in that direction. And we had learned that scientific theory is nothing without money back of it. The engineer cannot afford to be too proud, so long as he keeps his professional conscience clear. My man in those days would have swept James's office if that would have led to a decent and honorable job. And so would I!

James now was the man with a dream. He was risking everything he had, including his reputation, which was a big asset by this time, and a good deal of the money of his friends, on certain uncertain mining operations near Grass Valley, California — the first experiment in group mining ever tried in that region of old worked-out bonanzas.[1] The veil of business reserve, uncommonly dark in his case, covered all knowledge of these transactions that wasn't hearsay. He revealed his mind to A. only bit by bit. There were questions of sidelines and quieting titles and looking up absentee owners scattered far and wide, and the great question of all was the depth and permanence of the old North Star vein.

The North Star and Empire mines could look across the

[1] Concerning Hague's plans, and the mines at Grass Valley, see Introduction, p. 36. A photographic history of the North Star and Empire mines, with explanatory comments, is available in Jack R. Wagner's *Gold Mines of California* (Berkeley, 1970), pp. 176-229, and a comparable photographic history of the two towns has been assembled by Jim Morley and Doris Foley, *Gold Cities: Grass Valley and Nevada City* (Berkeley, 1965).

town of Grass Valley and Boston Ravine, with Wolf Creek in the bottom of it, from their opposite hillsides backed with pinewoods — a goodly view. Both were part of the Bourn family inheritance, of statewide fame. James and his friends had interests in both mines and at this time he was president of both. Later, Mr. W. B. Bourn bought back his ownership in the Empire and sold most of his North Star stock, and in 1886 the later North Star Mining Company was organized, a star that rose as to capital in the East.[2] It was said to have all kinds of money back of it, but this could not have been the case at the time I am writing of, when we began to look to the rising of that star as the hope of our own fortunes in a modest way. Owners we never expected to be; operators would be enough.

But as to risks, it took more than geology, it took the sternest stuff that faith is made of to launch these underground explorations then, and abide their heartbreaking delays and disappointments. I remember, in those early years at the North Star Cottage, when James used to spend weeks with us at a

---

[2] Quartz, or vein, mining at Grass Valley dated back to 1851, but like most quartz districts, Grass Valley's mines had experienced sharp fluctuations in profitability. Two of the best-known mines at Grass Valley, the North Star and the Empire, were at low ebb in the later 1870s, when the North Star was regarded as having been "worked out," while the mining experts were gloomy as to the future of the Empire. William B. Bourn, Jr., had just inherited a substantial interest in the Empire from his father, a native of Massachusetts who had become a prosperous San Francisco merchant and investor. During the early 1880s the younger Bourn first put the Empire back into very profitable operation, then bought the North Star and began its rehabilitation, retaining John Hays Hammond, the well-known mining engineer, as his adviser. James D. Hague, whose clients included some of the most substantial names in American business and finance, put together a syndicate of investors to purchase control of the North Star in January 1887. The corporate structure of the mine was reorganized in 1899 and the company took over a series of adjacent mines and claims that Hague wished to consolidate into North Star ownership. For a time Hague also had control of the Empire, but in the late 1890s sold that mine back to Bourn. Hague, the Footes, and the Bourns were well acquainted with one another. Mrs. Bourn's friendship with Mary Hallock Foote became close. The two ladies seem to have known each other since before their respective marriages.

time watching and studying the vein underground and walking the pinewoods on top, he came in very warm to luncheon one day and I imprudently asked where he had been that hot morning: and he answered with a smile, dropping into the Cornish dialect, "I've been to the Gold 'Ill and the New York 'Ill and the Massachusetts 'Ill and the Granite 'Ill and all the ills that man is heir to." The Massachusetts Hill mine had been dewatered and a good discovery dug out, but there was nothing more in sight at this time and the other claims — the other "Ills" — were as barren to all appearances as God made them.[3] But one never can tell: that is the bewitchment of mining, and "Nature," as any mining man will say, "has a very good poker face."

James Hague was like Nature in this respect; the workings of his mind were not visible to the eye. He was one who waited and considered long before deciding to act upon his own knowledge or that of any other man, but he was not what is called a quitter and he gave a man a free hand. In my husband's case there were no past results to encourage faith in his ability — James measured him by long personal observation of the man. The two were counterparts in temperament and complemental in the qualities and experience each brought to this association. James was the finished man of society, the deliberate and witty talker, one of that inner circle, professionally, which included some of the cleverest and most charming men of their time, to whom Henry Adams gave the name of "the men of the Fortieth Parallel."[4] He was a wise observer of all classes of men, but not the ordinary man's man in the sense of the material these two were handling at Grass Valley, the Cornish miner being in some respects a type by himself. And he used to say that he "hated a machine" — A. loved them and humored them and understood their little

[3] These were adjacent claims that had been consolidated into the North Star holdings.

[4] Adams, *Education*, p. 313.

contrary ways, and if they hadn't souls given them in the forging fires, he treated them as if they might have had. And so he handled his men; there might have been specimen thieves among them, but he would not have had them stripped and examined to find out; he said no honest man would stand that sort of thing.[5]

---

[5] Specimen thieves, or "high-graders," were employees who stole and smuggled out of the mine chunks of ore of especially high value — a very difficult practice to stop. Some mines insisted on searching the men's clothing and lunch pails.

⟨ 35 ⟩

AFTER THE Riverside report there was a pause; then A. was sent across the continent to the Calumet and Hecla to examine the electric pumping plant there, a new one of the latest design.[1] He stopped with us in Boise on his return, and having no office he worked up his notes on my writing table under the dormer window in our "snug little kingdom up three flights of stairs." One day he let drop that he had not liked altogether what he had seen of electricity underground at the Calumet and Hecla, and his wife's blood ran cold. He had been sent there, as she supposed, to learn, not to criticise. He did learn — and so did the Calumet and Hecla! A year or two later he had the satisfaction of telling the family misbeliever that he was right: the Calumet and Hecla had scrapped their new electric pumps and put in compressed air.

But in the meantime he had been sent to Grass Valley [January 1895] to install a pumping plant and hoisting works for dewatering the Massachusetts Hill mine and, acting on his own conclusions, he turned his back on electricity, which James had advised, and put in compressed air — because the dangerous man believed he was right. And when his wife heard of it she could not sleep o' nights till she had accustomed herself to this last act of irrepressible initiative. He never could

[1] The Calumet and Hecla copper mines were on Lake Superior, in northern Michigan. Having been consolidated into one company in 1871 and exploited very successfully under the leadership of Alexander Agassiz, by the 1890s they constituted one of the world's great mining enterprises. It was natural that Hague should wish to profit from the Calumet and Hecla's experience, the more so since Hague himself had been employed in the Lake Superior copper mines.

take another man's opinion unless his agreed — he would sooner have thrown up the job. The Calumet and Hecla, he argued, had money to burn on experiments, but if it came to scrapping new machinery at the Massachusetts Hill shaft, the work might have to stop and then the engineer would be scrapped. Later there was all manner of electric power applied at the North Star mines, but its captive giant at this time was "applied air compression."

But we were not *at* the North Star when this chapter begins; we never knew James's intentions for more than a step ahead nor how far he would require "our" services; possibly he did not know himself. It was very interesting but quite anxious. In view of these uncertainties we wrote Dr. Coit, with all thanks for the two years past, that the obligation ought to go no further; our circumstances had not improved and our son must be trained to meet them. He was now a fifth-form boy, too young for the stiff course at Boston Tech which he was preparing for, but we thought he should be able to take his first exams at the end of the [school] year; and we spoke of our plan to give him a year in the open on an engineering party under a personal friend who would be the best of influences in every way. I, who wrote the letter, was amused at myself answering for Mr. Wiley's character as a guide for Youth.

The Doctor answered in one of his condensed and perfect notes:

Arthur ought to see you and you him, this summer, but he is young for the work you propose, and I wish you would spare him for another year. It shall cost him nothing for tuition and residence, and there need be no burden of obligation felt, for my own great interest in him prompts this suggestion. The summer with you will set him up physically I hope and then another year here will mature him mentally and morally, so that the work undertaken hereafter will be made more effective and successful. May I hope that you and Mr. Foote will be willing to make this sacrifice? And will you remember that no debt has been or will be incurred?

How could we have resisted that letter — we had to — and if we might have troubled the great Doctor, with three hundred boys on his hands, with our detailed and sordid reasons, he perhaps would have understood, though he was abstracted and unconscious about money. But even so, unyielding and spiritually mistaken as we must have seemed, his final word came like a benediction — as it was a farewell. I was never to see his revered handwriting again. It was the last of those communications my heart hung upon for five years, our son's first years away from us. I wonder how many mothers of St. Paul's boys have kept those exquisitely simple but searching little notes put away in the sacred places of their lives? This was his beautiful answer: "I have a keen regret that I shall not have your dear Arthur here again. He will always have a welcome here. His life has been a sweet, wholesome one, to the best of my knowledge unstained in any way, and I pray that God's blessing may prevent and follow him in all he does and undertakes, now and always." . . . He wrote to the boy himself — who was never to go back for that welcome. The great Rector died the following winter. . . . How very seldom we hear "prevent" used in connection with the Blessing we crave for our beloveds in its positive forms. There is so much in *not* doing, *not* having, in withholding and being withheld from! But the world is not on that tack in these days.

Sonny passed his exams in Boston without conditions but under the harrow of a constant cough which he brought out with him to Idaho to hurt the joy of seeing him again — so tall, but underweight. He had worked hard and the cough had worked him still harder. Being an owlish person I lay awake nights over it and being a talkative person I spoke of it to our friends, the Murrays — though it spoke for itself with harassing monotony. The troopers of the Fourth Cavalry were about to start on their Long March for practice in the field: Captain Murray looked the boy over with a professional eye: "Let me have him with us on the March and I'll engage to bring him back without that cough." An invitation the heir to millions might have coveted — it was unique, an opportunity of a boy's lifetime, and never forgotten by our boy. Poor old son! he had not put leg over a saddle since the Cañon days when his legs were pretty short, and he never went far on Lollo without his pockets stuffed with oats to catch the little cayuse with should he buck his rider off and stroll home without him.

There were no cayuses on this trip. There were the troopers' matched-bay mounts and the roll of the army wagons behind them and 200 miles of noble country to roam over, all its bridgeless streams to ford and fish in, all its forests to hunt and its wild fodder to graze. There was a cot in the captain's tent, one of his horses to ride, and an orderly at every turn; and besides the West Point form and finish there was the spectacle of well-drilled men every day at work or exercise under the stern eye of their sergeant-major. Neither money nor influence could have procured this wonderful trip for our happy boy, and it is a thing we have never ceased to thank our good friend Captain Murray for.

Boise Barracks was an insignificant little army post left over from the days of Indian troubles with a half-savage white frontier; it was no longer needed either as a protection or a menace, but Boise wanted it as a very good customer that promptly paid its bills, and wires were pulled to keep it there.[2] Its officers were the same who in turn would be stationed at the Presidio or Fort Sherman or any of the big posts. Here it did its duty unnoticed for the most part and unpraised, and its technique was perfect from day to day. That satisfaction it had all unto itself and the admiring ladies of the garrison. "Nobody," as Mrs. Ewing says, "loves to look at the pretty sol-

---

[2] This was characteristic of a western community in this era. With few other customers, governmental expenditures and the governmental payroll were very important to every local merchant, contractor, teamster, farmer, and lumberman who could supply goods or services.

diers more than the pretty soldiers' wives and sweethearts."[3]
Here they made men out of such material as the recruiting
offices in time of peace could send them. It was not unlike a
boys' camp with grown-up men for pupils, and they taught
many things up there besides the art of war. . . . The captain
was as good as his word: in about three weeks the boy came
back without his chest cough and with a rested look of happiness in his eyes as he stumped up the walk and the captain's
orderly saluted and rode away leading his knightly charger
back to barracks. The style and romance were gone. Now to
get down to plain job — buy one's first working outfit, take
the Grand View stage and tramp a ditch line carrying the
"rod."

Mr. Wiley at this time was chief engineer of the Bruneau
Valley irrigation scheme, in its hopeful stage. He was building a "mighty clever dam," my husband called it, on the
Bruneau River, another tributary of the Snake about fifty
miles from Boise. His company had bought the Grand View
Hotel, both the roadhouse and the ferry; the house served for
the engineers' headquarters, and the chief incidentally ran it,
and the Grand View ferry too — all these Grands referring to
the scenery which well deserved the name.[4] Gerald, Bessie's
son, to his mother's heart's content, had come out with his C.E.
from Columbia — all that a widow's only son should be. He
was going on this same work as transitman and Sonny would

---

3 Juliana Horatia (Gatty) Ewing (1841-85), an English writer of stories for
young people, married a British Army officer and thereafter made soldier
stories one of her specialties.

4 Grand View was on the south bank of the Snake River, below the Snake's
junction with the Bruneau River. Mountain Home, which Mary Hallock
Foote later mentions (p. 383), was directly north of the Snake but was on the
railroad and therefore was a logical place for supplies. Oreana, to which she
saw freight wagons going (p. 383), was south of the Snake and west of Grand
View and on the way to Silver City, which Arthur Foote hoped to supply with
electric power.

be under him — almost a family arrangement, counting Mr. Wiley as part of the Cañon family in former days. Nobody could have imagined such a domestic arrangement in such a place! We did rash things with our children in some ways, but we were as cunning as serpents in choosing their friends. And now it rested with themselves to keep those friends. The Cañon days were not forgotten; they made the evenings at the Grand View Hotel more extraordinary in their likeness to a home, but there was no friendship nor kinship on the work. Mr. Wiley was not playing favorites with his company's money.

Eighteen ninety-four was another year of suspense and waiting. My chief of waiting had time to think of things, meanwhile, and his mind being now turned to electric transmission, he began to think of that. Silver City, in the Owyhee Mountains, was an old mining camp rejuvenated through some recent discoveries; it was calling for power, all kinds of power, and had the means to pay for it. He began to look for a head of water going to waste which could be located as the site for a power plant to carry its lines to Silver City. He tried first at the Thousand Springs, and took his wife on this trip, for here beauty as well as power was going to waste.

The Thousand Springs is one of the wonders of southern Idaho. It may be a summer resort today, but at that time not a thousand persons had ever visited it for its own sake since white men knew it was there. Here Nature has done some of her mysterious plumber's work, taking her time, after the manner of the trade — aeons of time. She carried her pipes through fifty miles of country to the face of the lava rock where the river cuts down its bed, turned on the taps as a fine surprise to whatever creatures walked the valley in those days, and left them running — how long no one can count: a broadside of cascades that breaks out of the rim rock 100 feet from the top, with a fall of from 200 to 400 feet, more or less on one line of cleavage. On top of the bluffs for fifty miles in every direction, endless lifts and swells of land but not one sign of living water. This is a region where water "sinks," as they say who know little what it does after it has disappeared — it finds a way through "sunless rivers" and "caverns measureless to man." [5] Around a shoulder of the bluffs where a rock staircase is formed by the broken debris, a flashing, churned up torrent tumbles down, called the Snow Bank, and farther again, falling sheer from the top, is the beautiful Sand Spring's fall, a dropping veil. We made our camp on a little reedy, grassy peninsula where we could see it from our tent door.

My schemer studied this enchanting place for days making his cold-blooded calculations. It was, however, 100 miles from anywhere. Electric power could be carried for distances like these, the Westinghouse people said, but it never had been done at that time. Nothing came of the trip to his account, but I made profit of it in my fashion of Ruth in the field of Boaz. I wove it impertinently into a story, a thing of barter and sale called "The Harshaw Bride." There were no Harshaws of course and no bride, but there was a moon after sunset above the Sand Spring's fall — no distinct shadows, rocks in pale afterglow, and a sky of twilight blue. There was the shadow of a mimosa-leaved plant stirring at night, printed on our canvas wall on the moon side of the tent. This by-product of electrical transmission was accepted by the *Century* and gave the effect, I was told, of having been written in the highest spirits at a time when our fortunes were "far, far from gay"![6] Which must have been due to pure intoxication and surprise at the loveliness hidden there — to come upon it after miles of desert

5 It was typical of Mary Hallock Foote to weave phrases from Coleridge's "Kubla Khan" into her prose, but it was equally typical for her to get one of the quotations not quite right. In the next sentence the phrase "dropping veils" is from Tennyson's "Lotus-Eaters."

6 Published in two installments as "The Harshaw Bride," *Century Magazine*, 52 (May and June 1896), 90-104, 228-41, with illustrations by the author.

travel (four days to be exact) and drink in, day by day, its silent, sustained appeal. I was a made-over woman after that trip.

But the next time my man went on this same errand he left me behind, and that time he was successful in his search for the power, which is only the beginning of a power scheme. He fitted it to the ground, but he had not found his angel with capital. The Swan Falls Power Plant was located, on this trip, at the rapids of that name on the Snake River — a much more accessible place, but there it stayed and waited. Nobody would look at it then.

The only angel he had was A. J. Wiley, who went with him and had more than a friendly interest in this scheme — he probably paid for the outfit — and to him it reverted with all its future possibilities when my man could wait no longer. The call had come at last. James Hague had wired him to meet him in Grass Valley, which meant the work there had begun. James was the man with the Vision laid on him now — his were the financial risks, the worry and the waiting. But if any man might successfully woo that coy lady, Eastern Capital, it would be he. Henry Janin used to say: "I wish I were half as wise as Hague looks."

BOOK VII

The Safer Life,

or

Dreams Kept Under

36

I<small>T WAS</small> six years later and we were anchored at the North Star at last, deep in deep mining, when the old Idaho dream came back to us with its sound of wild waters between dark basalt bluffs that cut the sky. We saw our own country again — in a book of great splendid photographs that opened wide on the table before us (a notable feat, the making those photographs alone), and inside we read in a hand we knew well: "The Swan Falls Power Plant — for A. D. Foote, the originator of this work; with the compliments of A. J. Wiley."

There it was finished — the last of our dreams in Idaho, the only one to be realized then. A little thing of four stone walls planted on stone pillars sitting on a rock shelf in the riverbed, with that splendid rush of waters sweeping past and that great stretch of country far and wide — there was no stingy crowding in these pictures — they were the very land itself in its true proportions; the small but mighty work of man and the vast overpowering Nature to be used and controlled. That little stone building would not have sat there long if it had not been planted on laws known to man as fixed as the bluffs that looked down on it — a toy in that whirl of waters which it parted smoothly and ordered to pass. What insolence — what a gesture! The river stopped on the one hand in its headlong rush and gave its force to the dynamos in that little pile of stone, and on the other hand it poured in one great silken sweep over the breast of the wasteweir. And in that mountain city sixty miles away the heart throbs of those dynamos could be felt in every fiber of its clanging activities. And the dyna-

375

mos (there was a photograph of them too) in their stone sanctuary lit with sunbeams hummed quietly as a hive of bees.

My flattered old "originator" took out his fountain pen and added, as before witnesses: "Designed and built by A. J. Wiley, M. Am. Soc. C. E." And he might have added, "Because I respect and love him." [1] . . . So they handed it to each other across a thousand miles and the years of work between 1901 and 1895, when they first talked of the scheme together.

The Swan Falls Power Plant is now incorporated with other properties as part of a much greater scheme under a name which I have forgotten. I go back to it foolishly because those pictures were sent by one who thought of us and knew what my husband's joy in them would be. A. was not so fortunate always in his collaborators. He had to see at times his truths distorted, his prophecies mocked, "the work he gave his heart to broken," discredited, and thrown away. In short, he bore what all men of strong initiative have had to bear who try to do things in advance of their time. He was an "originator" and one might as well be a madman on the whole. Yet they cannot be beaten, those men, and in time, in a measure, a few of them have come to their own.

He was not so old when the greatest of his dreams, the broken work I speak of, came to its accomplishment, with the government behind it; but his mind was turned to other lines of work, he was past the time of life when success lifts the heart up or failure casts it down; he had learned to "treat those two impostors just the same." I have to tell of this in the newspaper style as it came to us, composed on the date and on the spot, which after all is most appropriate to what was intended as a public tribute. It was a day of rejoicing in the Boise Valley when the head gates were opened and the first water was turned into the Big Ditch — the old New York Canal. The *Idaho Statesman* of that date set the name of a man unknown

[1] For Mary Hallock Foote's earlier use of this quotation, in a scene that had some of the same connotations, see above, p. 297.

to the later generation at the head of its leading article, over the words "An Appreciation." It was the name of the originator of that scheme — whose moustaches were white and whose brows were numb to the pricking of thorns or laurels; he had known chiefly the thorns.[2]

Most highly honored — most revered — are those who, as the years pass, are found to have stood upon elevations during their day from which they commanded a horizon far beyond the sight or understanding of the masses of the people. We know not what we owe them until they have passed out of the field of our activities and, in our halting way, we have come to a comprehension of what it was they saw and of which in our blindness we thought they were dreaming. . . . A quarter of a century ago Mr. Foote saw these possibilities which we now so fully realize; he saw where water could be diverted; he saw where it could be stored, and, in the reach of his precise imagination, he could see these lands peopled with thousands of prosperous families.

Mr. Foote was the father of the New York canal, through which that vivifying stream is flowing to-day . . . he laid out the line along which the canal has been constructed; he arranged to drop the water to the lands through the natural channels met with along the way. . . . Likewise he recognized the necessity of impounding the flood waters of the spring season, and, with thoroughness characteristic of his career, he found and charted all the possible reservoir sites on the upper reaches of this river. The capacity of these was so nicely estimated that his figures vary but little from those of later exploration.

But it was not alone to the valley of the Boise his attention was given; he was almost a generation ahead of his times in foreseeing

[2] The "day of rejoicing" when the New York Canal was at last opened was February 22, 1909, and the article of appreciation that Mary Hallock Foote here quotes was published in the Boise *Idaho Statesman*, February 24, 1909. It was written by D. W. Ross, state reclamation engineer. The editor of the *Idaho Statesman*, it will be remembered, was Calvin Cobb, who by 1909 must have been one of the few men still in Boise who had known Foote really well. About 3,000 people were lined up along the banks of the canal to watch what was regarded as a great moment in the development of the Boise Valley.

the probable development of many other projects that then slept as beautiful works in his imagination, but which are becoming actual achievements. Knowing that, with all the water in our streams, . . . a time would come when the demands of the people would make it necessary to supply more, he made exhaustive investigations to determine where a supply could be stored, and, in this branch of his tireless activities, he was the first to explore the Jackson's lake region in Wyoming to determine how much water could be held there to minister to the necessities of the population which he knew would be found in the valley of the Snake.

Mr. Foote ran the line for what is now the Fort Hall canal; he grasped the opportunity upon which the Clover creek project now rests. . . . One day in that long ago, this engineer, so deeply inspired through his enthusiasm, made a journey with some companions through a portion of the territory which is now known as the Twin Falls section. His unerring eye saw how the levels ran, and when, that evening, they camped at the Cedars, near what is now the Milner dam, he announced that the Snake would at no very distant time be diverted there to water that broad plain. That engineer who, following after, initiated the Twin Falls development, freely admits that he owes the thought entirely to his great chief of the former days.

It would be impossible to even briefly refer to every project suggested by Mr. Foote which has become an actuality, but the narration should not close without mentioning the Emmett bench project and that for generating electric power at Swan Falls for supplying the mines at Silver City.

The man of "precise imagination" writhed over certain expressions in these paragraphs, as I suppose a man of one profession always will when a man of another is handling his themes. I found no fault with any of it, but when I made the mistake of asking if Mr. Wiley could have written it, he snorted: "Wiley!" — that was enough. Still I cut it out and pasted it into a scrapbook which my husband had given me for my own best book reviews, and there it remains in proof of a wife's ingenuous vanity, and a record of all we didn't do in Idaho. In *The Light That Failed*, Dick says to Maisie who had showed him some of her poor little notices in the provincial press, "Do you value these things? Chuck 'em into the waste-paper basket!" "Not till I get something better," Maisie answered.[3] My man had got something better — his hands were full of work at this time. He had harnessed his imagination to the scheme of another man with a better grasp on the means of carrying it out — namely, money.

At the time I write of, Mr. Wiley was our only correspondent left in Idaho and he wrote only occasionally, for he was a busy man. The Murrays had been ordered to other posts, the Cobbs were still affectionately remembered but they were not letter writers — they were living full lives of their own. I wrote and thanked Mr. Cobb myself for that tribute to my husband in his paper, and he replied: "I knew how you would feel about it and it is only part of what is due your Old Man." . . . Gerald's work and Birney's marriage took my sister's children from her and she had followed them, disposing of her interests in Boise wisely as she did most things, though she always decried herself as a person of no business capacity. She has been a very capable grandmother and has lived to be a great-grandmother, and her influence, though seldom consciously exerted, is felt by all who know her well. In that hardest time of her life when she was called upon to decide for her children which way their futures should trend, she showed what the "gentle Elia," speaking of the Quaker bearing under trial, called a sort of "heroic tranquillity."[4]

3 From Kipling's *The Light That Failed*, Chapter V.
4 From Lamb's "A Quakers' Meeting," in *The Essays of Elia*, the same sketch from which Mary Hallock Foote quoted the phrase with which she closed the very first chapter of these reminisences (above, p. 50).

$\mathcal{C}37\mathcal{D}$

HERE ENDED our Vision in the Desert and with it the first cycle of my husband's work. And I think in submitting his powers to the judgment of another, less haughtily inspired but with more practical wisdom, he became master of them in a greater degree than ever before. But this is an opinion not without prejudice: the woman with children to plan for is very apt to play safe.

But James Hague had the creative imagination also, and a gift of prophecy, and he paid like the prince of financiers, when he had to, but the working out of mechanical details was hateful to him and he could not make the quick decisions called for on a widely extended scheme as the North Star plant became. And during those first and hardest years when both men were working full power, each at his own end of the job, it would have spoiled his nerve and broken his heart if he had known in New York every minor disaster and loss of time his executive took in hot blood and refused to count in the sum of what had to be done out here. They were fighting water as they went down deep and deeper in the North Star, and pumps and ever more pumps were in demand. To lose the fight with water was to drown the pumps and lose the mine.

But when the great trial of faith came and it was for Hague to say "shut down or go down," he said the word and the new Central shaft went down, and it was his judgment that pointed to the spot where it should start. Hundreds of feet had walked over that ground in the North Star woods and passed it in ignorance — his stopped there and he said, "Sink," and they kept on sinking till they struck the old North Star vein 1,600 feet underground at the spot where he prophesied it would be found, and there was gold in the bottom of the shaft which the last blast uncovered. And, as a personal detail showing how our fortunes were interlinked, it was Gerald Sherman, Bessie's son, who made the surveys for that shaft and was shaken by the hand when the new vertical and the old incline met, 1,600 feet underground.[1]

Grass Valley was scarcely our idea of heaven, though going there at last was not unlike dying in some respects.[2] We had contemplated the change a long time before it came to pass; we left our old mistakes and failures behind us for others to explain; we were done with our petty rages and humiliations that had ceased to burn within us. We parted with some true friends whom we never forget, as we trust to remember in the next life (or whatever is to come) the best that has happened to us here. These sweeping changes in environment are little lessons in dying, if we choose to see them so — it hurts but it does not really end things that are worth keeping, and it gives one a chance to begin again. Ah, but one gets so tired of these new beginnings! — and we were now in our forties instead of our twenties when we first took the Long Trail together.

[1] The importance of Hague's reputation among eastern financial interests was shown by the stockholders' willingness to let Hague and Foote spend about a million dollars on sinking this shaft and doing other development work, at a time when the mine was paying very little. In 1902 the mine finally began to pay richly, but until then the risk to the other stockholders and to Hague himself was very high.

[2] According to the 1890 census, Grass Valley township had a population of 6,798, which represented an increase of about 100 since 1880. The local business directory for the year of 1895, when the Footes arrived, boasted of the "large and palatial residences," which were in fact few in number, of the "neat cottages" of those miners who owned their own homes, and of the many "well-cultivated gardens" and fruit trees. There were several "business blocks," several churches, and a new public school building. The community was proud of having both gas and electricity. John E. Poingdestre, comp., *Nevada County Mining and Business Directory, 1895* (Oakland, 1895). A local journalist-historian estimated that at that time probably three-fourths of the population "were of Cornish birth or descent." Edmund Kinyon, *The Northern Mines: Factual Narratives of the Counties of Nevada* (Grass Valley, 1949), p. 159.

Arthur was sent for in January 1895, but he alone; there was no talk of "Mary and the children" then. He was a young man again, back at his beginnings; on a young man's uncertain job, breaking the road ahead but not sure where it might lead. In May of that year I took the little girls over to Grand View — my only "view" being to get the remnants of the family together under one roof, if only for nights and Sundays. Boy was there, and Gerald, and Mr. Wiley had invited us on Agnes' account, who had had influenza and still kept her cough and needed, the doctor said, plenty of sun and fresh air. And I knew there was space and silence over there, and beauty all around us. When I say silence, I mean the great valley's silence with its mysterious river sliding through — with a force it gives no sign of on the surface. The Snake River has a name for treachery and intentions that it keeps to itself.[3]

Our little girls were poetry-mad like others we have known. Their heads were ringing just then with the rhythm of "The Lady of Shalott" and all the rich heritage bound up in the same covers. I knew we could take them anywhere we liked — they never would know loneliness nor find life drag on their hands. Mr. Wiley came for us with the Grand View team and we drove the fifty miles, the happiest load it had ever hauled, I do believe, through the dust and sage.

It was next morning — one of those solemn, wide-eyed mornings in the great high valley — when our richness burst upon us. Here was the "margin willow-veiled," here the aspens quivered, and there ran the wave that flows forever round an island in the river — and even the "silent isle" itself, though subsequent acquaintance revealed the fact that it embowered wildcats and not mysterious ladies under a spell.[4] There were spells enough all around us. Here was a wider valley and a deeper river, and the mountain peaks that marched

---

3 For location of places near Grand View, see above, p. 369 n. 4.

4 The girls' enthusiastic quoting from Tennyson's "Lady of Shalott" gives an interesting insight into the reading standards of the Foote children. This chapter is speckled with phrases and lines from that poem.

with the valley kept their heads higher in the snows. Of course there was a rugged side to it and there were doubts as to the food and the cooking. Mr. Wiley had other things to do than keep house — he left that to the only sort of people he could hire. And we made our own beds and slept on them in great content and thankfulness.

We were the star boarders, being the only ones, and all day we were alone and the only persons of our kind and sex in the region probably, but we did not ask. The little girls made a playhouse of many rooms in the river brakes, creeping from room to room by passages they had cleared under low willow boughs shot through with sunlight, with gleams of the river through their flickering walls. They watched the queer fitful life of the road and the ferry pass by — not to towered Camelot, but to Oreana, from Mountain Home. Every day at noon the stage stopped for dinner and that gentle giant who drove it, Charley Chitwood was his name, sat opposite us at table and smiled at the little girls and combed his yellow moustache with his fork while the plates were changed. They inquired about certain wild flowers they had been looking for which were late that season: had he seen any on the road? "I haven't saw them," he answered in his gentle drawl, "but they may have came."

We spoke to no one of womankind that summer except the young lady we called Diana of the Ditch Camp — daughter of the contractor who had engaged to "move the dirt" on the Bruneau ditch line. His camp was a few miles above us. She ran the men's boardinghouse and the commissariat, sometimes with the help or company of a younger sister, sometimes alone, even without her father who often had to leave her on business trips. But not Diana of the silver bow was safer among the shepherds by her woods and streams than this black-eyed goddess of the dust and sage who used to whirl past us with her team and wagon to buy supplies at Mountain Home. She had a blighting way with anything like "freshness," but she was good to her shepherds too; when one of them had a run of fever she ordered his tent brought next to her own where she could nurse him day and night — if thereafter she had wanted a watchdog or a gun fighter, he was hers. She needed no guard but her own personality, the conviction and dash with which she did things that had to be done. She had beauty too and was probably better educated than any pupil of the ancient female seminary class. But there she was, more or less in charge of a hundred or two men with such morals as nature gave them, scratched up from anywhere. She occupied my mind to such an extent that to lay the spell I put her into a story; but I did not succeed in making her convincing to my editors of the *Century* — they gave me my first refusal and the MS went into the wastebasket. I knew they were right. We used to observe — we pair of apprentices — that when my bees were hiving his were, generally speaking, on the wing. He had enough to do now and little time to talk of it in letters. What he did tell us was that there was a Catherine Mermet rose in bloom that one could reach from the piazza railing at the North Star Cottage, and ripe strawberries in the North Star garden. We knew what he was thinking as he wrote this news.[5]

Did I say we talked to no woman? — we talked by the hour to our dear Mrs. Murray when she and Captain Murray and the little girls drove over to see us in the Post ambulance behind four army mules, changed with relays on the road. The captain said he was on "hunting leave" and his eyes twinkled. They are human in the Army — certainly Colonel Cook, then in command at Boise Barracks, was human;[6] but every move outside the fixed routine had to have its official excuse and sanction.

5 Arthur Foote was a dedicated and discriminating gardener, and did especially well with roses. His comments on this particular rose suggest how eager he was to resume the normal life of a householder. The Catherine Mermet has been described as "one of the most perfectly formed of all roses." Richard Thomson, *Old Roses for Modern Gardens* (Princeton, 1959), p. 73.

6 Possibly Lt. Col. Henry C. Cook of the Fourth Infantry.

38

An accent of peculiar kindness from everyone we knew clings to these last memories of Idaho. It was the note of farewell; our time now was short, and still we did not know, as to the children and myself, to what haven we were bound. James had suggested that I should start east with [young] Arthur when he went to Boston to enter Tech — branch off with the little girls and make their father a visit at the North Star Cottage; further than that nothing had been said.

"Visit" was distinctly the word he used in sending us this invitation. There was no intimation that the North Star Cottage might be our abiding place. There was no future to anything James could have offered my husband, at that time, equal to his needs of a man with a son to train to a profession and two daughters at the most expensive ages for schools. He could not offer him even a decent salary then. . . . "Isn't it enough?" he asked dryly, after a silence following his first naming the sum. "You know it's not enough," said Arthur, "but I am in no position to refuse it." Each knew the other's bonds — and "except these bonds," things would have been very different. No account with James Hague ever in the end left a balance due on his side. He was no ready promiser and he never explained, but in friendship or in business he had a long memory.

Our way through Portland, after we parted with Sonny, was smoothed for us by Mr. Cobb who had written to his friend the editor of the *Oregonian*[1] that Mrs. F. and children

[1] Harvey W. Scott (1838-1910) had been editor of the *Portland Oregonian* for most of the preceding thirty years, and had developed it into the strongest newspaper in the Pacific Northwest.

were arriving thus and so. He met our train and escorted us to our hotel where an introduction awaited me to a charming young woman, Louise Herrick Wall, just coming into notice as a writer of promise. Her mother, Mrs. Herrick, I might have called an old friend, though I had never seen her in the years when my manuscripts were passing through her hands on their way to the editorial desk. She was one of the readers on the staff of the *Century Magazine*.[2] We dined with her daughter and Mr. Wall that evening and our host saw us aboard our train on one of Portland's wet and foggy nights.

All the rich valley of the Sacramento was veiled in fog as we crossed it going up into the foothills. At Colfax Junction, where we boarded the little narrow gauge, we looked up as we plunged into the pinewoods and saw the great train we had left, with its two engines, rounding Cape Horn — five days now to the other side instead of seven, for that mighty shuttle between East and West.[3] The one passenger car was stuffy and filled with that underground smell which men who have worked in the mines for years cannot wash out of the pores of their skin, it is said. We heard the gruff voices that come out of chests as big as flour barrels, and the Cornish accent again was welcome to our ears. The ends of the circle had met. Not a great harvest for a twenty years' reaping, but some experience we had gathered, besides those two faces beaming at us in the seat opposite and the eighteen-year-old son on his way east to begin his life in precisely the way we might have hoped when he was our New Almaden baby.

The Rockwell cousins had had it in mind to ask him to live

[2] Sophia M'Ilvaine Bledsoe Herrick, born in 1837, had served on the *Southern Review* before joining the editorial staff of *Scribner's* and its successor, *Century Magazine*, in 1878.

[3] At Colfax the Nevada County Narrow Gauge Railroad began its run of seventeen miles to Grass Valley, over what was advertised as "a picturesque route." The main transcontinental line, in the meantime, continued on its eastward climb over and through the Sierra Nevada, but with a pause at "Cape Horn" to let passengers enjoy the spectacular view down into the cañon of the American River, far below.

with them while he was at Tech, but on second thoughts they believed it best, as they wrote us, for him to have his own rooms and keep his own hours, but they expected him regularly to Sunday night supper; and Kate wrote me as one human mother to another, after the Sunday when he first appeared in his new frock coat, to say how well he looked in it, poor child! He left it behind him in the things of the East when his four years in Boston were over; the high hat for church, and the symphony concerts, and his cousin Di's introductions to the Early Florentine painters and the fair nieces of Henry Adams — all that atmosphere of a culture which left him seemingly untouched, but we need more impressions than we can use all at once — we need a bank account to draw upon.

All the above is a look into the future. We had no future then, look as hard as we might, and economy was our watchword. . . . Ah, but our little girls were happy in the North Star Cottage — little impoverished ones rich in imagination! The boss carpenter on the work sent them at Christmas a music box that played two tunes, a wistful air by Mozart and a gay little waltz. It might not have been a wholly disinterested offering but we took it so — all faces were kind that looked at them. When the sitting room grew dusk early on the shortening days, and their father came home and lighted the fire and set the shadows dancing in the back of the room, they wound up their music and danced themselves to the trickle of those tunes over and over — they did not know how to dance; it was a fantasy of pure happiness. They were used to not knowing where their next home would be — they were not used to their father coming home to light the fire and smoke his pipe beside it and look at them in silence.

On Christmas morning the miners' bus drove out to the cottage filled with singers and they raised a carol as they came. They gave another, grouped on the grass below the piazza — grass that was still green. Invited in, there was handshaking all around and then the room rang to their voices as they sang — not the church carols, but quaint old chapel tunes and catches, older than Methodism, which are in the Cornish blood from father to son. But the great singing was on Christmas Eve when the day shift came up and the night shift was there waiting in their underground clothes, and they sang as one family grouped around the shaft the old country carols before scattering to their work and their little new western homes.[4]

We were still there in February when the almond trees were in blossom in the little shut-in dooryard of the cottage. And Mr. R. was still there, the superfluous superintendent, as we thought him.[5] If A. were merely the engineer on construction, there could be nothing to stay for much longer; the plant was finished; it only remained to operate it by one who would not brutalize its parts. James obviously was nervous at letting Arthur go; and still he said nothing.

The steel pipeline was in its bed, over a mile and a half long with a head of 800 feet, pitching down the hill from the Empire side of Wolf Creek, which it crossed on the arches of a little stone bridge built as they build in the Old Country. The crooked roofs of the powerhouse sat tight in the bottom of Boston Ravine and direct-acting air compressors rammed their power through pipes that carried it up to the new hoisting works on Massachusetts Hill, where the old shaft was being dewatered at the rate of seven or eight hundred gallons a minute.[6] The North Star plant had some rather heroic fea-

---

4 Grass Valley became almost as famous for its Cornish miners' Christmas singing as for the work that those same Cornishmen did down in the mines. The annual custom continues at Grass Valley even now that the mines are no longer active.

5 R. R. Roberts.

6 The handsome stone powerhouse and aqueduct, and the huge Pelton wheel, can still be seen at Grass Valley, where they are now part of a small mining museum. Water was brought down the steep slope from the Empire to the powerhouse, under high pressure, so as to be shot out of a nozzle against the buckets of the Pelton wheel, which by turning very rapidly compressed air in the cylinders. This compressed air was then used to drive the mine's machinery. Arthur Foote's design and construction was hailed as a pioneering achievement and was widely studied.

tures, the size of the Pelton waterwheel, for one; it worked so well that its author was asked (some time later) to prepare the article on the application of compressed air for the *Encyclopedia Britannica*. He had no assistant engineer, nor even a draftsman, on this work; he made his drawings himself evenings under a fierce electric light, and hurt his eyes — he was a careless man under the intoxication of his work. One who had watched him said he went at it like an artist. After those dry, frustrate years in Idaho, he went at it "as pants the hart—."

We could not worry about the future as parents should, seeing our little hostages so happy on fortune's ragged edge. There was no bedroom to spare for them inside the cottage; they slept in an end of the piazza partitioned off outside our bedroom door. We woke one dark morning and heard the rain trampling on the piazza roof and giggles on the other side of the door. The roof had sprung a leak just over the foot of their bed; they had spread out the rubber bathtub to catch the drips and were moving the little puddles it had gathered, with their toes underneath the bedclothes, as merry as grigs and no harm done.

They had given up the Lady of Shalott. Agnes was now the Primitive Woman weaving hammocks for her dolls to sleep in under the manzanita bushes on the knoll. Behind the cottage grounds a high board fence had a door in it through which you passed into the pinewoods and followed the trails made by the dinner-pail men going to and from their work. When their father took the little girls into the change house on Massachusetts Hill, where the miners leave their surface clothes when they are underground or their underground clothes to dry while they are on top — each man his own peg with his hat on it and his boots ranged beside other boots on the floor beneath — they gazed down the long stone passage lined in this way, and the notion popped into both their quaint little minds at once. They went away chanting to each other:

> Nine-and-twenty knights of fame
> Hung their shields in Branksome Hall —[7]

They never saw anything "plain"; everything suggested something else.

And so we lived in this bird on the bough fashion and nothing was said as to our going or staying; but whenever A. became restive, the chief, who was still with us, urged him to wait awhile. Mr. R., kind, cheerful, inefficient and fatally economical (too economical to be even tidy) seemed a fixture. The visiting wife endeavored to keep out of things and wrote her stories with the new backgrounds, trying to capture something of the atmosphere around us. The heats came on and we were still there [1896]. . . . Richard Watson Gilder wrote (as a friend, not an editor) that Mrs. Robert Carter was about to resign her position as Principal of the Cooper School of Design for Women and had expressed a wish that I might be her successor. He thought I could have the place if I cared for it by authorizing some friend to present my name as a candidate at the next meeting of the Trustees. . . . Did I want it? — I did not! It came as a shock that a near friend should think that I might want it — that I might be thankful to get it. I was thankful to my friends. The hours were from nine to two — one would not have to give up one's own work and the salary would keep three of us decently in New York where the children could go to some good school. I was sick with that decision; I was left to make it alone. My man said humbly that he did not wonder I feared the future, judging by the past — and I must decide the question for myself. I sent in my name, and after some wretched nights of facing what seemed like failure from the foundation, failure to "stick together," I gave in; discarded prudence and common sense and withdrew my name.

It was so soon after this that it seemed like an answer to

[7] From Scott's "Lay of the Last Minstrel."

faith when a letter came which put the decision up to James. I am sure it had been his intention from the first that we should stay if the plant of Arthur's designing answered expectations, only it took him so long to make up that slow but wise and faithful mind of his. The letter was from another mining company with eastern backing asking A. to take charge of their operations in Colorado, and what would he come for? . . . "What will you stay for?" James asked; and then the matter was very quickly settled. It was the work itself — he must have it in his own hands — that A. wanted, and a living salary, no more. Mr. R. left us in the most gracious humor. He was not in need of work. His children were all grown and he was well to do, with a wife rich in her own right and a great manager. We rather surmised that he left his handsome home in Michigan and sought these distant jobs to escape from so much management. He had the manner of a henpecked man on a stolen holiday.

And then we sent for Nelly Linton to finish her job with us, and began to plan how we could enlarge the cottage to hold us all with a room fit for the president when he was with us. One would have to know his habits and standards in his own home to appreciate the consideration he showed as our guest, if one may call a man your guest who puts a roof over your head and can bid you go or stay as he decides. I have found it very chastening to live in houses not one's own, on these terms.

Boise, ca. 1894-95: l. to r. (back row) Mary Hallock Foote, Bessie Sherman, Nelly Linton; (front row) Mary Birney Sherman, Agnes, Betty, and Arthur B. Foote.

North Star House

The Footes at North Star Cottage

❨ 39 ❩

For twenty years the mines went on under the same management, developing their double life of the Surface and the Underground. The story of the North Star vein has been told in the Company's reports; they made excellent reading for the stockholders in those years before the Great War — which changed things. Still, twenty years is a long lease of life for a mine which cannot reap the same field twice nor return the same rock to the crusher. The Surface has gone on spreading its boundary marks, keeping pace with the development underground; it covers now over a thousand acres of woods and pastures and old trails, with new roads crossing them and power-lines and light lines cut through the woods where they pass. An old prospector's or squatter's cabin erased here and there has left a well hole or a few foundation stones or a rose bush blossoming year after year. The miners live in town convenient to church and the shows of an evening. We see few dinner-pail men on our wood walks, but a hundred cars or more are parked in the sheds or around the works at quitting time. I once thought that when I was done writing stories I would take the stories that have been lived on the North Star Surface for a theme, but I have waited too long: I know it all too well; its roots are too deep in my own life in these thirty years we have lived here.

There are other things, not on the surface, which I shall pass over in silence; beautiful friendships we never dreamed were in store for us — these are not to be talked about as things of the past. They are too close to my daily thoughts; the perspective is lacking, and we cannot say things to the "faces" of

394

those we hold in delicate regard, more than we could write them letters to be passed around.

We shall never cease to miss our friend and brother who brought us here. From the moment when he looked me over at Oakland Ferry and saw that I needed warmer clothes, his touch upon my life was humorous and beneficent, and no blood brother could have been better loved by my husband than he. They strove mightily at times, as two strong men must with a common object and such different minds and temperaments to work with, yet James would have been my husband's model if he could have formed himself after the pattern of any other man. There was an understanding deeper than words between them, and none of the condescension on the side of the elder which the advantage of years and equipment might have excused. I marvel still at the trust he put in A. when he sent him here to act upon his own judgment; for none of those fine things had been said about him, in Idaho or anywhere else, when he came here stripped of everything but courage, after that twelve years' siege and surrender. And for myself, I never forgot those two words which comforted my doubts after our first failure, when I scarcely knew my husband's powers, from a man who never set his name to a flattery or undersigned a lie.

James died in 1908, at the height of the mines' prosperity. He saw this house[1] go up on the hill of the great view, once the property of a neighboring claim. When the time (and the price) were ripe he acquired it all for the sake of the surface rights and the beauty; he could afford to pay for beauty then. This was the house of success, but sorrow was built into its walls. "We cannot bribe thee, Death." Mary Hague died suddenly [in 1898], during one of James's inevitable absences — no preparation for the news had been possible, no last words

---

[1] I.e., North Star House, the large, elaborate stone structure that replaced North Star Cottage as the superintendent's residence and the place where Hague himself was to stay during his visits to the mine.

before the thread was snapped. He was losing old friends and comrades all those years. It was well for him that he went before the war and the death of his only son in France [in 1918]. He never saw Billy's young wife whom he would have loved, nor held his little grandsons on his knee, but he was spared the sorrow left for the young to bear. . . . The Rockwell cousins died within two years of each other and left Di [Katherine Diana], the last of that line, alone in the empty house on Beacon Street, mocked by everything the world can give, with nothing left that she had lived for. But that story ended well by waiting awhile; it will tell itself in the next generation; that line is not extinct.

James "sat at the springs of fate" for us and for our children in many and far-reaching ways. He gave Gerald Sherman his first opportunity on this coast, and when he had earned promotion he spoke for him before the gods of the Copper Queen,[2] and today Gerald is consulting engineer for the Phelps-Dodge combination. He mentioned our son to the president of the Unsan Mining Company of Korea, and he was sent out there on a three years' job, to serve his apprenticeship under strangers, as his father thought best. When Gerald went up higher [in 1904], Arthur was cabled to come home, if he wanted his place; he might have stayed in Korea and been promoted, but he came.

They were all coming home, from Korea, from Boston and from San Francisco, our three children — and now, we thought, the question of schools and apprenticeships might rest for awhile. They could practice at home what they had been learning in these long separations. Arthur scarcely knew the little sister he had not seen in three years, now a grown maiden of seventeen. She had been only as far as San Francisco to school, that winter, and she came first. We had her alone to ourselves watching her at the age when a young soul almost from day to day seems to mold the countenance it informs. We

[2] An important mine in Bisbee, Arizona.

said to each other, when she had kissed us good night and given us her backward look and smile before closing the door, "She is perfect." She was in our eyes: "Stillness with love and day with light."

Arthur was on shipboard, Betty on the train coming west in company with her Uncle James and his daughter Eleanor, who was to visit us while her father went on a long-dreamed-of voyage in search of his "lost island" (he never found it). Betty had been sent for that winter to stay with Di who had just suffered her last shock of bereavement by the sudden death of her father, as peremptory as a bullet through the brain. She was on the verge of a nervous collapse. The two girls had been together since this tragedy, alone with the servants in that ghostly house of memories. It had been a year of tense and hurried developments for our girl just entering her twenties. There were talks between us which did not include the younger sister; she must have missed, in those first crowded days, the all-sufficient companionship of their childhood. The darling! — so wiser than all of us in her ignorance of life. She stood alone, a little apart on the threshold of her woman's experience, regarding us in our intense preoccupation, not curiously nor wistfully but with that detachment which we recognized as one of the signs of genius feeling its way but not come yet to its full expression.

There were signs of genius in everything she did, but there was danger in that poise and power of repression. . . . We wasted one whole night, when she needed help at once but would not wake us to tell of her suffering. The next day was lost studying symptoms and sending messages; the young doctor who watched the case said it was acute appendicitis but he was afraid to operate. A midnight special was sent over to Colfax to meet the surgeon and nurse from San Francisco; there were two young assistants waiting — we could do no more. Four days after the operation which they said was "just in time," she died. In one week from that confused day of arrivals when the travelers returned, she was gone on her own great adventure. We called it fate — or freedom, for a soul that escaped before our eyes in that sudden whitening of her lovely face.

Superstition said it was the price for the attainment of everything else we had prayed for when we had our three children safe and well. Two weeks later, after a happy voyage filled with anticipation, Arthur's liner came into dock at San Francisco and he too walked into that ambush of fate.

That was in June 1904; she died on the twelfth of May— a month we have ever since connected with a recurrence of vital happenings. The autumn following we moved up into this house on the hill, and that is over twenty years ago. The fences around the old cottage were covered with Banksia roses that blossom early in May; their long, clustered garlands were casting perfume on the southwest wind. We smelled them all through the rooms of the cottage, we covered her with them when they carried her out of the gate. They send their message to us every May on that southwest wind that scatters their petals on the grass. . . . "Sleep is a thornless rose upon Life's breast" was one of the new sonnets we had just been reading that spring — forever after to be one of the perpetual, haunting reminders: the common experience — all poetry, all beauty is for each one of us alone, and our secret pang answers when the nerve is touched. . . . Here is her portrait by the one who knew her best. The sisters were thousands of miles apart when this came on Christmas Eve to Agnes, alone with us at the mine, from her sister at her art school in Philadelphia.

> Little rider where the trails are steep,
> Little gazer from the hills above,
> Little wanderer where the woods are deep
> Over the roads I love.
>
> Little dreamer on the gusty knoll,
> Little listener where the dark trees blow,

Pines with voices like a human soul —
Those are the woods I know.

Little reader by the firelight,
Little sleeper at a lonely mine,
Little One, I long for thee tonight
And for my home and thine!

All that has happened here since would be too difficult to tell for one so deeply implicated through her relations to the chief actors, yet so powerless, as myself. The next generation took the lead in household and mining affairs and made their own decisions, as we made ours; though never did I achieve that extraordinary self-effacement which ruled my own parents when their children's problems called for action. In 1912 my husband resigned his place as general manager and his son succeeded him under Mr. George B. Agnew of New York, who is now president of the North Star Mines Company.[3] The work is being extended, if one may use such a word for sinking deeper and still deeper in the ground; it may end in finding another mine beneath, or it may lead to that fatal word "shut down." There are highly interesting visits of geologists and long talks in the office, and more and more cars are parked around the works. It is a year of suspense — to suit the times. History must pause. But the North Star House now has its own flock of children, little Californians to whom this place will always be home; its memories will haunt them as the desert wind and the sound of that cañon river rising to our windows at night has stayed with our own children all their lives.

One of my family critics wrote after going through these pages: "All the characters, of course, are weakened — to be

[3] George Bliss Agnew (1868-1941), a prominent New York businessman, was president of the North Star Mines Company from the death of James D. Hague in 1908 until that company was merged with the Empire mine to form the Empire Star Mines Company, in 1929, at which time Agnew became vice-president.

paradoxical — by leaving out their weaknesses." Of course! If anything has been left out connected with the weaknesses of those I love (since I haven't mentioned any of my own), I am glad of it. I should distrust my touch in attempting analysis of these characters that I know are great stuff of biography, but not for me! I ought to know my own limitations by this time. These fragments of my past are presented merely as backgrounds and the figures upon them are placed by instinct in a selected light and seen from a certain point of view. To that extent I suppose I am still the artist I tried to be, and the old romancer too. And everyone knows the magic perspectives of memory — it keeps what we loved and alters the relative size and value of many things that we did not love enough — that we hated and resisted and made mountains of at the time. It turns the dust of our valleys of humiliation, now that the sun of our working hours has set, into a sad and dreamy splendor which will fade into depths beyond depths of unknown worlds of stars.

Bibliographical Note

The most important collections of Mary Hallock Foote material are divided between the Huntington and Stanford libraries and the descendants of Mary Hallock Foote. The Huntington Library has more than 100 letters from Mary Hallock Foote to members of the Hague family, especially the elder James D. Hague and his wife, Mary (Foote) Hague. Many notations concerning the Footes appear in James Hague's diaries, and some business correspondence with Arthur D. Foote has been preserved in James Hague's files of correspondence. The Huntington Library has also obtained, by purchase from a New York dealer, about thirty letters and telegrams from Mary Hallock Foote to the editors of the *Century Magazine*, and a complete set of her novels and collected short stories, mostly in first editions and mostly presentation copies to Rodman Gilder, son of her close friend, Helena de Kay Gilder. The Huntington Library has files of the periodicals that published most of Mary Hallock Foote's stories: *Century Magazine*, *Atlantic Monthly*, and *St. Nicholas*. Through the courtesy of the Foote and Hague descendants, there is a growing collection of pictorial material. Two of Bessie Sherman's grandchildren, Mrs. Helena Sherman Sims and Mrs. Mary Sherman Harper, have made available to the Huntington Library reminiscent accounts by Bessie Sherman, her son Gerald, and other members of the family, together with many photographs and some genealogical material.

The Stanford Library has about 500 letters from Mary Hallock Foote to her lifelong friend Helena de Kay Gilder, plus a scattering of other letters of related interest. Through the courtesy of the Stanford Library and Miss Rosamond Gilder, facsimiles of these letters have been obtained for the Huntington's collection. A microfilm of these same letters can be seen in the Bancroft Library, University of California, Berkeley, which also has the manuscript originals of some of Arthur D. Foote's business correspondence.

A small but informative collection of biographical material concerning Mary Hallock Foote has been preserved in the John M. Winterbotham Papers at the State Historical Society of Wisconsin, Madison. Included are Mary Hallock Foote's summary of her life and ancestry, as prepared at the request of the editors of a biographical dictionary, and her correction of the dictionary's proposed version. Through the courtesy of the State Historical Society of Wisconsin, facsimiles of these papers have been obtained for the Huntington's collection.

Cooper Union, New York City, and the Library of Congress both have small collections of drawings by Mary Hallock Foote. Those in the Cooper Union collection have been copied on microfilm for the National Portrait Gallery, Washington. The National Portrait Gallery also has on microfilm a small collection of letters and telegrams from Mary Hallock Foote to the editors of *Century Magazine*, obtained from the Archives of American Art.

Until recently few modern writers have shown interest in Mary Hallock Foote, but that neglect disappeared suddenly when Wallace Stegner of Stanford University won the Pulitzer Prize for his novel *Angle of Repose*. Any reader of Mary Hallock Foote's reminiscences will see that *Angle of Repose* is a fictional account of Mary Hallock Foote's life. The word "fictional" should be stressed, especially in regard to treatment of the Idaho years.

Stegner's novel is based upon study of the materials in the Stanford Library. Those materials include a typescript of a version of these reminiscences and the 500 letters from Mary

Hallock Foote to Richard and Helena Gilder. Comparison of the novel with the reminiscences and letters yields some fascinating insights into the freedom a writer feels when he is functioning as novelist rather than as historian or biographer. Although the basic settings and the cast of characters have been re-created out of Mary Hallock Foote's own descriptions, with few changes and only the thin disguise of a slight alteration of names, nevertheless the personalities and their individual destinies have been developed through a blending of fact, perceptive interpretation, and sheer invention — at times, unrestrained invention. Both the personalities and individual scenes have been given dramatic authenticity by the use of colorful incidents incorporated ready-made from the reminiscences or letters, and by the introduction of bits of prose from those same sources. The whole is fleshed out with dialogue and expressed inner thoughts that are based sometimes on inferences derived from the letters, but sometimes on nothing more than the novelist's sense of what would help to complete his development of character and plot. The result is a book that has high value as a novel but should not be regarded as a factual explanation of Mary Hallock Foote and her career.

A very good brief review of writing about Mary Hallock Foote has just been published by Richard W. Etulain, "Mary Hallock Foote (1847-1938)," *American Literary Realism*, 5 (Spring 1972), 144-50. Professor Etulain's essay is especially valuable for its summary of contemporary critical comment. Apparently we can anticipate a further and more extensive study by Professor Etulain.

In the meantime Professor James H. Maguire is completing a fifty-page pamphlet on Mary Hallock Foote's life and work. This is to be published in a new Western Writers Series sponsored by Boise State College.

Prior to the studies by Professors Etulain and Maguire, the principal scholarly examination of Mary Hallock Foote's career had been carried out by Mary Lou Benn (Mrs. Harold W. Benn) as part of her work for the master's degree at the University of Wyoming. Mrs. Benn's master's thesis, "Mary Hallock Foote: Pioneer Woman Novelist," is on deposit at the University of Wyoming and in the Western History Room of the Denver Public Library. Substantial chunks of it have been published in two articles: "Mary Hallock Foote: Early Leadville Writer," *Colorado Magazine*, 33 (April 1956), 93-108; and "Mary Hallock Foote in Idaho," *University of Wyoming Publications*, 20 (July 15, 1956), 157-78. The latter essay includes a list of Mary Hallock Foote's stories and books and was published as part of a notable special issue of the *University of Wyoming Publications*. Under the editorship of Ruth Hudson, and with the collective title of "Studies in Literature of the West," this special issue prints portions of three master's theses that deal with Mary Hallock Foote. In addition to Mrs. Benn's essay, Mary Hallock Foote is discussed in Lawana J. Shaul's "The West in Magazine Fiction, 1870-1900," pp. 29-56, and Harry H. Jones's "The Mining Theme in Western Fiction," pp. 101-29.

INDEX

Index

407

THE HALLOCK AND FOOTE GENEALOGICAL TABLES

These genealogical tables represent the Hallock and Foote families at the time Mary Hallock Foote was writing her reminiscences in the early 1920s. Members of the families not mentioned in the reminiscences are not included in the tables.

HALLOCK FAMILY TREE

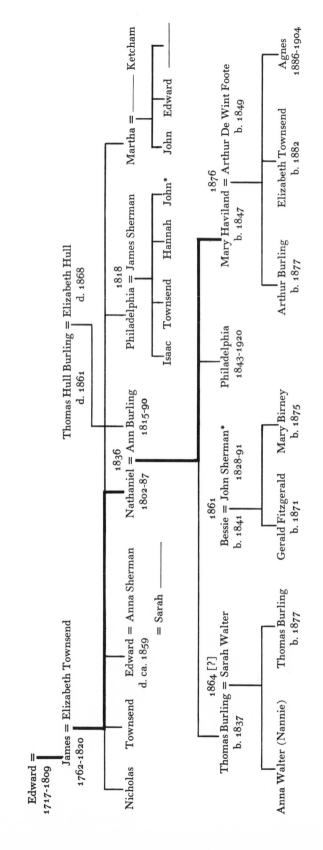

*John Sherman's name appears twice since he married his first cousin.

FOOTE FAMILY TREE

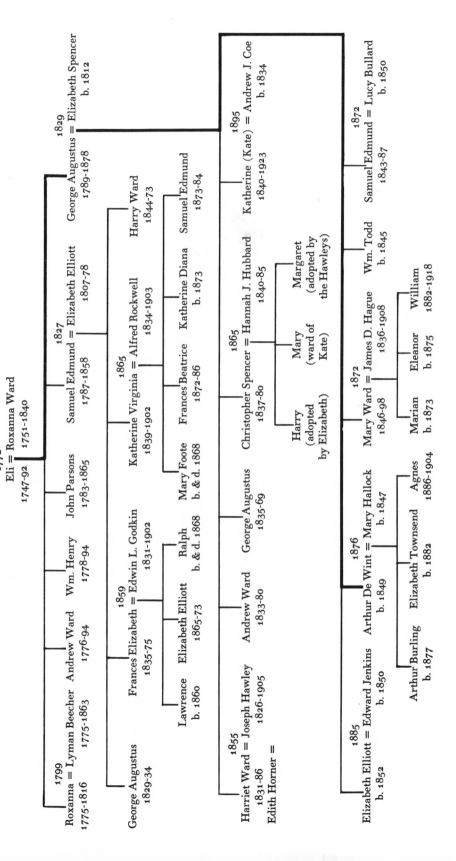